Definitive
XML
Schema

Second Edition

The Charles F. Goldfarb Definitive XML Series

Priscilla Walmsley
- Definitive XML Schema Second Edition

Charles F. Goldfarb and Paul Prescod
- Charles F. Goldfarb's XML Handbook™ Fifth Edition

Rick Jelliffe
- The XML and SGML Cookbook: Recipes for Structured Information

Charles F. Goldfarb, Steve Pepper, and Chet Ensign
- SGML Buyer's Guide: Choosing the Right XML and SGML Products and Services

G. Ken Holman
- Definitive XSL-FO
- Definitive XSLT and XPath

Bob DuCharme
- XML: The Annotated Specification
- SGML CD

Truly Donovan
- Industrial-Strength SGML: An Introduction to Enterprise Publishing

Lars Marius Garshol
- Definitive XML Application Development

JP Morgenthal with Bill la Forge
- Enterprise Application Integration with XML and Java

Michael Leventhal, David Lewis, and Matthew Fuchs
- Designing XML Internet Applications

Adam Hocek and David Cuddihy
- Definitive VoiceXML

Dmitry Kirsanov
- XSLT 2.0 Web Development

Yuri Rubinsky and Murray Maloney
- SGML on the Web: Small Steps Beyond HTML

David Megginson
- Structuring XML Documents

Sean McGrath
- XML Processing with Python
- XML by Example: Building E-commerce Applications
- ParseMe.1st: SGML for Software Developers

Chet Ensign
- $GML: The Billion Dollar Secret

Ron Turner, Tim Douglass, and Audrey Turner
- ReadMe.1st: SGML for Writers and Editors

Charles F. Goldfarb and Priscilla Walmsley
- XML in Office 2003: Information Sharing with Desktop XML

Michael Floyd
- Building Web Sites with XML

Fredrick Thomas Martin
- TOP SECRET Intranet: How U.S. Intelligence Built Intelink—The World's Largest, Most Secure Network

J. Craig Cleaveland
- Program Generators with XML and Java

About the Series Author

Charles F. Goldfarb is the father of XML technology. He invented SGML, the Standard Generalized Markup Language on which both XML and HTML are based. You can find him on the Web at: www.xmlbooks.com.

About the Series Logo

The rebus is an ancient literary tradition, dating from 16th century Picardy, and is especially appropriate to a series involving fine distinctions between markup and text, metadata and data. The logo is a rebus incorporating the series name within a stylized XML comment declaration.

Definitive XML Schema

Second Edition

 Priscilla Walmsley

PRENTICE
HALL

Upper Saddle River, NJ • Boston • Indianapolis • San Francisco
New York • Toronto • Montreal • London • Munich • Paris • Madrid
Cape Town • Sydney • Tokyo • Singapore • Mexico City

Titles in this series are produced using XML, SGML, and/or XSL. XSL-FO documents are rendered into PDF by the XEP Rendering Engine from RenderX: www.renderx.com.

The publisher offers excellent discounts on this book when ordered in quantity for bulk purchases or special sales, which may include electronic versions and/or custom covers and content particular to your business, training goals, marketing focus, and branding interests. For more information, please contact:

U.S. Corporate and Government Sales
(800) 382–3419
corpsales@pearsontechgroup.com

For sales outside the United States, please contact:

International Sales
international@pearsoned.com

Visit us on the Web: informit.com/ph

Library of Congress Cataloging-in-Publication Data is on file

ISBN-13: 978-0-132-88672-7
ISBN-10: 0-132-88672-3
Text printed in the United States on recycled paper at Edwards Brothers Malloy in Ann Arbor, MI.
First printing: September 2012

Editor-in-Chief: Mark L. Taub
Managing Editor: Kristy Hart
Book Packager: Alina Kirsanova
Cover Designer: Alan Clements

To Doug, my SH

Overview

Contents

Foreword

clas·sic *(adjective)*
judged over a period of time to be important and of the highest quality:

> *a classic novel*
> *a classic car*

Neither this definition, nor any of the leading dictionary definitions, has a usage example anything like:

> *a classic work on high-tech software*

After all, it is a rare book on software that even survives long enough to be "judged over a period of time."

Nevertheless, *Definitive XML Schema* satisfies every definition of "classic." It is one of the elite few software books that have been in print continuously for over ten years, and an essential trustworthy guide for tens of thousands of readers.

This *Second Edition* continues to be an essential and trustworthy classic:

Essential because in the last ten years XML has become the accepted standard for data interchange, and XML Schema 1.0 is largely responsible. Now version 1.1 has extended the ability to specify and validate document data, to a degree previously possible only for databases. These updates are covered in this book by extensive revisions—the most significant 250 of which are flagged in the text and table of contents. Hundreds more unflagged revisions reflect W3C corrections of XML Schema errata, and ten years of evolving "best practices."

Trustworthy because it is both authoritative and accurate.

- The **author(ity)**, Priscilla Walmsley, is a noted consultant who has been using XML Schema ever since she helped develop it as a member of the W3C XML Schema Group. She personally devised many of the current "best practices" described in this book. Priscilla is the Editor of the W3C XML Schema Primer, Second Edition.

- **Accuracy** was preserved by using the same XML-based production system that was used in 2002, operated by the same team of XML experts who read and thoroughly understood the book. Priscilla's original XML source (in which she had personally tagged the version 1.1 revisions) was used throughout production. Dmitry Kirsanov copy-edited and proofed it, while Alina Kirsanova prepared the index, coded the XSL transformations, and generated the camera-ready PDFs.

The result, as you will see, retains the structure, clarity, patient explanations, validated examples (over 450!), and well-reasoned advice that critics praised in the 2002 edition—but now they are ten years more up-to-date.

And after you've read *Definitive XML Schema, Second Edition*, it won't take another ten years for you, too, to judge it a classic.

Charles F. Goldfarb
Belmont, CA
August 2012

Acknowledgments

First and foremost, I would like to thank Charles Goldfarb for his invaluable guidance and support. Alina Kirsanova and Dmitry Kirsanov did an excellent job preparing this book for publication. I would also like to thank Mark Taub at Prentice Hall for his hand in the making this work possible.

Of course, this book would not have been possible without the efforts of all of the members of the W3C XML Schema Working Group, with whom I have had the pleasure of working for six years. The content of this book was shaped by the questions and comments of the people who contribute to XML-DEV and xmlschema-dev.

Finally, I'd like to thank my Dad for teaching me to "get stuck into it," a skill which allowed me to complete this substantial project.

Priscilla Walmsley
Traverse City, Michigan
March 2012

How to use this book

This book covers the two versions of XML Schema—1.0 and 1.1—and provides revision bars to assist access to just one or the other. In referring to both versions as "XML Schema," the book follows customary practice, despite the official name of 1.1 being "W3C XML Schema Definition Language (XSD) 1.1." For either version, the book is useable as both a tutorial and a reference.

As a tutorial, the book can be read from cover to cover with confidence that each topic builds logically on the information that was previously covered. (Of course, knowledge of XML itself is always a prerequisite to learning about XML Schema, and is assumed in this book.)

When using this book as a reference, you have several access options available to you:

- A comprehensive index starts on page 699.

- An alphabetical list of all the elements and attributes that make up the XML Schema syntax is in Appendix A on p. 648. For each there is a reference to further coverage in the body of the book.

- XML Schema includes a basic set of datatypes, known formally as the "built-in simple types." They are listed in Appendix B on p. 690. This appendix also refers to more detailed descriptions in the body of the book.

- The major changes in version 1.1 of XML Schema are summarized in Section 23.5.1 on p. 640, with references to detailed coverage elsewhere in the book.

Revisions in the Second Edition

This edition of *Definitive XML Schema* contains more than 500 revisions, covering such new and updated topics as:

- W3C published corrections for errata in XML Schema 1.0
- Current "best practices" after ten years of experience
- XML information modeling for relational and object-oriented modeling paradigms
- Schema design: evaluating pros and cons of alternatives
- Schema strategy: formulating a coherent strategy for schema development and maintenance
- Version 1.1 updates and additions to XML Schema

Identifying 1.1-related revisions

The author has chosen a "1.1 subset" of the book revisions, comprising the 250 most significant revisions that deal with version 1.1. If a section, table, example, or paragraph has content entirely from the "1.1 subset," there is a solid gray revision bar on its right. If other material might be included, the bar is a gray dotted line.

Strategies for using the revision bars

If your interest is **solely 1.0** (perhaps because your software does not yet support 1.1), you may decide to focus on content that either has a dotted revision bar or no bar at all.

If you are interested only in what is **new in 1.1** (presumably because you already know 1.0), consider content having either a solid or dotted revision bar in deciding where to focus your reading.

Finally, if your interest is **all of 1.1** (because you don't already know 1.0), you can easily disregard the revision bars (that's why they are grayed out ☺).

Syntax tables

This book contains syntax tables, each summarizing the allowed syntax of an XML Schema component. The first such table does not occur until Section 4.2 on p. 58, by which point the undefined terms in this explanation will have been introduced.

Syntax tables, whose captions all start with "XSD Syntax," look like the example below, which shows the syntax for named simple types. It contains the following information:

- The element name(s) used for this XML Schema component.
- The possible parent element name(s). Note that "1.1", printed white on a gray box, precedes `override` to identify it as a construct that is only permitted in version 1.1. This convention is followed in all syntax tables; it occurs once more in this table.
- A list of allowed attributes, along with their types, valid values, and brief descriptions. The names of required attributes appear in bold font. Default values appear in italics in the *Type* column.
- The allowed child elements, shown as a content model that uses, for compactness, the XML DTD syntax. Commas indicate that child elements must appear in the order shown, while vertical bars (|) indicate a choice among child elements. Occurrence constraints indicate how many of each may appear: ? means zero or one, * means zero or more, and + means one or more. Otherwise, one and only one is required. In this example, the allowed content is zero or one `annotation` element, followed by a choice of either one `restriction`, one `list`, or one `union` element.

Table XSD Syntax: named simple type definition

Name			
`simpleType`			

Parents			
`schema, redefine,` [1.1]`override`			

Attribute name	Type		Description
`id`	`ID`		Unique ID.
name	`NCName`		Simple type name.
`final`	`"#all"  |  `list of `("restriction"  |  "list"  | "union"  |  `[1.1]`"extension")`		Whether other types can be derived from this one.

Content			
`annotation?, (restriction  |  list  |  union)`			

In some cases, there is more than one syntax table for the same element name, because certain element names in XML Schema have multiple uses. For example, `simpleType` is used for both named simple types and anonymous simple types. Each of these use cases of `simpleType` allows different attributes and a different set of parent elements, so each is described with its own table.

Companion website

This book has a companion website, maintained by the author, at www.datypic.com/books/defxmlschema2. On the website, you can view any errata and download the examples from this book. In addition to the examples that appear in the book, which are generally concise in order to illustrate a particular point, the website also has larger, more comprehensive instances and schemas that can be copied or used to test validation.

Schemas:
An introduction

T his chapter provides a brief introduction to schemas and explains why they are important. It also discusses the basic schema design goals and describes the various existing schema languages.

1.1 | What is a schema?

The word *schema* means a diagram, plan, or framework. In XML, it refers to a document that describes an XML document. Suppose you have the XML instance shown in Example 1–1.

Example 1–1. Product instance

```
<product effDate="2001-04-12">
  <number>557</number>
  <size>10</size>
</product>
```

The instance consists of a `product` element that has two children (`number` and `size`) and an attribute (`effDate`).

The sentence you just read could be a schema because it describes the instance document, and all other instances of a `product` with the same kind of children and attribute. However, **to be useful with XML and benefit from computer processing**, this kind of schema won't do. The schema must be defined in a *schema document* using a formal *schema language*.

Example 1–2 shows a schema document that describes the instance. It contains element and attribute declarations that assign types and names to elements and attributes. The document is written in the XML Schema Definition Language (XSD).

Example 1–2. Product schema in XSD schema language

```
<xs:schema xmlns:xs="http://www.w3.org/2001/XMLSchema">
  <xs:element name="product" type="ProductType"/>
  <xs:complexType name="ProductType">
    <xs:sequence>
      <xs:element name="number" type="xs:integer"/>
      <xs:element name="size" type="SizeType"/>
    </xs:sequence>
    <xs:attribute name="effDate" type="xs:date"/>
  </xs:complexType>
  <xs:simpleType name="SizeType">
    <xs:restriction base="xs:integer">
      <xs:minInclusive value="2"/>
      <xs:maxInclusive value="18"/>
    </xs:restriction>
  </xs:simpleType>
</xs:schema>
```

In contrast, Example 1–3 on p. 9 shows an equally valid schema in the familiar Document Type Definition (DTD) language of XML. The disproportionate sizes of the two schema documents roughly reflect the capabilities of the two languages. The extensive features of XML Schema, when to use them, and how to use them effectively, form the subject matter of this book.

1.2 | The purpose of schemas

Schemas are developed for many purposes. How effectively a schema can achieve them depends on the capabilities of the schema language and the schema processor, as well as the quality of the schema design.

1.2.1 *Data validation*

One of the most common uses for schemas is to verify that an XML document is valid according to a defined set of rules. A schema can be used to validate:

- The structure of elements and attributes. For example, a `product` must have a `number` and a `size`, and may optionally have an `effDate` (effective date).
- The order of elements. For example, `number` must appear before `size`.
- The data values of elements and attributes, based on ranges, enumerations, and pattern matching. For example, `size` must be an integer between `2` and `18`, and `effDate` must be a valid date.
- The uniqueness of values in an instance. For example, all product numbers in an instance must be unique.

1.2.2 *A contract with trading partners*

Often, XML instances are passed between organizations. A schema may act as a contract with your trading partners. It clearly lays out the rules for document structure and what is required. Since an instance can be validated against a schema, the "contract" can be enforced using available tools.

1.2.3   *System documentation*

Schemas can provide documentation about the data in an XML instance. Anyone who needs to understand the data can refer to the schema for information about names, structures, and data types of the items. To include further documentation, you can add annotations to any schema component.

1.2.4   *Providing information to processors*

Schemas contain information about the type and structure of elements that is useful to have when processing the document. For example, if a processor knows the data type of a value, it knows how to sort it or compare it to other values, and it knows what operations it can reasonably perform on that data. Providing information to the processor can also be useful for debugging: If the processor knows that a certain element is not allowed by a schema, it can signal an error to the processing code.

1.2.5   *Augmentation of data*

Schema processing can also add to the instance. A schema can insert default and fixed values for elements and attributes and normalize whitespace according to the type.

1.2.6   *Application information*

Schemas provide a way for additional information about the data to be supplied to the application when processing a particular type of document. For example, you could include information on how to map the `product` element instances to a database table, and have the application use this information to automatically update that particular table with the data.

In addition to being available at processing time, such information in a schema can be used to generate code, such as:

- User interfaces for editing the information. For example, if you know that `size` is between `2` and `18`, you can generate an interface with a slider bar that has these values as the limits.
- Stylesheets to transform instance data into a reader-friendly representation such as XHTML. For example, if you know that the human-readable name for the content of a `number` element is "Product Number" you can use this as a column header.
- Code to insert or extract the data from a database. For example, if you know that the product number maps to the `PROD_NUM` column on the `PRODUCTS` table, you can generate an efficient routine to insert it into that column.

1.3 | Schema design

Schema languages often provide several ways to accurately describe the same thing. The decisions made during the design stage can affect a schema's usability, accuracy, and applicability. Therefore, it is important to keep in mind your design objectives when creating a schema. These objectives may vary depending on how you are using XML, but some are common to all use cases.

1.3.1 *Accuracy and precision*

Obviously, a schema should accurately describe an XML instance and allow it to be validated. Schemas should also be precise in describing data. Precision can result in more complete validation as well as better documentation. Precision can be achieved by defining restrictive types that truly represent valid values.

1.3.2 *Clarity*

Schemas should be very clear, allowing a reader to instantly understand the structure and characteristics of the instance being described. Clarity can be achieved by

- Appropriate choice of names
- Consistency in naming
- Consistency in structure
- Good documentation
- Avoiding unnecessary complexity

1.3.3 *Broad applicability*

There is a temptation to create schemas that are useful only for a specific application. In some cases, this may be appropriate. However, it is better to create a schema that has broader applicability. For example, a business unit that handles only domestic accounts may not use a `country` element declaration as part of an `address`. They should consider adding it in as an optional element for the purposes of consistency and future usability.

There are two components to a schema's broad applicability: reusability and extensibility. Reusable schema components are modular and well documented, encouraging schema authors to reuse them in other schemas. Extensible components are flexible and open, allowing other schema authors to build on them for future uses.

Since designing schemas well is so important, this book offers sections labeled "Design Hint" to address pros and cons of various alternatives in schema design. In addition, Chapters 21, 22, and 23 pull these principles together into a coherent design strategy.

1.4 | Schema languages

1.4.1 *Document Type Definition (DTD)*

Document Type Definitions (DTDs) are a commonly used method of describing XML documents. The DTD syntax is the original W3C schema language, built into XML 1.0 itself. A DTD allows you to define the basic structure of an XML instance, including

- The structure and order of elements
- The allowed attributes for elements
- Basic data typing for attributes
- Default and fixed values for attributes
- Notations to represent other data formats

Example 1–3 shows a DTD that is roughly equivalent to our schema in Example 1–2.

Example 1–3. Product schema in DTD schema language

```
<!ELEMENT product (number, size?)>
<!ELEMENT number (#PCDATA)>
<!ELEMENT size (#PCDATA)>
<!ATTLIST product effDate CDATA #IMPLIED>
```

DTDs have many advantages. They are relatively simple, have a compact syntax, and are widely understood by XML software implementers.

However, DTDs also have some shortcomings. They do not support namespaces easily, and they provide very limited data typing, for attributes only. Also, because they have a non-XML syntax, they cannot be parsed as XML, which is useful for generating documentation or making wholesale changes. However, conversion tools such as James Clark's open source Trang (www.relaxng.org) and other free and commercial products can convert DTDs to other schema languages for this purpose.

1.4.2   *Schema requirements expand*

As XML became increasingly popular for applications such as e-commerce and enterprise application integration (EAI), a more robust schema language was needed. Specifically, XML developers wanted:

- The ability to constrain data based on common data types such as integer and date.
- The ability to define their own types in order to further constrain data.
- Support for namespaces.
- The ability to specify multiple element declarations with the same name in different contexts.
- Object-oriented features such as type derivation. The ability to express types as extensions or restrictions of other types allows them to be processed similarly and substituted for each other.
- A schema language that uses XML syntax. This is advantageous because it is extensible, can represent more advanced models, and can be processed by many available tools.
- The ability to add structured documentation and application information that is passed to the application during processing.

DTDs have not disappeared since newer schema languages arrived on the scene. They are supported in many tools, are widely understood, and are still in use in many applications, especially in the publishing arena. In addition, they continue to be useful as a lightweight alternative to newer schema languages.

1.4.3   *W3C XML Schema*

Four schema languages were developed before work began on XML Schema: XDR (XML Data Reduced), DCD, SOX, and DDML. These four languages were considered, together, as a starting point for XML Schema, and many of their originators were involved in the creation of XML Schema.

The World Wide Web Consortium (W3C) began work on XML Schema in 1998, and it became an official recommendation on May 2, 2001.

On April 5, 2012, version 1.1 of XML Schema became official. It includes several significant enhancements as well as many small changes. One change was the name, which is officially "W3C XML Schema Definition Language (XSD) 1.1." Understandably, this book follows the common practice of continuing to use the name "XML Schema," along with "XSD" in syntax tables and other formal language contexts.[1]

XML Schema 1.1 is backward-compatible with 1.0, and schema authors do not need to specify in their schema documents the version to which they conform. A list of the major changes in 1.1 can be found in Section 23.5.1 on p. 640 of this book.

The formal recommendation is in three parts:

- *XML Schema Part 0: Primer* is a non-normative introduction to XML Schema 1.0 that provides a lot of examples and explanations. It can be found at www.w3.org/TR/xmlschema-0.

- *XML Schema Part 1: Structures* describes most of the components of XML Schema. The most recent version (1.1) can be found at www.w3.org/TR/xmlschema11-1.

- *XML Schema Part 2: Datatypes* covers simple types. It explains the built-in types and the facets that may be used to restrict

---

1.   *Outside this book*, two earlier unofficial names may also be in use: XML Schema Definition Language (XSDL) and W3C XML Schema (WXS).

them. It is a separate document so that other specifications may use it, without including all of XML Schema. The most recent version (1.1) can be found at www.w3.org/TR/xmlschema11-2.

1.4.4   *Other schema languages*

XML Schema and DTDs are not always the most appropriate schema languages for all cases. This section describes two other schema languages.

1.4.4.1   RELAX NG

RELAX NG covers some of the same ground as DTDs and XML Schema. RELAX NG was developed by an OASIS technical committee and was adopted as an ISO standard (*ISO/IEC 19757-2*). RELAX NG is intended only for validation; the processor does not pass documentation or application information from the schema to the application. RELAX NG does not have a complete built-in type library; it is designed to use other type libraries (such as that of XML Schema).

Some of the benefits of RELAX NG over XML Schema 1.0 have been addressed as new features in XML Schema 1.1. However, RELAX NG still has some advantages as compared to XML Schema 1.1:

- Many people consider the syntax of RELAX NG to be simpler and more elegant than that of XML Schema.
- It has a convenient, compact non-XML syntax.
- It includes attributes in the elements' content models. For example, you can specify that a `product` element must either have an `effectiveDate` attribute or a `startDate` attribute. XML Schema does not directly provide a way to do this.
- It allows the definition of components from multiple namespaces in the same document. In XML Schema, multiple schema documents are required.

- It does not require content models to be deterministic. This is explained in Section 12.5.6 on p. 279.

However, RELAX NG also has some limitations compared to XML Schema:

- It has no equivalent of XML Schema 1.1 assertions, which allow complex XPath expressions to be used to determine the validity of an element or attribute.
- It has no type derivation capabilities. XML Schema's restriction and extension mechanisms allow type substitution and many other benefits, described in Section 13.1 on p. 301.
- It has no equivalent of identity constraints. XML Schema's identity constraint mechanism is useful in data-oriented applications, as described in Chapter 17.
- Because it is only intended for validation, it does not provide application information to the processor. In fact, the RELAX NG processor passes to the application the exact same information that is available from a DTD. This is not a disadvantage if your only objective is validation, but it does not allow you to use the schema to help you understand how to process the instance.

For more information on RELAX NG, see http://relaxng.org.

1.4.4.2 Schematron

XML Schema, DTDs, and RELAX NG are all grammar-based schema languages. They specify what must appear in an instance, and in what order.

Schematron, on the other hand, is rule-based. It allows you to define a series of rules to which the document must conform. These rules are expressed using XPath. In contrast to grammar-based languages, Schematron considers anything that does not violate a rule to be valid.

There is no need to have declarations for every element and attribute that may appear in the instance.

Schematron, sometimes referred to as "ISO Schematron", is an ISO standard (*ISO/IEC 19757-3*). Like RELAX NG, Schematron is intended only for validation of instances. It has a number of advantages over XML Schema 1.1:

- It is easy to learn and use. It uses XPath, which is familiar to many people already using XML.

- The use of XPath allows it to very flexibly and succinctly express relationships between elements in a way that is not possible with other schema languages.

- Assertions in a Schematron rule can access XML data anywhere in a particular instance document. XML Schema 1.1 assertions, by contrast, can only be based on the contents of a particular type.

The limitations of Schematron compared to XML Schema are:

- It does not provide a model of the instance data. A person cannot gain an understanding of what instance data is expected by looking at the schema.

- It is intended only for validation and cannot be used to pass any information about the instance, such as types or default values, to an application.

- Anything is valid unless it is specifically prohibited. This puts a burden to anticipate all possible errors on the schema author.

As Schematron and XML Schema complement each other, it makes sense to combine the two. For more information on Schematron, see www.schematron.com.

A quick tour
of XML Schema

his chapter provides a quick tour of the main components of XML Schema. It also introduces a simple example of a schema and a conforming instance that will be used and built upon throughout the book.

2.1 | An example schema

Suppose you have the instance shown in Example 2–1. It consists of a product element that has two children (number and size) and an attribute (effDate).

Example 2–1. Product instance

```
<product effDate="2001-04-12">
  <number>557</number>
  <size>10</size>
</product>
```

Example 2–2 shows a schema that might be used to validate our instance. Its three element declarations and one attribute declaration assign names and types to the components they declare.

Example 2–2. Product schema

```
<xs:schema xmlns:xs="http://www.w3.org/2001/XMLSchema">
  <xs:element name="product" type="ProductType"/>
  <xs:complexType name="ProductType">
    <xs:sequence>
      <xs:element name="number" type="xs:integer"/>
      <xs:element name="size" type="SizeType"/>
    </xs:sequence>
    <xs:attribute name="effDate" type="xs:date"/>
  </xs:complexType>
  <xs:simpleType name="SizeType">
    <xs:restriction base="xs:integer">
      <xs:minInclusive value="2"/>
      <xs:maxInclusive value="18"/>
    </xs:restriction>
  </xs:simpleType>
</xs:schema>
```

2.2 | The components of XML Schema

Schemas are made up of a number of components of different kinds, listed in Table 2–1. All of the components of XML Schema are discussed in detail in this book, in the chapters indicated in Table 2–1.

2.2.1 *Declarations vs. definitions*

Schemas contain both declarations and definitions. The term *declaration* is used for components that can appear in the instance and be validated by name. This includes elements, attributes, and notations. The term *definition* is used for other components that are internal to the schema, such as complex and simple types, model groups, attribute groups, and identity constraints. Throughout this book, you will see the terms

Table 2–1   XML Schema components

Component	Can be named?	Can be unnamed?	Can be global?	Can be local?	Chapter
Element	yes	no	yes	yes	6
Attribute	yes	no	yes	yes	7
Simple type	yes	yes	yes	yes	8–11
Complex type	yes	yes	yes	yes	12–13
Notation	yes	no	yes	no	19
Named model group	yes	no	yes	no	15
Attribute group	yes	no	yes	no	15
Identity constraint	yes	no	no	yes	17

"element declaration" and "type definition," but not "element definition" or "type declaration."

The order of declarations and definitions in the schema document is insignificant. A declaration can refer to other declarations or definitions that appear before or after it, or even those that appear in another schema document.

2.2.2   *Global vs. local components*

Components can be declared (or defined) *globally* or *locally*. Global components appear at the top level of a schema document, and they are always named. Their names must be unique, within their component type, within the entire schema. For example, it is not legal to have two global element declarations with the same name in the same schema. However, it is legal to have an element declaration and a complex type definition with the same name.

Local components, on the other hand, are scoped to the definition or declaration that contains them. Element and attribute declarations can be local, which means their scope is the complex type in which they are declared. Simple types and complex types can also be locally defined, in which case they are anonymous and cannot be used by any element or attribute declaration other than the one in which they are defined.

2.3 | Elements and attributes

Elements and attributes are the basic building blocks of XML documents. The instance in Example 2–1 contains three elements (product, number, and size) and one attribute (effDate). As a result, the schema contains three element declarations and one attribute declaration. The product element declaration is global, since it appears at the top level of the schema document. The other two element declarations, as well as the attribute declaration, are local, and their scope is the ProductType type in which they are declared. Elements and attributes are covered in detail in Chapters 6 and 7, respectively.

2.3.1   *The tag/type distinction*

Each of the elements and attributes is associated with a *type*. XML Schema separates the concepts of elements and attributes from their types. This allows using different names for data that is structurally the same. For example, you can write two element declarations, shippingAddress and billingAddress, which have the exact same structure but different names. You are only required to define one type, AddressType, and use it in both element declarations. In addition to using different names, you can place the corresponding elements in different places in the document. A shippingAddress element may only be relevant in the shipment information section of a purchase order, while a billingAddress may appear only in the billing section.

You can also have two element declarations with the same name, but different types, in different contexts. For example, a size element can contain an integer when it is a child of shirt, or a value S, M, or L when it is a child of hat.

2.4 | Types

Types allow for validation of the content of elements and the values of attributes. They can be either *simple types* or *complex types*. The term "type" is used throughout this book to mean "simple or complex type."

2.4.1 *Simple vs. complex types*

Elements that have been assigned simple types have character data content, but no child elements or attributes. Example 2–3 shows the size, comment, and availableSizes elements that have simple types.

By contrast, elements that have been assigned complex types may have child elements or attributes. Example 2–4 shows the size, comment, and availableSizes elements with complex types.

Example 2–3. Elements with simple types

```
<size>10</size>
<comment>Runs large.</comment>
<availableSizes>10 large 2</availableSizes>
```

Example 2–4. Elements with complex types

```
<size system="US-DRESS">10</size>
<comment>Runs <b>large</b>.</comment>
<availableSizes><size>10</size><size>2</size></availableSizes>
```

Attributes always have simple types, not complex types. This makes sense, because attributes themselves cannot have children or other attributes. Example 2–5 shows some attributes that have simple types.

Example 2–5. Attributes with simple types

```
system="US-DRESS"
availableSizes="10 large 2"
```

2.4.2   *Named vs. anonymous types*

Types can be either *named* or *anonymous*. Named types are always defined globally (at the top level of a schema document) and are required to have a unique name. Anonymous types, on the other hand, must not have names. They are always defined entirely within an element or attribute declaration, and may only be used once, by that declaration. The two types in Example 2–2 are both named types. An anonymous type is shown in Example 2–6.

Example 2–6. Anonymous type

```
<xs:element name="size">
  <xs:simpleType>
    <xs:restriction base="xs:integer">
      <xs:minInclusive value="2"/>
      <xs:maxInclusive value="18"/>
    </xs:restriction>
  </xs:simpleType>
</xs:element>
```

2.4.3   *The type definition hierarchy*

XML Schema allows types to be *derived* from other types. In Example 2–2, the simple type `SizeType` is derived from the `integer` simple type. A complex type can also be derived from another type, either simple or complex. It can either restrict or extend the other type. For example, you could define a complex type `UKAddressType` that extends `AddressType` to add more children.

The derivation of types from other types forms a type definition hierarchy. Derived types are related to their ancestors and inherit qualities from them. They can also be substituted for each other in instances. If the `shippingAddress` element declaration refers to the type `AddressType`, a corresponding element can also have the type `UKAddressType` in the instance.

This is very powerful because applications designed to process generic `AddressType` elements can also process `UKAddressType` elements without caring about the differences. Other processors that do care about the differences between them can distinguish between the different types.

2.5 | Simple types

2.5.1 *Built-in simple types*

Forty-nine simple types are built into the XML Schema recommendation. These simple types represent common data types such as strings, numbers, date and time values, and also include types for each of the valid attribute types in XML DTDs. The built-in types are summarized in Table 2–2 and discussed in detail in Chapter 11.

Example 2–2 assigned the built-in simple type `integer` to the `number` elements, and the built-in simple type `date` to the `effDate` attribute.

Table 2–2 Built-in simple type summary

Category	*Built-in types*
Strings and names	`string`, `normalizedString`, `token`, `Name`, `NCName`, `QName`, `language`
Numeric	`float`, `double`, `decimal`, `integer`, `long`, `int`, `short`, `byte`, `positiveInteger`, `nonPositiveInteger`, `negativeInteger`, `nonNegativeInteger`, `unsignedLong`, `unsignedInt`, `unsignedShort`, `unsignedByte`
Date and time	`duration`, `dateTime`, `date`, `time`, `gYear`, `gYearMonth`, `gMonth`, `gMonthDay`, `gDay`, ▪`dayTimeDuration`, ▪`yearMonthDuration`, ▪`dateTimeStamp`
XML DTD types	`ID`, `IDREF`, `IDREFS`, `ENTITY`, `ENTITIES`, `NMTOKEN`, `NMTOKENS`, `NOTATION`
Other	`boolean`, `hexBinary`, `base64Binary`, `anyURI`

2.5.2   *Restricting simple types*

New simple types may be derived from other simple types by *restricting* them. Example 2–2 showed the definition of a simple type `SizeType` that restricts the built-in type `integer`. We applied the *facets* `minInclusive` and `maxInclusive` to restrict the valid values of the `size` elements to be between `2` and `18`. Using the fourteen facets that are part of XML Schema, you can specify a valid range of values, constrain the length and precision of values, enumerate a list of valid values, or specify a regular expression that valid values must match. These fourteen facets are summarized in Table 2–3. Chapter 8 explains how to derive new simple types.

Table 2–3   Facets

Category	*Facets*
Bounds	`minInclusive, maxInclusive, minExclusive, maxExclusive`
Length	`length, minLength, maxLength`
Precision	`totalDigits, fractionDigits`
Enumerated values	`enumeration`
Pattern matching	`pattern`
Whitespace processing	`whiteSpace`
XPath-based assertions	`assertion`
Time zone requirements	`explicitTimezone`

2.5.3   *List and union types*

Most simple types, including those we have seen so far, are *atomic types*. They contain values that are indivisible, such as `10`. There are two other varieties of simple types: list and union types.

List types have values that are whitespace-separated lists of atomic values, such as `<availableSizes>10 large 2</availableSizes>`.

Union types may have values that are either atomic values or list values. What differentiates them is that the set of valid values, or "value space," for the type is the union of the value spaces of two or more other simple types. For example, to represent a dress size, you may define a union type that allows a value to be either an integer from 2 through 18 or one of the string values `small`, `medium`, or `large`.

List and union types are covered in Chapter 10.

2.6 | Complex types

2.6.1 *Content types*

The "content" of an element is the character data and child elements that are between its tags. There are four types of content for complex types: *simple, element-only, mixed,* and *empty.* The content type is independent of attributes; all of these content types allow attributes. Example 2–7 shows the instance elements `size`, `product`, `letter`, and `color` that have complex types. They represent the four different content types.

- The `size` element has simple content, because it contains only character data.
- The `product` element has element-only content, because it has child elements, but no character data content.

Example 2–7. Elements with complex types

```
<size system="US-DRESS">10</size>

<product>
  <number>557</number>
  <size>10</size>
</product>

<letter>Dear <custName>Priscilla Walmsley</custName>...</letter>

<color value="blue"/>
```

- The `letter` element has mixed content, because it has both child elements and character data content.

- The `color` element has empty content, because it does not have any content (just attributes).

2.6.2   *Content models*

The order and structure of the child elements of a complex type are known as its *content model*. Content models are defined using a combination of model groups, element declarations or references, and wildcards. In Example 2–2, the content model of `ProductType` was a single `sequence` model group containing two element declarations. There are three kinds of model groups:

- `sequence` groups require that the child elements appear in the order specified.

- `choice` groups allow any one of several child elements to appear.

- `all` groups allow child elements to appear in any order.

These groups can be nested and may occur multiple times, allowing you to create sophisticated content models. Example 2–8 shows a more complex content model for `ProductType`. Instances of this new definition of `ProductType` must have a `number` child, optionally followed

Example 2–8. More complicated content model

```
<xs:complexType name="ProductType">
  <xs:sequence>
    <xs:element name="number" type="xs:integer"/>
    <xs:choice minOccurs="0" maxOccurs="3">
      <xs:element name="size" type="SizeType"/>
      <xs:element name="color" type="ColorType"/>
    </xs:choice>
    <xs:any namespace="##other"/>
  </xs:sequence>
  <xs:attribute name="effDate" type="xs:date"/>
</xs:complexType>
```

by up to three children which may be either `size` or `color` elements, followed by any one element from another namespace.

An `any` element is known as a wildcard, and it allows for open content models. There is an equivalent wildcard for attributes, `anyAttribute`, which allows any attribute to appear in a complex type.

2.6.3 *Deriving complex types*

Complex types may be derived from other types either by restriction or by extension.

Restriction, as the name suggests, restricts the valid contents of a type. The values for the new type are a subset of those for the base type. All values of the restricted type are also valid according to the base type.

Extension allows for adding additional child elements and/or attributes to a type, thus extending the contents of the type. Values of the base type are not necessarily valid for the extended type, since required elements or attributes may be added. Example 2–9 shows the definition of `ShirtType` that is a complex type extension. It adds another element declaration, `color`, and another attribute declaration, `id`, to `ProductType`. New element declarations or references may only be added to the end of a content model, so instances of `ShirtType` must have the children `number`, `size`, and `color`, in that order.

Example 2–9. Complex type extension

```
<xs:complexType name="ShirtType">
  <xs:complexContent>
    <xs:extension base="ProductType">
      <xs:sequence>
        <xs:element name="color" type="ColorType"/>
      </xs:sequence>
      <xs:attribute name="id" type="xs:ID" use="required"/>
    </xs:extension>
  </xs:complexContent>
</xs:complexType>
```

2.7 | Namespaces and XML Schema

Namespaces are an important part of XML Schema, and they are discussed in detail in Chapter 3. Example 2–10 shows our now-familiar schema, this time with a target namespace declared. Let's take a closer look at the attributes of a `schema` element.

1. The namespace `http://www.w3.org/2001/XMLSchema` is mapped to the `xs:` prefix. This indicates that the elements used in the schema document itself, such as `schema`, `element`, and `complexType`, are part of the XML Schema namespace.

2. A target namespace, `http://datypic.com/prod`, is declared. Any schema document may have a target namespace, which applies to the global (and some local) components declared or defined in it. Although a schema document can only have one target namespace, multiple schema documents with different

Example 2–10. Product schema document with target namespace

```
<xs:schema xmlns:xs="http://www.w3.org/2001/XMLSchema"
           targetNamespace="http://datypic.com/prod"
           xmlns:prod="http://datypic.com/prod">

  <xs:element name="product" type="prod:ProductType"/>
  <xs:complexType name="ProductType">
    <xs:sequence>
      <xs:element name="number" type="xs:integer"/>
      <xs:element name="size" type="prod:SizeType"/>
    </xs:sequence>
    <xs:attribute name="effDate" type="xs:date"/>
  </xs:complexType>
  <xs:simpleType name="SizeType">
    <xs:restriction base="xs:integer">
      <xs:minInclusive value="2"/>
      <xs:maxInclusive value="18"/>
    </xs:restriction>
  </xs:simpleType>
</xs:schema>
```

target namespaces can be assembled together to represent a schema.

3. The target namespace is mapped to the `prod` prefix.

Example 2–11 shows a new instance, where a namespace is declared. In order for an instance to be valid according to a schema, the namespace declaration in the instance must match the target namespace of the schema document.

Example 2–11. Instance with namespace

```
<prod:product xmlns:prod="http://datypic.com/prod"
              effDate="2001-04-12">
  <number>557</number>
  <size>10</size>
</prod:product>
```

In this case, only the `product` element has a prefixed name. This is because the other two elements and the attribute are declared locally. By default, locally declared components do not take on the target namespace. However, this can be overridden by specifying `elementFormDefault` and `attributeFormDefault` for the schema document. This is discussed in detail in Chapters 6 and 7.

2.8 | Schema composition

An XSD schema is a set of components such as type definitions and element declarations. Example 2–2 showed a schema document that was used alone to validate an instance. It contained the declarations and definitions for all of the components of the schema.

However, a schema could also be represented by an assembly of schema documents. One way to compose them is through the include and import mechanisms. Include is used when the other schema document has the same target namespace as the "main" schema document. Import is used when the other schema document has a different target

Example 2–12. Schema composition using `include` and `import`

```
<xs:schema xmlns:xs="http://www.w3.org/2001/XMLSchema"
           xmlns="http://datypic.com/ord"
           targetNamespace="http://datypic.com/ord">

  <xs:include schemaLocation="moreOrderInfo.xsd"/>

  <xs:import namespace="http://datypic.com/prod"
             schemaLocation="productInfo.xsd"/>
  <!--...-->
</xs:schema>
```

namespace. Example 2–12 shows how you might include and import other schema documents.

The include and import mechanisms are not the only way for processors to assemble schema documents into a schema. Unfortunately, there is not always a "main" schema document that represents the whole schema. Instead, a processor might join schema documents from various predefined locations, or take multiple hints from the instance. See Chapter 4 for more information on schema composition.

2.9 | Instances and schemas

A document that conforms to a schema is known as an instance. An instance can be validated against a particular schema, which may be made up of the schema components defined in multiple schema documents. A number of different ways exist for the schema documents to be located for a particular instance. One way is using the `xsi:schemaLocation` attribute. Example 2–13 shows an instance that uses the `xsi:schemaLocation` attribute to map a namespace to a particular schema document.

Using `xsi:schemaLocation` is not the only way to tell the processor where to find the schema. XML Schema is deliberately flexible on this topic, allowing processors to use different methods for choosing schema documents to validate a particular instance. These

Example 2–13. Using `xsi:schemaLocation`

```
<prod:product xmlns:prod="http://datypic.com/prod"
              xmlns:xsi="http://www.w3.org/2001/XMLSchema-instance"
              xsi:schemaLocation="http://datypic.com/prod prod.xsd"
              effDate="2001-04-12">
  <number>557</number>
  <size>10</size>
</prod:product>
```

methods include built-in schemas, use of internal catalogs, use of the `xsi:schemaLocation` attribute, and dereferencing of namespaces. Chapter 5 covers the validation of instances in detail.

2.10 | Annotations

XML Schema provides many mechanisms for describing the structure of XML documents. However, it cannot express everything there is to know about an instance or the data it contains. For this reason, XML Schema allows annotations to be added to almost any schema component. These annotations can contain human-readable information (under `documentation`) or application information (under `appinfo`). Example 2–14 shows an annotation for the `product` element declaration. Annotations are covered in Chapter 21.

Example 2–14. Annotation

```
<xs:schema xmlns:xs="http://www.w3.org/2001/XMLSchema"
           xmlns:doc="http://datypic.com/doc">
  <xs:element name="product" type="ProductType">
    <xs:annotation>
      <xs:documentation xml:lang="en"
        source="http://datypic.com/prod.html#product">
        <doc:description>This element represents a product.
        </doc:description>
      </xs:documentation>
    </xs:annotation>
  </xs:element>
</xs:schema>
```

2.11 | Advanced features

XML Schema has some more advanced features. These features are available if you need them, but are certainly not an integral part of every schema. Keep in mind that you are not required to use all of XML Schema. You should choose a subset that is appropriate for your needs.

2.11.1 *Named groups*

XML Schema provides the ability to define groups of element and attribute declarations that are reusable by many complex types. This facility promotes reuse of schema components and eases maintenance. Named model groups are fragments of content models, and attribute groups are bundles of related attributes that are commonly used together. Chapter 15 explains named groups.

2.11.2 *Identity constraints*

Identity constraints allow you to uniquely identify nodes in a document and ensure the integrity of references between them. They are similar to the primary and foreign keys in databases. They are described in detail in Chapter 17.

2.11.3 *Substitution groups*

Substitution groups are a flexible way to designate certain element declarations as substitutes for other element declarations in content models. If you have a group of related elements that may appear inter-changeably in instances, you can reference the substitution group as a whole in content models. You can easily add new element declarations to the substitution groups, from other schema documents, and even other namespaces, without changing the original declarations in any way. Substitution groups are covered in Chapter 16.

2.11.4 *Redefinition and overriding*

Redefinition and overriding allow you to define a new version of a schema component while keeping the same name. This is useful for extending or creating a subset of an existing schema document, or overriding the definitions of components in a schema document. Redefinition and overriding are covered in Chapter 18.

2.11.5 *Assertions*

Assertions are XPath constraints on XML data, which allow complex validation above and beyond what can be specified in a content model. This is especially useful for co-constraints, where the values or existence of certain child elements or attributes affect the validity of other child elements or attributes. For example, "If the value of `newCustomer` is false, then `customerID` must appear." Chapter 14 covers assertions in detail.

Namespaces

nderstanding namespaces is essential to understanding XML Schema. This chapter introduces namespaces and explains their relationship to schemas.

3.1 | Namespaces in XML

Before we delve into the use of namespaces in schema documents, let's take a minute to learn about namespaces in general. Namespaces are a surprisingly simple concept considering how much confusion and controversy it causes. The purpose of namespaces is to provide containers for the names used in XML. A name, such as `table`, can have several meanings. Its meaning in XHTML is very different from its meaning in a hypothetical language for describing office furniture, FurnitureML. An element or attribute name in an instance can be declared to be in a namespace, which provides context and identifies the XML vocabulary to which the element or attribute belongs.

Namespaces are defined by a separate W3C recommendation called *Namespaces in XML*, which is in two versions: 1.0 and 1.1. XML Schema 1.0 uses Namespaces 1.0, and XML Schema 1.1 uses Namespaces 1.1. There are few substantive differences between them, mentioned in the appropriate sections of this chapter.

3.1.1 *Namespace names*

Namespace names are Uniform Resource Identifiers (URIs). URIs encompass URLs of various schemes (e.g., HTTP, FTP, gopher, telnet), as well as URNs (Uniform Resource Names). Many namespaces are written in the form of HTTP URLs, such as `http://datypic.com/prod`. It is also legal to use a URN, such as `urn:example:org`.

The main purpose of a namespace is not to point to a location where a resource resides. Instead, much like a Java package name, it is intended to provide a unique name that can be associated with a particular person or organization. Therefore, namespace names are not required to be dereferenceable. That is, there does not necessarily need to be an HTML page or other resource that can be accessed at `http://datypic.com/prod`. The namespace URI could point to a schema, an HTML page, a directory of resources, or nothing at all. This is explained further in Section 21.8.5 on p. 589.

Namespace names are case-sensitive. Two namespaces are considered different if their capitalization is different, even if you might consider them equivalent URLs. For example, `http://DATYPIC.COM/prod` and `http://datypic.com/prod` represent different namespaces, because they are capitalized differently.

Although relative URI references, such as `../prod` or just plain `prod` are legal as URIs, they are not appropriate namespace names. A namespace name should be unique, and it is difficult to ensure the uniqueness of `../prod`. In fact, version 1.1 of the Namespaces recommendation says that they are deprecated.

The URI syntax only allows basic Latin letters and digits, with a few special punctuation characters. Non-Latin characters can be represented, but they must be escaped. In Namespaces 1.1, and therefore when using XML Schema 1.1, namespace names are actually IRIs (Internationalized Resource Identifiers) rather than URIs, which means that non-Latin characters can be directly represented in namespace names.

3.1.2 *Namespace declarations and prefixes*

An instance may include one or more namespace declarations that relate elements and attributes to namespaces. This happens through a prefix, which serves as a proxy for the namespace.

A namespace is declared using a special attribute whose name starts with the letters `xmlns`. Example 3–1 shows an instance whose root element has a namespace declaration. This declaration maps the namespace `http://datypic.com/prod` to the prefix `prod`. All of the element names in the document, namely `product`, `number`, and `size`, are prefixed with `prod`. The `system` attribute does not have a prefixed name, so it is not "in" the namespace.

Example 3–1. Namespace declaration

```
<prod:product xmlns:prod="http://datypic.com/prod">
  <prod:number>557</prod:number>
  <prod:size system="US-DRESS">10</prod:size>
</prod:product>
```

Prefixes are convenient because they are generally shorter than namespace names, so they make the document more readable. A more important reason for prefixes, though, is that namespace names may contain characters that are not permitted in XML names. Prefixes are constrained by the rules for XML non-colonized names, as described in Section 3.1.4 on p. 40. There is no limit to how many characters long a prefix can be, but it is best to keep prefixes short for readability.

Although the instance author may choose prefixes arbitrarily, there are commonly used prefixes for some namespaces. For example, the xsl prefix is usually mapped to the Extensible Stylesheet Language (XSL) namespace. It is legal to map the prefix bob to the XSL namespace and write a stylesheet with every XSL element name prefixed with bob. However, this is not recommended because it is confusing. For the XML Schema Namespace, the commonly used prefixes are xsd and xs.

You can declare more than one namespace in the same instance, as shown in Example 3–2. Two prefixes, ord and prod, are mapped to the namespaces http://datypic.com/ord and http://datypic.com/prod, respectively. The element names in the document are prefixed with either ord or prod to relate them to one of the two namespaces.

Example 3–2. Multiple namespace declarations

```
<ord:order xmlns:ord="http://datypic.com/ord"
           xmlns:prod="http://datypic.com/prod">
  <ord:number>123ABBCC123</ord:number>
  <ord:items>
    <prod:product>
      <prod:number>557</prod:number>
      <prod:size system="US-DRESS">10</prod:size>
    </prod:product>
  </ord:items>
</ord:order>
```

Note that number appears twice, with two different prefixes. This illustrates the usefulness of namespaces which make it obvious whether it is a product number or an order number. In most cases, the two can be distinguished based on their context in the instance, but not always.

You do not need to declare xmlns:ord and xmlns:prod as attributes in the order element declaration in your schema. In fact, it is illegal to declare them. All schema processors understand that attributes prefixed with xmlns and the unprefixed attribute with the name xmlns are always permitted.

3.1.3   *Default namespace declarations*

An instance may also include a default namespace declaration that maps unprefixed element names to a namespace. The default namespace declaration uses the attribute xmlns, with no colon or prefix. In Example 3–3, the start order tag contains a default namespace declaration. This declaration relates the namespace http://datypic.com/ord to all of the unprefixed element names in the document, namely order, number, and items.

Example 3–3. Default namespace declaration

```
<order xmlns="http://datypic.com/ord"
       xmlns:prod="http://datypic.com/prod">
  <number>123ABBCC123</number>
  <items>
    <prod:product>
      <prod:number>557</prod:number>
      <prod:size system="US-DRESS">10</prod:size>
    </prod:product>
  </items>
</order>
```

Note that the default namespace declaration can be combined with other namespace declarations in the same document and even in the same tag.

Default namespace declarations do not directly apply to attributes. In this case, the system attribute, although its name is not prefixed, is not in the default namespace http://datypic.com/ord. It is not directly in any namespace at all. For further explanation of the relationship between attributes and namespaces, see Section 3.1.8 on p. 44.

3.1.4 *Name terminology*

In the context of namespaces, there are several different kinds of names. They include:

Qualified names, known as QNames, are names that are qualified with a namespace name. This may happen one of two ways:

1. The name contains a prefix that is mapped to a namespace. In Example 3–3, `prod:product` is a prefixed, qualified name.

2. The name does not contain a prefix, but there is a default namespace declared for that element. In Example 3–3, `items` is an unprefixed, qualified name. This applies only to elements; there is no such thing as an unprefixed, qualified attribute name, as you will see in Section 3.1.8 on p. 44.

Unqualified names, on the other hand, are names that are not in any namespace. For element names, this means they are unprefixed and there is no default namespace declaration. For attribute names, this means they are unprefixed, period.

Prefixed names are names that contain a namespace prefix, such as `prod:product`. Prefixed names are qualified names, assuming there is a namespace declaration for that prefix in scope.

Unprefixed names are names that do not contain a prefix, such as `items`. Unprefixed element names can be either qualified or unqualified, depending on whether there is a default namespace declaration.

A *local name* is the part of a qualified name that is not the prefix. In Example 3–3, local names include `items` and `product`.

Non-colonized names, known as NCNames, are simply XML names that do not contain colons. That means that they are case-sensitive, they may start with a letter or underscore (_), and contain letters, digits, underscores (_), dashes (-), and periods (.). They cannot start with the letters "XML" either in lower or uppercase. All local names and

unprefixed names are NCNames. Prefixes are also NCNames, because
they follow these same rules.

3.1.5 *Scope of namespace declarations*

In the previous examples, namespace declarations appeared in the start
tag of the root element. Namespace declarations, including default
namespace declarations, can appear in any start tag in the document.
Example 3–4 shows the previous `order` example, but with the
namespace declaration for the `http://datypic.com/prod` namespace
moved down to the `product` tag.

Example 3–4. Namespace declarations in multiple tags

```
<order xmlns="http://datypic.com/ord">
  <number>123ABBCC123</number>
  <items>
    <prod:product xmlns:prod="http://datypic.com/prod">
      <prod:number>557</prod:number>
      <prod:size system="US-DRESS">10</prod:size>
    </prod:product>
  </items>
</order>
```

The scope of a namespace declaration is the element in whose start
tag it appears, and all of its children, grandchildren, and so on. In
Example 3–4, it would be invalid to use the `prod` prefix outside of
the `product` element and its children. In Example 3–5, the second
`product` element uses the `prod` prefix, which is illegal because the
namespace declaration is outside its scope.

Generally, it is preferable to put all your namespace declarations in
the root element's start tag. It allows you to see at a glance what
namespaces a document uses, there is no confusion about their scopes,
and it keeps them from cluttering the rest of the document.

Example 3–5. Invalid prefix outside of scope

```
<order xmlns="http://datypic.com/ord">
  <number>123ABBCC123</number>
  <items>
    <prod:product xmlns:prod="http://datypic.com/prod">
      <prod:number>557</prod:number>
      <prod:size system="US-DRESS">10</prod:size>
    </prod:product>
    <prod:product>
      <prod:number>559</prod:number>
      <prod:size system="US-DRESS">10</prod:size>
    </prod:product>
  </items>
</order>
```

3.1.6 *Overriding namespace declarations*

Namespace declarations can also be overridden. If a namespace declaration appears within the scope of another namespace declaration with the same prefix, it overrides it. Example 3–6 illustrates this. In the order tag, the prefix prod is mapped to http://datypic.com/prod. In number, it is mapped to http://datypic.com/prod2. The second namespace declaration overrides the first within the scope of the number element. This includes the number element itself.

Example 3–6. Overriding a namespace declaration

```
<order xmlns="http://datypic.com/ord"
       xmlns:prod="http://datypic.com/prod">
  <number>123ABBCC123</number>
  <items>
    <prod:product>
      <prod:number xmlns:prod="http://datypic.com/prod2">
        557</prod:number>
      <prod:size system="US-DRESS">10</prod:size>
    </prod:product>
  </items>
</order>
```

Likewise, if a default namespace declaration appears within the scope of another default namespace declaration, it overrides it, as shown in Example 3–7. The default namespace declaration in the `product` start tag overrides the one on the root element, meaning that `product` and its children are in the `http://datypic.com/prod` namespace.

Example 3–7. Overriding a default namespace declaration

```
<order xmlns="http://datypic.com/ord">
  <number>123ABBCC123</number>
  <items>
    <product xmlns="http://datypic.com/prod">
      <number>557</number>
      <size system="US-DRESS">10</size>
    </product>
  </items>
</order>
```

3.1.7   *Undeclaring namespaces*

A default namespace declaration may also be the empty string (that is, `xmlns=""`). This means that unprefixed element names in its scope are not in any namespace. This can be used to essentially "undeclare" the default namespace.

Example 3–8 is similar to Example 3–7 except that it uses the empty string. This means that `product` and its children are in no namespace.

Example 3–8. Undeclaring a default namespace

```
<order xmlns="http://datypic.com/ord">
  <number>123ABBCC123</number>
  <items>
    <product xmlns="">
      <number>557</number>
      <size system="US-DRESS">10</size>
    </product>
  </items>
</order>
```

In version 1.1 (but not in 1.0), you can also undeclare a prefix by using an empty string. In Example 3–9, the namespace declaration for the ord prefix in the product start tag undeclares the one on the root element, meaning that the ord prefix is undefined within the scope of product.

Example 3–9. Undeclaring a prefixed namespace

```
<ord:order xmlns:ord="http://datypic.com/ord">
  <ord:number>123ABBCC123</ord:number>
  <ord:items>
    <prod:product xmlns:ord="" xmlns:prod="http://datypic.com/prod">
      <prod:number>557</prod:number>
      <prod:size system="US-DRESS">10</prod:size>
    </prod:product>
  </ord:items>
</ord:order>
```

3.1.8 *Attributes and namespaces*

The relationship between attributes and namespaces is slightly simpler than the relationship between elements and namespaces. Prefixed attribute names, as you would expect, are in whichever namespace is mapped to that prefix. Attributes with prefixed names are sometimes referred to as global attributes. Unprefixed attribute names, however, are never in a namespace. This is because they are not affected by default namespace declarations.

Some people make the argument that an unprefixed attribute is (or should be) in the namespace of its parent element. While it may be indirectly associated with that namespace, it is not directly in it. For the purposes of writing schemas and using other XML technologies such as XSLT and XQuery, you should treat an unprefixed attribute as if it were in no namespace at all.

Example 3–10 shows a size element that has two attributes: app:system and system. app:system is associated with the namespace `http://datypic.com/app` through the `app` prefix. The unprefixed `system` attribute is not in any namespace at all, despite the default namespace declaration.

Example 3–10. Two attributes with the same local name

```
<product xmlns="http://datypic.com/prod"
         xmlns:app="http://datypic.com/app">
  <number>557</number>
  <size app:system="R32" system="US-DRESS">10</size>
</product>
```

Although an element cannot have two attributes with the same name, this example is valid because the attribute names are in different namespaces (or rather, one is in a namespace and one is not), and they therefore are considered to have different names.

Example 3–11 is also valid, even though the default namespace and the namespace mapped to the `prod` prefix are the same. This is again because the unprefixed `system` attribute is not in any namespace.

Example 3–11. Two more attributes with the same local name

```
<product xmlns="http://datypic.com/prod"
         xmlns:prod="http://datypic.com/prod">
  <number>557</number>
  <size system="US-DRESS" prod:system="R32">10</size>
</product>
```

Example 3–12 shows an invalid duplication of attributes. The problem is not that two different prefixes are mapped to the same namespace; this is perfectly acceptable. However, it is not valid for an element to have two attributes with the same name that are in the same namespace, even if they have different prefixes.

Example 3–12. Invalid duplicate attributes

```
<product xmlns:prod="http://datypic.com/prod"
         xmlns:prod2="http://datypic.com/prod">
  <number>557</number>
  <size prod:system="US-DRESS" prod2:system="R32">10</size>
</product>
```

This example illustrates an important point: The prefix itself has no particular meaning. Instead, it is the namespace to which it is mapped that matters when validating and comparing names. The two qualified names `prod:system` and `prod2:system` are equal, even though the prefixes differ.

3.1.9   *A summary example*

To summarize our discussion of namespaces, Example 3–13 provides a more complex instance that shows various combinations of namespace declarations in different scopes.

Example 3–13. A summary example

```
<envelope>
  <order xmlns="http://datypic.com/ord"
         xmlns:prod="http://datypic.com/prod">
    <number>123ABBCC123</number>
    <items>
      <product xmlns="http://datypic.com/prod">
        <number prod:id="prod557">557</number>
        <name xmlns="">Short-Sleeved Linen Blouse</name>
        <prod:size system="US-DRESS">10</prod:size>
        <prod:color xmlns:prod="http://datypic.com/prod2"
                    prod:value="blue"/>
      </product>
    </items>
  </order>
</envelope>
```

Table 3–1 explains which namespace each name is in, and why.

Table 3–1   Explanation of the summary example

Name	*Namespace (http://datypic.com/ . . .)*	*Explanation*
envelope	none	No prefix, no default namespace in scope.
order	ord	Takes default namespace from order (itself).
number (child of order)	ord	Takes default namespace from order.
product	prod	Takes default namespace from product (itself).
number (child of product)	prod	Takes default namespace from product.
prod:id	prod	Prefix ties it to namespace declaration in order.
name	none	Default namespace set to empty string, which is equivalent to saying that it has no namespace.
prod:size	prod	Prefix ties it to the namespace declaration in order.
system	none	Unprefixed attribute names are never in a namespace, even if there is a default namespace declaration.
prod:color	prod2	Prefix ties it to the namespace declaration in color (itself).
prod:value	prod2	Prefix ties it to the namespace declaration in color.

3.2 | The relationship between namespaces and schemas

Namespaces and schemas have a many-to-many relationship.

A namespace can have names defined in any number of schemas. A namespace can exist without any schema. Some namespaces have one schema that defines its names. Other namespaces have multiple schemas. These schemas may be designed to be used together, or be completely incompatible with each other. They could present different perspectives on the same information, or be designed for different purposes such as varying levels of validation or system documentation. They could be different versions of each other. There are no rules that prevent several schemas from utilizing the same namespace, with overlapping declarations. As long as the processor does not try to validate an instance against all of them at once, this is completely legal.

A schema can declare names for any number of target namespaces. Some schemas have no target namespace at all. Other schemas are represented by composing multiple schema documents, each with its own target namespace. This is described in detail in Chapter 4.

3.3 | Using namespaces in schemas

3.3.1 *Target namespaces*

Each schema document can declare and define components for one namespace, known as its target namespace. Every globally declared or defined component (element, attribute, type, named group, or notation) is associated with that target namespace. Example 3–14 shows a schema document that declares a target namespace of `http://datypic.com/prod`. Three element declarations are global, and therefore all of them are in the namespace `http://datypic.com/prod`. Local element declarations may or may not use the target namespace of the schema document, as described in Section 6.3 on p. 98.

Example 3–14. Declaring a target namespace

```
<xs:schema xmlns:xs="http://www.w3.org/2001/XMLSchema"
           xmlns="http://datypic.com/prod"
           targetNamespace="http://datypic.com/prod">

  <xs:element name="product" type="ProductType"/>
  <xs:element name="number" type="xs:integer"/>
  <xs:element name="size" type="SizeType"/>

  <xs:complexType name="ProductType">
    <xs:sequence>
      <xs:element ref="number"/>
      <xs:element ref="size"/>
    </xs:sequence>
  </xs:complexType>
  <!--...-->
</xs:schema>
```

Adding a target namespace to a schema is not just informational; the target namespace becomes an important part of the names, and it must be reflected in the instance documents. Example 3–15 shows how the elements from the previous example could appear in an instance. Since they are associated with the `http://datypic.com/prod` namespace, they must be qualified in some way, either through a prefix or by a default namespace declaration.

Example 3–15. Prefixed names in an instance

```
<prod:product xmlns:prod="http://datypic.com/prod">
  <prod:number>557</prod:number>
  <prod:size>10</prod:size>
</prod:product>
```

A schema document cannot have more than one target namespace. However, you can link together schema documents that have different target namespaces, using an `import`. This is described in Section 4.3.2 on p. 66.

If you do not plan to use namespaces, you are not required to specify a target namespace. In this case, omit the `targetNamespace` attribute entirely.

3.3.2 *The XML Schema Namespace*

Since schema documents are XML, namespaces also apply to them. For example, all the elements used in schemas, such as `schema`, `element`, and `simpleType`, are in the XML Schema Namespace, whose namespace name is `http://www.w3.org/2001/XMLSchema`. In addition, the names of the built-in simple types are in this namespace.

The prefixes most commonly mapped to this namespace are `xsd` or `xs`. It is recommended that you use one of these for clarity, although you could just as easily use any other prefix. Example 3–16 shows a schema document that maps the XML Schema Namespace to `xs` and prefixes all of the element names in the schema document.

Example 3–16. Declaring the XML Schema Namespace

```
<xs:schema xmlns:xs="http://www.w3.org/2001/XMLSchema">
  <xs:element name="number" type="xs:integer"/>
  <xs:element name="size" type="SizeType"/>
  <xs:simpleType name="SizeType">
    <!--...-->
  </xs:simpleType>
</xs:schema>
```

It is interesting to note that while all the element names are prefixed, all of the attribute names are unprefixed. This is because none of the attributes in the XML Schema Namespace is declared globally. This is explained further in Section 7.4 on p. 122.

The `xs` prefix is also used when referring to the built-in type `integer`. This is because `integer` is a simple type that is defined in the schema for schemas, whose target namespace is the XML Schema Namespace.

Mapping a prefix such as `xs` to the XML Schema Namespace is one of the three options for namespace declarations in schema documents. See Section 3.3.5 on p. 52 for more information.

3.3.3 *The XML Schema Instance Namespace*

The XML Schema Instance Namespace is a separate namespace for the four schema-related attributes that may appear in instances. Its namespace name is `http://www.w3.org/2001/XMLSchema-instance`. These attributes, whose names are commonly prefixed with `xsi`, are: `type`, `nil`, `schemaLocation`, and `noNamespaceSchemaLocation`. They are described in Section 5.1 on p. 79.

3.3.4 *The Version Control Namespace*

The XML Schema Version Control Namespace is a namespace used by six attributes that signal to processors the conditions under which they should pay attention to particular schema components. Its namespace name is `http://www.w3.org/2007/XMLSchema-versioning`, and it is commonly associated with the prefix `vc`. Four of these attributes control the portability of implementation-defined facets and types and are covered in Section 23.5.3 on p. 642. The other two indicate versions of the XML Schema language and are described in Section 23.5.2 on p. 641.

3.3.5 *Namespace declarations in schema documents*

Schema documents must contain namespace declarations of both the XML Schema Namespace and the target namespace in order to resolve the references between schema components. There are three ways to set up the namespace declarations in your schema document, each of which is described in this section.

3.3.5.1 Map a prefix to the XML Schema Namespace

You can map the XML Schema Namespace to a prefix such as xsd or xs, and make the target namespace the default namespace. Example 3–17 shows a schema document that uses this approach. This method is used throughout this book. Its advantage is that it makes it clear which components are defined by XML Schema, especially when it comes to referencing built-in types.

Example 3–17. Prefixing the XML Schema Namespace

```
<xs:schema xmlns:xs="http://www.w3.org/2001/XMLSchema"
           xmlns="http://datypic.com/prod"
           targetNamespace="http://datypic.com/prod">
  <xs:element name="number" type="xs:integer"/>
  <xs:element name="size" type="SizeType"/>
  <xs:simpleType name="SizeType">
    <!--...-->
  </xs:simpleType>
</xs:schema>
```

If your schema document does not have a target namespace, you *must* map a prefix to the XML Schema Namespace. Otherwise, you will have no way of referencing other schema components that are defined in your schema document. Example 3–18 shows a schema document that does not have a target namespace and defaults the XML Schema Namespace. This is invalid, because the declaration of size references the type SizeType. Since the default namespace is the XML Schema

Namespace, the processor will look unsuccessfully for a definition of `SizeType` in the XML Schema Namespace.

Example 3–18. Invalid absence of prefixes

```
<schema xmlns="http://www.w3.org/2001/XMLSchema">
  <element name="number" type="integer"/>
  <element name="size" type="SizeType"/>
  <simpleType name="SizeType">
    <!--...-->
  </simpleType>
</schema>
```

3.3.5.2 Map a prefix to the target namespace

Another alternative is to map a prefix to the target namespace, and make the XML Schema Namespace the default namespace. Example 3–19 shows a schema document that uses this approach. The names in the declarations themselves do not need to be prefixed because they automatically become part of the target namespace. The only place the prefix is used is in references to other components. For example, the declaration of `size` references the type `SizeType` by its qualified name. If it did not prefix the name of the type, the processor would look unsuccessfully for a definition of `SizeType` in the XML Schema Namespace.

Example 3–19. Prefixing the target namespace

```
<schema xmlns="http://www.w3.org/2001/XMLSchema"
        xmlns:prod="http://datypic.com/prod"
        targetNamespace="http://datypic.com/prod">
  <element name="number" type="integer"/>
  <element name="size" type="prod:SizeType"/>
  <simpleType name="SizeType">
    <!--...-->
  </simpleType>
</schema>
```

If you plan to use identity constraints, you may be required to map a prefix to the target namespace. See Section 17.9 on p. 439 for more information.

3.3.5.3   Map prefixes to all namespaces

It is also possible to map prefixes to all the namespaces, as shown in Example 3–20. This has the advantage of clarity, particularly when your schema documents import other namespaces.

Example 3–20. Prefixing all namespaces

```
<xs:schema xmlns:xs="http://www.w3.org/2001/XMLSchema"
           xmlns:prod="http://datypic.com/prod"
           targetNamespace="http://datypic.com/prod">
  <xs:element name="number" type="xs:integer"/>
  <xs:element name="size" type="prod:SizeType"/>
  <xs:simpleType name="SizeType">
    <!--...-->
  </xs:simpleType>
</xs:schema>
```

Note that the prefix used for the target namespace in the schema does not necessarily correspond to the prefix used in the instance document. While the schema in the previous example uses the prefix prod for the target namespace, a valid instance document could use prod, foo, or any other prefix, or make that namespace the default. It is the namespace names that must match, not prefixes.

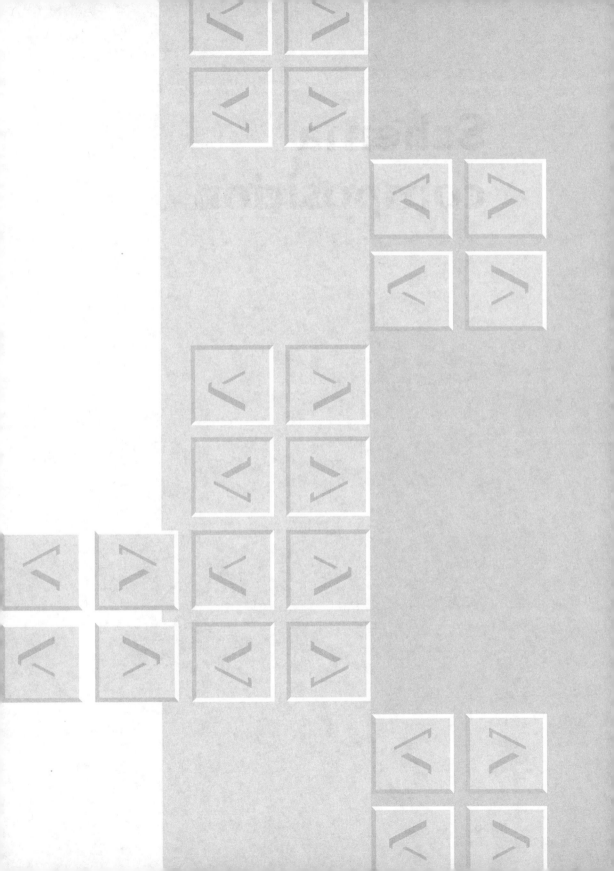

Schema
composition

I t is convenient to think of a schema as an individual schema document. However, in XML Schema, a schema can be composed of components defined in one or more schema documents. This chapter explains how schema documents are assembled together to represent a schema through various mechanisms, including those built into XML Schema and processor-specific handling.

4.1 | Modularizing schema documents

Breaking a schema document into multiple documents has a number of advantages such as promoting reuse, easing maintenance, and providing more granular access or versioning. The modularization can be based on subject areas, areas of responsibility, or the likely containers of reuse. How best to do it is a design decision that is covered in more detail in Section 21.5.2 on p. 557.

4.2 | Defining schema documents

A schema document is most typically a physical XML file whose root element is schema, but this is only one form of schema document. A schema document may also be a fragment of another XML document referenced using a fragment identifier or an XPointer, a DOM tree in memory, or some other physical representation.

Each schema document describes components for at most one namespace, known as its target namespace. Several schema documents can describe components in the same namespace. Some schema documents have no target namespace at all. Figure 4–1 shows several schema documents in different namespaces.

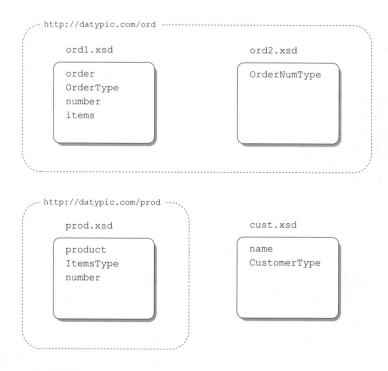

Figure 4–1   Schema documents

Each schema document is represented by a schema element whose syntax is shown in Table 4–1.

Table 4–1   XSD Syntax: schema document

Name		
schema		

Parents		
none		

Attribute name	Type	Description
id	ID	Unique ID.
version	token	Version of the schema document (not the version of the XML Schema language).
xml:lang	language	Natural language of the schema document.
targetNamespace	anyURI	Namespace to which all global schema components belong, see Section 3.3.1.
attributeFormDefault	"qualified" | "unqualified" : *"unqualified"*	Whether local attribute declarations should use qualified names, see Section 7.4.

(Continues)

Table 4–1   (Continued)

Attribute name	Type	Description
elementFormDefault	"qualified" | "unqualified" : *"unqualified"*	Whether local element declarations should use qualified names, see Section 6.3.
blockDefault	"#all" | list of ("substitution" | "extension" | "restriction")	Whether to block element substitution or type substitution, see Section 13.7.
finalDefault	"#all" | list of ("extension" | "restriction" | "list" | "union")	Whether to disallow type derivation; see Section 16.7.1 for element declarations, Section 13.7.1 for complex types, Section 8.5 for simple types.
[1.1]defaultAttributes	QName	Name of the default attribute group, see Section 15.3.3.
[1.1]xpathDefault-Namespace	anyURI | "##defaultNamespace" | "##targetNamespace" | "##local"	The default namespace for XPath expressions.

Content

(include | import | redefine | [1.1]override | annotation)*,
[1.1]defaultOpenContent?, (simpleType | complexType | group |
attributeGroup | element | attribute | notation | annotation)*

As you can see from the content model, there are two distinct sections of a schema document. At the beginning, you specify all the includes, imports, redefines, and overrides that are used to refer to other schema documents. After that come the global, or *top-level*, components of the schema, such as elements, attributes, named types, and groups. These components can appear in the schema document in any order. Annotations can appear at the top level throughout the schema document.

4.3 | Combining multiple schema documents

There are several methods of explicitly combining multiple schema documents.

- Includes are used to combine schema documents that have the same target namespace.
- Imports are used to combine schema documents that have different target namespaces.
- Redefines and overrides are used to combine schema documents that have the same target namespace, while revising the definition of the included components.

Includes and imports are covered in this section. Because of the complexities of redefines and overrides, all of Chapter 18 is devoted to them.

Although includes and imports are very common, they are not the only way to assemble schema documents. There is not always a "main" schema document that represents the whole schema. Some other alternatives are:

- The instance author can specify multiple schema locations in the instance, as described in Section 5.3.1 on p. 84.
- The processor can assemble schema documents from predefined locations.

- Multiple command-line parameters can be used to list the locations of the schema documents.

4.3.1   `include`

An `include` is used when you want to include other schema documents in a schema document that has the same target namespace. This provides for modularization of schema documents. For example, you may want to break your schema into several documents: two different order schema documents and a customer schema document. This is depicted in Figure 4–2.

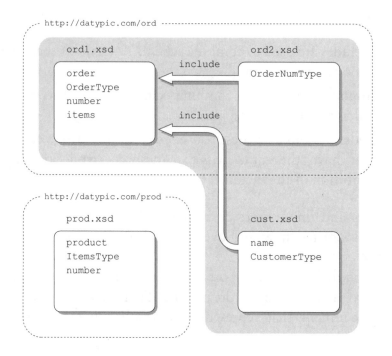

Figure 4–2   Includes

4.3.1.1 The syntax of includes

Includes are represented by `include` elements, whose syntax is shown in Table 4–2.

Table 4–2   XSD Syntax: include

Name		
include		
Parents		
schema		
Attribute name	**Type**	**Description**
id	ID	Unique ID.
schemaLocation	anyURI	Location of the included schema document.
Content		
annotation?		

The `include` elements may only appear at the top level of a schema document, and they must appear at the beginning (along with the `import`, `redefine`, and `override` elements).

The `schemaLocation` attribute indicates where the included schema document is located. This attribute is required, although the location is not required to be resolvable. However, if it is resolvable, it must be a complete schema document.

Example 4–1 shows the use of `include` in a schema document. The schema author wants to use the type `OrderNumType` in the `number` element declaration. However, `OrderNumType` is defined in a different schema document. The `include` statement references the location of the schema document, `ord2.xsd`, that contains the definition of `OrderNumType`. In this example, the including document is referring to a simple type in the included document, but it could similarly refer to elements, attributes, complex types, or any other global components in the included document.

Example 4–1. Include

---

ord1.xsd:

```
<xs:schema xmlns:xs="http://www.w3.org/2001/XMLSchema"
           xmlns="http://datypic.com/ord"
           targetNamespace="http://datypic.com/ord">

  <xs:include schemaLocation="ord2.xsd"/>

  <xs:element name="order" type="OrderType"/>
  <xs:complexType name="OrderType">
    <xs:sequence>
      <xs:element name="number" type="OrderNumType"/>
      <!--...-->
    </xs:sequence>
  </xs:complexType>

</xs:schema>
```

ord2.xsd:

```
<xs:schema xmlns:xs="http://www.w3.org/2001/XMLSchema"
           xmlns="http://datypic.com/ord"
           targetNamespace="http://datypic.com/ord">

  <xs:simpleType name="OrderNumType">
    <xs:restriction base="xs:string"/>
  </xs:simpleType>
</xs:schema>
```

The schema documents `ord1.xsd` and `ord2.xsd` have the same target namespace. When you use includes, one of the following must be true:

- Both schema documents have the same target namespace.
- Neither schema document has a target namespace.

- The including schema document has a target namespace, and the included schema document does not have a target namespace.

There can be multiple `include` elements in a schema document. There can also be multiple levels of includes in schema documents. For example, `ord1.xsd` can include `ord2.xsd`, which includes `cust.xsd`, and so on. It is not an error to include the exact same schema document twice.

4.3.1.2 Chameleon includes

In the case where the included schema document has no target namespace, all components of the included schema document take on the namespace of the including schema document. These components are sometimes called chameleon components, because their namespace changes depending on where they are included. This is shown in Example 4–2.

Example 4–2. Chameleon include

ord1.xsd:

```
<xs:schema xmlns:xs="http://www.w3.org/2001/XMLSchema"
           xmlns="http://datypic.com/ord"
           targetNamespace="http://datypic.com/ord">

  <xs:include schemaLocation="cust.xsd"/>

  <xs:element name="order" type="OrderType"/>
  <xs:complexType name="OrderType">
    <xs:sequence>
      <xs:element name="number" type="xs:string"/>
      <xs:element name="customer" type="CustomerType"/>
      <!--...-->
    </xs:sequence>
  </xs:complexType>
</xs:schema>
```

(Continues)

Example 4–2. **(Continued)**

cust.xsd:

```
<xs:schema xmlns:xs="http://www.w3.org/2001/XMLSchema">

  <xs:complexType name="CustomerType">
    <xs:sequence>
      <xs:element name="name" type="CustNameType"/>
      <!--...-->
    </xs:sequence>
  </xs:complexType>
  <xs:simpleType name="CustNameType">
    <xs:restriction base="xs:string"/>
  </xs:simpleType>
</xs:schema>
```

Note that in cust.xsd, the element declaration of name can reference the type CustNameType without any namespace. Even though
these components will take on the target namespace of the ord.xsd
schema document, the unqualified references between components in
cust.xsd will be honored.

However, in ord1.xsd, the references to the cust.xsd components
such as CustomerType *do* have to be qualified. This example works
because ord1.xsd declares http://datypic.com/ord as the default
namespace (in addition to being the target namespace). This means
that any unprefixed references, such as the one to CustomerType, are
considered to be in that namespace.

4.3.2 import

An import is used to tell the processor that you will be referring to
components from other namespaces. For example, if you want to reference an attribute from another namespace in your complex type definition, or you want to derive your type from a type in another namespace,
you must import this namespace. This is depicted in Figure 4–3.

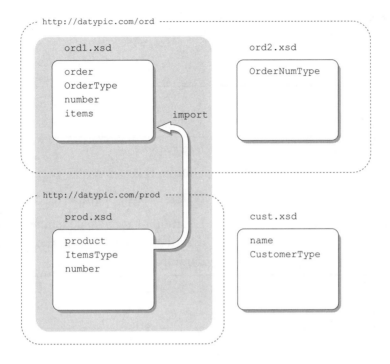

Figure 4–3   Import

Imports differ from includes in two important ways. First, includes only take place within a namespace, while imports take place across namespaces. The second, subtler distinction is their general purpose. The purpose of an include is specifically to pull in other schema documents, while the purpose of an import is to record a dependency on another namespace, not necessarily another schema document. Import does allow you to specify the location of a schema document for that namespace, but it is just a hint, and the processor is not required to try to resolve it.

4.3.2.1 The syntax of imports

Imports are represented by import elements, whose syntax is shown in Table 4–3.

Table 4–3   XSD Syntax: import

Name		
import		

Parents		
schema		

Attribute name	Type	Description
id	ID	Unique ID.
namespace	anyURI	Namespace to be imported.
schemaLocation	anyURI	Location of a schema document which describes components in the imported namespace.

Content		
annotation?		

The import elements may only appear at the top level of a schema document, and must appear at the beginning (along with the include, redefine, and override elements).

The namespace attribute indicates the namespace that you wish to import. If you do not specify a namespace, it means that you are importing components that are not in any namespace. The imported namespace cannot be the same as the target namespace of the importing schema document. If the importing schema document has no target namespace, the import element must have a namespace attribute.

The schemaLocation attribute provides a hint to the processor as to where to find a schema document that declares components for that namespace. If you do not specify a schemaLocation, it is assumed that the processor somehow knows where to find the schema document, perhaps because it was specified by the user or built into the processor. When schemaLocation is present and the processor is able to resolve the location to some resource, it must resolve to a schema document.

That schema document's target namespace must be equal to the value of the `namespace` attribute of the `import` element.

Looping references (`ord1.xsd` imports `prod.xsd`'s namespace, and `prod.xsd` imports `ord1.xsd`'s namespace) are also acceptable, because this just indicates the interdependence of the components.

Example 4–3 shows the use of `import` in a schema document. The schema author wants to use the type `ItemsType` in an element declaration. However, `ItemsType` is defined in a different namespace. The `import` statement references the namespace and location of the schema document that contains `ItemsType`. The declaration of `items` is then able to reference `ItemsType` using the appropriate prefix.

Note that the target namespace of `prod.xsd` must also be declared as a namespace in the importing schema document. This is necessary so that the `items` element declaration can refer to the type `ItemsType` using its appropriate namespace prefix.

***Example 4–3.** Import*

ord1.xsd:

```
<xs:schema xmlns:xs="http://www.w3.org/2001/XMLSchema"
           xmlns="http://datypic.com/ord"
           xmlns:prod="http://datypic.com/prod"
           targetNamespace="http://datypic.com/ord">

  <xs:import namespace="http://datypic.com/prod"
             schemaLocation="prod.xsd"/>

  <xs:element name="order" type="OrderType"/>
  <xs:complexType name="OrderType">
    <xs:sequence>
      <xs:element name="number" type="xs:string"/>
      <xs:element name="items" type="prod:ItemsType"/>
      <!--...-->
    </xs:sequence>
  </xs:complexType>
</xs:schema>
```

(Continues)

Example 4–3.   (Continued)

---

prod.xsd:

```
<xs:schema xmlns:xs="http://www.w3.org/2001/XMLSchema"
           xmlns="http://datypic.com/prod"
           targetNamespace="http://datypic.com/prod">

  <xs:complexType name="ItemsType">
    <xs:sequence>
      <xs:element name="product" type="ProductType"/>
    </xs:sequence>
  </xs:complexType>
  <!-- ... -->
</xs:schema>
```

4.3.2.2 Multiple levels of imports

As with includes, imports can be chained together. That is, `ord1.xsd` can import `prod.xsd` which itself imports a third schema document, `extension.xsd`. However, imports are subtly different from includes in this regard. With multilevel includes, `ord1.xsd` would automatically be able to refer to components from `extension.xsd`. With imports, if `ord1.xsd` wants to directly refer to components in `extension.xsd`, it would have to also directly import the target namespace of `extension.xsd`. This is because the import is also used to record a dependency on another namespace, not just incorporate another schema document.

This is shown in Example 4–4, where `ord1.xsd` directly references `ext:ExtensionType` from `extension.xsd`. This requires it to import `extension.xsd` (or at least the `ext` namespace), which it does. If it did not directly refer to a component in that namespace, it would not need to import it.

Example 4–4. Multiple levels of import

ord1.xsd:

```
<xs:schema xmlns:xs="http://www.w3.org/2001/XMLSchema"
           xmlns="http://datypic.com/ord"
           xmlns:prod="http://datypic.com/prod"
           xmlns:ext="http://datypic.com/ext"
           targetNamespace="http://datypic.com/ord">

  <xs:import namespace="http://datypic.com/prod"
             schemaLocation="prod.xsd"/>
  <xs:import namespace="http://datypic.com/ext"
             schemaLocation="extension.xsd"/>

  <xs:element name="order" type="OrderType"/>
  <xs:complexType name="OrderType">
    <xs:sequence>
      <xs:element name="number" type="xs:string"/>
      <xs:element name="items" type="prod:ItemsType"/>
      <!--...-->
      <xs:element name="extension" type="ext:ExtensionType"/>
    </xs:sequence>
  </xs:complexType>
</xs:schema>
```

prod.xsd:

```
<xs:schema xmlns:xs="http://www.w3.org/2001/XMLSchema"
           xmlns="http://datypic.com/prod"
           xmlns:ext="http://datypic.com/ext"
           targetNamespace="http://datypic.com/prod">

  <xs:import namespace="http://datypic.com/ext"
             schemaLocation="extension.xsd"/>

  <xs:complexType name="ItemsType">
    <xs:sequence>
      <!-- ... -->
      <xs:element name="extension" type="ext:ExtensionType"/>
    </xs:sequence>
  </xs:complexType>
</xs:schema>
```

(Continues)

Example 4–4. (Continued)

extension.xsd:

```
<xs:schema xmlns:xs="http://www.w3.org/2001/XMLSchema"
           xmlns="http://datypic.com/ext"
           targetNamespace="http://datypic.com/ext">

  <xs:complexType name="ExtensionType">
    <!-- ... -->
  </xs:complexType>
</xs:schema>
```

4.3.2.3 Multiple imports of the same namespace

It is legal to have multiple imports of the same namespace in the same schema document or a set of assembled schema documents. If they refer to the same schema document, the processor will determine that they are the same components and will not raise errors about duplicate definitions. This was the case in Example 4–4, where both ord1.xsd and prod.xsd import the same schema document, extension.xsd.

However, if multiple imports of the same namespace refer to different schema documents, most processors will ignore all but the first one they encounter. This is permissible (if not always convenient) because imports, unlike includes, are considered to be just "hints" that the processor can choose to ignore.

Suppose, for example, that a schema document root.xsd declares a root element root that has two children: orderSummary and orderDetails. The two child elements are in the same namespace but declared in different schema documents. You might expect to be able to import both Summary.xsd and Detail.xsd into root.xsd, as shown in Example 4–5. However, when you validate an instance against root.xsd, most processors will ignore the import of Detail.xsd and raise an error because no declaration of orderDetails could be found.

Example 4–5. Multiple imports of the same namespace

---

root.xsd:

```
<xs:schema xmlns:xs="http://www.w3.org/2001/XMLSchema"
           xmlns="http://datypic.com/root"
           xmlns:ord="http://datypic.com/ord"
           targetNamespace="http://datypic.com/root">

  <xs:import namespace="http://datypic.com/ord"
             schemaLocation="Summary.xsd"/>
  <xs:import namespace="http://datypic.com/ord"
             schemaLocation="Detail.xsd"/>

  <xs:element name="root" type="RootType"/>
  <xs:complexType name="RootType">
    <xs:sequence>
      <xs:element ref="ord:orderSummary"/>
      <xs:element ref="ord:orderDetails"/>
      <!--...-->
    </xs:sequence>
  </xs:complexType>

</xs:schema>
```

Summary.xsd:

```
<xs:schema xmlns:xs="http://www.w3.org/2001/XMLSchema"
           xmlns="http://datypic.com/ord"
           targetNamespace="http://datypic.com/ord">

  <xs:element name="orderSummary"/>
  <!-- ... -->
</xs:schema>
```

Detail.xsd:

```
<xs:schema xmlns:xs="http://www.w3.org/2001/XMLSchema"
           xmlns="http://datypic.com/ord"
           targetNamespace="http://datypic.com/ord">

  <xs:element name="orderDetails"/>
  <!-- ... -->
</xs:schema>
```

One way to get around this is to declare a single schema document, sometimes called a *proxy schema*, for the `ord` namespace and include all the necessary schema documents in that namespace, as shown in Example 4–6. This will work because there is only one import for that namespace in `root.xsd` and the includes in `Orders.xsd` cannot be ignored.

Example 4–6. Proxy schema to avoid multiple imports

root.xsd:

```
<xs:schema xmlns:xs="http://www.w3.org/2001/XMLSchema"
           xmlns="http://datypic.com/root"
           xmlns:ord="http://datypic.com/ord"
           targetNamespace="http://datypic.com/root">

  <xs:import namespace="http://datypic.com/ord"
             schemaLocation="Orders.xsd"/>

  <xs:element name="root" type="RootType"/>
  <xs:complexType name="RootType">
    <xs:sequence>
      <xs:element ref="ord:orderSummary"/>
      <xs:element ref="ord:orderDetails"/>
      <!-- ... -->
    </xs:sequence>
  </xs:complexType>

</xs:schema>
```

Orders.xsd:

```
<xs:schema xmlns:xs="http://www.w3.org/2001/XMLSchema"
           xmlns="http://datypic.com/ord"
           targetNamespace="http://datypic.com/ord">

  <xs:include schemaLocation="Summary.xsd"/>
  <xs:include schemaLocation="Detail.xsd"/>
  <!-- ... -->
</xs:schema>
```

4.4 | Schema assembly considerations

Whether you are using includes, imports, redefines, or overrides, there are several factors to take into consideration when combining multiple schema documents into a single schema. These factors are discussed in this section.

4.4.1 *Uniqueness of qualified names*

The qualified names of globally declared components must be unique in the schema, not just a schema document. When assembling a schema from multiple schema documents, be careful not to introduce duplicate qualified names. Example 4–7 shows two schema documents, both of which contain global element declarations for order.

Example 4–7. Illegal duplication of element names

ord1.xsd:

```
<xs:schema xmlns:xs="http://www.w3.org/2001/XMLSchema"
           xmlns="http://datypic.com/ord"
           targetNamespace="http://datypic.com/ord">
  <xs:include schemaLocation="ord2.xsd"/>
  <xs:element name="order" type="OrderType"/>
</xs:schema>
```

ord2.xsd:

```
<xs:schema xmlns:xs="http://www.w3.org/2001/XMLSchema"
           xmlns="http://datypic.com/ord"
           targetNamespace="http://datypic.com/ord">
  <xs:element name="order" type="OrderType"/>
</xs:schema>
```

It is not illegal for two schema documents to exist that have duplicate names, since they may be used at different times in different situations. However, since ord1.xsd includes ord2.xsd, they will be used together, and this is illegal. Remember, the qualified name includes the namespace name, so this example would be valid if the two schema documents had different target namespaces (and `ord2.xsd` had been imported rather than included).

This rule holds true for all named, global components, including attributes, simple and complex types, named model groups, attribute groups, identity constraints, and notations. The uniqueness of qualified names is within the type of component. For example, it is illegal to have two global element declarations for `order`, but it is legal to have both an element declaration and a simple type definition with that name. However, simple and complex types cannot share the same qualified name.

4.4.2 *Missing components*

In some cases, declarations or definitions will refer to components that are outside the schema document. In Example 4–8, the `order` element declaration uses the type `OrderType` that is not defined in the schema document. This is not illegal unless a processor tries to use that declaration and cannot find a definition of `OrderType`.

Example 4–8. Missing component

```
<xs:schema xmlns:xs="http://www.w3.org/2001/XMLSchema"
           xmlns="http://datypic.com/ord"
           targetNamespace="http://datypic.com/ord">

  <xs:element name="number" type="xs:integer"/>
  <xs:element name="order" type="OrderType"/>
</xs:schema>
```

In this case, the processor might obtain access to a schema document that contains the `OrderType` definition by some other means, as described in Section 4.3 on p. 61.

Even if a schema document containing the definition of `OrderType` is never found, the processor will still be able to validate a `number` element. The fact that there are unresolved references in the schema is only an error if such a reference is directly involved in the validation.

4.4.3 *Schema document defaults*

As we saw in Section 4.2 on p. 58, schema documents can have four defaults specified: `attributeFormDefault`, `elementFormDefault`, `blockDefault`, and `finalDefault`. As schema documents are assembled into schemas, these defaults are not overridden in any way. The defaults of a schema document still apply to all components defined or declared in that particular schema document. For example, if `ord2.xsd` has `elementFormDefault` set to `unqualified`, all of the local element declarations in `ord2.xsd` will have unqualified names, even if `ord2.xsd` is included in another schema document that has `elementFormDefault` set to `qualified`.

Instances
and schemas

Chapter

5

There is a many-to-many relationship between instances and schemas. A schema can describe many valid instances, possibly with different root element names. Likewise, an instance may be described by many schemas, depending on the circumstances. For example, you may have multiple schemas for an instance, with different levels of validation. One may just validate the structure, while another checks every data item against a type. There may also be multiple schemas with different application information to be used at processing time. This chapter explains the interaction between schemas and instances.

5.1 | Using the instance attributes

There are four attributes that can apply to any element in an instance. These four attributes, which are described in Table 5–1, are all in the XML Schema Instance Namespace, `http://www.w3.org/2001/XMLSchema-instance`. This namespace is commonly mapped to the prefix `xsi`.[1]

Table 5–1   Instance attributes

Attribute name	Type	Description
`nil`	`boolean`: *false*	Whether the element's value is `nil`, see Section 6.5.
`type`	`QName`	The name of a type that is being substituted for the element's declared type, see Section 13.6.
`schemaLocation`	list of `anyURI`	List of the locations of schema documents for designated namespaces, see Section 5.3.1.1.
`noNamespaceSchemaLocation`	`anyURI`	Location of a schema document with no target namespace, see Section 5.3.1.2.

Example 5–1 shows the use of `xsi:type` in an instance.

Because these four attributes are globally declared, their names must be prefixed in instances. You are required to declare the XML Schema Instance Namespace and map a prefix (preferably `xsi`) to it. However, you are not required to specify a schema location for these four attributes. You are also *not* required or even permitted to declare `xsi:type` as an attribute in the type definition for `number`. The attributes in the XML Schema Instance Namespace, like namespace

---

1.   While any prefix may be mapped to the namespace, this book uses the prefix `xsi` as a shorthand, sometimes without explicitly stating that it is mapped to `http://www.w3.org/2001/XMLSchema-instance`.

Example 5–1. Using an instance attribute

```
<product xmlns="http://datypic.com/prod"
         xmlns:xsi="http://www.w3.org/2001/XMLSchema-instance">
  <number xsi:type="ShortProdNumType">557</number>
  <size>10</size>
</product>
```

declarations, are special attributes that a schema processor always recognizes without explicit declarations.

In fact, the number element in this example can have a simple type, even though elements with simple types are normally not allowed to have attributes.

5.2 | Schema processing

5.2.1 *Validation*

Validation is an important part of schema processing. Validation determines whether an instance conforms to all of the constraints described in the schema. It involves checking all of the elements and attributes in an instance to determine that they have declarations and that they conform to those declarations and to the corresponding type definitions.

The validation process verifies:

- *Correctness of the data.* Validating against a schema does not provide a 100% guarantee that the data is correct, but it can signal invalid formats or out-of-range values.
- *Completeness of the data.* Validation can check that all required information is present.
- *Shared understanding of the data.* Validation can make sure that the way you perceive the document is the same way that the sender perceives it.

Whether to validate your instances on a regular basis depends on a number of factors.

- *Where the instances originate.* Within your organization, perhaps you have control over the application that generates instances. After some initial testing, you may trust that all documents coming from that application are valid, without performing validation. However, often the instances you are processing are originating outside your organization. You may be less likely to trust these documents.
- *Whether the instances were application-generated or user-generated.* Human involvement can introduce typographical and other errors. Even with validating XML editors, it is still possible to introduce errors inadvertently during the handling of the documents.
- *Data quality.* For example, if the instances are generated directly from an existing database, they may not be complete or 100% correct.
- *Performance.* Obviously, it takes extra time to validate. If performance is critical, you may want to avoid some validation or write application-specific code that can validate more efficiently than a schema processor.

5.2.2 *Augmenting the instance*

In addition to validating the instance, a schema processor may alter the instance by

- Adding default and fixed values for elements and attributes
- Normalizing whitespace in element and attribute values that contain character data

Because of this, it is important that the sender and receiver of the document agree on the schema to use. If the receiver processes an element with a declaration that has a default value different from that of the sender's declaration, it can alter the data of the element in ways unintended by the sender.

5.3 | Relating instances to schemas

Instances can be related to schemas in a number of ways.

- *Using hints in the instance.* The `xsi:schemaLocation` and `xsi:noNamespaceSchemaLocation` attributes can be used in the instance to provide a hint to the processor where to find the schema documents.

- *Application's choice.* Most applications will be processing the same type of instances repeatedly. These applications may already know where the appropriate schema documents are on the web, or locally, or even have them built in. In this case, the processor could either (1) ignore `xsi:schemaLocation`, or (2) reject documents containing `xsi:schemaLocation` attributes, or (3) reject documents in which the `xsi:schemaLocation` does not match the intended schema document.

- *User's choice.* The location of the schema document(s) can be specified, at processing time, by a command-line instruction or user dialog.

- *Dereferencing the namespace.* The namespace name can be dereferenced to retrieve a schema document or resource directory. However, this is not typically done by XML Schema processors.

5.3.1   *Using hints in the instance*

XML Schema provides two attributes that act as hints to where the processor might find the schema document(s) for the instance. Different processors may ignore or acknowledge these hints in different ways.

These two attributes are: `xsi:schemaLocation`, for use with schema documents that have target namespaces, and `xsi:noNamespaceSchemaLocation`, for use with schema documents without target namespaces.

5.3.1.1   The `xsi:schemaLocation` attribute

The `xsi:schemaLocation` attribute allows you to specify a list of pairs that match namespace names with schema locations. Example 5–2 shows an instance that uses `xsi:schemaLocation`. The default namespace for the document is `http://datypic.com/prod`. The `xsi` prefix is assigned to the XML Schema Instance Namespace, so that the processor will recognize the `xsi:schemaLocation` attribute. Then, the `xsi:schemaLocation` attribute is specified to relate the namespace `http://datypic.com/prod` to the schema location `prod.xsd`.

Example 5–2. Using `xsi:schemaLocation`

```
<product xmlns="http://datypic.com/prod"
         xmlns:xsi="http://www.w3.org/2001/XMLSchema-instance"
         xsi:schemaLocation="http://datypic.com/prod prod.xsd">
  <number>557</number>
  <size>10</size>
</product>
```

The value of the `xsi:schemaLocation` attribute is actually at least two values separated by whitespace. The first value is the namespace name (in this example `http://datypic.com/prod`), and the second value is the URL for the schema location (in this example `prod.xsd`, a relative URI). The processor will retrieve the schema document from the schema location and make sure that its target namespace matches that of the namespace it is paired with in xsi:schemaLocation.

Since spaces are used to separate values in this attribute, you should not have spaces in your schema location path. You can replace a space with %20, which is standard for URLs. For example, instead of my schema.xsd, use my%20schema.xsd. To use an absolute path rather than a relative path, some processors require that you start your schema location with file:/// (with three forward slashes), as in file:///C:/Users/PW/Documents/prod.xsd.

If multiple namespaces are used in the document, xsi:schemaLocation can contain more than one pair of values, as shown in Example 5–3.

Example 5–3. Using xsi:schemaLocation with multiple pairs

```
<order xmlns="http://datypic.com/ord"
       xmlns:xsi="http://www.w3.org/2001/XMLSchema-instance"
       xsi:schemaLocation="http://datypic.com/prod prod.xsd
                           http://datypic.com/ord ord1.xsd">
  <items>
    <product xmlns="http://datypic.com/prod">
      <number>557</number>
      <size>10</size>
    </product>
  </items>
</order>
```

If you have a schema document that imports schema documents with different target namespaces, you do not have to specify schema locations for all the namespaces (if the processor has some other way of finding the schema documents, such as the schemaLocation attribute of import). For example, if ord1.xsd imports prod.xsd, it is not necessary to specify prod.xsd in the xsi:schemaLocation in the instance. You do still need to declare your namespaces using the xmlns attributes, as shown in the example.

It is not illegal to list two or more pairs of values that refer to the same namespace. In Example 5–3, you could refer to both `ord1.xsd` and `ord2.xsd`, repeating the same namespace name for each. However, this is not recommended because many processors will ignore all but the first schema location for a particular namespace.

It is generally a good practice to use one main schema document that includes or imports all other schema documents needed for validation. This simplifies the instance and makes name collisions more obvious.

The `xsi:schemaLocation` attribute may appear anywhere in an instance, in the tags of any number of elements. Its appearance in a particular tag does not signify its scope. However, it must appear before any elements that it would validate. It is most typical to put the `xsi:schemaLocation` attribute on the root element, for simplicity.

5.3.1.2   The `xsi:noNamespaceSchemaLocation` attribute

The `xsi:noNamespaceSchemaLocation` attribute is used to reference a schema document with no target namespace. `xsi:noNamespaceSchemaLocation` does not take a list of values; only one schema location may be specified. The schema document referenced cannot have a target namespace. Example 5–4 shows the use of `xsi:noNamespaceSchemaLocation` in an instance.

Example 5–4. Using `xsi:noNamespaceSchemaLocation`

```
<product xmlns:xsi="http://www.w3.org/2001/XMLSchema-instance"
         xsi:noNamespaceSchemaLocation="prod.xsd">
  <number>557</number>
  <size>10</size>
</product>
```

It is legal according to XML Schema to have both `xsi:noNamespaceSchemaLocation` and `xsi:schemaLocation` specified, but once again, you should check with your processor to see what it will accept.

5.4 | The root element

Sometimes you want to be able to specify which element declaration is for the root element of the instance. For example, you may not want the document shown in Example 5–5 to be considered a valid instance, although the element itself is valid according to its declaration.

Example 5–5. A valid instance?

```
<number>557</number>
```

Schemas work similarly to DTDs in this regard. There is no way to designate the root. Any element conforming to a global element declaration can be a root element for validation purposes.

You can work around this by having only one global element declaration. If the number declaration is local, Example 5–5 is not valid on its own. However, there are times that you cannot avoid global element declarations either because you are using substitution groups or because you are importing element declarations over which you have no control. A better approach is to use the application to verify that the root element is the one you expect.

Using some schema processors, validation may not necessarily start at the root. It is possible to validate sections of instance documents with different schema documents using different xsi:schemaLocation hints, or to validate fragments of instance documents identified by IDs or XPointer expressions. Also, one schema document may describe several related types of instance documents (e.g., purchase orders and invoices) which may have different root elements.

Element
declarations

Chapter

6

This chapter covers the basic building blocks of XML: elements. It explains how to use element declarations to assign names and types to elements. It also describes element properties that can be set via element declarations, such as default and fixed values, nillability, and qualified versus unqualified name forms.

6.1 | Global and local element declarations

Element declarations are used to assign names and types to elements. This is accomplished using an `element` element. Element declarations can be either global or local.

6.1.1 *Global element declarations*

Global element declarations appear at the top level of the schema document, meaning that their parent must be `schema`. These global element declarations can then be used in multiple complex types, as described in Section 12.4.2 on p. 267. Table 6–1 shows the syntax for a global element declaration.

Table 6–1   XSD Syntax: global element declaration

Name
element

Parents
schema, ▪override

Attribute name	Type	Description
id	ID	Unique ID.
name	NCName	Element name.
type	QName	Type, see Section 6.2.
default	string	Default value, see Section 6.4.1.
fixed	string	Fixed value, see Section 6.4.2.
nillable	boolean: *false*	Whether xsi:nil can be used in the instance, see Section 6.5.
abstract	boolean: *false*	Whether the declaration can apply to an instance element (as opposed to being just the head of a substitution group), see Section 16.7.3.
substitutionGroup	QName or ▪list of QName	Head of the substitution group to which it belongs, see Section 16.3.

(Continues)

Table 6–1 (Continued)

Attribute name	Type	Description
block	"#all" | list of ("substitution" | "extension" | "restriction")	Whether type and/or element substitutions should be blocked from the instance (see Section 13.7.3 for type substitutions, Section 16.7.2 for element substitutions); defaults to blockDefault of schema.
final	"#all" | list of ("extension" | "restriction")	Whether the declaration can be the head of a substitution group (see Section 16.7.1); defaults to finalDefault of schema.

Content

```
annotation?, (simpleType | complexType)?, alternative*,
(key | keyref | unique)*
```

Example 6–1 shows two global element declarations: name and size. A complex type is then defined which references these element declarations by name using the ref attribute.

The qualified names used by global element declarations must be unique in the schema. This includes not just the schema document in which they appear, but also any other schema documents that are used with it.

The name specified in an element declaration must be an XML non-colonized name, which means that it must start with a letter or underscore (_), and may only contain letters, digits, underscores (_), hyphens (-), and periods (.). The qualified element name consists of the target namespace of the schema document, plus the local name in the declaration. In Example 6–1, the name and size element declarations take on the target namespace http://datypic.com/prod.

Example 6–1. Global element declarations

```
<xs:schema xmlns:xs="http://www.w3.org/2001/XMLSchema"
           xmlns="http://datypic.com/prod"
           targetNamespace="http://datypic.com/prod">

  <xs:element name="name" type="xs:string"/>
  <xs:element name="size" type="xs:integer"/>

  <xs:complexType name="ProductType">
    <xs:sequence>
      <xs:element ref="name"/>
      <xs:element ref="size" minOccurs="0"/>
    </xs:sequence>
  </xs:complexType>

</xs:schema>
```

Since globally declared element names are qualified by the target namespace of the schema document, it is not legal to include a namespace prefix in the value of the `name` attribute, as shown in Example 6–2. If you want to declare elements in a different namespace, you must create a separate schema document with that target namespace and import it into the original schema document.

Example 6–2. Illegal attempt to prefix an element name

```
<xs:schema xmlns:xs="http://www.w3.org/2001/XMLSchema"
           xmlns:prod="http://datypic.com/prod"
           targetNamespace="http://datypic.com/prod">
  <xs:element name="name" type="xs:string"/>
  <xs:element name="prod:size" type="xs:integer"/>
</xs:schema>
```

Occurrence constraints (`minOccurs` and `maxOccurs`) appear in an element reference rather than the global element declaration. This is because they are related to the appearance of an element in a particular content model. Element references are covered in Section 12.4.2 on p. 267.

6.1.2 *Local element declarations*

Local element declarations, on the other hand, appear entirely within a complex type definition. Local element declarations can only be used in that type definition, never referenced by other complex types or used in a substitution group. Table 6–2 shows the syntax for a local element declaration.

Table 6–2 XSD Syntax: local element declaration

Name
element

Parents
all, choice, sequence

Attribute name	Type	Description
id	ID	Unique ID.
name	NCName	Element name.
form	"qualified" | "unqualified"	Whether the element name must be qualified in the instance (see Section 6.3); defaults to elementFormDefault of schema, which defaults to unqualified.
type	QName	Type, see Section 6.2.
minOccurs	nonNegativeInteger: *1*	Minimum number of element occurrences, see Section 12.4.2.
maxOccurs	nonNegativeInteger | "unbounded" : *1*	Maximum number of element occurrences, see Section 12.4.2.

(Continues)

Table 6–2   (Continued)

Attribute name	Type	Description
default	string	Default value, see Section 6.4.1.
fixed	string	Fixed value, see Section 6.4.2.
nillable	boolean: *false*	Whether xsi:nil can be used in the instance, see Section 6.5.
block	"#all" | list of ("extension" | "restriction")	Whether type substitutions should be blocked from the instance (see Section 13.7.3); defaults to blockDefault of schema.
▣targetNamespace	anyURI	The target namespace, if restricting a type in another namespace, see Section 13.5.7.

Content

annotation?, (simpleType | complexType)?, ▣alternative*, (key | keyref | unique)*

Example 6–3 shows two local element declarations, name and size, which appear entirely within a complex type definition.

Occurrence constraints (minOccurs and maxOccurs) can appear in local element declarations. Some attributes, namely substitutionGroup, final, and abstract, are valid in global element declarations but not in local element declarations. This is because these attributes all relate to substitution groups, in which local element declarations cannot participate.

The name specified in a local element declaration must also be an XML non-colonized name. If its form is qualified, it takes on the target

Example 6–3. Local element declarations

```
<xs:schema xmlns:xs="http://www.w3.org/2001/XMLSchema"
           xmlns="http://datypic.com/prod"
           targetNamespace="http://datypic.com/prod">
  <xs:complexType name="ProductType">
    <xs:sequence>
      <xs:element name="name" type="xs:string"/>
      <xs:element name="size" type="xs:integer" minOccurs="0"/>
    </xs:sequence>
  </xs:complexType>
</xs:schema>
```

namespace of the schema document. If it is unqualified, it is considered to be in no namespace. See Section 6.3 on p. 98 for more information.

Names used in local element declarations are scoped to the complex type within which they are declared. You can have two completely different local element declarations with the same element name, as long as they are in different complex types. You can also have two local element declarations with the same element name in the same complex type, provided that they themselves have the same type. This is explained further in Section 12.4.3 on p. 268.

6.1.3   *Design hint: Should I use global or local element declarations?*

Use global element declarations if:

- The element declaration could ever apply to the root element during validation. Such a declaration should be global so that the schema processor can access it.

- You want to use the exact same element declaration in more than one complex type.

- You want to use the element declaration in a substitution group. Local element declarations cannot participate in substitution groups (see Chapter 16).

Use local element declarations if:

- You want to allow unqualified element names in the instance. In this case, make all of the element declarations local except for the root element declaration. If you mix global and local declarations, and you want the element names in local declarations to be unqualified, you will require your instance authors to know which element declarations are global and which are local. Global element names are always qualified in the instance (see Section 6.3 on p. 98).

- You want to have several element declarations with the same name but different types or other properties. Using local declarations, you can have two element declarations for `size`: One that is a child of `shoe` has the type `ShoeSizeType`, and one that is a child of `hat` has the type `HatSizeType`. If the `size` declaration is global, it can only occur once, and therefore use only one type, in that schema. The same holds true for default and fixed values as well as nillability.

6.2 | Declaring the types of elements

Regardless of whether they are local or global, all element declarations associate an element name with a type, which may be either simple or complex. There are four ways to associate a type with an element name:

1. Reference a named type by specifying the `type` attribute in the element declaration. This may be either a built-in type or a user-defined type.

2. Define an anonymous type by specifying either a `simpleType` or a `complexType` child.

3. Use no particular type, by specifying neither a `type` attribute nor a `simpleType` or `complexType` child. In this case, the

actual type is `anyType` which allows any children and/or character data content, and any attributes, as long as it is well-formed XML.[1]

4. Define one or more type alternatives using `alternative` children. This more advanced feature of version 1.1 is described separately in Section 14.2 on p. 375.

Example 6–4 shows four element declarations with different type assignment methods.

Example 6–4. Assigning types to elements

```
<xs:element name="size" type="SizeType"/>

<xs:element name="name" type="xs:string"/>

<xs:element name="product">
  <xs:complexType>
    <xs:sequence>
      <xs:element ref="name"/>
      <xs:element ref="size"/>
    </xs:sequence>
  </xs:complexType>
</xs:element>

<xs:element name="anything"/>
```

The first example uses the `type` attribute to specify `SizeType` as the type of `size`. The second example also uses the `type` attribute, this time to assign a built-in type `string` to `name`. The `xs` prefix is used because built-in types are part of the XML Schema Namespace. For a complete explanation of the use of prefixes in schema documents, see Section 3.3.5 on p. 52.

The third example uses an in-line anonymous complex type, which is defined entirely within the `product` declaration. Finally, the fourth

---

1.   Unless it is in a substitution group, as described in Chapter 16.

element declaration, `anything`, does not specify a particular type, which means that `anything` elements can have any well-formed content and any attributes.

For a detailed discussion of using named or anonymous types, see Section 8.2.3 on p. 133.

6.3 | Qualified vs. unqualified forms

When an element declaration is local—that is, when it isn't at the top level of a schema document—you have the choice of putting those element names into the target namespace of the schema or not. Let's explore the two alternatives.

6.3.1   Qualified local names

Example 6–5 shows an instance where all element names are qualified. Every element name has a prefix that maps it to the product namespace.

Example 6–5. Qualified local names

```
<prod:product xmlns:prod="http://datypic.com/prod">
  <prod:number>557</prod:number>
  <prod:size>10</prod:size>
</prod:product>
```

6.3.2   Unqualified local names

Example 6–6, on the other hand, shows an instance where only the root element name, `product`, is qualified. The other element names have no prefix, and since there is no default namespace declaration, they are not in any namespace.

Example 6–6. Unqualified local names

```
<prod:product xmlns:prod="http://datypic.com/prod">
  <number>557</number>
  <size>10</size>
</prod:product>
```

6.3.3 *Using* elementFormDefault

Let's look at the schemas that would describe these two instances. Example 6–7 shows a schema for the instance in Example 6–5, which has qualified element names.

Example 6–7. Schema for qualified local element names

```
<xs:schema xmlns:xs="http://www.w3.org/2001/XMLSchema"
           xmlns="http://datypic.com/prod"
           targetNamespace="http://datypic.com/prod"
           elementFormDefault="qualified">
  <xs:element name="product" type="ProductType"/>
  <xs:complexType name="ProductType">
    <xs:sequence>
      <xs:element name="number" type="xs:integer"/>
      <xs:element name="size" type="xs:integer"/>
    </xs:sequence>
  </xs:complexType>
</xs:schema>
```

The schema document has elementFormDefault set to qualified. As a result, elements conforming to local declarations must use qualified element names in the instance. In this example, the declaration for product is global and the declarations for number and size are local.

To create a schema for the instance in Example 6–6, which has unqualified names, you can simply change the value of elementFormDefault in the schema document to unqualified. Or, since the default value is unqualified, you could simply omit the attribute. In this case, elements conforming to global declarations must still use qualified element names—hence the use of `prod:product` in the instance.

6.3.4 Using `form`

It is also possible to specify the form on a particular element declaration using a `form` attribute whose value, like `elementFormDefault`, is either `qualified` or `unqualified`. Example 6–8 shows a revised schema that uses the `form` attribute on the `number` element declaration to override `elementFormDefault` and make it unqualified.

Example 6–8. Using the `form` attribute

```
<xs:schema xmlns:xs="http://www.w3.org/2001/XMLSchema"
           xmlns="http://datypic.com/prod"
           targetNamespace="http://datypic.com/prod"
           elementFormDefault="qualified">
  <xs:element name="product" type="ProductType"/>
  <xs:complexType name="ProductType">
    <xs:sequence>
      <xs:element name="number" type="xs:integer"
                        form="unqualified"/>
      <xs:element name="size" type="xs:integer"/>
    </xs:sequence>
  </xs:complexType>
</xs:schema>
```

A valid instance is shown in Example 6–9.

Example 6–9. Overridden form

```
<prod:product xmlns:prod="http://datypic.com/prod">
  <number>557</number>
  <prod:size>10</prod:size>
</prod:product>
```

6.3.5   *Default namespaces and unqualified names*

Default namespaces do not mix well with unqualified element names. The instance in Example 6–10 declares the `prod` namespace as the default namespace. However, this will not work with a schema document where `elementFormDefault` is set to `unqualified`, because it will be unsuccessfully looking for the elements `number` and `size` in the `prod` namespace whereas they are in fact not in any namespace.

Example 6–10. Invalid mixing of unqualified names and a default namespace

```
<product xmlns="http://datypic.com/prod">
  <number>557</number>
  <size>10</size>
</product>
```

Although unqualified element names may seem confusing, they do have some advantages when combining multiple namespaces. Section 21.7.3 on p. 575 provides a more complete coverage of the pros and cons of unqualified local names.

6.4 | Default and fixed values

Default and fixed values are used to augment an instance by adding values to empty elements. The schema processor will insert a default or fixed value if the element in question is empty. If the element is absent from the instance, it will not be inserted. This is different from the treatment of default and fixed values for attributes.

Default and fixed values are specified by the `default` and `fixed` attributes, respectively. Only one of the two attributes (`default` or `fixed`) may appear; they are mutually exclusive. Default and fixed values can be specified in element declarations with:

- Simple types
- Complex types with simple content
- Complex types with mixed content, if all children are optional

The default or fixed value must be valid for the type of that element. For example, it is not legal to specify a default value of xyz if the type of the element is integer.[1]

The specification of fixed and default values in element declarations is independent of their occurrence constraints (minOccurs and maxOccurs). Unlike defaulted attributes, a defaulted element may be required (i.e., minOccurs in its declaration may be more than 0). If an element with a default value is required, it may still appear empty and have its default value filled in.

6.4.1   Default values

The default value is filled in if the element is empty. Example 6–11 shows the declaration of product with two children, name and size, that have default values specified.

Example 6–11. Specifying an element's default value

```
<xs:element name="product">
  <xs:complexType>
    <xs:choice minOccurs="0" maxOccurs="unbounded">
      <xs:element name="name" type="xs:string" default="N/A"/>
      <xs:element name="size" type="xs:integer" default="12"/>
    </xs:choice>
  </xs:complexType>
</xs:element>
```

---

1.   This is not considered an error in the schema, but any instance that relies on the value would be in error.

It is important to note that certain types allow an empty value. This includes `string`, `normalizedString`, `token`, and any types derived from them that do not specifically disallow the empty string as a value. Additionally, unrestricted list types allow empty values. For any type that allows an empty string value, the element will never be considered to have that empty string value because the default value will be filled in. However, if an element has the `xsi:nil` attribute set to `true`, its default value is *not* inserted.

Table 6–3 describes how element default values are inserted in different situations, based on the declaration in Example 6–11.

Table 6–3   Default value behavior for elements

Situation	*Result*	*Before example*	*After example*
Value specified	Original value kept	`<size>10</size>`	`<size>10</size>`
Empty element	Value filled in	`<size/>`	`<size>12</size>`
		`<size></size>`	`<size>12</size>`
		`<name/>`	`<name>N/A</name>`
		`<name></name>`	`<name>N/A</name>`
Value is just whitespace	No value filled in	`<size> </size>`	`<size></size>`
		`<name> </name>`	*(error is raised)*
			`<name> </name>`
Element is nil	No value filled in	`<size xsi:nil="true"/>`	`<size xsi:nil="true"/>`
Element does not appear	No element added	`<product/>`	`<product/>`

6.4.2   *Fixed values*

Fixed values are added in all the same situations as default values. The only difference is that if the element has a value, its value must be equivalent to the fixed value. When the schema processor determines whether the value of the element is in fact equivalent to the fixed value, it takes into account the element's type.

Table 6–4 shows some valid and invalid instances for elements declared with fixed values. The `size` element has the type `integer`, so all forms of the integer "1" are accepted in the instance, including "01", "+1", and " 1 " surrounded by whitespace. Whitespace around a value is acceptable because the `whiteSpace` facet value for `integer` is `collapse`, meaning that whitespace is stripped before validation takes place. A value that contains only whitespace, like `<size> </size>`, is not valid because it is not considered empty but also is not equal to 1.

The `name` element, on the other hand, has the type `string`. The string "01" is invalid because it is not considered to be equal to the string "1". The string " 1 " is also invalid because the `whiteSpace` facet value for `string` is `preserve`, meaning that the leading and trailing spaces are kept. For more information on type equality, see Section 11.7 on p. 253.

Table 6–4   Elements with fixed values

Schema

```
<xs:element name="name" type="xs:string" fixed="1"/>
<xs:element name="size" type="xs:integer" fixed="1"/>
```

Valid instances	*Invalid instances*
`<size>1</size>`	`<size>2</size>`
`<size>01</size>`	`<size> </size>`
`<size>+1</size>`	
`<size> 1 </size>`	
`<size/>`	
`<size></size>`	
`<name>1</name>`	`<name>01</name>`
`<name/>`	`<name>+1</name>`
`<name></name>`	`<name> 1 </name>`
	`<name> </name>`
	`<name>2</name>`

6.5 | Nils and nillability

In some cases, an element may be either absent from an instance or empty (contain no value). The instance shown in Example 6–12 is a purchase order with some absent and empty elements.

Example 6–12. Missing values

```
<order>
  <giftWrap>ADULT BDAY</giftWrap>
  <customer>
    <name>
      <first>Priscilla</first>
      <middle/>
      <last>Walmsley</last>
    </name>
  </customer>
  <items>
    <shirt>
      <giftWrap/>
      <number>557</number>
      <name>Short-Sleeved Linen Blouse</name>
      <size></size>
    </shirt>
    <umbrella>
      <number>443</number>
      <name>Deluxe Golf Umbrella</name>
      <size></size>
    </umbrella>
  </items>
</order>
```

There are many possible reasons for an element value to be missing in an instance:

- The information is not applicable: Umbrellas do not come in different sizes.
- We do not know whether the information is applicable: We do not know whether the customer has a middle name.

- It is not relevant to this particular application of the data: The billing application does not care about product sizes.

- It is the default, so it is not specified: The customer's title should default to "Mr."

- It actually is present and the value is an empty string: The gift wrap value for the shirt is empty, meaning "none," which should override the gift wrap value of the order.

- It is erroneously missing because of a user error or technical bug: We should have a size for the shirt.

Different applications treat missing values in different ways. One application might treat an absent element as not applicable, and an empty element as an error. Another might treat an empty element as not applicable, and an absent element as an error. The treatment of missing values may vary within the same schema. In our example, we used a combination of absent and empty elements to signify different reasons for missing values.

XML Schema offers a third method of indicating a missing value: *nils*. By marking an element as nil, you are telling the processor "I know this element is empty, but I want it to be valid anyway." The actual reason why it is empty, or what the application should do with it, is entirely up to you. XML Schema does not associate any particular semantics with this absence. It only offers an additional way to express a missing value, with the following benefits:

- You do not have to weaken the type by allowing empty content and/or making attributes optional.

- You are making a deliberate statement that the information does not exist. This is a clearer message than simply omitting the element, which would mean that we do not know if it exists.

- If for some reason an application is relying on that element being there, for example as a placeholder, nil provides a way for it to exist without imparting any additional information.

- You can easily turn off default value processing. The default value for the element will not be added if it is marked as nil.

An approach for our purchase order document is outlined below. It uses nils, derived types, simple type restrictions, and default values to better constrain missing values. The resulting instance is shown in Example 6–13.

Example 6–13. Missing values, revisited

```
<order xmlns:xsi="http://www.w3.org/2001/XMLSchema-instance">
  <giftWrap>ADULT BDAY</giftWrap>
  <customer>
    <name>
      <title/>               <!--default will be filled in-->
      <first>Priscilla</first>
      <middle xsi:nil="true"/>
      <last>Walmsley</last>
    </name>
  </customer>
  <items>
    <shirt>
      <giftWrap/>
      <number>557</number>
      <name>Short-Sleeved Linen Blouse</name>
      <size></size>                    <!--INVALID! -->
    </shirt>
    <umbrella>
      <number>443</number>
      <name>Deluxe Golf Umbrella</name>
    </umbrella>
  </items>
</order>
```

- The information is not applicable: Give `shirt` and `umbrella` different types and do not include the `size` element declaration in `UmbrellaType`.
- We do not know whether the information is applicable: Make `middle` nillable and set `xsi:nil` to `true` if it is not present.

- It is not relevant to this particular application of the data: Give the billing application a separate schema document and insert a wildcard where the `size` and other optional element declarations or references may appear.
- It is the default, so it is not specified: Specify a default value of "Mr." for `title`.
- It actually is present and the value is an empty string: Allow `giftWrap` to appear empty.
- It is erroneously missing because of a user error or technical bug: Make `size` required and make it an `integer` or other type that does not accept empty values.

This is one of the many reasonable approaches for handling absent values. The important thing is to define a strategy that provides all the information your application needs and ensures that all errors are caught.

6.5.1   *Using* `xsi:nil` *in an instance*

To indicate that the value of an instance element is nil, specify the `xsi:nil` attribute on that element. Example 6–14 shows five instances of `size` that use the `xsi:nil` attribute. The `xsi:nil` attribute applies to the element in whose tag it appears, not any of the attributes. There is no way to specify that an attribute value is nil.

Example 6–14. `xsi:nil` in instance elements

```
<size xsi:nil="true"/>
<size xsi:nil="true"></size>
<size xsi:nil="true" system="US-DRESS"/>
<size xsi:nil="false">10</size>
<size xsi:nil="true">10</size> <!--INVALID! -->
```

The `xsi:nil` attribute is in the XML Schema Instance Namespace (`http://www.w3.org/2001/XMLSchema-instance`). This namespace must be declared in the instance, but it is not necessary to specify a schema location for it. Any schema processor will recognize the `xsi:nil` attribute of any XML element.

If the `xsi:nil` attribute appears on an element, and its value is set to `true`, that element must be empty. It cannot contain any child elements or character data, even if its type requires content. The last instance of the `size` element in Example 6–14 is invalid because `xsi:nil` is `true` but it contains data. However, it is valid for a nil element to have other attributes, as long as they are declared for that type.

6.5.2 *Making elements nillable*

In order to allow an element to appear in the instance with the `xsi:nil` attribute, its element declaration must indicate that it is *nillable*. Nillability is indicated by setting the `nillable` attribute in the element declaration to `true`. Example 6–15 shows an element declaration illustrating this.

Example 6–15. Making `size` elements nillable

```
<xs:element name="size" type="xs:integer" nillable="true"/>
```

Specifying `nillable="true"` in the declaration allows elements to have the `xsi:nil` attribute. Otherwise, the `xsi:nil` attribute cannot appear, even with its value set to `false`. It is not necessary (or even legal) to separately declare the `xsi:nil` attribute for the type used in the element declaration. In Example 6–15, we gave `size` a simple type. Normally this would mean that it cannot have attributes, but the `xsi:nil` attribute is given special treatment. Elements with either complex or simple types can be nillable.

If `nillable` is set to `true`, a fixed value may not be specified in the declaration.[1] However, it is legal to specify a default value. If an element

---

1.   This would be considered an error in the instance, not the schema.

has an `xsi:nil` set to `true`, the default value is not filled in even though the element is empty.

Elements should not be declared nillable if they will ever be used as fields in an identity constraint, such as a key or a uniqueness constraint. See Section 17.7.2 on p. 434 for more information on identity constraint fields.

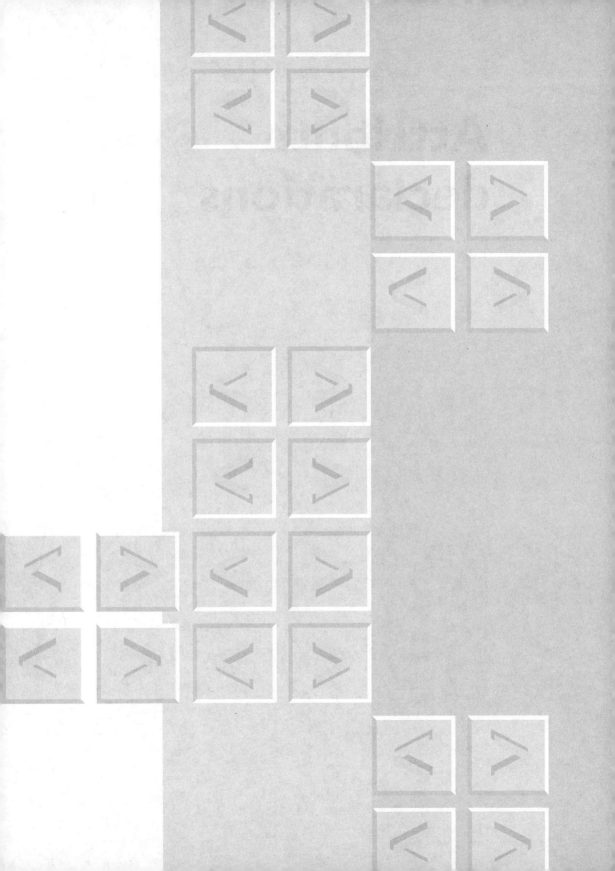

Attribute
declarations

Chapter

7

T his chapter covers the other basic building block of XML: attributes. It explains how to declare attributes and assign types to them. It also describes fixed and default values as they apply to attributes.

7.1 | Attributes vs. elements

Whether to model data values as elements or attributes is an often-discussed question. XML Schema, with its ability to define data types for elements, eliminates many of the advantages of attributes in DTDs. The advantages of using attributes are:

- They are less verbose.
- For narrative content, attributes are typically used for values that should not appear in the content—that is, for metadata. In a typical (X)HTML document, elements are used for the content that appears on a page, while attributes specify style

and other information that is used by the browser but not directly by the end user. This is a convenient separation for some narrative XML vocabularies.

- If you plan to validate using DTDs as well as schemas, you can perform some minimal type checking on attribute values. For example, `color` can be constrained to a certain set of values. Elements' values character data content cannot be validated using DTDs.

- Attributes can be added to the instance by specifying default values; elements cannot (they must appear to receive a default value).

- Attributes can be inherited by descendant elements, as described in Section 7.6 on p. 126.

The advantages of using elements are:

- They are more extensible because attributes can later be added to them without affecting a processing application. For example, if you realized that you needed to keep track of what currency a price is expressed in, you can declare a `currency` attribute in the `price` element declaration. If `price` is an attribute, this is not possible.

- They can contain other elements. For example, if you want to mark up a textual description using XHTML tags, this is not possible if `description` is an attribute.

- They can be repeated. An element may only appear once now, but later you may wish to extend it to appear multiple times. For example, if you decide later that a product can have multiple colors, you can allow a `color` child to appear more than once. Attributes may only appear once per element.

- You have more control over the rules of their appearance. For example, you can say that a `product` can have either a `number` or a `productCode` child. This is not possible for attributes.

- They can be used in substitution groups.

- They can be given nil values.
- They can use type substitution to substitute derived types in the instance.
- Their order is significant, while the order of attributes is not. Obviously, this is only an advantage if you care about the order.
- When the values are lengthy, elements tend to be more readable than attributes.

As you can see, there are many more advantages to using elements than attributes, but attributes are useful in some cases. A general recommendation is to use attributes for metadata and elements for data. For example, use an attribute to describe the units, language, or time dependence of an element value. Additionally, attributes should be used for ID and IDREF values as well as XLink expressions. Elements should be used for everything else.

7.2 | Global and local attribute declarations

Attribute declarations are used to name an attribute and associate it with a particular simple type. This is accomplished using an attribute element. Attribute declarations may be either global or local.

7.2.1 *Global attribute declarations*

Global attribute declarations appear at the top level of the schema document, meaning that their parent must be the schema element. These global attribute declarations can then be used in multiple complex types, as described in Section 12.6 on p. 281. Table 7–1 shows the syntax of a global attribute declaration.

Example 7–1 shows two global attribute declarations: system and dim. A complex type is then defined which references those attribute declarations by name using the ref attribute.

Table 7–1 XSD Syntax: global attribute declaration

Name
attribute

Parents
schema, ▪ override

Attribute name	Type	Description
id	ID	Unique ID.
name	NCName	Unique name.
type	QName	Type, see Section 7.3.
default	string	Default value, see Section 7.5.1.
fixed	string	Fixed value, see Section 7.5.2.
▪ inheritable	boolean: *false*	Whether the value can be inherited by descendant elements, see Section 7.6.

Content
annotation?, simpleType?

Example 7–1. Global attribute declarations

```
<xs:schema xmlns:xs="http://www.w3.org/2001/XMLSchema"
           xmlns="http://datypic.com/prod"
           targetNamespace="http://datypic.com/prod">

  <xs:attribute name="system" type="xs:string"/>
  <xs:attribute name="dim" type="xs:integer"/>

  <xs:complexType name="SizeType">
    <xs:attribute ref="system" use="required"/>
    <xs:attribute ref="dim"/>
  </xs:complexType>

</xs:schema>
```

The qualified names used by global attribute declarations must be unique in the schema. This includes not just the schema document in which they appear, but any other schema documents that are used with it.

The use attribute, which indicates whether an attribute is required or optional, appears in the attribute reference rather than attribute declaration. This is because it applies to the appearance of that attribute in a complex type, not the attribute itself. Attribute references are covered in Section 12.6 on p. 281.

The name specified in an attribute declaration must be an XML non-colonized name, which means that it must start with a letter or under-score, and may only contain letters, digits, underscores, hyphens, and periods. The qualified name consists of the target namespace of the schema document plus the local name in the declaration. In Exam-ple 7–1, the system and dim attributes take on the target namespace http://datypic.com/prod.

Since globally declared attribute names are qualified by the target namespace of the schema document, it is not legal to include a namespace prefix in the value of the name attribute. If you want to declare attributes in another namespace, you must create a separate schema document with that namespace as target and import it into the original schema document. If you simply want to specify an attribute from another namespace, such as xml:lang, use the ref attribute to reference it in a complex type.

7.2.2 *Local attribute declarations*

Local attribute declarations, on the other hand, appear entirely within a complex type definition. They may only be used in that type defini-tion, and are never reused by other types. Table 7–2 shows the syntax for a local attribute declaration.

Table 7–2   XSD Syntax: local attribute declaration

Name

`attribute`

Parents

`complexType, restriction, extension, attributeGroup`

Attribute name	Type	Description
`id`	`ID`	Unique ID.
name	`NCName`	Unique name.
`type`	`QName`	Simple type, see Section 7.3.
`form`	`"qualified"` | `"unqualified"`	Whether the attribute name must be qualified in the instance (see Section 7.4); defaults to `attributeFormDefault` of `schema`, which defaults to `unqualified`.
`use`	`"optional"` | `"prohibited"` | `"required"` : *optional*	Whether it is required or optional, see Section 12.6.2.
`default`	`string`	Default value, see Section 7.5.1.
`fixed`	`string`	Fixed value, see Section 7.5.2.
▪ `targetNamespace`	`anyURI`	The target namespace if restricting a type in another namespace, see Section 13.5.7.
▪ `inheritable`	`boolean:` *false*	Whether the value can be inherited by descendant elements, see Section 7.6.

Content

`annotation?, simpleType?`

Example 7–2 shows two local attribute declarations, system and dim, which appear entirely within a complex type definition.

Example 7–2. Local attribute declarations

```
<xs:schema xmlns:xs="http://www.w3.org/2001/XMLSchema"
           xmlns="http://datypic.com/prod"
           targetNamespace="http://datypic.com/prod">

  <xs:complexType name="SizeType">
    <xs:attribute name="system" type="xs:string" use="required"/>
    <xs:attribute name="dim" type="xs:integer"/>
  </xs:complexType>

</xs:schema>
```

Unlike global attribute declarations, local attribute declarations can have a use attribute, which indicates whether an attribute is required or optional.

The name specified in a local attribute declaration must also be an XML non-colonized name. If its form is qualified, it takes on the target namespace of the schema document. If it is unqualified, it is considered to be in no namespace. See Section 7.4 on p. 122 for more information on qualified versus unqualified attribute names.

Locally declared attribute names are scoped to the complex type in which they are declared. It is illegal to have two attributes with the same qualified name in the same complex type definition. This is explained further in Section 12.6 on p. 281.

7.2.3 *Design hint: Should I use global or local attribute declarations?*

Global attribute declarations are discouraged unless the attribute is used in a variety of element declarations which are in a variety of namespaces. This is because globally declared attribute names must be prefixed in instances, resulting in an instance element that looks like this:

```
<prod:size prod:system="US-DRESS" prod:dim="1"/>
```

Prefixing every attribute is not what users generally expect, and it adds a lot of extra text without any additional meaning.

Two examples of global attributes are the `xml:lang` attribute that is part of XML and the `xsi:type` attribute that is part of XML Schema. Virtually any element in any namespace may have these two attributes, so in this case it is desirable to distinguish them by their namespace.

If you are tempted to use a global attribute declaration because you want to be able to reuse it multiple times, consider these two alternatives:

- Put it into an attribute group. This makes it, effectively, a local attribute declaration, while still allowing you to reuse it.
- Define a named simple type that can be reused by multiple local attribute declarations.

7.3 | Declaring the types of attributes

Regardless of whether they are local or global, all attribute declarations associate an attribute name with a simple type. All attributes have simple types rather than complex types, which makes sense since they cannot themselves have child elements or attributes. There are three ways to assign a simple type to an attribute.

1. Reference a named simple type by specifying the `type` attribute in the attribute declaration. This may be either a built-in type or a user-derived type.
2. Define an anonymous type by specifying a `simpleType` child.

3. Use no particular type, by specifying neither a `type` attribute
    nor a `simpleType` child. In this case, the actual type is
    `anySimpleType`, which may have any value, as long as it
    is well-formed XML.

Example 7–3 shows four attribute declarations with different type
assignment methods.

Example 7–3. Declaring the types of attributes

```
<xs:attribute name="color" type="ColorType"/>

<xs:attribute name="dim" type="xs:integer"/>

<xs:attribute name="system">
  <xs:simpleType>
    <xs:restriction base="xs:string">
      <xs:enumeration value="US-DRESS"/>
      <!--...-->
    </xs:restriction>
  </xs:simpleType>
</xs:attribute>

<xs:attribute name="anything"/>
```

The first example uses the `type` attribute to assign `ColorType` to
the attribute `color`. The second example also uses the `type` attribute, this time to assign the built-in type `integer` to the attribute `dim`.
The `xs` prefix is used because the built-in types are part of the XML
Schema Namespace. For a complete explanation of the use of prefixes
in schema documents, see Section 3.3.5 on p. 52.

The third example uses an inline anonymous simple type, which is
defined entirely within the `system` attribute declaration. Finally, the
fourth attribute, `anything`, does not specify a particular type, which
means that any value is valid.

For a detailed discussion of using named or anonymous types, see
Section 8.2.3 on p. 133.

7.4 | Qualified vs. unqualified forms

XML Schema allows you to exert some control over using namespace-qualified or unqualified attribute names in the instance. Since default namespace declarations do not apply to attributes, this is essentially a question of whether you want the attribute names to be prefixed or unprefixed.

This is indicated by the `form` attribute, which may be set to `qualified` or `unqualified`. If the `form` attribute is not present in a local attribute declaration, the value defaults to the value of the `attributeFormDefault` attribute of the `schema` element. If neither attribute is present, the default is `unqualified`. The `form` and `attributeFormDefault` attributes only apply to locally declared attributes. If an attribute is declared globally (at the top level of the schema document), it must always have a qualified (prefixed) name in the instance.

Example 7–4 shows a schema that declares several attributes, along with a valid instance. In the instance, the `global` attribute's name is qualified (prefixed) because it is globally declared. The attributes `unqual` and `qual` both have a `form` attribute specified, and their names appear in the instance as designated. The `unspec` attribute's name is unqualified (unprefixed) because that is the default when neither `form` nor `attributeFormDefault` are present.

Qualified attribute names should only be used for attributes that apply to a variety of elements in a variety of namespaces, such as `xml:lang` or `xsi:type`. For locally declared attributes, whose scope is limited to the type definition in which they appear, prefixes add extra text without any additional meaning.

The best way to handle qualification of attribute names is to ignore the `form` and `attributeFormDefault` attributes completely. Then, globally declared attributes will have qualified names, and locally declared attributes will have unqualified names, which makes sense. Section 21.7.3 on p. 575 provides a more complete coverage of the pros and cons of unqualified local names for both elements and attributes.

Example 7–4. Qualified and unqualified attribute names

Schema:

```
<xs:schema xmlns:xs="http://www.w3.org/2001/XMLSchema"
           xmlns="http://datypic.com/prod"
           targetNamespace="http://datypic.com/prod">
  <xs:attribute name="global" type="xs:string"/>
  <xs:element name="size" type="SizeType"/>
  <xs:complexType name="SizeType">
    <xs:attribute ref="global"/>
    <xs:attribute name="unqual" form="unqualified"/>
    <xs:attribute name="qual" form="qualified"/>
    <xs:attribute name="unspec"/>
  </xs:complexType>
</xs:schema>
```

Valid instance:

```
<prod:size xmlns:prod="http://datypic.com/prod"
           prod:global="x" unqual="x" prod:qual="x" unspec="x"/>
```

7.5 | Default and fixed values

Default and fixed values are used to augment an instance by adding attributes when they are not present. If an attribute is absent, and a default or fixed value is specified in its declaration, the schema processor will insert the attribute and give it the default or fixed value.

Default and fixed values are specified by the default and fixed attributes, respectively. Only one of the two attributes (default or fixed) may appear; they are mutually exclusive. If an attribute has a default value specified, it cannot be a required attribute. This makes sense, because if the attribute is required, it will always appear in instances, and the default value will never be used.

The default or fixed value must be valid for the type of that attribute. For example, it is not legal to specify a default value of xyz if the type of the attribute is integer.

7.5.1   *Default values*

A default value is filled in if the attribute is absent from the element. If the attribute appears, with any value, it is left alone. Example 7–5 shows the declaration of `size` with one attribute, `dim`, that has a default value specified.

Example 7–5. Declaring a default value for an attribute

```
<xs:element name="size">
  <xs:complexType>
    <xs:attribute name="dim" type="xs:integer" default="1"/>
  </xs:complexType>
</xs:element>
```

Table 7–3 describes how attribute default values are inserted in different situations, based on the declaration in Example 7–5. Note that the only time the default value is inserted is when the attribute is absent. If the attribute's value is the empty string, it is left as is. In that case, if an empty string is not valid for that type, which it is not for `integer`, an error is raised. This is different from the behavior of default values for elements, described in Section 6.4.1 on p. 102.

Table 7–3   Default value behavior for attributes

Situation	Result	Before example	After example
Attribute is absent.	Attribute is added with the default value.	`<size/>`	`<size dim="1"/>`
Attribute appears with a value.	Original value is kept.	`<size dim="2"/>`	`<size dim="2"/>`
Attribute appears with empty string as its value.	Empty string is kept.	`<size dim=""/>`	`<size dim=""/>` *(Error is raised.)*

7.5.2   *Fixed values*

Fixed values are inserted in all the same situations as default values. The only difference is that if the attribute appears, its value must be equal to the fixed value. When the schema processor determines whether the value of the attribute is in fact equal to the fixed value, it takes into account the attribute's type.

Table 7–4 shows some valid and invalid instances for attributes declared with fixed values. The `dim` attribute has the type `integer`, so all forms of the integer "1" are accepted in the instance, including "01", "+1", and " 1 " surrounded by whitespace. The whitespace is acceptable because the `whiteSpace` facet value for `integer` is `collapse`, meaning that leading and trailing whitespace is stripped before validation takes place.

Table 7–4   Attributes with fixed values

Schema

```
<xs:element name="size">
  <xs:complexType>
    <xs:attribute name="system" type="xs:string" fixed="1"/>
    <xs:attribute name="dim" type="xs:integer" fixed="1"/>
  </xs:complexType>
</xs:element>
```

Valid instances	*Invalid instances*
`<size system="1" dim="1"/>`	`<size system="3" dim="3"/>`
`<size/>`	`<size dim=""/>`
`<size dim="01"/>`	`<size dim=" "/>`
`<size dim="+1"/>`	`<size system="01"/>`
`<size dim=" 1 "/>`	`<size system="+1"/>`
	`<size system=" 1 "/>`
	`<size system=""/>`

The `system` attribute, on the other hand, has the type `string`. The string "01" is invalid because it is not considered equal to the string "1". The string " 1 " is also invalid because the `whiteSpace` facet value for `string` is `preserve`, meaning that the leading and trailing spaces are kept. For more information on type equality, please see Section 11.7 on p. 253.

7.6 | Inherited attributes

In version 1.1, it is possible to declare an attribute to be *inheritable*. Conceptually, this means that it is relevant not just to the element on which it appears, but to the descendant elements as well. A good example is a `language` attribute which could be declared as an allowed attribute of a `chapter` element, but could be overridden in a descendant `p` element, as shown in Example 7–6.

Example 7–6. Instance containing an inherited attribute

```
<chapter language="en">
  <p>This is not a pipe.</p>
  <p language="fr">Ceci n'est pas une pipe.</p>
</chapter>
```

The implication is that the language of the chapter is English (`en`), and all descendant elements have that language unless otherwise specified with another `language` attribute. In this case, the first paragraph doesn't have a `language` attribute, so it inherits the value `en` from the chapter. The second paragraph does not inherit the value, because it overrides it by saying its language is French (`fr`).

Example 7–7 is a schema for the example. The `language` attribute declaration uses `inheritable="true"` to indicate that `language` attributes are inheritable from chapters down to their descendants.

Note that using an inheritable `language` attribute declaration in `ChapterType` does not mean that the attribute can be automatically

Example 7–7. Declaring an inheritable attribute

```
<xs:element name="chapter" type="ChapterType"/>
<xs:complexType name="ChapterType">
  <xs:sequence>
    <xs:element name="p" type="ParaType" maxOccurs="unbounded"/>
  </xs:sequence>
  <xs:attribute name="language" type="xs:language"
                inheritable="true"/>
</xs:complexType>
<xs:complexType name="ParaType">
  <xs:simpleContent>
    <xs:extension base="xs:string">
      <xs:attribute name="language" type="xs:language"/>
    </xs:extension>
  </xs:simpleContent>
</xs:complexType>
```

valid on all descendants of a `chapter`. In fact, this example requires a separate `language` attribute declaration within `ParaType`.[1]

A practical implication of declaring an attribute inheritable is that inherited attributes can be used in the type alternatives that are defined for the descendant elements. This is described further in Section 14.2.6 on p. 382.

---

1. In this example, making `language` inheritable with `ParaType` would have no meaning, since there are no allowed descendants. But otherwise it is good practice to make `language` inheritable.

Simple types

B oth element and attribute declarations can use simple types to describe their data content. This chapter introduces simple types and explains how to define your own atomic simple types for use in your schemas.

8.1 | Simple type varieties

There are three varieties of simple types: atomic types, list types, and union types.

1. *Atomic types* have values that are indivisible, such as 10 or large.

2. *List types* have values that are whitespace-separated lists of atomic values, such as `<availableSizes>10 large 2</availableSizes>`.

3. *Union types* may have values that are either atomic values or list values. What differentiates them is that the set of valid values, or "value space," for the type is the union of the value spaces of

two or more other simple types. For example, to represent a dress size, you may define a union type that allows a value to be either an integer from 2 through 18, or one of the string values small, medium, or large.

List and union types are covered in Chapter 10.

8.1.1 *Design hint: How much should I break down my data values?*

Data values should be broken down to the most atomic level possible. This allows them to be processed in a variety of ways for different uses, such as display, mathematical operations, and validation. It is much easier to concatenate two data values back together than it is to split them apart. In addition, more granular data is easier to validate.

It is a fairly common practice to put a data value and its units in the same element, for example `<length>3cm</length>`. However, the preferred approach is to have a separate data value, preferably an attribute, for the units, for example `<length units="cm">3</length>`.

Using a single concatenated value is limiting because:

- It is extremely cumbersome to validate. You have to apply a complicated pattern that would need to change every time a unit type is added.

- You cannot perform comparisons, conversions, or mathematical operations on the data without splitting it apart.

- If you want to display the data item differently (for example, as "3 centimeters" or "3 cm" or just "3", you have to split it apart. This complicates the stylesheets and applications that process instance documents.

It is possible to go too far, though. For example, you may break a date down as follows:

```
<orderDate>
  <year>2001</year>
  <month>06</month>
  <day>15</day>
</orderDate>
```

This is probably overkill unless you have a special need to process these items separately.

8.2 | Simple type definitions

8.2.1   *Named simple types*

Simple types can be either named or anonymous. Named simple types are always defined globally (i.e., their parent is always `schema`[1]) and are required to have a name that is unique among the types (both simple and complex) in the schema. The syntax for a named simple type definition is shown in Table 8–1.

The `name` of a simple type must be an XML non-colonized name, which means that it must start with a letter or underscore, and may only contain letters, digits, underscores, hyphens, and periods. You cannot include a namespace prefix when defining the type; it takes its namespace from the target namespace of the schema document.

All examples of named types in this book have the word "Type" at the end of their names to clearly distinguish them from element and attribute names. However, this is a convention and not a requirement. You can even have a type definition and an element declaration using the same name, but this is not recommended because it can be confusing.

Example 8–1 shows the definition of a named simple type `DressSizeType` along with an element declaration that references it. Named types can be used in multiple element and attribute declarations.

---

1.   Except in the case of a redefine or override.

Table 8–1   XSD Syntax: named simple type definition

Name
simpleType

Parents
schema, redefine, ▪️override

Attribute name	Type	Description
id	ID	Unique ID.
name	NCName	Simple type name.
final	"#all" | list of ("restriction" | "list" | "union" | ▪️"extension")	Whether other types can be derived from this one (see Section 8.5); defaults to finalDefault of schema.

Content
annotation?, (restriction | list | union)

Example 8–1. Defining and referencing a named simple type

```
<xs:simpleType name="DressSizeType">
  <xs:restriction base="xs:integer">
    <xs:minInclusive value="2"/>
    <xs:maxInclusive value="18"/>
  </xs:restriction>
</xs:simpleType>

<xs:element name="size" type="DressSizeType"/>
```

8.2.2   *Anonymous simple types*

Anonymous types, on the other hand, must not have names. They are always defined entirely within an element or attribute declaration, and may only be used once, by that declaration. Defining a type anonymously prevents it from ever being restricted, used in a list or union, redefined, or overridden. The syntax to define an anonymous simple type is shown in Table 8–2.

Table 8–2   XSD Syntax: anonymous simple type definition

Name
simpleType

Parents
element, attribute, restriction, list, union, **1.1** alternative

Attribute name	*Type*	*Description*
id	ID	Unique ID.

Content
annotation?, (restriction | list | union)

Example 8–2 shows the definition of an anonymous simple type within an element declaration.

Example 8–2. Defining an anonymous simple type

```
<xs:element name="size">
  <xs:simpleType>
    <xs:restriction base="xs:integer">
      <xs:minInclusive value="2"/>
      <xs:maxInclusive value="18"/>
    </xs:restriction>
  </xs:simpleType>
</xs:element>
```

8.2.3   *Design hint: Should I use named or anonymous types?*

The advantage of named types is that they may be defined once and used many times. For example, you may define a type named

`ProductCodeType` that lists all of the valid product codes in your organization. This type can then be used in many element and attribute declarations in many schemas. This has the advantages of

- Encouraging consistency throughout the organization
- Reducing the possibility of error
- Requiring less time to define new schemas
- Simplifying maintenance, because new product codes need only be added in one place

If a type is named, you can also derive new types from it, which is another way to promote reuse and consistency.

Named types can also make a schema more readable when its type definitions are complicated.

An anonymous type, on the other hand, can be used only in the element or attribute declaration that contains it. It can never be redefined, overridden, have types derived from it, or be used in a list or union type. This can seriously limit its reusability, extensibility, and ability to change over time.

However, there are cases where anonymous types are preferable to named types. If the type is unlikely to ever be reused, the advantages listed above no longer apply. Also, there is such a thing as too much reuse. For example, if an element can contain the values 1 through 10, it does not make sense to define a type named `OneToTenType` to be reused by other unrelated element declarations with the same value space. If the value space for one of the element declarations using that named type changes but the other element declarations stay the same, it actually makes maintenance more difficult, because a new type would need to be defined at that time.

In addition, anonymous types can be more readable when they are relatively simple. It is sometimes desirable to have the definition of the type right there with the element or attribute declaration.

8.3 | Simple type restrictions

Every simple type is a restriction of another simple type, known as its base type. It is not possible to extend a simple type, except by adding attributes which results in a complex type. This is described in Section 13.4.1 on p. 306.

Every new simple type restricts the value space of its base type in some way. Example 8–3 shows a definition of DressSizeType that restricts the built-in type integer.

Example 8–3. Deriving a simple type from a built-in simple type

```
<xs:simpleType name="DressSizeType">
  <xs:restriction base="xs:integer">
    <xs:minInclusive value="2"/>
    <xs:maxInclusive value="18"/>
    <xs:pattern value="\d{1,2}"/>
  </xs:restriction>
</xs:simpleType>
```

Simple types may also restrict user-derived simple types that are defined in the same schema document, or even in a different schema document. For example, you could further restrict DressSizeType by defining another simple type, MediumDressSizeType, as shown in Example 8–4.

A simple type restricts its base type by applying facets to restrict its values. In Example 8–4, the facets minInclusive and maxInclusive are used to restrict the value of MediumDressSizeType to be between 8 and 12 inclusive.

Example 8–4. Deriving a simple type from a user-derived simple type

```
<xs:simpleType name="MediumDressSizeType">
  <xs:restriction base="DressSizeType">
    <xs:minInclusive value="8"/>
    <xs:maxInclusive value="12"/>
  </xs:restriction>
</xs:simpleType>
```

8.3.1   *Defining a restriction*

The syntax for a `restriction` element is shown in Table 8–3. You must specify one base type either by using the `base` attribute or by defining the simple type anonymously using a `simpleType` child. The option of using a `simpleType` child is generally only useful when restricting list types, as described in Section 10.3.3 on p. 190.

Table 8–3   XSD Syntax: simple type restriction

Name
restriction

Parents
simpleType

Attribute name	Type	Description
id	ID	Unique ID.
base	QName	Simple type that is being restricted; either a `base` attribute or a `simpleType` child is required.

Content
annotation?, simpleType?, (minExclusive | minInclusive | maxExclusive | maxInclusive | length | minLength | maxLength | totalDigits | fractionDigits | enumeration | pattern | whiteSpace | ▥assertion | ▥explicitTimezone | ▥*{any element in another namespace}*) *

Within a `restriction` element, you can specify any of the facets, in any order. However, the only facets that may appear more than once in the same restriction are `pattern`, `enumeration`, and `assertion`. It is legal to define a restriction that has no facets specified. In this case, the derived type allows the same values as the base type.

8.3.2   *Overview of the facets*

The available facets are listed in Table 8–4.

Table 8–4   Facets

Facet	Meaning
minExclusive	Value must be greater than *x*.
minInclusive	Value must be greater than or equal to *x*.
maxInclusive	Value must be less than or equal to *x*.
maxExclusive	Value must be less than *x*.
length	The length of the value must be equal to *x*.
minLength	The length of the value must be greater than or equal to *x*.
maxLength	The length of the value must be less than or equal to *x*.
totalDigits	The number of significant digits must be less than or equal to *x*.
fractionDigits	The number of fractional digits must be less than or equal to *x*.
whiteSpace	The schema processor should either preserve, replace, or collapse whitespace depending on *x*.
enumeration	*x* is one of the valid values.
pattern	*x* is one of the regular expressions that the value may match.
explicitTimezone	The time zone part of the date/time value is required, optional, or prohibited depending on *x*.
assertion	The value must conform to a constraint in the XPath expression.

The syntax for applying a facet is shown in Table 8–5. All facets (except assertion) must have a value attribute, which has different valid values depending on the facet. Most facets may also have a `fixed` attribute, as described in Section 8.3.4 on p. 140.

Table 8–5   XSD Syntax: facet

Name		
`minExclusive, minInclusive, maxExclusive, maxInclusive, length, minLength, maxLength, totalDigits, fractionDigits, enumeration, pattern, whiteSpace,` `explicitTimezone`[†]		

Parents		
`restriction`		

Attribute name	*Type*	*Description*
`id`	`ID`	Unique ID.
value	various	Value of the restricting facet.
`fixed`	`boolean:` `false`	Whether the facet is fixed and therefore cannot be restricted further (see Section 8.3.4); not applicable for `pattern, enumeration`.

Content		
`annotation?`		

[†]   The `assertion` facet has a different syntax that is described in Table 14–1.

Certain facets are not applicable to some types. For example, it does not make sense to apply the `fractionDigits` facet to a character string type. There is a defined set of applicable facets for each of the built-in types.[1] If a facet is applicable to a built-in type, it is also applicable to atomic types that are derived from it. For example, since the `length` facet is applicable to `string`, if you derive a new type from

---

1.   Technically, it is the primitive types that have applicable facets, with the rest of the built-in types inheriting that applicability from their base types. However, since most people do not have the built-in type hierarchy memorized, it is easier to list applicable facets for all the built-in types.

string, the `length` facet is also applicable to your new type. Section 8.4 on p. 142 describes each of the facets in detail and lists the built-in types to which the facet can apply.

8.3.3 *Inheriting and restricting facets*

When a simple type restricts its base type, it inherits all of the facets of its base type, its base type's base type, and so on back through its ancestors. Example 8–4 showed a simple type `MediumDressSizeType` whose base type is `DressSizeType`. `DressSizeType` has a `pattern` facet which restricts its value space to one- or two-digit numbers. Since `MediumDressSizeType` inherits all of the facets from `DressSizeType`, this same `pattern` facet applies to `MediumDressSizeType` also. Example 8–5 shows an equivalent definition of `MediumDressSizeType` where it restricts `integer` and has the `pattern` facet applied.

Example 8–5. Effective definition of `MediumDressSizeType`

```
<xs:simpleType name="MediumDressSizeType">
  <xs:restriction base="xs:integer">
    <xs:minInclusive value="8"/>
    <xs:maxInclusive value="12"/>
    <xs:pattern value="\d{1,2}"/>
  </xs:restriction>
</xs:simpleType>
```

Sometimes a simple type definition will include facets that are also specified for one of its ancestors. In Example 8–4, `MediumDressSizeType` includes `minInclusive` and `maxInclusive`, which are also applied to its base type, `DressSizeType`. The `minInclusive` and `maxInclusive` facets of `MediumDressSizeType` (whose values are `8` and `12`, respectively) override those of `DressSizeType` (`2` and `18`, respectively).

It is a requirement that the facets of a derived type (in this case `MediumDressSizeType`) be more restrictive than those of the base type. In Example 8–6, we define a new restriction of `DressSizeType`, called `SmallDressSizeType`, and set `minInclusive` to 0. This type definition is illegal, because it attempts to expand the value space by allowing 0, which was not valid for `DressSizeType`.

Example 8–6. Illegal attempt to extend a simple type

```
<xs:simpleType name="SmallDressSizeType">
  <xs:restriction base="DressSizeType">
    <xs:minInclusive value="0"/>
    <xs:maxInclusive value="6"/>
  </xs:restriction>
</xs:simpleType>
```

This rule also applies when you are restricting the built-in types. For example, the `short` type has a `maxInclusive` value of 32767. It is illegal to define a restriction of `short` that sets `maxInclusive` to 32768.

Although `enumeration` facets can appear multiple times in the same type definition, they are treated in much the same way. If both a derived type and its ancestor have a set of `enumeration` facets, the values of the derived type must be a subset of the values of the ancestor. An example of this is provided in Section 8.4.4 on p. 145.

Likewise, the `pattern` facets specified in a derived type must allow a subset of the values allowed by the ancestor types. A schema processor will not necessarily check that the regular expressions represent a subset; instead, it will validate instances against the patterns of both the derived type and all the ancestor types, effectively taking the intersection of the pattern values.

8.3.4   *Fixed facets*

When you define a simple type, you can fix one or more of the facets. This means that further restrictions of this type cannot change the value of the facet. Any of the facets may be fixed, with the exception of `pattern`, `enumeration`, and `assertion`. Example 8–7 shows our

DressSizeType with fixed minInclusive and maxInclusive facets, as indicated by a fixed attribute set to true.

Example 8–7. Fixed facets

```
<xs:simpleType name="DressSizeType">
  <xs:restriction base="xs:integer">
    <xs:minInclusive value="2" fixed="true"/>
    <xs:maxInclusive value="18" fixed="true"/>
    <xs:pattern value="\d{1,2}"/>
  </xs:restriction>
</xs:simpleType>
```

With this definition of DressSizeType, it would have been illegal to define the MediumDressSizeType as shown in Example 8–4 because it attempts to override the minInclusive and maxInclusive facets which are now fixed. Some of the built-in types have fixed facets that cannot be overridden. For example, the built-in type integer has its fractionDigits facet fixed at 0, so it is illegal to derive a type from integer and specify a fractionDigits that is not 0.

8.3.4.1 Design hint: When should I fix a facet?

Fixing facets makes your type less flexible and discourages other schema authors from reusing it. Keep in mind that any types that may be derived from your type must be more restrictive, so you are not at risk that your type will be dramatically changed if its facets are unfixed.

A justification for fixing facets might be that changing that facet value would significantly alter the meaning of the type. For example, suppose you want to define a simple type that represents price. You define a Price type and fix the fractionDigits at 2. This still allows other schema authors to restrict Price to define other types, for example, by limiting it to a certain range of values. However, they cannot modify the fractionDigits of the type, because this would result in a type not representing a price in dollars and cents.

8.4 | Facets

8.4.1 *Bounds facets*

The four bounds facets (minInclusive, maxInclusive, minExclusive, and maxExclusive) restrict a value to a specified range. Our previous examples applied minInclusive and maxInclusive to restrict the value space of DressSizeType. While minInclusive and maxInclusive specify boundary values that are included in the valid range, minExclusive and maxExclusive specify bounds that are excluded from the valid range.

There are several constraints associated with the bounds facets:

- minInclusive and minExclusive cannot both be applied to the same type. Likewise, maxInclusive and maxExclusive cannot both be applied to the same type. You may, however, mix and match, applying, for example, minInclusive and maxExclusive together. You may also apply just one end of the range, such as minInclusive only.

- The value for the lower bound (minInclusive or minExclusive) must be less than or equal to the value for the upper bound (maxInclusive or maxExclusive).

- The facet value must be a valid value for the base type. For example, when restricting integer, it is illegal to specify a maxInclusive value of 18.5, because 18.5 is not a valid integer.

The four bounds facets can be applied only to the date/time and numeric types, and the types derived from them. Special consideration should be given to time zones when applying bounds facets to date/time types. For more information, see Section 11.4.15 on p. 235.

8.4.2   *Length facets*

The length facet allows you to limit values to a specific length. If it is a string-based type, length is measured in number of characters. This includes the XML DTD types and anyURI. If it is a binary type, length is measured in octets of binary data. If it is a list type, length is measured as the number of items in the list. The facet value for length must be a nonnegative integer.

The minLength and maxLength facets allow you to limit a value's length to a specific range. Either of both of these facets may be applied. If they are both applied, minLength must be less than or equal to maxLength. If the length facet is applied, neither minLength nor maxLength may be applied. The facet values for minLength and maxLength must be nonnegative integers.

The three length facets (length, minLength, maxLength) can be applied to any string-based types (including the XML DTD types), the binary types, and anyURI. They cannot be applied to the date/time types, numeric types, or boolean.

8.4.2.1   Design hint: What if I want to allow empty values?

Many of the built-in types do not allow empty values. Types other than string, normalizedString, token, hexBinary, base64Binary, and anyURI do not allow empty values unless xsi:nil appears in the element tag.

You may have an integer that you want to be either between 2 and 18, or empty. First, consider whether you want to make the element (or attribute) optional. In this case, if the data is absent, the element will not appear at all. However, sometimes it is desirable for the element to appear, as a placeholder, or perhaps it is unavoidable because of the technology used to generate the instance.

If you do determine that the elements must be able to appear empty, you must define a union type that includes both the integer type and an empty string, as shown in Example 8–8.

Example 8–8. Union allowing an empty value

```
<xs:simpleType name="DressSizeType">
  <xs:union>
    <xs:simpleType>
      <xs:restriction base="xs:integer">
        <xs:minInclusive value="2"/>
        <xs:maxInclusive value="18"/>
      </xs:restriction>
    </xs:simpleType>
    <xs:simpleType>
      <xs:restriction base="xs:token">
        <xs:enumeration value=""/>
      </xs:restriction>
    </xs:simpleType>
  </xs:union>
</xs:simpleType>
```

8.4.2.2   Design hint: What if I want to restrict the length of an integer?

The length facet only applies to the string-based types, the XML DTD types, the binary types, and anyURI. It does not make sense to try to limit the length of the date/time types because they have fixed lexical representations. But what if you want to restrict the length of an integer value?

You can restrict the lower and upper bounds of an integer by applying bounds facets, as discussed in Section 8.4.1 on p. 142. You can also control the number of significant digits in an integer using the totalDigits facet, as discussed in Section 8.4.3 on p. 145. However, these facets do not consider leading zeros as significant. Therefore, they cannot force an integer to appear in the instance with a specific number of digits. To do this, you need a pattern. For example, the pattern \d{1,2} used in our DressSizeType example forces the size to be one or two digits long, so 012 would be invalid.

Before taking this approach, however, you should reconsider whether it is really an integer or a string. See Section 11.3.3.1 on p. 220 for a discussion of this issue.

8.4.3   `totalDigits` *and* `fractionDigits`

The `totalDigits` facet allows you to specify the maximum number of digits in a number. The facet value for `totalDigits` must be a positive integer.

The `fractionDigits` facet allows you to specify the maximum number of digits in the fractional part of a number. The facet value for `fractionDigits` must be a nonnegative integer, and it must not exceed the value for `totalDigits`, if one exists.

The `totalDigits` facet can be applied to `decimal` or any of the integer types, as well as types derived from them. The `fractionDigits` facet may only be applied to `decimal`, because it is fixed at `0` for all integer types.

8.4.4   *Enumeration*

The `enumeration` facet allows you to specify a distinct set of valid values for a type. Unlike most other facets (except `pattern` and `assertion`), the `enumeration` facet can appear multiple times in a single restriction. Each enumerated value must be unique, and must be valid for that type. If it is a string-based or binary type, you may also specify the empty string in an enumeration value, which allows elements or attributes of that type to have empty values.

Example 8–9 shows a simple type `SMLXSizeType` that allows the values `small`, `medium`, `large`, and `extra large`.

Example 8–9. Applying the enumeration facet

```
<xs:simpleType name="SMLXSizeType">
  <xs:restriction base="xs:token">
    <xs:enumeration value="small"/>
    <xs:enumeration value="medium"/>
    <xs:enumeration value="large"/>
    <xs:enumeration value="extra large"/>
  </xs:restriction>
</xs:simpleType>
```

When restricting types that have enumerations, it is important to note that you must *restrict*, rather than *extend*, the set of enumeration values. For example, if you want to restrict the valid values of SMLSizeType to only be small, medium, and large, you could define a simple type as in Example 8–10.

Example 8–10. Restricting an enumeration

```
<xs:simpleType name="SMLSizeType">
  <xs:restriction base="SMLXSizeType">
    <xs:enumeration value="small"/>
    <xs:enumeration value="medium"/>
    <xs:enumeration value="large"/>
  </xs:restriction>
</xs:simpleType>
```

Note that you need to repeat all of the enumeration values that apply to the new type. This example is legal because the values for SMLSizeType (small, medium, and large) are a subset of the values for SMLXSizeType. By contrast, Example 8–11 attempts to add an enumeration facet to allow the value extra small. This type definition is illegal because it attempts to extend rather than restrict the value space of SMLXSizeType.

Example 8–11. Illegal attempt to extend an enumeration

```
<xs:simpleType name="XSMLXSizeType">
  <xs:restriction base="SMLXSizeType">
    <xs:enumeration value="extra small"/>
    <xs:enumeration value="small"/>
    <xs:enumeration value="medium"/>
    <xs:enumeration value="large"/>
    <xs:enumeration value="extra large"/>
  </xs:restriction>
</xs:simpleType>
```

The only way to add an enumeration value to a type is by defining a union type. Example 8–12 shows a union type that adds the value

Example 8–12. Using a union to extend an enumeration

```
<xs:simpleType name="XSMLXSizeType">
  <xs:union memberTypes="SMLXSizeType">
    <xs:simpleType>
      <xs:restriction base="xs:token">
        <xs:enumeration value="extra small"/>
      </xs:restriction>
    </xs:simpleType>
  </xs:union>
</xs:simpleType>
```

extra small to the set of valid values. Union types are described in detail in Section 10.2 on p. 183.

When enumerating numbers, it is important to remember that the enumeration facet works on the actual value of the number, not its lexical representation as it appears in an XML instance. Example 8–13 shows a simple type NewSmallDressSizeType that is based on integer, and specifies an enumeration of 2, 4, and 6. The two instance elements shown, which contain 2 and 02, are both valid. This is because 02 is equivalent to 2 for integer-based types. However, if the base type of NewSmallDressSizeType had been string, the

Example 8–13. Enumerating numeric values

Schema:

```
<xs:simpleType name="NewSmallDressSizeType">
  <xs:restriction base="xs:integer">
    <xs:enumeration value="2"/>
    <xs:enumeration value="4"/>
    <xs:enumeration value="6"/>
  </xs:restriction>
</xs:simpleType>
```

Valid instances:

```
<size>2</size>
<size>02</size>
```

value 02 would not be valid, because the strings 2 and 02 are not the same. If you wish to constrain the lexical representation of a numeric type, you should apply the pattern facet instead. For more information on type equality in XML Schema, see Section 11.7 on p. 253.

The enumeration facet can be applied to any type except boolean.

8.4.5 *Pattern*

The pattern facet allows you to restrict values to a particular pattern, represented by a regular expression. Chapter 9 provides more detail on the rules for the regular expression syntax. Unlike most other facets (except enumeration and assertion), the pattern facet can be specified multiple times in a single restriction. If multiple pattern facets are specified in the same restriction, the instance value must match at least one of the patterns. It is not required to match all of the patterns.

Example 8–14 shows a simple type DressSizeType that includes the pattern \d{1,2}, which restricts the size to one or two digits.

Example 8–14. Applying the pattern facet

```
<xs:simpleType name="DressSizeType">
  <xs:restriction base="xs:integer">
    <xs:minInclusive value="2"/>
    <xs:maxInclusive value="18"/>
    <xs:pattern value="\d{1,2}"/>
  </xs:restriction>
</xs:simpleType>
```

When restricting types that have patterns, it is important to note that you must *restrict*, rather than *extend*, the set of valid values that the patterns represent. In Example 8–15, we define a simple type SmallDressSizeType that is derived from DressSizeType, and add an additional pattern facet that restricts the size to one digit.

Example 8–15. Restricting a pattern

```
<xs:simpleType name="SmallDressSizeType">
  <xs:restriction base="DressSizeType">
    <xs:minInclusive value="2"/>
    <xs:maxInclusive value="6"/>
    <xs:pattern value="\d{1}"/>
  </xs:restriction>
</xs:simpleType>
```

It is not technically an error to apply a pattern facet that does not represent a subset of the ancestors' pattern facets. However, the schema processor tries to match the instance value against the pattern facets of both the type and its ancestors, ensuring that it is in fact a subset. Example 8–16 shows an illegal attempt to define a new size type that allows the size value to be up to three digits long. While the schema is not in error, it will not have the desired effect because the schema processor will check values against both the pattern of LongerDressSizeType and the pattern of DressSizeType. The value 004 would not be considered a valid instance of LongerDressSizeType because it does not conform to the pattern of DressSizeType.

Example 8–16. Illegal attempt to extend a pattern

```
<xs:simpleType name="LongerDressSizeType">
  <xs:restriction base="DressSizeType">
    <xs:pattern value="\d{1,3}"/>
  </xs:restriction>
</xs:simpleType>
```

Unlike the enumeration facet, the pattern facet applies to the lexical representation of the value. If the value 02 appears in an instance, the pattern is applied to the digits 02, not 2 or +2 or any other form of the integer.

The pattern facet can be applied to any type.

8.4.6   *Assertion*

The `assertion` facet allows you to specify additional constraints on values using XPath 2.0. Example 8–17 is a simple type with an assertion, namely that the value must be divisible by 2. It uses a facet named `assertion` with a `test` attribute that contains the XPath expression.

Simple type assertions are a flexible and powerful feature covered in more detail, along with complex type assertions, in Chapter 14.

Example 8–17. Simple type assertion

```
<xs:simpleType name="EvenDressSizeType">
  <xs:restriction base="DressSizeType">
    <xs:assertion test="$value mod 2 = 0" />
  </xs:restriction>
</xs:simpleType>
```

8.4.7   *Explicit Time Zone*

The `explicitTimezone` facet allows you to control the presence of an explicit time zone on a date/time value. Example 8–18 is a simple type based on `time` but with an explicit time zone required. The syntax of time zones is described in more detail in Section 11.4.13 on p. 233.

The `value` attribute of `explicitTimezone` has three possible values:

1. `optional`, making the time zone optional (the value for most built-in date/time types)
2. `required`, making the time zone required (the value for the `dateTimeStamp` built-in type)
3. `prohibited`, disallowing the time zone

Example 8–18. Explicit time zone

```
<xs:simpleType name="SpecificTimeType">
  <xs:restriction base="xs:time">
    <xs:explicitTimezone value="required"/>
  </xs:restriction>
</xs:simpleType>
```

8.4.8 *Whitespace*

The whitespace facet allows you to specify the whitespace normalization rules which apply to this value. Unlike the other facets, which restrict the value space of the type, the whitespace facet is an instruction to the schema processor on to what to do with whitespace. This type of facet is known as a *prelexical* facet because it results in some processing of the value before the other constraining facets are applied. The valid values for the whitespace facet are:

- preserve: All whitespace is preserved; the value is not changed.
- replace: Each occurrence of tab (#x9), line feed (#xA), and carriage return (#xD) is replaced with a single space (#x20).
- collapse: As with replace, each occurrence of tab (#x9), line feed (#xA), and carriage return (#xD) is replaced with a single space (#x20). After the replacement, all consecutive spaces are collapsed into a single space. In addition, leading and trailing spaces are deleted.

Table 8–6 shows examples of how values of a string-based type will be handled depending on its whitespace facet.

Table 8–6 Handling of string values depending on whitespace facet

Original string	string (preserve)	normalizedString (replace)	token (collapse)
a string	a string	a string	a string
on two lines	on two lines	on two lines	on two lines
has spaces	has spaces	has spaces	has spaces
leading tab	leading tab	leading tab	leading tab
leading spaces	leading spaces	leading spaces	leading spaces

The whitespace processing, if any, will happen first, before any validation takes place. In Example 8–9, the base type of SMLXSizeType is token, which has a whiteSpace facet of collapse. Example 8–19 shows valid instances of SMLXSizeType. They are valid because the leading and trailing spaces are removed, and the line feed is turned into a space. If the base type of SMLXSizeType had been string, the whitespace would have been left as is, and these values would have been invalid.

Example 8–19. Valid instances of SMLXSizeType

```
<size> small </size>

<size>extra
large</size>
```

Although you should understand what the whiteSpace facet represents, it is unlikely that you will ever apply it directly in your schemas. The whiteSpace facet is fixed at collapse for most built-in types. Only the string-based types can be restricted by a whiteSpace facet, but this is not recommended. Instead, select a base type that already has the whiteSpace facet you want. The types string, normalizedString, and token have the whiteSpace values preserve, replace, and collapse, respectively. For example, if you wish to define a string-based type that will have its whitespace collapsed, base your type on token, instead of basing it on string and applying a whiteSpace facet. Section 11.2.1 on p. 205 provides a discussion of these three types.

8.5 | Preventing simple type derivation

XML Schema allows you to prevent derivation of other types from your type. By specifying the final attribute with a value of #all in your simple type definition, you prevent derivation of any kind (restriction, extension, list, or union). If you want more granular control, the value of final can be a whitespace-separated list of any of the keywords restriction, extension, list, or union. The extension value refers to the extension of simple types to derive complex types, described in Section 13.4.1 on p. 306. Example 8–20 shows some valid values for final.

Example 8–20. Valid values for the final attribute in simple type definitions

```
final="#all"
final="restriction list union"
final="list restriction extension"
final="union"
final=""
```

Example 8–21 shows a simple type that cannot be restricted by any other type or used as the item type of a list. With this definition of DressSizeType, it would have been illegal to define MediumDressSizeType in Example 8–4 because it attempts to restrict DressSizeType.

Example 8–21. Preventing type derivation

```
<xs:simpleType name="DressSizeType" final="restriction list">
  <xs:restriction base="xs:integer">
    <xs:minInclusive value="2"/>
    <xs:maxInclusive value="18"/>
  </xs:restriction>
</xs:simpleType>
```

If no final attribute is specified, it defaults to the value of the finalDefault attribute of the schema element. If neither final nor finalDefault is specified, there are no restrictions on derivation from that type. You can specify the empty string ("") for the final value if you want to override the finalDefault value.

8.6 | Implementation-defined types and facets

Starting with version 1.1, additional simple types and facets may be defined and supported by a particular XML Schema implementation.

8.6.1   *Implementation-defined types*

An implementation can choose to support a set of primitive simple types in addition to those built into XML Schema (described in Chapter 11).

Suppose that an implementation defines a special primitive type `ordinalDate` that represents an ordinal date: a year, followed by a hyphen, followed by a number from 001 to 366 indicating the day of the year. Although an ordinal date value could be represented as a string, it may be beneficial to promote it to its own primitive type if it has special considerations for ordering or validation of its values, or special operations that can be performed on it (for example, subtracting two ordinal dates to get a duration).

A schema author can use an implementation-defined type just like a built-in type, except that it will be in a different namespace defined by the implementation. The schema in Example 8–22

Example 8–22. Using an implementation-defined type

```
<xs:schema xmlns:xs="http://www.w3.org/2001/XMLSchema"
           xmlns:ext="http://example.org/extensions">
  <xs:element name="anyOrdinalDate" type="ext:ordinalDate"/>
  <xs:element name="recentOrdinalDate" type="OrdinalDateIn2011"/>
  <xs:simpleType name="OrdinalDateIn2011">
    <xs:restriction base="ext:ordinalDate">
      <xs:minInclusive value="2011-001"/>
      <xs:maxInclusive value="2011-365"/>
    </xs:restriction>
  </xs:simpleType>
</xs:schema>
```

contains two references to the `ordinalDate` type, which is in the hypothetical `http://example.org/extensions` namespace. The `anyOrdinalDate` element declaration refers to the type directly by its qualified name. The `OrdinalDateIn2011` user-defined simple type is a restriction of `ordinalDate` using bounds facets to specify a range of allowed values.

8.6.2   *Implementation-defined facets*

Implementation-defined facets might specify additional constraints on the valid values, or even signal to the processor how to process the value. An example is the Saxon processor's `preprocess` facet which allows you to specify an XPath expression that transforms the value in some way before validation.

In Example 8–23, the `saxon:preprocess` facet appears among the children of `restriction`. You can tell that it is an implementation-defined facet because it is in a different namespace, `http://saxon.sf.net/`. This particular example is telling the processor to convert the value to upper case before validating it against the enumeration facets. It is essentially implementing a case-insensitive enumeration.

Example 8–23. Using the Saxon preprocess facet

```
<xs:schema xmlns:xs="http://www.w3.org/2001/XMLSchema"
           xmlns:saxon="http://saxon.sf.net/">
  <xs:simpleType name="SMLXSizeType">
    <xs:restriction base="xs:token">
      <saxon:preprocess action="upper-case($value)"/>
      <xs:enumeration value="SMALL"/>
      <xs:enumeration value="MEDIUM"/>
      <xs:enumeration value="LARGE"/>
      <xs:enumeration value="EXTRA LARGE"/>
    </xs:restriction>
  </xs:simpleType>
</xs:schema>
```

Implementation-defined facets can apply to the XML Schema built-in types (and user-defined restrictions of them); they can also apply to any implementation-defined types such as the `ordinalDate` example type described in the previous section.

While implementation-defined types and facets can be useful, they do affect the portability of your schema. With the schema in Example 8–23, if you try to validate a document that contains lower-case "small" for a size, it would be valid when using Saxon but not when using a different implementation. Therefore, implementation-defined facets should be used only in controlled situations. Section 23.5.3 on p. 642 provides more information on how to make your schemas more portable across implementations when using implementation-defined types and facets.

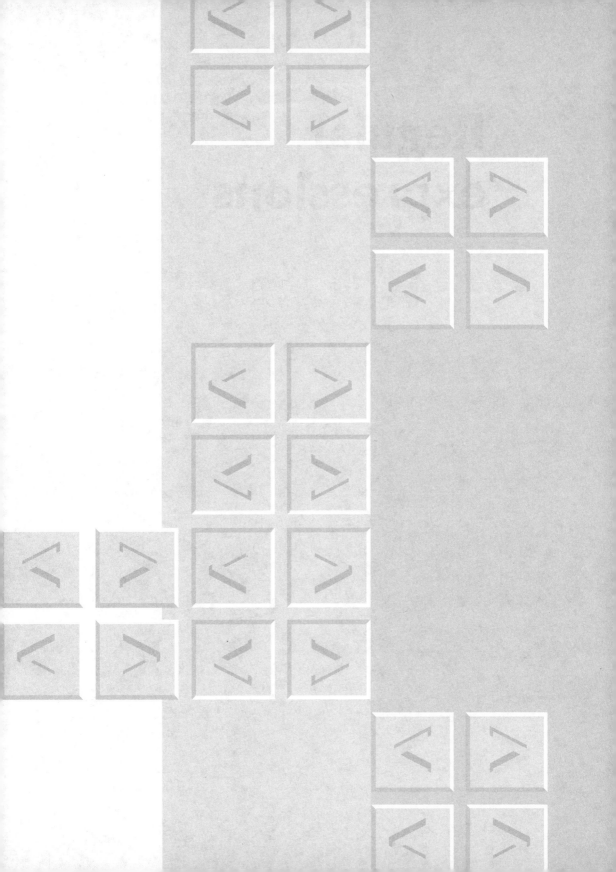

Regular expressions

Chapter
9

R egular expressions are used in XML Schema to restrict the values of simple types to certain patterns of characters. For example, a pattern could specify that an SKU must be three digits, followed by a hyphen, followed by two uppercase letters. This chapter explains the XML Schema syntax for regular expressions.

9.1 | The structure of a regular expression

XML Schema's regular expression language is very similar to that of the Perl programming language. Regular expressions, also known as "regexes," are made up of *branches*, which are in turn made up of *pieces*. Each piece consists of one *atom* and an optional *quantifier*.

For example, suppose the product number in your organization can either be an SKU or a 7-digit number. The SKU format is three digits, followed by a hyphen, followed by two uppercase letters—for example,

Example 9–1. A simple type with a pattern

```
<xs:simpleType name="ProductNumberType">
  <xs:restriction base="xs:string">
    <xs:pattern value="\d{3}-[A-Z]{2}|\d{7}"/>
  </xs:restriction>
</xs:simpleType>
```

123-AB. We could represent this pattern by defining the simple type shown in Example 9–1.

One difference between XML Schema regular expressions and other regular expression languages is that XML Schema assumes anchors to be present at the beginning and end of the expression. This means that the whole value, not just a substring, must match the expression. In the previous example, the whole product number must be a 6-digit SKU or a 7-digit number, with no characters before or after it.

Figure 9–1 shows the structure of the regular expression from the previous example.

It has two branches separated by a vertical bar (|): the first to represent an SKU, and the second to represent a seven-digit number. If there is more than one branch in a regular expression, a matching string must

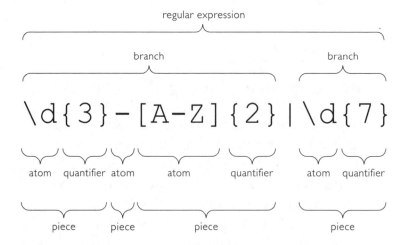

Figure 9–1   Structure of a regular expression

match at least one of the branches; it is not required to match all of the branches. In this case, the first branch consists of three pieces:

- \d{3} represents the initial three digits. The atom, \d, is a character class escape that represents any digit. The quantifier, {3}, indicates how many times this atom (a digit) may appear.
- \- represents the hyphen. The atom in this case is the hyphen, which represents itself as a normal character. This piece does not contain a quantifier, so the hyphen must appear once and only once.
- [A-Z]{2} represents the two letters. The atom, [A-Z], is a character class expression which represents any one of the letters A through Z. The quantifier, {2}, indicates how many times this atom (a letter) may appear.

The second branch, \d{7}, consists of only one piece which represents the seven digits.

The rest of this chapter explains these concepts in detail.

9.2 | Atoms

An atom describes one or more characters. It may be any one of the following:

- A normal character, such as a.
- Another regular expression, enclosed in parentheses, such as (a|b).
- An escape, indicated by a backslash, such as \d or \p{IsBasicLatin}.
- A character class expression, indicated by square brackets, such as [A-Z].

Each of these types of atoms is described in the sections that follow.

9.2.1 *Normal characters*

An atom can be a single character, as shown in Table 9–1. Each of the characters a, b, and c is an atom.

Table 9–1   Using normal characters

Regular expression	Matching strings	Nonmatching strings
a	a	b
a|b|c	a, b, c	abc

Most characters that can be entered from a keyboard can be represented directly in a regular expression. Some characters, known as *metacharacters*, have special meaning and must be escaped[1] in order to be treated like normal characters. They are: ., \, ?, *, +, |, {, }, (,), [, and]. This is explained in Section 9.2.3.1 on p. 165.

The space character can be used to represent itself in a regular expression. This means that you may not put any extra whitespace in the regular expression that will not appear in the matching strings. For example, the regular expression "a | b" will only match "a followed by a space" or "a space followed by b".

Characters that are not easily entered on a keyboard may also be represented as they are in any XML document—by character references that specify the character's Unicode code point. XML character references take two forms:

- "&#" plus a sequence of decimal digits representing the character's code point, followed by ";"
- "&#x" plus a sequence of hexadecimal digits representing the character's code point, followed by ";"

---

1.   Except when they are within square brackets, as described in Section 9.2.4.6 on p. 175.

For example, a space can be represented as `&#x20;`. You can also include the predefined XML entities for the "less than," "greater than," ampersand, apostrophe, and quote characters. Table 9–2 lists some common XML character references and entities.

Table 9–2   Common XML character references and entities

Entity/Reference	Meaning
`&#x20;`	Space
`&#xA;`	Line feed (also represented by `\n`)
`&#xD;`	Carriage return (also represented by `\r`)
`&#x9;`	Tab (also represented by `\t`)
`&lt;`	Less than (<)
`&gt;`	Greater than (>)
`&amp;`	Ampersand (&)
`&apos;`	Apostrophe (')
`&quot;`	Quote (")

Table 9–3 illustrates the inclusion of character entities and references in regular expressions.

Table 9–3   Using character references

Regular expression	Matching strings	Nonmatching strings
`a&#x20;z`	`a z`	`az`
`a&#x20;*z`	`az, a z, a  z, a   z`	`a *z`
`PB&amp;J`	`PB&J`	`PBJ`

9.2.2   *The wildcard escape character*

The period (.) has special significance in regular expressions; it matches any one character except a carriage return or line feed. The period character, known as wildcard, represents only one matching character, but a quantifier (such as *) may be applied to it to represent multiple characters. Table 9–4 shows some examples of the wildcard escape character in use.

The period character is also useful at the beginning or end of a regular expression to signify a pattern that starts with, ends with, or contains a matching string, as shown in the last three examples of the table. This gets around the implicit anchors in XML Schema regular expressions.

It is important to note that the period loses its wildcard power when placed in a character class expression (within square brackets).

Table 9–4   Using the wildcard escape character

Regular expression	Matching strings	Nonmatching strings
a.z	aaz, abz, a2z	az, abbz
a..z	aaaz, abcz, a12z	az, abz
a.*z	az, abz, abcdez	a b
a\.z	a.z	abz
.*abc.*	abc, xxxabc, abcxxx, xxxabcxxx	xxx
.*abc	abc, xxxabc	abcxxx, xxxabcxxx
abc.*	abc, abcxxx	xxxabc, xxxabcxxx

9.2.3   *Character class escapes*

A character class escape uses the backslash (\) as an escape character to indicate any one of several characters. There are four categories of character class escapes:

- Single character escapes, which represent one specific character
- Multicharacter escapes, which represent any one of several characters
- Category escapes, which represent any one of a group of characters with similar characteristics (such as "Punctuation"), as defined in the Unicode standard
- Block escapes, which represent any one character within a range of code points, as defined in the Unicode standard

Note that each escape may be matched by only one character. You must apply a quantifier such as * to an escape to make it represent multiple characters.

This section describes each of the four types of character class escapes.

9.2.3.1 Single-character escapes

Single-character escapes are used for characters that are either difficult to read and write in their natural form, or have special meaning in regular expressions. Each escape represents only one possible matching character. Table 9–5 provides a complete list of single-character escapes.

Table 9–5 Single-character escapes

Escape	Meaning	Escape	Meaning
\n	Line feed (#xA)	*	*
\r	Carriage return (#xD)	\+	+
\t	Tab (#x9)	\{	{
\\	\	\}	}
|	|	\(	(
\.	.	\)	)
\-	–	\[	[
\^	^	\]	]
\?	?		

Table 9–6 illustrates single-character escapes in regular expressions. The first example has an unescaped plus sign (+). However, the plus sign has another meaning in regular expressions—it is treated as a quantifier on the atom consisting of the character 1. The second example escapes the plus sign, which results in it being treated as an atom itself that can appear in the matching string. The third example escapes the first plus sign, but not the second, resulting in the first one being interpreted as an atom and the second one being interpreted as a quantifier.

Table 9–6   Using single-character escapes

Regular expression	Matching strings	Nonmatching strings
1+2	12, 112, 1112	1+2
1\+2	1+2	12, 1\+2
1\++2	1+2, 1++2, 1+++2	12

9.2.3.2   Multicharacter escapes

A multicharacter escape may represent any one of several characters. Table 9–7 provides a complete list of multicharacter escapes.

Table 9–7   Multicharacter escapes

Escape	Meaning
\d	Any decimal digit.
\D	Any character that is not a decimal digit.
\s	A whitespace character (space, tab, carriage return, or line feed).
\S	Any character that is not a whitespace character.

(Continues)

Table 9–7   (Continued)

Escape	Meaning
\i	Any character that may be the first character of an XML name, namely a letter, an underscore (_), or a colon (:).
\I	Any character that is not permitted as the first character of an XML name.
\c	Any character that may be part of an XML name, namely a letter, a digit, an underscore (_), a colon (:), a hyphen (-), or a period (.).
\C	Any character that cannot be part of an XML name.
\w	A "word" character, that is, any character *not* in one of the categories Punctuation, Separators, and Other, described in the next section.
\W	Any character in one of the categories Punctuation, Separators, and Other, described in the next section.

Table 9–8 illustrates multicharacter escapes in regular expressions.

Table 9–8   Using multicharacter escapes

Regular expression	Matching strings	Nonmatching strings
a\dz	a0z, a1z	az, adz, a12z
a\s*z	az, a z	axz

9.2.3.3 Category escapes

Category escapes provide convenient groupings of characters, based on their characteristics. These categories are defined by the Unicode standard. More information about the Unicode standard can be found at www.unicode.org. Table 9–9 provides a complete list of category escapes.

Table 9–9   Category escapes

Category	Property	Meaning
	L	all letters
	Lu	uppercase
	Ll	lowercase
Letters	Lt	titlecase
	Lm	modifier
	Lo	other
	M	all marks
	Mn	non-spacing
Marks	Mc	spacing combining
	Me	enclosing
	N	all numbers
	Nd	decimal digit
Numbers	Nl	letter
	No	other
	P	all punctuation
	Pc	connector
	Pd	hyphen
	Ps	open
Punctuation	Pe	close
	Pi	initial quote
	Pf	final quote
	Po	other

(Continues)

Table 9–9   (Continued)

Category	Property	Meaning
Separators	Z	all separators
	Zs	space
	Zl	line
	Zp	paragraph
Symbols	S	all symbols
	Sm	math
	Sc	currency
	Sk	modifier
	So	other
Other	C	all others
	Cc	control
	Cf	format
	Co	private use
	Cn	not assigned

The syntax to use one of these escapes is \p{xx} where xx is the one- or two-character property. For example, \p{Nd} represents any decimal digit. It is also possible to represent the complement—that is, any character that is *not* part of the category, using a capital P. For example, \P{Nd} represents any character that is not a decimal digit. Table 9–10 illustrates category escapes in regular expressions.

Note that the category escapes include all character sets. If you only intend for an expression to match the capital letters A through Z, it is better to use [A-Z] than \p{Lu}, because \p{Lu} will allow uppercase letters of all alphabets, not just Latin. Likewise, if your intention is to allow only the decimal digits 0 through 9, use [0-9] rather than \p{Nd} or \d, because there are digits other than 0 through 9 in some languages' scripts.

Table 9–10   Using category escapes

Regular expression	Matching strings	Nonmatching strings
\p{Lu}	A, B, C	a, b, c, 1, 2, 3
\P{Lu}	a, b, c, 1, 2, 3	A, B, C
\p{Nd}	1, 2, 3	a, b, c, A, B, C
\P{Nd}	a, b, c, A, B, C	1, 2, 3

9.2.3.4 Block escapes

Block escapes represent a range of characters based on their Unicode code points. The Unicode standard provides names for these ranges, such as Basic Latin, Greek, Thai, Mongolian, etc. The block names used in regular expressions are these same names, with the spaces removed. Table 9–11 lists the first five block escape ranges as an example. A complete list of the most recent Unicode blocks can be downloaded from www.unicode.org/Public/UNIDATA/Blocks.txt.

Table 9–11   Partial list of block escapes

Start code	End code	Block name
#x0000	#x007F	BasicLatin
#x0080	#x00FF	Latin-1Supplement
#x0100	#x017F	LatinExtended-A
#x0180	#x024F	LatinExtended-B
#x0250	#x02AF	IPAExtensions
. . .	. . .	. . .

The syntax to use one of the block escapes is \p{Is*XX*} where *XX* is the block name. For example, \p{IsBasicLatin} represents any character in the range #x0000 to #x007F. It is also possible to represent the complement—that is, any character that is not part of the block—using a capital P. For example, \P{IsBasicLatin} represents any character that is not in that range. Table 9–12 illustrates block escapes in regular expressions.

Table 9–12   Using block escapes

Regular expression	Matching strings	Nonmatching strings
\p{IsBasicLatin}	a, b, c	â, ß, ç
\P{IsBasicLatin}	â, ß, ç	a, b, c

9.2.4   *Character class expressions*

A character class expression allows you to specify a choice from a set of characters. The expression, which appears in square brackets, may include a list of individual characters or character escapes, or a character range, or both. It is also possible to negate the specified set of characters, or subtract values from it. Like an escape, a character class expression may only represent one character in the matching string. To allow a matching character to appear multiple times, a quantifier may be applied to the expression.

9.2.4.1   Listing individual characters

The simplest case of a character class expression is a list of the matching characters or escapes. The expression represents one and only one of the characters listed. Table 9–13 illustrates a list of characters inside an expression. The first example can be read as "a or b or c, followed by z." The character class expression in the second example uses escapes to represent one character that is either an uppercase letter or a decimal digit.

Table 9–13   Specifying a list of characters

Regular expression	*Matching strings*	*Nonmatching strings*
`[abc]z`	`az, bz, cz`	`abz, z, abcz, abc`
`[\p{Lu}\d]z`	`Az, Bz, 1z, 2z`	`az, bz, cz, A1z`

9.2.4.2   Specifying a range

A range of characters may be specified in a character class expression. The lower and upper bounds are inclusive, and they are separated by a hyphen. For example, to allow the letters a through f, you can specify `[a-f]`. The bounds must be single characters or single character escapes. It is not valid to specify a range using multicharacter strings, such as `[(aa)-(fe)]`, or multicharacter escapes, such as `[\p{Lu}-\p{Ll}]`. The lower bound must have a code point that is less than or equal to that of the upper bound.

Multiple ranges may be specified in the same expression. If multiple ranges are specified, the character must match one of the ranges.

Table 9–14 illustrates ranges in expressions. The first example can be read as "a letter between a and f (inclusive), followed by z." The second example provides three ranges, namely the digits 0 to 9, lowercase a to f, and uppercase A to F. The first character of a matching string must conform to at least one of these ranges. The third example uses character entities to represent the bounds.

Table 9–14   Specifying a range

Regular expression	*Matching strings*	*Nonmatching strings*
`[a-f]z`	`az, fz`	`z, abz, gz, hz`
`[0-9a-fA-F]z`	`1z, az, Bz`	`z, gz, Gz, 1aBz`
`[&#x0020;-&#x007F;]z`	`az, bz, cz`	`âz`

9.2.4.3 Combining individual characters and ranges

It is also possible to combine ranges, individual characters, and escapes in an expression, in any order. Table 9–15 illustrates this. The first example allows the first character of the matching string to be either a digit 0 through 9, or one of the letters p, q, or r. The second example represents nearly the same thing, with a range on the letters instead of the numbers, and the escape \d to represent the digits. It is not exactly the same thing because \d also includes decimal digits from other character sets, not just the digits 0 through 9.

Table 9–15 Combining characters and ranges

Regular expression	*Matching strings*	*Nonmatching strings*
[0-9pqr]z	1z, 2z, pz, rz	cz,dz,0sz
[p-r\d]z	1z, 2z, pz, rz	cz,dz,0sz

9.2.4.4 Negating a character class expression

A character class expression can be negated to represent any character that is not in the specified set of characters. You can negate any expression, regardless of whether it is a range, a list of characters, or both. The negation character, ^, must appear directly after the opening bracket.

Table 9–16 illustrates this negation. The character class expression in the first example represents "any character except a or b." In the second example it is "any character that is not a digit." In the third, it is "any character that does not fall in the range 1 through 3 or a through c." Note that the negation in the third example applies to both ranges. It is *not* possible to negate one range but not another in the same expression. To represent this, use subtraction, which is described in the next section.

Table 9–16   Negating a character class expression

Regular expression	Matching strings	Nonmatching strings
[^ab]z	cz, dz, 1z	az, bz
[^\d]z	az, bz, cz	1z, 2z, 3z
[^1-3a-c]z	dz, 4z	1z, az

9.2.4.5 Subtracting from a character class expression

It is possible to subtract individual values or ranges of values from a specified set of characters. A minus sign (-) precedes the values to be subtracted, which are themselves enclosed in square brackets. Table 9–17 illustrates subtractions from character class expressions. The first example represents "any character between a and z, except for c, followed by z." The second is "any character between a and z, except for c and d, followed by z." The third example subtracts a range, namely c through e, from the range a through z. The net result is that the allowed values are a through b and f through z. The fourth example is a subtraction from a negation of a subtraction. The negation character applies only to the a-z range, and the 123 digits are subtracted from that. Essentially, the example allows the first character to be anything except the letters a to z or the digits 1, 2, or 3.

Table 9–17   Subtracting from a character class expression

Regular expression	Matching strings	Nonmatching strings
[a-z-[c]]z	az, dz, ez, zz	cz
[a-z-[cd]]z	az, ez, zz	cz, dz
[a-z-[c-e]]z	az, zz	cz, dz, ez, 1z
[^a-z-[123]]z	4z	az, 3z, zz

9.2.4.6 Escaping rules for character class expressions

Special escaping rules apply to character class expressions. They are as follows:

- The characters [,], \, and - should be escaped when included as individual characters or bounds in a range.[1]
- The character ^ should be escaped if it appears first in the character class expression, directly after the opening bracket ([).

The other metacharacters do not need to be escaped when used in a character class expression, because they have no special meaning in that context. This includes the period character, which does not serve as a wildcard escape character when inside a character class expression. However, it is never an error to escape any of the metacharacters, and getting into the habit of always escaping them eliminates the need to remember these rules.

9.2.5 *Parenthesized regular expressions*

A parenthesized regular expression may be used as an atom in a larger regular expression. Any regular expression may be included in the parentheses, including those containing normal characters, characters entities, escapes, and character class expressions.

Parenthesized expressions are useful for repeating certain sequences of characters. For example, suppose you want to indicate a repetition of the string ab. The expression ab* will match abbb, but not abab because the quantifier applies to the final atom, not the entire string. To allow abab, you need to parenthesize the two characters: (ab)*.

Parenthesized expressions are also useful when you want to allow a choice between several different patterns. For example, to allow either

---

1. The rules are actually slightly more complex and less strict than this; they also differ between versions 1.0 and 1.1. However, it is never an error to escape these characters inside a character class expression.

the string ab or the string cd to come before z, you can use the expression (ab|cd)z. This example makes use of branches, which are described further in Section 9.4 on p. 177. Table 9–18 shows some examples of parenthesizing within regular expressions.

Table 9–18   Using parenthesized regular expressions

Regular expression	Matching strings	Nonmatching strings
(ab)*z	z, abz, ababz	az, bz, aabbz
(ab|cd)z	abz, cdz	abcdz, z
(a+b)*z	z, abz, aabz, abaabz	az, abbz
([a-f]x)*z	z, axz, bxfxfxz	gxz, xz
(\db)*z	z, 1bz, 1b2bz	1z, bz

9.3 | Quantifiers

A quantifier indicates how many times the atom may appear in a matching string. Table 9–19 lists the quantifiers.

Table 9–19   Quantifiers

Quantifier	Meaning
none	Must appear once.
?	May appear 0 or 1 times.
*	May appear 0 or more times.
+	May appear 1 or more times.
$\{n\}$	Must appear n times.
$\{n,\}$	May appear n or more times.
$\{n,m\}$	May appear n through m times.

Table 9–20 illustrates quantifiers in regular expressions. The first seven examples illustrate the seven types of quantifiers. They each have three atoms: a, b, and z, with the quantifier applying only to b. The remaining three examples show how quantifiers can apply not just to normal character atoms, but also to character class expressions, character class escapes, and parenthesized regular expressions, respectively.

Table 9–20   Using quantifiers

Regular expression	Matching strings	Nonmatching strings
abz	abz	az, abbz
ab?z	az, abz	abbz
ab*z	az, abz, abbz, abbbz, ...	a1z
ab+z	abz, abbz, abbbz, ...	az
ab{2}z	abbz	abz, abbbz
ab{2,}z	abbz, abbbz, abbbbz, ...	az, abz
ab{2,3}z	abbz, abbbz	az, abz, abbbbz
a[b-d]+z	abz, abdz, addbccdddz	az, aez, abez
a\p{Nd}+z	a1z, a11z, a234z	az, abcz
a(bc)+z	abcz, abcbcz, abcbcbcz, ...	az, abz, acbz

9.4 | Branches

As mentioned early in this chapter, a regular expression can consist of an unlimited number of branches. Branches, separated by the vertical bar (|) character, represent a choice between several expressions. The | character does not act on the atom immediately preceding it, but on the entire expression that precedes it (back to the previous | or an opening parenthesis). For example, the regular expression true|false indicates a choice between `true` and `false`, not "tru, followed by e or f, followed by alse". It is not necessary to put `true` and `false` in parentheses. Table 9–21 shows some examples that exhibit the interaction between branches, expressions, and parentheses.

Table 9–21   Branches, expressions, and parentheses

Regular expression	Matching strings	Nonmatching strings
true|false	true, false	trufalse
tru(e|f)alse	trufalse	true, false
yes|no|maybe	yes, no, maybe	yenoaybe
(a|b)c|d	ac, bc, d	c, ad

Union and list types

Chapter

10

I n Chapter 8, we learned how to define atomic simple types. This chapter covers the other two varieties of simple types: union types and list types.

10.1 | Varieties and derivation types

As we saw in Chapter 8, there are three varieties of simple types: atomic types, list types, and union types.

- *Atomic types* have values that are indivisible, such as 10 and large.
- *List types* have values that are whitespace-separated lists of atomic values, such as `<availableSizes>10 large 2</availableSizes>`.
- *Union types* may have values that are either atomic values or list values. What differentiates them is that the set of valid values,

181

or "value space," for the type is the union of the value spaces of two or more other simple types. For example, to represent a dress size, you may define a union type that allows a value to be either an integer from 2 through 18, or one of the string values small, medium, or large.

Each newly defined simple type must be based on an existing type, using one of the following methods:

- A restriction of another type, known as the base type of the restriction. This results in a type of the same variety as the base type, with a restricted set of valid values. For example, you can define a SmallInteger type that restricts the value space of the integer type.
- A list of another type (either an atomic or union type), known as the item type of the list. This results in a type that allows a whitespace-separated list of values of the item type. For example, you can define an IntegerList type that is a list of integer values.
- A union of one or more other types, known as the member types of the union. This results in a type that allows values that are valid for any of its member types. For example, you can define an IntegerOrString type that allows either an integer or a string.

The variety of the resulting type depends on both the derivation type and the variety of the original type. Table 10–1 shows all possible combinations of derivation types and original type varieties. The important thing to understand is that when you restrict, for example, a list type, the resulting type is still a list type. All the rules for list types, such as applicable facets, also apply to this new type.

Table 10–1   Varieties of derived types

		Derivation type		
		restriction	*list*	*union*
	atomic	atomic	list	union
Base type variety	*list*	list	*not legal*	union
	union	union	list†	union

† Legal only if the union type does not itself contain a list.

10.2 | Union types

10.2.1 *Defining union types*

Union types allow a value to conform to any one of several different simple types. The syntax to define a union type is shown in Table 10–2.

Table 10–2   XSD Syntax: union type

Name		
union		
Parents		
simpleType		
Attribute name	*Type*	*Description*
id	ID	Unique ID.
memberTypes	list of QName	Member types that make up the union type; either a memberTypes attribute or a simpleType child (or a combination) is required.
Content		
annotation?, simpleType*		

To continue with our `DressSizeType` example, perhaps we want to allow a value to be either an integer from 2 to 18, or one of the specific values `small`, `medium`, or `large`. Example 10–1 shows the definition of a union type that accomplishes this.

Example 10–1. Defining a union type

```
<xs:simpleType name="SizeType">
  <xs:union>
    <xs:simpleType>
      <xs:restriction base="xs:integer">
        <xs:minInclusive value="2"/>
        <xs:maxInclusive value="18"/>
      </xs:restriction>
    </xs:simpleType>
    <xs:simpleType>
      <xs:restriction base="xs:token">
        <xs:enumeration value="small"/>
        <xs:enumeration value="medium"/>
        <xs:enumeration value="large"/>
      </xs:restriction>
    </xs:simpleType>
  </xs:union>
</xs:simpleType>
```

The simple types that compose a union type are known as its member types. Member types must always be simple types; there is no such thing as a union of complex types. There must be at least one member type, and there is no limit for how many member types may be specified.

In Example 10–1, the member types are defined anonymously within the union, as `simpleType` children. It is also possible to specify the member types using a `memberTypes` attribute of the union element, as shown in Example 10–2. It is assumed that `DressSizeType` and `SMLSizeType` are defined elsewhere in the schema.

Example 10–2. Using the `memberTypes` attribute

```
<xs:simpleType name="SizeType">
  <xs:union memberTypes="DressSizeType SMLSizeType"/>
</xs:simpleType>
```

You can also combine the `memberTypes` attribute with `simpleType` children, as shown in Example 10–3.

Example 10–3. Combining `memberTypes` and `simpleType`

```
<xs:simpleType name="SizeType">
  <xs:union memberTypes="DressSizeType">
    <xs:simpleType>
      <xs:restriction base="xs:token">
        <xs:enumeration value="small"/>
        <xs:enumeration value="medium"/>
        <xs:enumeration value="large"/>
      </xs:restriction>
    </xs:simpleType>
  </xs:union>
</xs:simpleType>
```

10.2.2 *Restricting union types*

It is possible to restrict a union type. The syntax for restricting a union type is shown in Table 10–3.

Of all the facets, only three may be applied to union types: `pattern`, `enumeration`, and `assertion`. These restrictions are considered to be in addition to the restrictions of the individual member types. Example 10–4 shows a restriction of `SizeType` that only allows integers 2, 4, and 6, and the value `small`. A value of the type `SmallSizeType` is first validated against the enumerations defined in `SmallSizeType`, then validated against each of the member types of `SizeType` until it is successfully validated against one.

Table 10–3   XSD Syntax: union type restriction

Name
restriction

Parents
simpleType

Attribute name	Type	Description
id	ID	Unique ID.
base	QName	Base type of the restriction (in this case, the union type); either a base attribute or a simpleType child is required.

Content
annotation?, simpleType?, (enumeration | pattern | 🔳assertion)*

Example 10–4. Restricting a union

```
<xs:simpleType name="SmallSizeType">
  <xs:restriction base="SizeType">
    <xs:enumeration value="2"/>
    <xs:enumeration value="4"/>
    <xs:enumeration value="6"/>
    <xs:enumeration value="small"/>
  </xs:restriction>
</xs:simpleType>
```

10.2.3 *Unions of unions*

It is possible to define a union type that has another union type as its member type. For example, if you want to expand your size type yet again, to include non-US sizes, you might define a new type InternationalSizeType that is the union of SizeType (which is itself a union) and a new anonymous type, as shown in Example 10–5.

Example 10–5. A union of a union

```
<xs:simpleType name="InternationalSizeType">
  <xs:union memberTypes="SizeType">
    <xs:simpleType>
      <xs:restriction base="xs:integer">
        <xs:minInclusive value="24"/>
        <xs:maxInclusive value="54"/>
      </xs:restriction>
    </xs:simpleType>
  </xs:union>
</xs:simpleType>
```

The only caveat is that union type references cannot be circular, either directly or indirectly. For example, you cannot define a union type union1 that has another type union2 among its member types, if union2 also has union1 among its member types.

10.2.4 *Specifying the member type in the instance*

An instance element can optionally use the xsi:type attribute to specify its type. In the case of union types, you can use xsi:type to specify which of the member types the element conforms to. This allows more targeted validation and provides a clue to the application that processes the instance about what type of value to expect. Example 10–6 shows what an instance element might look like.

Example 10–6. Specifying the member type in the instance

```
<size xsi:type="DressSizeType">12</size>
```

Naturally, this technique only works for elements, not attributes. In the previous example, if size were an attribute, you would have no way of specifying its member type, because attributes cannot have attributes.

If the xsi:type attribute is not used in the instance, an element is considered to have the first member type for which it is valid.

10.3 | List types

10.3.1 *Defining list types*

List types are whitespace-separated lists of atomic values. A list type is defined by designating another simple type (an atomic or union type) as its item type. Table 10–4 shows the syntax for defining a list type.

Table 10–4   XSD Syntax: list type

Name		
list		
Parents		
simpleType		
Attribute name	**Type**	**Description**
id	ID	Unique ID.
itemType	QName	The simple type of each item in the list; either an itemType attribute or a simpleType child is required.
Content		
annotation?, simpleType?		

Example 10–7 shows a simple type that allows a list of available dress sizes.

Example 10–7. Defining a list type using an itemType attribute

```
<xs:simpleType name="AvailableSizesType">
  <xs:list itemType="DressSizeType"/>
</xs:simpleType>
```

An instance element of the type AvailableSizesType is shown in Example 10–8.

Example 10–8. List instance

```
<availableSizes>10 12  14</availableSizes>
```

Example 10–7 uses the `itemType` attribute to designate a global simple type named `DressSizeType` as its item type. Alternatively, the item type can be specified anonymously in a `simpleType` child within the list type definition, as shown in Example 10–9. Either the `itemType` attribute or the `simpleType` child must appear, not both.

Example 10–9. Defining a list type using a `simpleType` child

```
<xs:simpleType name="AvailableSizesType">
  <xs:list>
    <xs:simpleType>
      <xs:restriction base="xs:integer">
        <xs:minInclusive value="2"/>
        <xs:maxInclusive value="18"/>
      </xs:restriction>
    </xs:simpleType>
  </xs:list>
</xs:simpleType>
```

There is no way to represent an absent or nil item in a list. The `whiteSpace` facet for all list types is fixed at `collapse`, which means that if multiple whitespace characters appear consecutively, they are collapsed into one space. In Example 10–8, even though there are two spaces between the values `12` and `14`, there are only three items in the list.

10.3.2 *Design hint: When should I use lists?*

When representing sequences of like values, you are faced with a decision whether to use a list, such as:

```
<availableSizes>10 12 14</availableSizes>
```

or use markup to separate the distinct values, such as:

```
<availableSizes>
  <size>10</size>
  <size>12</size>
  <size>14</size>
</availableSizes>
```

The advantage of using a list is obvious: It is less verbose. However, there are a number of disadvantages of lists.

- They are not appropriate for values that may contain whitespace (see Section 10.3.4 on p. 195).
- If you later wish to expand the values by adding children or attributes, this will not be possible if you use a list. For example, if you use markup, you can later add an attribute to `size` to indicate the measurement system, such as `<size system="US-DRESS">`.
- There is no way to represent nil values.
- There may be limited support for lists in other XML technologies. For example, individual values in a list cannot be accessed via XPath 1.0 or XSLT 1.0.

10.3.3 *Restricting list types*

The syntax for restricting a list type is shown in Table 10–5. A limited number of facets may be applied to list types. These facets have a slightly different behavior when applied to a list type, because they apply to the list as a whole, not to the individual items in the list. To restrict the values of each item in the list, you should restrict the item type, not the list type itself.

Table 10–5   XSD Syntax: list type restriction

Name		
`restriction`		

Parents		
`simpleType`		

Attribute name	*Type*	*Description*
`id`	ID	Unique ID.
`base`	QName	The base type of the restriction (in this case, the list type); either a `base` attribute or a `simpleType` child is required.

Content
`annotation?, simpleType?, (length | minLength | maxLength | pattern | enumeration | whiteSpace | `▣`assertion)*`

When applying facets to a list type, you do not specify the facets directly in the list type definition. Instead, you define the list type, then define a restriction of that list type. This can be done with two separate named simple types, or it can be accomplished all in one definition as shown in Example 10–10.

Example 10–10. Length facet applied to a list

```
<xs:simpleType name="AvailableSizesType">
  <xs:restriction>
    <xs:simpleType>
      <xs:list itemType="SMLSizeType"/>
    </xs:simpleType>
    <xs:maxLength value="3"/>
  </xs:restriction>
</xs:simpleType>
```

10.3.3.1 Length facets

Length facets `length`, `minLength`, and `maxLength` may be used to restrict list types. The length is measured as number of items in the list, not the length of each item. Example 10–10 shows a list that is restricted by a `maxLength` facet.

Example 10–11 shows a valid instance of `AvailableSizesType`. It is valid because the number of items in the list is not more than three. The fact that the strings `medium` and `large` are longer than three characters is not relevant. To restrict the length of each item in the list, apply the `maxLength` facet to the item type itself (`SMLSizeType`), not to the list type.

Example 10–11. **Valid instance of a length-restricted list**

```
<availableSizes>medium large</availableSizes>
```

When you define a list type, there are no automatic restrictions on the length of the list. Therefore, a list with zero items (i.e., empty elements or just whitespace) is considered valid. If you do not want a list to be valid if it is empty, restrict the list type by setting its `minLength` to 1.

10.3.3.2 Enumeration facet

The `enumeration` facet may also be used to restrict list types. However, the enumeration specified applies to the whole list, not to each item in the list. For example, to restrict the values in a list to a specific set, you may be tempted to define a simple type like the one shown in Example 10–12.

Example 10–12. Enumeration applied inappropriately to a list type

```
<xs:simpleType name="AvailableSizesType">
  <xs:restriction>
    <xs:simpleType>
      <xs:list itemType="xs:token"/>
    </xs:simpleType>
    <xs:enumeration value="small"/>
    <xs:enumeration value="medium"/>
    <xs:enumeration value="large"/>
  </xs:restriction>
</xs:simpleType>
```

However, this would not behave as you expect. It would restrict the value of the entire list to only one of the values: small, medium, or large. Therefore, <availableSizes>small</availableSizes> would be valid, but <availableSizes>small medium</available-Sizes> would not. Instead, apply the enumeration to the item type, as shown in Example 10–13.

Example 10–13. Enumeration applied to the item type of a list

```
<xs:simpleType name="AvailableSizesType">
  <xs:list>
    <xs:simpleType>
      <xs:restriction base="xs:token">
        <xs:enumeration value="small"/>
        <xs:enumeration value="medium"/>
        <xs:enumeration value="large"/>
      </xs:restriction>
    </xs:simpleType>
  </xs:list>
</xs:simpleType>
```

There may be cases where you do want to restrict the entire list to certain values. Example 10–14 shows a list that may only have two values, as shown.

Example 10–14. Enumeration correctly applied to a list type

Schema:

```
<xs:simpleType name="ApplicableSizesType">
  <xs:restriction>
    <xs:simpleType>
      <xs:list itemType="SizeType"/>
    </xs:simpleType>
    <xs:enumeration value="small medium large"/>
    <xs:enumeration value="2 4 6 8 10 12 14 16 18"/>
  </xs:restriction>
</xs:simpleType>
```

Instance:

```
<applicableSizes>small medium large</applicableSizes>
<applicableSizes>2 4 6 8 10 12 14 16 18</applicableSizes>
```

10.3.3.3 Pattern facet

The `pattern` facet may also be applied to list types. Like the `length` and `enumeration` facets, the `pattern` facet in this case applies to the entire list, not the items in the list. For example, suppose you want to represent vector information as a list of integers. You want your list to always contain zero or more groups of three integers each, separated by whitespace. The restriction shown in Example 10–15 enforces this constraint.

Example 10–15. Pattern applied to a list type

```
<xs:simpleType name="VectorType">
  <xs:restriction>
    <xs:simpleType>
      <xs:list itemType="xs:unsignedInt"/>
    </xs:simpleType>
    <xs:pattern value="\d+\s+\d+\s+((\d+\s+){3})*\d+"/>
  </xs:restriction>
</xs:simpleType>
```

10.3.4 *Lists and strings*

Be careful when deriving list types from string-based types whose values may contain whitespace. This includes the built-in types `string`, `normalizedString`, and `token`, as well as user-defined types derived from them. Since list items are separated by whitespace, strings that contain whitespace may give unexpected results when included as items in a list. Example 10–16 shows the definition of `AvailableSizesType` as a list of `SMLXSizeType`, which is derived from `token` and allows the values `small`, `medium`, `large`, and `extra large`.

Example 10–16. Defining a list of a string-based type

```
<xs:simpleType name="AvailableSizesType">
  <xs:list itemType="SMLXSizeType"/>
</xs:simpleType>
<xs:simpleType name="SMLXSizeType">
  <xs:restriction base="xs:token">
    <xs:enumeration value="small"/>
    <xs:enumeration value="medium"/>
    <xs:enumeration value="large"/>
    <xs:enumeration value="extra large"/>
  </xs:restriction>
</xs:simpleType>
```

Example 10–17 shows an invalid instance of `AvailableSizesType`. The schema processor would consider this instance to be a list of three items ("`small`", "`extra`", and "`large`") rather than the expected two items ("`small`" and "`extra large`"). When it attempts to validate the value "`extra`" against the enumerated values, it will find it invalid.

Example 10–17. Invalid instance of `AvailableSizesType`

```
<availableSizes>
small
extra large
</availableSizes>
```

10.3.5 *Lists of unions*

Lists of union types are no different from lists of atomic types. Each item in the list must simply be a valid value of one of the member types of the union type. Example 10–18 defines our now familiar union type `SizeType`, then defines a list type `AvailableSizesType` whose item type is `SizeType`.

Example 10–18. Defining a list of a union

```
<xs:simpleType name="SizeType">
  <xs:union memberTypes="DressSizeType SMLXSizeType"/>
</xs:simpleType>

<xs:simpleType name="AvailableSizesType">
  <xs:list itemType="SizeType"/>
</xs:simpleType>
```

Example 10–19 shows a valid instance of `AvailableSizesType`. Note that both the integers and the enumerated `small`, `medium`, and `large` are valid list items, in any order.

Example 10–19. Instance of a list of a union

```
<availableSizes>10 large 2</availableSizes>
```

The only restriction on lists of unions is that the union type cannot have any list types among its member types. That would equate to a list of lists, which is not legal.

10.3.6 *Lists of lists*

Lists of lists are not legal. The item type of a list type cannot be a list type itself, nor can it be derived at any level from another list type (for example, as a restriction of a list, or a union of a list).

Example 10–20 is illegal as it attempts to define a simple type
TwoDimensionalArrayType as a list of lists.

Example 10–20. Illegal list of lists

```
<xs:simpleType name="RowType">
  <xs:list itemType="xs:integer"/>
</xs:simpleType>

<xs:simpleType name="TwoDimensionalArrayType">
  <xs:list itemType="RowType"/>
</xs:simpleType>
```

Instead, you should put markup around the items in the lists. Example 10–21 shows a complex type definition that accomplishes this and a valid instance.

Example 10–21. An array using markup

Schema:

```
<xs:complexType name="VectorType">
  <xs:sequence maxOccurs="unbounded">
    <xs:element name="e" type="xs:integer"/>
  </xs:sequence>
</xs:complexType>

<xs:complexType name="ArrayType">
  <xs:sequence maxOccurs="unbounded">
    <xs:element name="r" type="VectorType"/>
  </xs:sequence>
</xs:complexType>

<xs:element name="array" type="ArrayType"/>
```

Instance:

```
<array>
  <r>  <e>1</e>  <e>12</e> <e>15</e> </r>
  <r>  <e>44</e> <e>2</e>  <e>3</e>  </r>
</array>
```

10.3.7 *Restricting the item type*

Once you have defined a list type, you cannot derive another list type from it that restricts the item type. For example, it is impossible to derive a list of `MediumDressSizeType` from a list of `DressSizeType`. Instead, you must restrict the item type (in this case `DressSizeType`), then define a new list type of the new restricted atomic type (e.g., `MediumDressSizeType`).

Built-in simple types

Chapter

11

This chapter describes the 49 built-in simple types that are included in XML Schema. These simple types represent common types that can be used directly in schemas. They are also the foundation for deriving other simple types, as described in Chapter 8. A complete reference to the built-in simple types and the facets that apply to them can be found in Appendix B.

11.1 | The XML Schema type system

There are 49 simple types built into XML Schema. They are specified in Part 2 of the XML Schema recommendation. This part of the recommendation makes a distinction between "datatypes" and "simple types." Datatypes are abstract concepts of data, such as "integer." Simple types are the concrete representations of these datatypes. Most of the built-in types are atomic types, although there are three list types as well.

11.1.1 *The type hierarchy*

Types in the XML Schema type system form a hierarchy. Figure 11–1 depicts the hierarchy of the built-in types, showing that some built-in types are derived from other built-in types. The downward arrows represent derivation by restriction, so the types become more restrictive toward the bottom of the diagram. For example, `nonPositiveInteger`

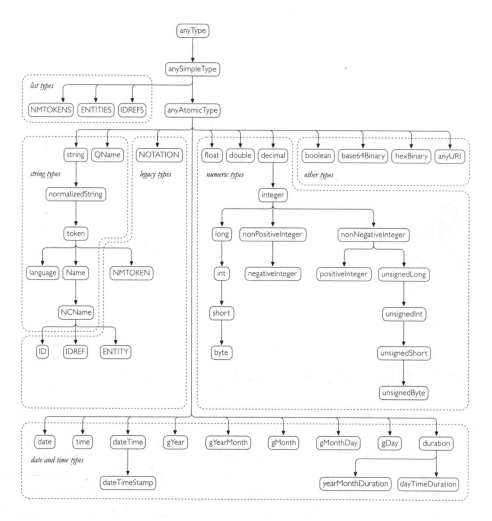

Figure 11–1 The built-in type hierarchy

is more restrictive than `integer`, which is more restrictive than `anyAtomicType`.

At the top of the hierarchy are three special types:

1. `anyType` is a generic complex type that allows anything: any attributes, any child elements, any text content.

2. `anySimpleType`, derived from `anyType`, is the base of all simple types, including atomic, list, and union types.

3. `anyAtomicType`, derived from `anySimpleType`, is a generic type from which all atomic types are derived.

`anyType` can be declared as the type of an element, in which case that element can have any content. It is also the default type for elements if none is specified. `anyType` can also be extended or restricted by complex type definitions. `anySimpleType` and `anyAtomicType` are special types that cannot be used as the base for user-defined types in a schema. However, they can be declared as the type of an element or attribute.

The types directly under `anyAtomicType` are known as *primitive* types, while the rest are *derived* built-in types. The primitive types represent basic type concepts, and all other built-in atomic types are restrictions of those types. When you define new simple types in your schema, they can never be primitive; they must be derived from a built-in primitive type.

Figure 11–1 shows that the three built-in list types (NMTOKENS, ENTITIES, and IDREFS) are derived from `anySimpleType`. Any user-defined list and union types are also derived from `anySimpleType`, although they have item types or member types that may be specific atomic types.

Starting in version 1.1, it is possible for implementations to support other primitive types, in addition to the built-in types described in this chapter. Consult the documentation of your XML Schema processor to determine whether you have access to any additional primitive types.

11.1.2 *Value spaces and lexical spaces*

Every type in the XML Schema type system has a *value space*. This value space represents the set of possible values for a type. For example, for the int type, it is the set of integers from –2147483648 to 2147483647. Every type also has a *lexical space*, which includes all the possible representations of those values. For int, each value in the value space might have several lexical representations. For example, the value 12 could also be written as 012 or +12. All of these values are considered equal for this type (but not if their type were string).

Of the lexical representations, one is considered the *canonical representation*: It maps one-to-one to a value in the value space and can be used to determine whether two values are equal. For the int type, the rule is that the canonical representation has no plus sign and no leading zeros. If you turn each of the three values 12, +12, and 012 into their canonical representation using that rule, they would all be 12 and therefore equal to each other. Some primitive types, such as string, only have one lexical representation, which becomes, by default, the canonical representation. In this chapter, the canonical representation of a particular type is only mentioned if there can be more than one lexical representation per value in the value space.

11.1.3 *Facets and built-in types*

As we saw in Chapter 8, simple types inherit the facets of their ancestors. For example, the integer type has a fractionDigits facet that is set to 0. This means that all of the twelve types derived (directly and indirectly) from integer also have a fractionDigits of 0.

However, it is not just the facet *value* that is inherited, but also the *applicability* of a facet. Each primitive type has certain facets that are applicable to it. For example, the string type has length as an applicable facet, but not totalDigits, because it does not make sense to apply totalDigits to a string. Therefore, the totalDigits facet cannot be applied to string or any of its derived types, whether they are built-in or user-defined.

It is not necessary to remember which types are primitive and which are derived. This chapter lists the applicable facets for *all* of the built-in types, not just the primitive types. When you derive new types from the built-in types, you may simply check which facets are applicable to the built-in type, regardless of whether it is primitive or derived.

11.2 | String-based types

11.2.1 `string`, `normalizedString`, *and* `token`

The types `string`, `normalizedString`, and `token` represent a character string that may contain any Unicode characters allowed by XML. Certain characters, namely the "less than" symbol (`<`) and the ampersand (`&`), must be escaped (using the entities `&lt;` and `&amp;`, respectively) when used in strings in XML instances. The only difference between the three types is in the way whitespace is handled by a schema-aware processor, as shown in Table 11–1.

Table 11–1   Whitespace handling of string types

Original string	string *(preserve)*	normalizedString *(replace)*	token *(collapse)*
A string	A string	A string	A string
On two lines	On two lines	On two lines	On two lines
Has spaces	Has spaces	Has spaces	Has spaces
Leading tab	Leading tab	Leading tab	Leading tab
Leading spaces	Leading spaces	Leading spaces	Leading spaces

The `string` type has a `whiteSpace` facet of `preserve`, which means that all whitespace characters (spaces, tabs, carriage returns, and line feeds) are preserved by the processor.

The `normalizedString` type has a `whiteSpace` facet of `replace`, which means that the processor replaces each carriage return, line feed, and tab by a single space. There is no collapsing of multiple consecutive spaces into a single space.

The `token` type represents a tokenized string. The name `token` may be slightly confusing because it implies that there may be only one token with no whitespace. In fact, there can be whitespace in a `token` value. The `token` type has a `whiteSpace` facet of `collapse`, which means that the processor replaces each carriage return, line feed, and tab by a single space. After this replacement, each group of consecutive spaces is collapsed into one space character, and all leading and trailing spaces are removed.

Table 11–2 shows some valid and invalid values of the string types.

Table 11–2   Values of the string types

Valid values	Comment
`This is a string!`	
`Édition française.`	
`12.5`	
	An empty string is valid.
`PB&amp;J`	When parsed, it will become `PB&J`.
`   Separated   by   3   spaces.`	
`This` `is on two lines.`	

Invalid values[†]	Comment
`AT&T`	Ampersand must be escaped.
`3 < 4`	The "less than" symbol must be escaped.

[†] In physical XML files.

The facets indicated in Table 11–3 can restrict `string`, `normalizedString`, and `token`, and their derived types.[1]

Table 11–3   **Facets applicable to** `string`, `normalizedString`, **and** `token` **types**

length	A	minExclusive		totalDigits	
minLength	A	minInclusive		fractionDigits	
maxLength	A	maxInclusive		pattern	A
whiteSpace	V	maxExclusive		enumeration	A
⊞explicitTimezone		⊞assertion	A		

`whiteSpace` is `preserve` for `string`, `replace` for `normalizedString`, and `collapse` for `token`.

11.2.1.1 Design hint: Should I use `string`, `normalizedString`, or `token`?

First, consider whether to use a string-based simple type at all. If it is a long string of general text, such as a letter or a long description of an item, this may not be wise. This is because simple types are not extensible. Later, you may want to allow XHTML markup in the letter, or break the item description down into more structured components. It will be impossible to do this without altering the schema in a way that is not backwards compatible.

Additionally, simple types cannot support internationalization requirements such as Ruby annotations and BIDI (bidirectionality) elements.

In these cases, you should instead declare a complex type with mixed content, and include a wildcard to allow for future extensions. The complex type definition shown in Example 11–1 accomplishes

---

1.   A—applicable, V—value specified, F—fixed value specified.

this purpose. The character data content of an element of this type will have its whitespace preserved.

Example 11–1. Extensible mixed content

```
<xs:complexType name="TextType" mixed="true">
  <xs:sequence>
    <xs:any namespace="##any" processContents="lax"
            minOccurs="0" maxOccurs="unbounded"/>
  </xs:sequence>
  <xs:attribute ref="xml:lang"/>
</xs:complexType>
```

For short, atomic items, such as a postal code or a gender, it does make sense to use `string`, `normalizedString`, or `token`. But which one? Here are some general guidelines:

- `string` should be used for text where formatting, such as tabs and line breaks, is significant. However, as mentioned above, it may be better to use mixed complex type in this case.
- `normalizedString` is used when formatting is not significant but consecutive whitespace characters are significant. This can be used when the information in the string is positional.
- `token` should be used for most short, atomic strings, especially ones that have an enumerated set of values. Basing your enumerated types on `token` means that `<gender> M </gender>` will be valid as well as `<gender>M</gender>`.

11.2.2 Name

The type `Name` represents an XML name, which can be used as an element name or attribute name, among other things. Values of this type must start with a letter, underscore (_), or colon (:), and may contain only letters, digits, underscores (_), colons (:), hyphens (-), and periods (.). Colons should only be used to separate namespace prefixes from local names.

Table 11–4 shows some valid and invalid values of the Name type.

Table 11–4   Values of the Name type

Valid values	Comment
myElement	
_my.Element	
my-element	
pre:myelement3	This is recommended only if pre is a namespace prefix; otherwise, colons should not be used.

Invalid values	Comment
-myelement	A Name must not start with a hyphen.
3rdElement	A Name must not start with a number.
	An empty value is not valid, unless xsi:nil is used.

The facets indicated in Table 11–5 can restrict Name and its derived types.

Table 11–5   Facets applicable to Name type

length	A	minExclusive		totalDigits	
minLength	A	minInclusive		fractionDigits	
maxLength	A	maxInclusive		pattern	V
whiteSpace	V	maxExclusive		enumeration	A
▣explicitTimezone		▣assertion	A		

whiteSpace is collapse, pattern is \i\c*.

11.2.3 NCName

The type NCName represents an XML non-colonized name, which is simply a name that does not contain colons. An NCName must start with either a letter or underscore (_) and may contain only letters, digits, underscores (_), hyphens (-), and periods (.). This is identical to the Name type, except that colons are not permitted.

Table 11–6 shows some valid and invalid values of the NCName type.

Table 11–6   Values of the NCName type

Valid values	Comment
myElement	
_my.Element	
my-element	

Invalid values	Comment
pre:myElement	An NCName must not contain a colon.
-myelement	An NCName must not start with a hyphen.
	An empty value is not valid, unless xsi:nil is used.

The facets indicated in Table 11–7 can restrict NCName and its derived types.

Table 11–7   Facets applicable to NCName type

length	A	minExclusive		totalDigits	
minLength	A	minInclusive		fractionDigits	
maxLength	A	maxInclusive		pattern	V
whiteSpace	V	maxExclusive		enumeration	A
▣explicitTimezone		▣assertion	A		

whiteSpace is collapse, pattern is [\i-[:]][\c-[:]]*.

11.2.4 `language`

The type `language` represents a natural language identifier, generally used to indicate the language of a document or a part of a document. Before creating a new attribute of type `language`, consider using the `xml:lang` attribute that is intended to indicate the natural language of the element and its content.

Values of the `language` type conform to RFC 3066, *Tags for the Identification of Languages*, in version 1.0 and to RFC 4646, *Tags for Identifying Languages*, and RFC 4647, *Matching of Language Tags*, in version 1.1. The three most common formats are:

- For ISO-recognized languages, the format is a two- or three-letter (usually lowercase) language code that conforms to ISO 639, optionally followed by a hyphen and a two-letter, usually uppercase, country code that conforms to ISO 3166. For example, `en` or `en-US`.

- For languages registered by the Internet Assigned Numbers Authority (IANA), the format is `i-`*langname*, where *langname* is the registered name. For example, `i-navajo`.

- For unofficial languages, the format is `x-`*langname*, where *langname* is a name of up to eight characters agreed upon by the two parties sharing the document. For example, `x-Newspeak`.

Any of these three formats may have additional parts, each preceded by a hyphen, which identify more countries or dialects. Schema processors will not verify that values of the `language` type conform to the above rules. They will simply validate them based on the pattern specified for this type, which says that it must consist of one or more parts of up to eight characters each, separated by hyphens.

Table 11–8 shows some valid and invalid values of the `language` type.

Table 11–8   Values of the `language` type

Valid values	Comment
en	English.
en-GB	UK English.
en-US	US English.
fr	French.
de	German.
es	Spanish.
it	Italian.
nl	Dutch.
zh	Chinese.
ja	Japanese.
ko	Korean.
i-navajo	IANA-registered language.
x-Newspeak	Private, unregistered language.
any-value-with-short-parts	Although a schema processor will consider this value valid, it does not follow RFC 3066 guidelines.
Invalid values	**Comment**
longerThan8	Parts may not exceed eight characters in length.
	An empty value is not valid, unless `xsi:nil` is used.

The facets indicated in Table 11–9 can restrict `language` and its derived types.

Table 11–9   Facets applicable to `language` type

length	A	minExclusive		totalDigits	
minLength	A	minInclusive		fractionDigits	
maxLength	A	maxInclusive		pattern	V
whiteSpace	V	maxExclusive		enumeration	A
1.1 explicitTimezone		**1.1** assertion	A		

whiteSpace is collapse, pattern is
([a-zA-Z]{1,8})(-[a-zA-Z0-9]{1,8})*.

11.3 | Numeric types

11.3.1 `float` *and* `double`

The type `float` represents an IEEE single-precision 32-bit floating-point number, and `double` represents an IEEE double-precision 64-bit floating-point number. The lexical representation of both `float` and `double` values is a mantissa (a number which conforms to the type `decimal` described in the next section) followed, optionally, by the character "E" or "e" followed by an exponent. The exponent must be an integer. For example, `3E2` represents 3 times 10 to the 2nd power, or 300.

In addition, the following values are valid: `INF` (infinity), `+INF` (positive infinity, version 1.1 only), `-INF` (negative infinity), `0` (positive 0), `-0` (negative 0), and `NaN` (Not a Number). `0` and `-0` are considered equal. `INF` and `+INF` are equal and are considered to be greater than all other values, while `-INF` is less than all other values. The value `NaN` cannot be compared to any other values.

The canonical representation for `float` and `double` always contains an uppercase letter `E` and a decimal point in the mantissa. No leading or trailing zeros are present, except that there is always at least one digit before and after the decimal point in the mantissa, and at least one digit in the exponent. No positive signs are included. For example, the canonical representation of the `float` value +12 is `12.0E0`.

Table 11–10 shows some valid and invalid values of the `float` and `double` types.

Table 11–10   Values of the `float` and `double` types

Valid values	Comment
-3E2	
4268.22752E11	
+24.3e-3	
12	
+3.5	Any value valid for `decimal` is also valid for `float` and `double`.
INF	Positive infinity.
-INF	Negative infinity.
+INF	▩Positive infinity, value allowed in version 1.1 but not in 1.0.
+0	Positive 0.
-0	Negative 0.
NaN	Not a Number.

Invalid values	Comment
-3E2.4	The exponent must be an integer.
12E	An exponent must be specified if "E" is present.
Inf	Values are case-sensitive and must be capitalized correctly.
NAN	Values are case-sensitive and must be capitalized correctly.
	An empty value is not valid, unless `xsi:nil` is used.

The facets indicated in Table 11–11 can restrict `float`, `double`, and their derived types.

Table 11–11   Facets applicable to `float` and `double` **types**

length		minExclusive	A	totalDigits	
minLength		minInclusive	A	fractionDigits	
maxLength		maxInclusive	A	pattern	A
whiteSpace	F	maxExclusive	A	enumeration	A
▣explicitTimezone		▣assertion	A		

`whiteSpace` is `collapse`.

11.3.2 `decimal`

The type `decimal` represents a decimal number of arbitrary precision. Schema processors vary in the number of significant digits they support, but a minimally conforming processor must support at least 16 significant digits. The lexical representation of `decimal` is a sequence of digits optionally preceded by a sign ("+" or "-") and optionally containing a period. If the fractional part is 0 then the period and trailing zeros may be omitted. Leading and trailing zeros are permitted but not considered significant. That is, the decimal values `3.0` and `3.0000` are considered equal.

The canonical representation of `decimal` always contains a decimal point. No leading or trailing zeros are present, except that there is always at least one digit before and after the decimal point. No positive signs are included.

Table 11–12 shows some valid and invalid values of the `decimal` type.

Table 11–12   Values of the `decimal` type

Valid values	Comment
3.0	
-3.0	A negative sign is permitted.
+3.5	A positive sign is permitted.
3	A decimal point is not required.
0	
-0.3	
0003.0	Leading zeros are permitted.
3.0000	Trailing zeros are permitted; considered equal to 3.0.

Invalid values	Comment
3,5	Commas are not permitted; the decimal separator must be a period.
24.3e-3	Exponents cannot be specified.
	An empty value is not valid, unless `xsi:nil` is used.

The facets indicated in Table 11–13 can restrict `decimal` and its derived types.

Table 11–13   Facets applicable to `decimal` type

length		minExclusive	A.	totalDigits	A
minLength		minInclusive	A	fractionDigits	A
maxLength		maxInclusive	A	pattern	A
whiteSpace	F	maxExclusive	A	enumeration	A
[1.1]explicitTimezone		[1.1]assertion	A		

whiteSpace is collapse.

11.3.3 *Integer types*

The type integer represents an arbitrarily large integer; from it, 12 other built-in integer types are derived (directly or indirectly). The lexical representation of the integer types is a sequence of digits. Some of the integer types allow or require a sign ("+" or "-") to precede the numbers, others prohibit it. Leading zeros are permitted, but decimal points are not.

The canonical representations of integer types do not contain leading zeros or positive signs. Table 11–14 lists all of the integer types, with their bounds and the rules for preceding signs.

Table 11–14   Integer types

Type name	minInclusive	maxInclusive	*Preceding sign*
integer	n/a	n/a	+ (optional) or -.
positive-Integer	1	n/a	+ (optional).
nonPositive-Integer	n/a	0	- or + (optional, and only if the value is 0).
negative-Integer	n/a	-1	- (required).
nonNegative-Integer	0	n/a	+ (optional) or - (optional, and only if the value is 0).
long	-9223372036854775808	9223372036854775807	+ (optional) or -.
int	-2147483648	2147483647	+ (optional) or -.

(Continues)

Table 11–14   (Continued)

Type name	minInclusive	maxInclusive	Preceding sign
short	-32768	32767	+ (optional) or -.
byte	-128	127	+ (optional) or -.
unsignedLong	0	18446744073709551615	In 1.0: prohibited. ▪1.1In 1.1: + (optional) or - (optional, and only if the value is 0).
unsignedInt	0	4294967295	In 1.0: prohibited. ▪1.1In 1.1: + (optional) or - (optional, and only if the value is 0).
unsignedShort	0	65535	In 1.0: prohibited. ▪1.1In 1.1: + (optional) or - (optional, and only if the value is 0).
unsignedByte	0	255	In 1.0: prohibited. ▪1.1In 1.1: + (optional) or - (optional, and only if the value is 0).

Table 11–15 shows some valid and invalid values of the integer types. The facets indicated in Table 11–16 can restrict the integer types and their derived types.

Table 11–15   Values of the integer types

Valid values	Comment
122	Valid for all integer types except `negativeInteger` and `nonPositiveInteger`.
00122	Leading zeros are permitted.
0	`0` is permitted for most integer types (except `positiveInteger` and `negativeInteger`).
-3	A negative sign is permitted for some integer types, see Table 11–14.
+3	A positive sign is permitted for some integer types, see Table 11–14.

Invalid values	Comment
3.	An integer must not contain a decimal point.
3.0	An integer must not contain a decimal point.
	An empty value is not valid, unless `xsi:nil` is used.

Table 11–16   Facets applicable to integer types

length		minExclusive	A	totalDigits	A
minLength		minInclusive	V	fractionDigits	F
maxLength		maxInclusive	V	pattern	V
whiteSpace	F	maxExclusive	A	enumeration	A
⬚explicitTimezone		⬚assertion	A		

`whiteSpace` is `collapse`, `fractionDigits` is 0, `pattern` is `[\-+]?[0-9]+`, `minInclusive` and `maxInclusive` are as specified in Table 11–14.

11.3.3.1 Design hint: Is it an integer or a string?

When defining types for values that are sequences of digits, it may be difficult to determine whether the type should be based on an integer or a string. For example, a quantity is an example of a value that is better treated as an integer than a string. 5-digit U.S. zip codes, on the other hand, are valid integers, but they are probably better interpreted as strings. Here are some general guidelines:

Use `integer` (or, more likely, `nonNegativeInteger`) if:

- You will ever compare two values of that type numerically. For example, if you compare the quantity 100 to the quantity 99, you obviously want 100 to be greater. But if you define them as strings, they will be compared as strings in languages such as XSLT 2.0 and XQuery, and `100` will be considered less than `99`.
- You will ever perform mathematical operations on values of that type. You might want to double a quantity, but you are unlikely to want to double a zip code.
- You want to restrict their values' bounds. For example, you may require that quantity must be between 0 and 100. While it can be possible to restrict a string in this way, by applying a pattern, it is more cumbersome.

Use `string` (or, more likely, `token`) if:

- You want to restrict your values' lexical length. For example, zip codes must be five digits long; `8540` is not a valid zip code, but `08540` is valid. While it is technically possible to restrict an integer to five digits by applying a pattern, it is more cumbersome.
- You will ever take a substring. For example, you may want to extract the central processing facility as the first three digits of a zip code.
- You plan to derive nonnumeric types from this type, or use it in a substitution group with nonnumeric types. For example,

if you plan to also define types for international postal codes, which may contain letters or other characters, it is safer to base your U.S. zip code elements on a string type, so that they can be used in a substitution group with other postal code elements.

11.4 | Date and time types

XML Schema provides a number of built-in date and time types, whose formats are based on ISO 8601. This section explains each of the date and time types and provides general information that applies to all date and time types.

11.4.1 `date`

The type `date` represents a Gregorian calendar date. The lexical representation of `date` is `YYYY-MM-DD` where `YY` represents the year, `MM` the month and `DD` the day. No left truncation is allowed for any part of the date. To represent years later than 9999, additional digits can be added to the left of the year value, but extra leading zeros are not permitted. To represent years before 0000, a preceding minus sign ("`-`") is allowed. An optional time zone expression may be added at the end, as described in Section 11.4.13 on p. 233.

Table 11–17 shows some valid and invalid values of the `date` type.

Table 11–17 Values of the `date` type

Valid values	Comment
`2004-04-12`	April 12, 2004.
`-0045-01-01`	January 1, 45 B.C.
`12004-04-12`	April 12, 12004.

(Continues)

Table 11–17   (Continued)

Valid values	Comment
2004-04-12-05:00	April 12, 2004, US Eastern Standard Time, which is 5 hours behind Coordinated Universal Time (UTC).
2004-04-12Z	April 12, 2004, Coordinated Universal Time (UTC).
0000-04-12	⚑The year zero is permitted in version 1.1, but not in version 1.0.

Invalid values	Comment
99-04-12	Left truncation of the century is not allowed.
2004-4-2	Month and day must be two digits each.
2004/04/02	Slashes are not valid separators.
04-12-2004	The value must be in YYYY-MM-DD order.
2004-04-31	The date must be a valid date (April has 30 days).
+2004-04-02	Positive signs are not permitted.
	An empty value is not valid, unless xsi:nil is used.

11.4.2 time

The type time represents a time of day. The lexical representation of time is hh:mm:ss.sss where hh represents the hour, mm the minutes, and ss.sss the seconds. An unlimited number of additional digits can be used to increase the precision of fractional seconds if desired. The time is based on a 24-hour time period, so hours should be represented as 00 through 24. Either of the values 00:00:00 or 24:00:00 can be used to represent midnight. An optional time zone expression may be added at the end, as described in Section 11.4.13 on p. 233.

Table 11–18 shows some valid and invalid values of the time type.

Table 11–18   Values of the `time` type

Valid values	Comment
13:20:00	1:20 P.M.
13:20:30.5555	1:20 P.M. and 30.5555 seconds.
13:20:00-05:00	1:20 P.M., US Eastern Standard Time.
13:20:00Z	1:20 P.M., Coordinated Universal Time (UTC).
00:00:00	Midnight.
24:00:00	Midnight.

Invalid values	Comment
5:20:00	Hours, minutes, and seconds must be two digits each.
13:20	Seconds must be specified, even if it is 00.
13:20.5:00	Values for hours and minutes must be integers.
13:65:00	The value must be a valid time of day.
30:05:00	The value must be a valid time of day; for a duration of 30 hours, use the `duration` type.
	An empty value is not valid, unless `xsi:nil` is used.

11.4.3   dateTime

The type `dateTime` represents a specific date and time. The lexical representation of `dateTime` is `YYYY-MM-DDThh:mm:ss.sss`, which is a concatenation of the `date` and `time` forms, separated by a literal letter `T`. All of the same rules that apply to the `date` and `time` types are applicable to `dateTime` as well. An optional time zone expression may be added at the end, as described in Section 11.4.13 on p. 233.

Table 11–19 shows some valid and invalid values of the `dateTime` type.

Table 11–19   Values of the `dateTime` type

Valid values	*Comment*
`2004-04-12T13:20:00`	1:20 P.M. on April 12, 2004.
`2004-04-12T13:20:15.5`	1:20 P.M. and 15.5 seconds on April 12, 2004.
`2004-04-12T13:20:00-05:00`	1:20 P.M. on April 12, 2004, US Eastern Standard Time.
`2004-04-12T13:20:00Z`	1:20 P.M. on April 12, 2004, Coordinated Universal Time (UTC).
Invalid values	*Comment*
`2004-04-12T13:00`	Seconds must be specified.
`2004-04-1213:20:00`	The letter `T` is required.
`2004-04-12t13:20:00`	The letter `T` must be upper case.
`99-04-12T13:00`	The century must not be left-truncated.
`2004-04-12`	The time is required.
	An empty value is not valid, unless `xsi:nil` is used.

11.4.4 `dateTimeStamp`

The type `dateTimeStamp` represents a specific date and time, but with a time zone required. It is derived from `dateTime` and has the same lexical representation and rules. The only difference is that a value is required to end in a time zone, as described in Section 11.4.13 on p. 233.

Table 11–20 shows some valid and invalid values of the `dateTimeStamp` type.

Table 11–20   Values of the `dateTimeStamp` type

Valid values	Comment
`2004-04-12T13:20:00-05:00`	1:20 P.M. on April 12, 2004, US Eastern Standard Time.
`2004-04-12T13:20:00Z`	1:20 P.M. on April 12, 2004, Coordinated Universal Time (UTC).

Invalid values	Comment
`2004-04-12T13:20:00`	A time zone is required.
`2004-04-12T13:20:15.5`	A time zone is required.
	An empty value is not valid, unless `xsi:nil` is used.

11.4.5 gYear

The type `gYear` represents a specific Gregorian calendar year. The letter `g` at the beginning of most date and time types signifies "Gregorian." The lexical representation of `gYear` is YYYY. No left truncation is allowed. To represent years later than 9999, additional digits can be added to the left of the year value. To represent years before 0000, a preceding minus sign ("-") is allowed. An optional time zone expression may be added at the end, as described in Section 11.4.13 on p. 233.

Table 11–21 shows some valid and invalid values of the `gYear` type.

Table 11–21   Values of the `gYear` type

Valid values	Comment
`2004`	2004.
`2004-05:00`	2004, US Eastern Standard Time.
`12004`	The year 12004.
`0922`	The year 922.
`-0045`	45 B.C.

(Continues)

Table 11–21   (Continued)

Invalid values	Comment
99	The century must not be truncated.
922	No left truncation is allowed; leading zeros should be added if necessary.
	An empty value is not valid, unless xsi:nil is used.

11.4.6 gYearMonth

The type gYearMonth represents a specific month of a specific year. The lexical representation of gYearMonth is YYYY-MM. No left truncation is allowed on either part. To represent years later than 9999, additional digits can be added to the left of the year value. To represent years before 0000, a preceding minus sign ("-") is permitted. An optional time zone expression may be added at the end, as described in Section 11.4.13 on p. 233.

Table 11–22 shows some valid and invalid values of the gYearMonth type.

Table 11–22   Values of the gYearMonth type

Valid values	Comment
2004-04	April 2004.
2004-04-05:00	April 2004, US Eastern Standard Time.
Invalid values	Comment
99-04	The century must not be truncated.
2004	The month is required.
2004-4	The month must be two digits.
2004-13	The month must be a valid month.
	An empty value is not valid, unless xsi:nil is used.

11.4.7 gMonth

The type gMonth represents a specific month that recurs every year. It can be used to indicate, for example, that fiscal year-end processing occurs in September of every year. To represent a duration in months, use the duration type instead. The lexical representation of gMonth is --MM. An optional time zone expression may be added at the end, as described in Section 11.4.13 on p. 233. No preceding sign is allowed.

Table 11–23 shows some valid and invalid values of the gMonth type.

Table 11–23   Values of the gMonth type

Valid values	Comment
--04	April.
--04-05:00	April, US Eastern Standard Time.
Invalid values	*Comment*
2004-04	The year must not be specified; use gYearMonth instead.
04	The leading hyphens are required.
--4	The month must be two digits.
--13	The month must be a valid month.
	An empty value is not valid, unless xsi:nil is used.

11.4.8 gMonthDay

The type gMonthDay represents a specific day that recurs every year. It can be used to say, for example, that your birthday is on the 12th of April every year. The lexical representation of gMonthDay is --MM-DD. An optional time zone expression may be added at the end, as described in Section 11.4.13 on p. 233.

Table 11–24 shows some valid and invalid values of the gMonthDay type.

Table 11–24 Values of the `gMonthDay` type

Valid values	Comment
`--04-12`	April 12.
`--04-12Z`	April 12, Coordinated Universal Time (UTC).

Invalid values	Comment
`04-12`	The leading hyphens are required.
`--04-31`	It must be a valid day of the year (April has 30 days).
`--4-6`	The month and day must be two digits each.
	An empty value is not valid, unless `xsi:nil` is used.

11.4.9 gDay

The type `gDay` represents a day that recurs every month. It can be used to say, for example, that checks are paid on the 5th of each month. To represent a duration in days, use the `duration` type instead. The lexical representation of `gDay` is `---DD`. An optional time zone expression may be added at the end, as described in Section 11.4.13 on p. 233.

Table 11–25 shows some valid and invalid values of the `gDay` type.

Table 11–25 Values of the `gDay` type

Valid values	Comment
`---02`	The 2nd of the month.

Invalid values	Comment
`02`	The leading hyphens are required.
`---2`	The day must be two digits.
`---32`	The day must be a valid day of the month; no month has 32 days.
	An empty value is not valid, unless `xsi:nil` is used.

11.4.10 duration

The type `duration` represents a duration of time expressed as a number of years, months, days, hours, minutes, and seconds. The lexical representation of `duration` is `PnYnMnDTnHnMnS`, where `P` is a literal value that starts the expression, `nY` is the number of years followed by a literal `Y`, `nM` is the number of months followed by a literal `M`, `nD` is the number of days followed by a literal `D`, `T` is a literal value that separates the date and time, `nH` is the number of hours followed by a literal `H`, `nM` is the number of minutes followed by a literal `M`, and `nS` is the number of seconds followed by a literal `S`. The following rules apply to `duration` values:

- Any of these numbers and corresponding designators may be absent if they are equal to 0, but at least one number and designator must appear.
- The numbers may be any unsigned integer, with the exception of the number of seconds, which may be an unsigned decimal number.
- If a decimal point appears in the number of seconds, there must be at least one digit after the decimal point.
- A minus sign may appear before the `P` to specify a negative duration.
- If no time items (hours, minutes, seconds) are present, the letter `T` must not appear.

In the canonical representation of `duration`, the months value must be less than 12, the hours value less than 24, and the minutes and seconds values less than 60. This means that `P15M` and `P1Y3M` are both valid (and equal) lexical representations that map to the same canonical value `P1Y3M`.

Table 11–26 shows some valid and invalid values of the `duration` type.

Table 11–26   Values of the `duration` type

Valid values	Comment
P2Y6M5DT12H35M30S	2 years, 6 months, 5 days, 12 hours, 35 minutes, 30 seconds.
P1DT2H	1 day, 2 hours.
P20M	20 months (the number of months can be more than 12).
PT20M	20 minutes.
P0Y20M0D	20 months (0 is permitted as a number, but is not required).
P0Y	0 years.
-P60D	Minus 60 days.
PT1M30.5S	1 minute, 30.5 seconds.

Invalid values	Comment
P-20M	The minus sign must appear first if it is present.
P20MT	No time items are present, so T must not be present.
P1YM5D	No value is specified for months, so M must not be present.
P15.5Y	Only the seconds can be expressed as a decimal.
P1D2H	T must be present to separate days and hours.
1Y2M	P must always be present.
P2M1Y	Years must appear before months.
P	At least one number and designator are required.
PT15.S	At least one digit must follow the decimal point if it appears.
	An empty value is not valid, unless `xsi:nil` is used.

When deriving types from `duration`, applying the bounds facets (`minExclusive`, `minInclusive`, `maxInclusive`, and maxExclusive) can have unexpected results. For example, if the maxInclusive value for a duration-based type is P1M, and an instance value contains P30D, it is ambiguous. Months may have 28, 29, 30, or 31 days, so is 30 days less than a month or not?

It is best to avoid the ambiguity by always specifying bounds for durations in the same unit in which the instance values will appear, in this case setting maxExclusive to P32D instead of P1M. You can use the pattern facet to force a particular unit of duration. For example, the pattern P\d+D applied to the duration type would force the duration to be expressed in days only.

Alternatively, if you are using version 1.1, you can use one of the two totally ordered duration types, yearMonthDuration or dayTimeDuration, described in the next two sections.

11.4.11 yearMonthDuration

The type yearMonthDuration, new in version 1.1, represents a duration of time expressed as a number of years and months. The lexical representation of duration is PnYnM, where P is a literal value that starts the expression, nY is the number of years followed by a literal Y, and nM is the number of months followed by a literal M.

yearMonthDuration is derived from duration, and all of the same lexical rules apply.

Table 11–27 shows some valid and invalid values of the yearMonthDuration type.

Table 11–27   Values of the yearMonthDuration type

Valid values	Comment
P1Y2M	1 year, 2 months.
P20M	20 months (the number of months can be more than 12).

(Continues)

Table 11–27   (Continued)

Valid values	Comment
P0Y20M	20 months (0 is permitted as a number, but is not required).
P0Y	0 years.
-P2Y	Minus 2 years.

Invalid values	Comment
P2Y6M5D	The value cannot contain a number of days.
P-20M	The minus sign must appear first if it is present.
P1YM	No value is specified for months, so M must not be present.
P15.5Y	Years cannot be expressed as a decimal.
1Y2M	P must always be present.
P2M1Y	Years must appear before months.
P	At least one number and designator are required.
	An empty value is not valid, unless xsi:nil is used.

11.4.12 dayTimeDuration

The type dayTimeDuration, new in version 1.1, represents a duration of time expressed as a number of days, hours, minutes, and seconds. The lexical representation of duration is PnDTnHnMnS, where P is a literal value that starts the expression, nD is the number of days followed by a literal D, T is a literal value that separates the date and time, nH is the number of hours followed by a literal H, nM is the number of minutes followed by a literal M, and nS is the number of seconds followed by a literal S.

dayTimeDuration is derived from duration, and all of the same lexical rules apply.

Table 11–28 shows some valid and invalid values of the dayTimeDuration type.

Table 11–28   Values of the `dayTimeDuration` type

Valid values	Comment
P5DT12H35M30S	5 days, 12 hours, 35 minutes, 30 seconds.
PT20M	20 minutes.
P0DT20M	20 minutes (0 is permitted as a number, but is not required).
P0D	0 days.
-P60D	Minus 60 days.
PT1M30.5S	1 minute, 30.5 seconds.

Invalid values	Comment
P-20D	The minus sign must appear first if it is present.
P20DT	No time items are present, so T must not be present.
PT5DM10S	No value is specified for minutes, so M must not be present.
P15.5D	Only the seconds can be expressed as a decimal.
P1D2H	T must be present to separate days and hours.
PT30S1H	Hours must appear before seconds.
P	At least one number and designator are required.
PT15.S	At least one digit must follow the decimal point if it appears.
	An empty value is not valid, unless `xsi:nil` is used.

11.4.13 *Representing time zones*

All of the date and time types, with the exception of the duration types, allow a time zone indicator at the end. The letter Z is used to indicate Coordinated Universal Time (UTC). All other time zones are represented by their difference from Coordinated Universal Time in the format +hh:mm or -hh:mm. These values may range from -14:00 to 14:00.

For example, US Eastern Standard Time, which is 5 hours behind UTC, is represented as -05:00. If no time zone value is present, it is considered unknown; it is not assumed to be UTC.

For most built-in types, a time zone is optional. However, for the dateTimeStamp type, it is required. This is because that type has its explicitTimezone facet set to required. In user-defined types derived from the date and time types, you can choose to leave the time zone optional, or require or prohibit a time zone using the explicitTimezone facet, as described in Section 8.4.7 on p. 150.

Table 11–29 shows some valid and invalid values of time zones.

Table 11–29   Time zone values

Valid values	Comment
Z	Coordinated Universal Time (UTC).
-05:00	US Eastern Standard Time, which is 5 hours behind UTC.
+09:00	UTC plus 9 hours, Japan's time zone.
	Unknown time zone.
Invalid values	Comment
+9:00	The hour must be two digits in length; use leading zeroes if necessary.
Z+05:00	The value may be Z or a time zone, but not both.
+20:00	The range is limited to -14:00 through +14:00.
-05	Minutes are required.

11.4.14 *Facets*

The facets indicated in Table 11–30 can restrict the date and time types as well as their derived types.

Table 11–30   Facets applicable to date and time types

length		minExclusive	A	totalDigits	
minLength		minInclusive	A	fractionDigits	
maxLength		maxInclusive	A	pattern	A
whiteSpace	F	maxExclusive	A	enumeration	A
▣explicitTimezone	V	▣assertion	A		

whiteSpace is collapse, explicitTimezone is required for dateTimeStamp, not applicable for duration types, and optional for all other date and time types.

11.4.15 *Date and time ordering*

When deriving types from date and time types (other than the duration types), it is important to note that applying the bounds facets (minExclusive, minInclusive, maxInclusive, and maxExclusive) can have unexpected results. If the values of the bounds facets specify time zones and the instance values do not, or vice versa, it may be impossible to compare the two. For example, if maxInclusive for a time-based type is 14:30:00Z, this means that the maximum value is 2:30 P.M. in UTC. If the value 13:30:00 appears in an instance, which is 1:30 P.M. with no time zone specified, it is impossible to tell if this value is valid. It could be 1:30 P.M. in UTC, which would be valid, or 1:30 P.M. US Eastern Standard Time, which would be 6:30 P.M. UTC, and therefore invalid. Since this is indeterminate, the schema processor will consider it an invalid value.

To avoid this problem, either use time zones in both bounds facet values and instance values, or do not use time zones at all. If both the bounds and the instance values have a time zone, the two values can be compared. Likewise, if neither has a time zone, the two values are assumed to be in the same time zone and compared as such.

11.5 | Legacy types

The XML DTD types described in this section are attribute types that are specified in the XML recommendation. It is recommended that these types are only used for attributes, in order to maintain compatibility with XML DTDs. However, it is not an error to use these types in element declarations.

11.5.1   ID

The type ID is used for an attribute that uniquely identifies an element in an XML document. An ID value must conform to the rules for an NCName, as described in Section 11.2.3 on p. 210. This means that it must start with a letter or underscore, and can only contain letters, digits, underscores, hyphens, and periods.

ID values must be unique within an XML instance, regardless of the attribute's name or its element name. Example 11–2 is invalid if attributes custID and orderID are both declared to be of type ID.

Example 11–2. Invalid nonunique IDs

```
<order orderID="A123">
  <customer custID="A123">...</customer>
</order>
```

In version 1.0, ID carries two additional constraints, both of which have been eliminated in version 1.1:

1. A complex type cannot include more than one attribute of type ID or of any type derived from ID. The type definition in Example 11–3 is illegal.
2. ID attributes cannot have default or fixed values specified. The attribute declarations in Example 11–4 are illegal.

Example 11–3. Illegal duplication of ID attributes (version 1.0)

```
<xs:complexType name="CustType">
  <xs:attribute name="id" type="xs:ID"/>
  <xs:attribute name="custID" type="xs:ID"/>
</xs:complexType>
```

Example 11–4. Illegal attribute declarations (version 1.0)

```
<xs:attribute name="id" type="xs:ID" fixed="A123"/>
<xs:attribute name="custID" type="xs:ID" default="C00000"/>
```

The facets indicated in Table 11–31 can restrict ID and its derived types.

Table 11–31   Facets applicable to ID type

length	A	minExclusive	totalDigits	
minLength	A	minInclusive	fractionDigits	
maxLength	A	maxInclusive	pattern	V
whiteSpace	V	maxExclusive	enumeration	A
explicitTimezone		assertion	A	

whiteSpace is collapse, pattern is [\i-[:]][\c-[:]]*.

11.5.2 IDREF

The type IDREF is used for an attribute that references an ID. A common use case for IDREF is to create a cross-reference to a particular section of a document. Like ID, an IDREF value must be an NCName, as described in Section 11.2.3 on p. 210.

All attributes of type IDREF must reference an ID in the same XML document. In Example 11–5, the ref attribute of quote is of type IDREF, and the id attribute of footnote is of type ID. The instance contains a reference between them.

Example 11–5. Using IDREF

Schema:

```
<xs:element name="quote">
  <xs:complexType>
    <!--content model-->
    <xs:attribute name="ref" type="xs:IDREF"/>
  </xs:complexType>
</xs:element>
<xs:element name="footnote">
  <xs:complexType>
    <!--content model-->
    <xs:attribute name="id" type="xs:ID" use="required"/>
  </xs:complexType>
</xs:element>
```

Instance:

```
<quote ref="fn1">...</quote>
<footnote id="fn1">...</footnote>
```

ID and IDREF are best used for referencing unique locations in document-oriented XML. To enforce complex uniqueness of data values, and primary and foreign key references, consider using identity constraints, which are described in Chapter 17.

The facets indicated in Table 11–32 can restrict IDREF and its derived types.

Table 11–32   Facets applicable to IDREF type

length	A	minExclusive		totalDigits	
minLength	A	minInclusive		fractionDigits	
maxLength	A	maxInclusive		pattern	V
whiteSpace	V	maxExclusive		enumeration	A
explicitTimezone		assertion	A		

whiteSpace is collapse, pattern is [\i-[:]][\c-[:]]*.

11.5.3 IDREFS

The type `IDREFS` represents a list of `IDREF` values separated by whitespace. There must be at least one `IDREF` in the list.

Each of the values in an attribute of type `IDREFS` must reference an ID in the same XML document. In Example 11–6, the `refs` attribute of `quote` is of type `IDREFS`, and the `id` attribute of `footnote` is of type `ID`. The instance contains a reference from the `quote` element to two `footnote` elements, with their IDs (`fn1` and `fn2`) separated by whitespace.

Example 11–6. Using `IDREFS`

Schema:

```
<xs:element name="quote">
  <xs:complexType>
    <!--content model-->
    <xs:attribute name="refs" type="xs:IDREFS"/>
  </xs:complexType>
</xs:element>
<xs:element name="footnote">
  <xs:complexType>
    <!--content model-->
    <xs:attribute name="id" type="xs:ID" use="required"/>
  </xs:complexType>
</xs:element>
```

Instance:

```
<quote refs="fn1 fn2">...</quote>
<footnote id="fn1">...</footnote>
<footnote id="fn2">...</footnote>
```

The facets indicated in Table 11–33 can restrict `IDREFS` and its derived types.

Table 11–33   Facets applicable to `IDREFS` type

length	A	minExclusive		totalDigits	
minLength	V	minInclusive		fractionDigits	
maxLength	A	maxInclusive		pattern	A
whiteSpace	V	maxExclusive		enumeration	A
▣explicitTimezone		▣assertion	A		

`whiteSpace` is `collapse`, `minLength` is `1`.

Since `IDREFS` is a list type, restricting an `IDREFS` value with these facets may not behave as you expect. The facets `length`, `minLength`, and `maxLength` apply to the number of items in the `IDREFS` list, not the length of each item. The `enumeration` facet applies to the whole list, not the individual items in the list. For more information, see Section 10.3.3 on p. 190.

11.5.4 ENTITY

The type `ENTITY` represents a reference to an unparsed entity. The `ENTITY` type is most often used to include information from another location that is not in XML format, such as graphics. An `ENTITY` value must be an `NCName`, as described in Section 11.2.3 on p. 210. An `ENTITY` value carries the additional constraint that it must match the name of an unparsed entity in a document type definition (DTD) for the instance.

Example 11–7 shows an XML document that links product numbers to pictures of the products. In the schema, the `picture` element declaration declares an attribute `location` that has the type `ENTITY`. In the instance, each value of the `location` attribute (in this case, `prod557` and `prod563`) matches the name of an entity declared in the internal DTD subset of the instance.

The facets indicated in Table 11–34 can restrict `ENTITY` and its derived types.

Example 11–7. Using an unparsed entity

Schema:

```
<xs:element name="picture">
  <xs:complexType>
    <xs:attribute name="location" type="xs:ENTITY"/>
  </xs:complexType>
</xs:element>
<!--...-->
```

Instance:

```
<!DOCTYPE catalog SYSTEM "catalog.dtd" [
<!NOTATION jpeg SYSTEM "JPG">
<!ENTITY prod557 SYSTEM "prod557.jpg" NDATA jpeg>
<!ENTITY prod563 SYSTEM "prod563.jpg" NDATA jpeg>
]>

<catalog>
  <product>
    <number>557</number>
    <picture location="prod557"/>
  </product>
  <product>
    <number>563</number>
    <picture location="prod563"/>
  </product>
</catalog>
```

Table 11–34 Facets applicable to ENTITY type

length	A	minExclusive		totalDigits	
minLength	A	minInclusive		fractionDigits	
maxLength	A	maxInclusive		pattern	V
whiteSpace	V	maxExclusive		enumeration	A
▪explicitTimezone		▪assertion	A		

whiteSpace is collapse, pattern is [\i-[:]][\c-[:]]*.

11.5.5 ENTITIES

The type ENTITIES represents a list of ENTITY values separated by whitespace. There must be at least one ENTITY in the list. Each of the ENTITY values must match the name of an unparsed entity that has been declared in a document type definition (DTD) for the instance.

Expanding on the example from the previous section, Example 11–8 shows the declaration of an attribute named location that is of type ENTITIES. In the instance, the location attribute can include a list of entity names. Each value (in this case there are two: prod557a and prod557b) matches the name of an entity that is declared in the internal DTD subset for the instance.

Example 11–8. Using ENTITIES

Schema:

```
<xs:element name="pictures">
  <xs:complexType>
    <xs:attribute name="location" type="xs:ENTITIES"/>
  </xs:complexType>
</xs:element>
```

Instance:

```
<!DOCTYPE catalog SYSTEM "catalog.dtd" [
<!NOTATION jpeg SYSTEM "JPG">
<!ENTITY prod557a SYSTEM "prod557a.jpg" NDATA jpeg>
<!ENTITY prod557b SYSTEM "prod557b.jpg" NDATA jpeg>
]>

<catalog>
  <product>
    <number>557</number>
    <pictures location="prod557a prod557b"/>
  </product>
</catalog>
```

The facets indicated in Table 11–35 can restrict ENTITIES and its derived types.

Table 11–35 Facets applicable to `ENTITIES` type

length	A	minExclusive		totalDigits	
minLength	V	minInclusive		fractionDigits	
maxLength	A	maxInclusive		pattern	A
whiteSpace	V	maxExclusive		enumeration	A
▣explicitTimezone		▣assertion	A		

`whiteSpace` is `collapse`, `minLength` is 1.

Since `ENTITIES` is a list type, restricting an `ENTITIES` value with these facets may not behave as you expect. The facets `length`, `minLength`, and `maxLength` apply to the number of items in the `ENTITIES` list, not the length of each item. The `enumeration` facet applies to the whole list, not the individual items in the list. For more information, see Section 10.3.3 on p. 190.

11.5.6 NMTOKEN

The type `NMTOKEN` represents a single string token. `NMTOKEN` values may consist of letters, digits, periods (.), hyphens (-), underscores (_), and colons (:). They may start with any of these characters. `NMTOKEN` has a `whiteSpace` facet value of `collapse`, so any leading or trailing whitespace will be removed. However, no whitespace may appear within the value itself. Table 11–36 shows some valid and invalid values of the `NMTOKEN` type.

Table 11–36 Values of the `NMTOKEN` type

Valid values	Comment
ABCD	
123_456	
starts_with_a_space	When parsed, leading spaces will be removed.

(Continues)

Table 11–36   (Continued)

Invalid values	Comment
`contains a space`	Value must not contain a space.
	An empty value is not valid, unless `xsi:nil` is used.

The facets indicated in Table 11–37 can restrict NMTOKEN and its derived types.

Table 11–37   Facets applicable to NMTOKEN type

`length`	A	`minExclusive`		`totalDigits`	
`minLength`	A	`minInclusive`		`fractionDigits`	
`maxLength`	A	`maxInclusive`		`pattern`	V
`whiteSpace`	V	`maxExclusive`		`enumeration`	A
▣`explicitTimezone`		▣`assertion`	A		

whiteSpace is `collapse`, pattern is `\c+`.

11.5.7 NMTOKENS

The type NMTOKENS represents a list of NMTOKEN values separated by whitespace. There must be at least one NMTOKEN in the list. Table 11–38 shows some valid and invalid values of the NMTOKENS type.

The facets indicated in Table 11–39 can restrict NMTOKENS and its derived types.

Since NMTOKENS is a list type, restricting an NMTOKENS value with these facets may not behave as you expect. The facets `length`, `minLength`, and `maxLength` apply to the number of items in the NMTOKENS list, not the length of each item. The `enumeration` facet applies to the whole list, not the individual items in the list. For more information, see Section 10.3.3 on p. 190.

Table 11–38   Values of the NMTOKENS type

Valid values	Comment
ABCD 123	
ABCD	One-item list.
Invalid values	*Comment*
	An empty value is not valid, unless xsi:nil is used.

Table 11–39   Facets applicable to NMTOKENS type

length	A	minExclusive		totalDigits	
minLength	V	minInclusive		fractionDigits	
maxLength	A	maxInclusive		pattern	A
whiteSpace	V	maxExclusive		enumeration	A
explicitTimezone		assertion	A		

whiteSpace is collapse, minLength is 1.

11.5.8 NOTATION

The type NOTATION represents a reference to a notation. A notation is a method of interpreting XML and non-XML content. For example, if an element in an XML document contains binary graphics data in JPEG format, a notation can be declared to indicate that this is JPEG data. An attribute of type NOTATION can then be used to indicate which notation applies to the element's content. A NOTATION value must be a QName as described in Section 11.6.1 on p. 246.

NOTATION is the only built-in type that cannot be the type of attributes or elements. Instead, you must define a new type that restricts NOTATION, applying one or more enumeration facets. Each of these enumeration values must match the name of a declared notation. For more information on declaring notations and NOTATION-based types, see Section 19.7 on p. 493.

The facets indicated in Table 11–40 can restrict NOTATION and its derived types.

Table 11–40 Facets applicable to NOTATION type

length	A	minExclusive		totalDigits	
minLength	A	minInclusive		fractionDigits	
maxLength	A	maxInclusive		pattern	A
whiteSpace	F	maxExclusive		enumeration	A
[1.1]explicitTimezone		[1.1]assertion	A		

whiteSpace is collapse.

11.6 | Other types

11.6.1 QName

The type QName represents an XML namespace-qualified name that consists of a namespace name and a local part.

When appearing in XML documents, the lexical representation of a QName consists of a prefix and a local part, separated by a colon, both of which are NCNames. The prefix and colon are optional.

The lexical structure is mapped onto the QName value in the context of namespace declarations, as described in Chapter 3. If the QName value is prefixed, the namespace name is that which is in scope for that prefix. If it is not prefixed, the default namespace declaration in scope (if any) becomes the QName's namespace.

QName is not based on string like the other name-related types, because it has this special two-part value with additional constraints that cannot be expressed with XML Schema facets. Table 11–41 shows some valid and invalid values of the QName type.

Table 11–41   Values of the `QName` type

Valid values	Comment
`pre:myElement`	Valid assuming the prefix `pre` is mapped to a namespace in scope.
`myElement`	Prefix and colon are optional.

Invalid values	Comment
`:myElement`	A `QName` must not start with a colon.
`pre:3rdElement`	The local part must not start with a number; it must be a valid `NCName`.
	An empty value is not valid, unless `xsi:nil` is used.

The facets indicated in Table 11–42 can restrict `QName` and its derived types.

Table 11–42   Facets applicable to `QName` type

`length`	A	`minExclusive`		`totalDigits`	
`minLength`	A	`minInclusive`		`fractionDigits`	
`maxLength`	A	`maxInclusive`		`pattern`	A
`whiteSpace`	F	`maxExclusive`		`enumeration`	A
`explicitTimezone`		`assertion`	A		

`whiteSpace` is `collapse`.

11.6.2 `boolean`

The type `boolean` represents logical yes/no values. The valid values for `boolean` are `true`, `false`, `0`, and `1`. Values that are capitalized (e.g., `TRUE`) or abbreviated (e.g., `T`) are not valid. Table 11–43 shows some valid and invalid values of the `boolean` type.

Table 11–43   Values of the `boolean` type

Valid values	Comment
true	
false	
0	false
1	true

Invalid values	Comment
TRUE	Values are case sensitive.
T	The word "true" must be spelled out.
	An empty value is not valid, unless `xsi:nil` is used.

The facets indicated in Table 11–44 can restrict `boolean` and its derived types.

Table 11–44   Facets applicable to `boolean` type

length		minExclusive		totalDigits	
minLength		minInclusive		fractionDigits	
maxLength		maxInclusive		pattern	A
whiteSpace	F	maxExclusive		enumeration	
explicitTimezone		assertion	A		

whiteSpace is collapse.

11.6.3 *The binary types*

The types `hexBinary` and `base64Binary` represent binary data. Their lexical representation is a sequence of binary octets.

The type `hexBinary` uses hexadecimal encoding, where each binary octet is a two-character hexadecimal number. Lowercase and uppercase letters A through F are permitted. For example, 0FB8 and 0fb8 are two equal hexBinary representations consisting of two octets. The canonical representation of hexBinary uses only uppercase letters.

The type base64Binary, typically used for embedding images and other binary content, uses base64 encoding, as described in RFC 3548. The following rules apply to base64Binary values:

- The following characters are allowed: the letters A to Z (upper and lower case), digits 0 through 9, the plus sign (+), the slash (/), the equals sign (=), and XML whitespace characters.
- XML whitespace characters may appear anywhere in the value.
- The number of nonwhitespace characters must be divisible by 4.
- Equals signs may only appear at the end of the value, and there may be zero, one, or two of them. If there are two equals signs, they must be preceded by one of the following characters: AQgw. If there is only one equals sign, it must be preceded by one of the following characters: AEIMQUYcgkosw048. In either case, there may be whitespace between the necessary characters and the equals sign(s).

The canonical representation of base64Binary removes all whitespace characters. For more information on base64 encoding, see RFC 3548, *The Base16, Base32, and Base64 Data Encodings*.

Table 11–45 shows some valid and invalid values of the binary types.

The facets indicated in Table 11–46 can restrict hexBinary, base64Binary, and their derived types.

The length facet for the binary types represents the number of binary octets (groups of 8 bits each). For example, the length of the hexBinary value 0FB8 is equal to 2. Since base64 characters represent 6 bits each, the length of the base64Binary value 0FB8 is equal to 3. Whitespace and equals signs are ignored when calculating the length of a base64Binary value.

Table 11–45   Values of the binary types

Valid values	Comment
0FB8	
0fb8	In hexBinary, the equivalent of 0FB8; in base64Binary represents a different value.
0 FB8 0F+9	base64Binary only; whitespace is allowed anywhere in the value (not valid for hexBinary).
0F+40A==	base64Binary only; equals signs are used for padding (not valid for hexBinary).
	An empty value is valid.

Invalid values	Comment
FB8	An odd number of characters is not valid; characters appear in pairs (in hexBinary) or groups of four (in base64Binary).
==0F	Equals signs may only appear at the end in base64Binary, and not at all in hexBinary.

Table 11–46   Facets applicable to binary types

length		A	minExclusive		totalDigits	
minLength		A	minInclusive		fractionDigits	
maxLength		A	maxInclusive		pattern	A
whiteSpace		F	maxExclusive		enumeration	A
[1.1]explicitTimezone			[1.1]assertion	A		

whiteSpace is collapse.

11.6.4 anyURI

The type anyURI represents a Uniform Resource Identifier (URI) reference. URIs are used to identify resources, and they may be absolute

or relative. Absolute URIs provide the entire context for locating a resource, such as `http://datypic.com/prod.html`. Relative URIs
are specified as the difference from a base URI, for example
`../prod.html`. It is also possible to specify a fragment identifier using
the # character, for example `../prod.html#shirt`.

The three previous examples happen to be HTTP URLs (Uniform
Resource Locators), but URIs also encompass URLs of other schemes
(e.g., FTP, gopher, telnet), as well as URNs (Uniform Resource Names).
URIs are not required to be dereferenceable; that is, it is not necessary
for there to be a web page at `http://datypic.com/prod.html` in
order for this to be a valid URI.

URIs require that some characters be escaped with their hexadecimal Unicode code point preceded by the % character. This
includes non-ASCII characters and some ASCII characters including
control characters, space, and certain punctuation characters. For
example, `../édition.html` must be represented instead as
`../%C3%A9dition.html`, with the é escaped as `%C3%A9`. However,
the `anyURI` type will accept these characters either escaped or unescaped. With the exception of the characters % and #, it will assume
that unescaped characters are intended to be escaped when used in an
actual URI, although the schema processor will do nothing to alter
them. It is valid for an `anyURI` value to contain a space, but this practice
is strongly discouraged. Spaces should instead be escaped using %20.
For more information on URIs, see RFC 2396, *Uniform Resource
Identifiers (URI): Generic Syntax.*

Version 1.1 expands the definition of `anyURI` to include IRfIs, or
Internationalized Resource Identifiers. Compared to URIs, IRIs allow
a much broader range of characters without requiring them to be escaped. Since the `anyURI` type does not require escaping anyway, this
has little practical impact on your schemas. For more information about
IRIs, see RFC 3987, *Internationalized Resource Identifiers (IRIs).*

Note that when relative URI references such as `../prod` are used
as values of `anyURI`, no attempt is made by the schema processor to
determine or keep track of the base URI to which they may be applied.
For example, it will not attempt to resolve the value relative to the URL

of the containing document, or any `xml:base` attributes that may appear in it.

Table 11–47 shows some examples of valid and invalid `anyURI` values. The schema processor is not required to parse the contents of an `anyURI` value to determine whether it is valid according to any particular URI scheme. Since the bare minimum rules for valid URI references are fairly generic, the schema processor will accept most character strings, including an empty value. The only values that are not accepted are ones that make inappropriate use of reserved characters, such as those containing multiple # characters or % characters not followed by two hexadecimal digits.

Table 11–47   Valid values of `anyURI` type

Valid values	*Comment*
`http://datypic.com`	Absolute URI (also a URL).
`mailto:info@datypic.com`	Absolute URI.
`../%C3%A9dition.html`	Relative URI containing escaped non-ASCII character.
`../édition.html`	Relative URI containing unescaped non-ASCII character.
`http://datypic.com/prod.html#shirt`	URI with fragment identifier.
`../prod.html#shirt`	Relative URI with fragment identifier.
`urn:example:org`	URN.
	An empty value is allowed.
Invalid values	*Comment*
`http://datypic.com#frag1#frag2`	Too many # characters.
`http://datypic.com#f% rag`	% character followed by something other than two hexadecimal digits.

The facets indicated in Table 11–48 can restrict `anyURI` and its derived types.

Table 11–48   Facets applicable to `anyURI` type

length	A	minExclusive		totalDigits	
minLength	A	minInclusive		fractionDigits	
maxLength	A	maxInclusive		pattern	A
whiteSpace	F	maxExclusive		enumeration	A
▦explicitTimezone		▦assertion	A		

`whiteSpace` is `collapse`.

11.7 | Comparing typed values

When a schema processor is comparing two values, it does more than compare lexical values as if they were strings. It takes into account the types of the values. This comes into play during validation of an instance in several places:

- Validating fixed values
- Validating enumerated values
- Validating values against bounds facets
- Determining uniqueness of identity constraint fields
- Validating key references
- Comparisons in assertions

This is also important to consider when using schema-aware languages, such as XSLT 2.0 and XQuery, which allow a processor to use type information from the schema when comparing values.

One of the factors used in determining the equality of two values is the relationship of their types in the derivation hierarchy. Types that are related to each other by restriction, list, or union can have values that are equal. For example, the value 2 of type `integer` and the value 2 of type `positiveInteger` are considered equal, since `positiveInteger` is derived from `integer`. Types that are not related in the hierarchy can never have values that are equal. This means that an `integer` value will never equal a `string` value, even if they are both 2. This is true of both the built-in and user-derived types. Example 11–9 illustrates this point.[1]

Example 11–9. Equality based on type definition hierarchy

```
<integer>2</integer> does not equal <string>2</string>
<integer>2</integer> equals <positiveInteger>2</positiveInteger>
<string>abc</string> equals <NCName>abc</NCName>
<string>abc</string> does not equal <QName>abc</QName>
<IDREFS>abc</IDREFS> equals <IDREF>abc</IDREF>
```

Some of the built-in types have multiple lexical representations that are equivalent. For example, an `integer` may be represented as 2, 02, +2, or +00002. These values are all considered equal if they have the type `integer`, because they all represent the same canonical value. However, these same lexical values are unequal if they have the type `string`. Example 11–10 illustrates this point.

Another factor to take into account is whitespace normalization. Whitespace is normalized before any validation takes place. Therefore, it plays a role in determining whether two values are equal. For example, the `string` type has a `whiteSpace` facet value of `preserve`, while

---

1.   Assume for this section that there are element declarations with names that are the same as their type names. For example, `<xs:element name="integer" type="xs:integer"/>`.

the token type's is collapse. The value " a " that has the type string will not equal " a " that has the type token, because the leading and trailing spaces will be stripped for the token value. Example 11–11 illustrates this point.

Example 11–10. Equality based on equivalent lexical representations

```
<integer>2</integer> equals <integer>02</integer>
<integer>2</integer> equals <positiveInteger>02</positiveInteger>
<string>2</string> does not equal <string>02</string>
<boolean>true</boolean> equals <boolean>1</boolean>
<hexBinary>0fb8</hexBinary> equals <hexBinary>0FB8</hexBinary>
<time>13:20:00-05:00</time> equals <time>12:20:00-06:00</time>
```

Example 11–11. Equality based on whitespace normalization

```
<string> a </string> does not equal <token> a </token>
<string>a</string> equals <token> a </token>
<token>a</token> equals <token> a </token>
```

Complex types

Chapter

12

C omplex types are used to define the content model and attributes of elements. This chapter introduces complex types. It covers the four content types (simple, element-only, mixed, and empty) and the use of element declarations, model groups, attribute declarations, and wildcards to define complex types.

12.1 | What are complex types?

Elements that have complex types have child elements or attributes. They may also have character content. Example 12–1 shows the elements size, product, letter, and color that have complex types. They have the four different content types that are described in this chapter (simple, element-only, mixed, and empty, respectively).

Attributes can never have complex types; they always have simple types. This makes sense, because attributes cannot themselves have children or attributes.

Example 12–1. Elements with complex types

```
<size system="US-DRESS">10</size>

<product>
  <number>557</number>
  <name>Short-Sleeved Linen Blouse</name>
</product>

<letter>Dear <custName>Priscilla Walmsley</custName>...</letter>

<color value="blue"/>
```

12.2 | Defining complex types

12.2.1 *Named complex types*

Complex types may be either named or anonymous. Named types can be used by multiple element and attribute declarations. They are always defined globally (i.e., their parent is always schema[1]) and are required to have a name that is unique among the types (both simple and complex) in the schema. The syntax to define a named complex type is shown in Table 12–1.

The name of a complex type must be an XML non-colonized name, which means that it must start with a letter or underscore, and may only contain letters, digits, underscores, hyphens, and periods. You cannot include a namespace prefix when defining the type; it takes its namespace from the target namespace of the schema document. All of the examples of types in this book have the word "Type" at the end of their names, to clearly distinguish them from element names. However, this is a convention and not a requirement. You can even have a type definition and an element declaration using the same name, but this is not recommended because it can be confusing.

---

1.   Except in the case of a redefine or override.

Table 12–1 XSD Syntax: named complex type definition

Name
`complexType`

Parents
`schema`, `redefine`, ▪▪`override`

Attribute name	Type	Description
`id`	`ID`	Unique ID.
`name`	`NCName`	Complex type name.
`mixed`	`boolean`: *false*	Whether the complex type allows mixed content, see Section 12.3.3.
`abstract`	`boolean`: *false*	Whether the type can be used in an instance, see Section 13.7.4.
`block`	`"#all"` | list of (`"extension"` | `"restriction"`)	Whether to block type substitution in the instance, see Section 13.7.2; defaults to `blockDefault` of `schema`.
`final`	`"#all"` | list of (`"extension"` | `"restriction"`)	Whether other types can be derived from this one, see Section 13.7.1; defaults to `finalDefault` of `schema`.
▪▪`defaultAttributes-Apply`	`boolean`: *true*	Whether the default attribute group applies to this complex type, see Section 15.3.3.

Content
`annotation?, (simpleContent	complexContent	(`▪▪`openContent?, (group | all | choice | sequence)?, ((attribute | attributeGroup)*, anyAttribute?),` ▪▪`assert*))`

Example 12–2 shows the definition of the named complex type
ProductType, along with an element declaration that references it.

Example 12–2. Named complex type

```
<xs:complexType name="ProductType">
  <xs:sequence>
    <xs:element name="number" type="xs:integer"/>
    <xs:element name="name" type="xs:string"/>
    <xs:element name="size" type="SizeType"/>
  </xs:sequence>
</xs:complexType>

<xs:element name="product" type="ProductType"/>
```

12.2.2 *Anonymous complex types*

Anonymous complex types, on the other hand, must not have names.
They are always defined entirely within an element declaration, and
may only be used once, by that declaration. Defining a type anonymously prevents it from ever being restricted, extended, redefined, or
overridden. The syntax to define an anonymous complex type is shown
in Table 12–2.

Example 12–3 shows the definition of an anonymous complex type
within an element declaration.

Example 12–3. Anonymous complex type

```
<xs:element name="product">
  <xs:complexType>
    <xs:sequence>
      <xs:element name="number" type="xs:integer"/>
      <xs:element name="name" type="xs:string"/>
      <xs:element name="size" type="SizeType"/>
    </xs:sequence>
  </xs:complexType>
</xs:element>
```

Table 12–2   XSD Syntax: anonymous complex type definition

Name
complexType

Parents
element, [1.1]alternative

Attribute name	Type	Description
id	ID	Unique ID.
mixed	boolean: *false*	Whether the complex type allows mixed content.
[1.1]defaultAttributes-Apply	boolean: *true*	Whether the default attribute group applies to this complex type, see Section 15.3.3.

Content
annotation?, (simpleContent | complexContent | ([1.1]openContent?, (group | all | choice | sequence)?, ((attribute | attributeGroup)*, anyAttribute?), [1.1]assert*))

The question of whether to use named or anonymous types is covered in Section 8.2.3 on p. 133.

12.2.3 *Complex type alternatives*

There are four different possible structures for the children of complexType elements, representing four different methods of creating complex types:

- A single complexContent child, which is used to derive a complex type from another complex type. It is covered in detail in the next chapter, Chapter 13.

- A single simpleContent child, which is used to derive a complex type from a simple type. This is covered briefly in

Section 12.3.1 of this chapter, and in more detail in the next chapter.

- A group (group, all, choice, or sequence) and/or attribute declarations. This is used to define a complex type without deriving it from any particular type. We will cover this method in this chapter.

- No content at all, in which case the type allows no attributes and no content.

The various declarations that make up the content of a complex type are known collectively as *particles*. Particles include local element declarations, element references, model groups (all, choice, or sequence), named model group references, and element wildcards. All of these kinds of particles are described in detail in this chapter.

12.3 | Content types

The contents of an element are the character data and child elements that are between its tags. The order and structure of the children allowed by a complex type are known as its *content model*. There are four types of content for complex types: simple, element-only, mixed, and empty. The content type is independent of attributes; all of these content types allow attributes. Figure 12–1 shows the decision tree needed to determine the appropriate content type. This section explains the four content types and provides an example of how each is represented in a schema.

12.3.1 *Simple content*

Simple content allows character data only, with no children. Example 12–4 shows the element size that has character data (the value 10) but no child elements. Generally, the only thing that distinguishes a simple type from a complex type with simple content is that the latter

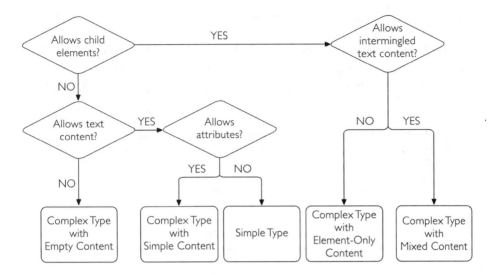

Figure 12–1   Content type decision tree

may have attributes. If a `size` element could never have a `system` attribute, you could just give `size` a simple type, as described in Chapter 8.

Example 12–5 shows a complex type definition that might be assigned to the `size` element that appears in Example 12–4. It defines `SizeType` whose character data content conforms to the simple type `integer`. It extends `integer` to add the attribute `system`.

Example 12–4. Instance element with simple content

```
<size system="US-DRESS">10</size>
```

Example 12–5. Complex type with simple content

```
<xs:complexType name="SizeType">
  <xs:simpleContent>
    <xs:extension base="xs:integer">
      <xs:attribute name="system" type="xs:token"/>
    </xs:extension>
  </xs:simpleContent>
</xs:complexType>
```

12.3.2 *Element-only content*

Element-only content allows only children, with no character data content. Example 12–6 shows an element `product` that has element-only content. It has four children: `number`, `name`, `size`, and `color`.

Example 12–6. Instance element with element-only content

```
<product>
  <number>557</number>
  <name>Short-Sleeved Linen Blouse</name>
  <size system="US-DRESS">10</size>
  <color value="blue"/>
</product>
```

Example 12–7 shows a complex type definition that might be used by the `product` element declaration.

Example 12–7. Complex type with element-only content

```
<xs:complexType name="ProductType">
  <xs:sequence>
    <xs:element name="number" type="xs:integer"/>
    <xs:element name="name" type="xs:string"/>
    <xs:element name="size" type="SizeType"/>
    <xs:element name="color" type="ColorType"/>
  </xs:sequence>
</xs:complexType>
```

12.3.3 *Mixed content*

Mixed content allows character data as well as child elements. This is most often used for freeform text such as letters and documents. Example 12–8 shows an element `desc` with mixed content. Note that there is character data directly contained in the `desc` element, as well as children `i`, `b`, and `u`.

Example 12–8. Instance element with mixed content

```
<desc>This is our <i>best-selling</i> shirt.
 <b>Note: </b> runs <u>large</u>.</desc>
```

Example 12–9 shows a type definition that describes the `letter` element shown in Example 12–8. To indicate that character data content is permitted, the `complexType` element in Example 12–9 has an attribute `mixed` that is set to `true`. The default value for `mixed` is `false`, meaning that character data content is not permitted.

Example 12–9. Complex type with mixed content

```
<xs:element name="desc" type="DescType"/>
<xs:complexType name="DescType" mixed="true">
  <xs:choice minOccurs="0" maxOccurs="unbounded">
    <xs:element name="i" type="xs:string"/>
    <xs:element name="b" type="xs:string"/>
    <xs:element name="u" type="xs:string"/>
    <!--...-->
  </xs:choice>
</xs:complexType>
```

It is important to note that the character data that is directly contained in the `desc` element (e.g., "`This is our `", "`shirt`", etc.) is not assigned a type. It is completely unrestricted in terms of its type and where (and whether) it appears. Therefore, you should not use mixed content types for data that you wish to constrain in any way.

12.3.4 *Empty content*

Empty content allows neither character data nor child elements. Elements with empty content often have values in attributes. In some cases, they may not even have attributes; their presence alone is meaningful. For example, a `<br/>` element in XHTML indicates a line break, without providing any data other than its presence. Example 12–10 shows an element `color` with empty content.

Example 12–10. Instance element with empty content

```
<color value="blue"/>
```

Example 12–11 shows a type definition that might be assigned to the `color` element in Example 12–10. Note that there is no special attribute in the complex type definition to indicate that the content is empty. The fact that only an attribute, with no content model, is specified for the complex type is enough to indicate this.

Example 12–11. Complex type with empty content

```
<xs:complexType name="ColorType">
  <xs:attribute name="value" type="ColorValueType"/>
</xs:complexType>
```

12.4 | Using element declarations

Element declarations can be included in complex-type content models in three ways: as local element declarations, as references to global element declarations, and as wildcards.

12.4.1 *Local element declarations*

Complex types can contain local element declarations. Such an element declaration specifies a name, a type, and other properties within the complex type. The scope of that element declaration is limited to the complex type within which it appears. Local element declarations are described in detail in Section 6.1.2 on p. 93. All of the prior examples in this chapter have local element declarations, as evidenced by the `name` attributes of the `element` elements.

12.4.2 *Element references*

Complex types can also contain references to global element declarations. Global element declarations themselves are covered in detail in Section 6.1.1 on p. 89. The syntax to reference a global element declaration is shown in Table 12–3. An `element` element is used to make the reference, though it uses a `ref` attribute instead of a `name` attribute.

Table 12–3   XSD Syntax: element reference

Name		
`element`		

Parents		
`all, choice, sequence`		

Attribute name	Type	Description
`id`	`ID`	Unique ID.
ref	`QName`	Name of the global element declaration being referenced.
`minOccurs`	`nonNegativeInteger:` *1*	Minimum number of element occurrences.
`maxOccurs`	`nonNegativeInteger |` `"unbounded"` : *1*	Maximum number of element occurrences.

Content		
`annotation?`		

Example 12–12 shows four global element declarations, with the `ProductType` definition referencing them through the `ref` attribute. Note that the `type` attribute appears in the global element declaration, while the `minOccurs` attribute is in the element reference. Occurrence constraints (`minOccurs` and `maxOccurs`) may only appear within

Example 12–12. Element references

```
<xs:schema xmlns:xs="http://www.w3.org/2001/XMLSchema">
  <xs:element name="number" type="xs:integer"/>
  <xs:element name="name" type="xs:string"/>
  <xs:element name="size" type="SizeType"/>
  <xs:element name="color" type="ColorType"/>

  <xs:complexType name="ProductType">
    <xs:sequence>
      <xs:element ref="number"/>
      <xs:element ref="name"/>
      <xs:element ref="size" minOccurs="0"/>
      <xs:element ref="color" minOccurs="0"/>
    </xs:sequence>
  </xs:complexType>

  <!--...-->
</xs:schema>
```

complex type definitions, that is, in element references or local element declarations but not in global element declarations.

For a detailed discussion of local or global element declarations see Section 6.1.3 on p. 95.

12.4.3 *Duplication of element names*

If two element declarations or references with the same name appear anywhere in the same complex type, they must have the same type. Example 12–13 shows a complex type definition that includes two declarations for name. This content model represents "either number or name or both." It is valid because both name declarations refer to the exact same type, string.

Example 12–14, on the other hand, is illegal because the two declarations of name refer to different types.

Example 12–13. Legal duplication of element names

```
<xs:complexType name="ProductType">
  <xs:choice>
    <xs:sequence>
      <xs:element name="number" type="xs:integer"/>
      <xs:element name="name" type="xs:string" minOccurs="0"/>
    </xs:sequence>
    <xs:element name="name" type="xs:string"/>
  </xs:choice>
</xs:complexType>
```

Example 12–14. Illegal duplication of element names

```
<xs:complexType name="ProductType">
  <xs:choice>
    <xs:sequence>
      <xs:element name="number" type="xs:integer"/>
      <xs:element name="name" type="xs:string" minOccurs="0"/>
    </xs:sequence>
    <xs:element name="name" type="xs:token"/>
  </xs:choice>
</xs:complexType>
```

Anonymous types are never considered equal, even if they have identical content models. If either of the name declarations used an anonymous type, it would automatically be illegal.

It is the *qualified* name that is relevant here. If one of the name element names had been qualified, or both had been qualified with different namespace names, Example 12–14 would have been legal. This applies regardless of whether the element declarations are global or local.

It is only the type name that must be consistent. It is legal for the two name element declarations to specify different default values, annotations, or other properties.

12.5 | Using model groups

Model groups allow you to group child element declarations or references together to construct more meaningful content models. There are three kinds of model groups: `all` groups, `choice` groups, and `sequence` groups.

Every complex type (except empty-content types) has exactly one model group child. This model group child contains the element declarations or references, or other model groups that make up the content model. Element declarations are never directly contained in the `complexType` element.

12.5.1 sequence *groups*

A `sequence` group is used to indicate that elements should appear in a specified order. In all previous examples, we specified a `sequence` group using a `sequence` element, whose syntax is shown in Table 12–4.

Table 12–4   XSD Syntax: `sequence` **group**

Name		
`sequence`		

Parents		
`complexType, restriction, extension, group, choice, sequence`		

Attribute name	Type	Description
`id`	`ID`	Unique ID.
`minOccurs`	`nonNegativeInteger: 1`	Minimum occurrences of the entire sequence.
`maxOccurs`	`nonNegativeInteger | "unbounded" : 1`	Maximum occurrences of the entire sequence.

Content		
`annotation?, (element | group | choice | sequence | any)*`		

Example 12–15 shows a complex type definition that contains a sequence group. All of the children (number, name, size, and color), if they appear, must appear in that order. The fact that the minOccurs attribute of the size and color element declarations is set to 0 means that they are optional.

Example 12–15. A sequence group

```
<xs:complexType name="ProductType">
  <xs:sequence>
    <xs:element name="number" type="xs:integer"/>
    <xs:element name="name" type="xs:string"/>
    <xs:element name="size" type="SizeType" minOccurs="0"/>
    <xs:element name="color" type="ColorType" minOccurs="0"/>
  </xs:sequence>
</xs:complexType>
```

Example 12–16 shows some valid instances of ProductType. They are valid because the elements that are required (i.e., do not have their minOccurs set to 0) do appear and the elements that appear are in the correct order.

Example 12–16. Valid instances of ProductType

```
<product>
  <number>557</number>
  <name>Short-Sleeved Linen Blouse</name>
  <size system="US-DRESS">10</size>
  <color value="blue"/>
</product>

<product>
  <number>557</number>
  <name>Short-Sleeved Linen Blouse</name>
</product>

<product>
  <number>557</number>
  <name>Short-Sleeved Linen Blouse</name>
  <color value="blue"/>
</product>
```

Example 12–17 shows an invalid instance of `ProductType`. It is invalid because the elements appear in the wrong order.

Example 12–17. Invalid instance of `ProductType`

```
<product>
  <number>557</number>
  <size system="US-DRESS">10</size>
  <name>Short-Sleeved Linen Blouse</name>
  <color value="blue"/>
</product>
```

12.5.1.1 Design hint: Should I care about the order of elements?

You may not be concerned about the order in which an element's children appear. However, some constraints will only work if you enforce an order. For example, in version 1.0, it is not possible to say that a `product` may have one `number`, one `name`, and up to three `color` children, in any order. You could use an `all` group if you only want to allow each element once, or you could use a `choice` group if you do not mind there being more than one `number` or `name`. You could also use a `choice` group containing several `sequence` groups to iterate over all the possible orders of the child elements, but this is rather cumbersome and becomes explosively more cumbersome as more children are added. In order to ensure that you will only have one `number` and one `name`, and allow more than one `color`, the best approach is to enforce the order and use a `sequence` group, as shown in Example 12–18.

Version 1.1 relaxes some constraints on `all` groups, making it possible to express the above constraint without forcing a particular order. However, `sequence` groups still have a slight advantage of clarity and ease of processing over `all` groups.

Example 12–18. Enforcing order for better constraints

```
<xs:complexType name="ProductType">
  <xs:sequence>
    <xs:element name="number" type="xs:integer"/>
    <xs:element name="name" type="xs:string"/>
    <xs:element name="color" type="ColorType" maxOccurs="3"/>
  </xs:sequence>
</xs:complexType>
```

12.5.2 choice *groups*

A `choice` group is used to indicate that only one of the declared elements must appear. This is accomplished using a `choice` element, whose syntax is shown in Table 12–5.

Table 12–5 XSD Syntax: `choice` group

Name
choice

Parents
complexType, restriction, extension, group, choice, sequence

Attribute name	Type	Description
id	ID	Unique ID.
minOccurs	nonNegativeInteger: *1*	Minimum occurrences of the choice.
maxOccurs	nonNegativeInteger | "unbounded" : *1*	Maximum occurrences of the choice.

Content
annotation?, (element | group | choice | sequence | any)*

Example 12–19 shows a choice group that specifies that any one of the elements (shirt, hat, or umbrella) must appear.

Example 12–19. A choice group

```
<xs:complexType name="ItemsType">
  <xs:choice>
    <xs:element name="shirt" type="ShirtType"/>
    <xs:element name="hat" type="HatType"/>
    <xs:element name="umbrella" type="UmbrellaType"/>
  </xs:choice>
</xs:complexType>
```

Example 12–20 shows some valid instances of ItemsType. They are valid because each contains exactly one element declared in the choice group. If more than one element appeared, or no elements at all appeared, it would be invalid.

Example 12–20. Valid instances of ItemsType

```
<items>
  <shirt>...</shirt>
</items>

<items>
  <hat>...</hat>
</items>
```

A common use case for choice groups is to allow any number of children to appear in any order. If, in our example above, we allowed the choice group to repeat itself by setting its maxOccurs attribute to unbounded, as shown in Example 12–21, that would entirely change the meaning of the group. Now it allows any of the children, any number of times, in any order.

Example 12–22 shows a valid instance of the new definition of ItemsType.

Example 12–21. A repeating `choice` group

```
<xs:complexType name="ItemsType">
  <xs:choice minOccurs="0" maxOccurs="unbounded">
    <xs:element name="shirt" type="ShirtType"/>
    <xs:element name="umbrella" type="UmbrellaType"/>
    <xs:element name="hat" type="HatType"/>
  </xs:choice>
</xs:complexType>
```

Example 12–22. Valid instance of `ItemsType`

```
<items>
  <shirt>...</shirt>
  <hat>...</hat>
  <umbrella>...</umbrella>
  <shirt>...</shirt>
  <shirt>...</shirt>
</items>
```

In Example 12–21, we also set the `minOccurs` attribute of the `choice` group to `0`. This means that `items` would also be valid if it were completely empty.

Use of repeating `choice` groups is especially common in narrative document-oriented XML, where child elements can be intermingled with character data content and their number and position needs to be very flexible. Example 12–9 on p. 265 showed a typical mixed-content complex type that uses a repeating choice group to allow any number of `i`, `b`, and `u` elements to appear any number of times, in any order. Substitution groups, described in Chapter 16, are another approach to defining such a structure.

12.5.3 *Nesting of* sequence *and* choice *groups*

In order to specify more advanced content models, `sequence` and `choice` groups can be nested within each other as many levels deep as necessary. Example 12–23 shows a slightly more complicated definition of `ProductType`. With this definition, `number` must appear first, then name, then any number of the properties (such as size or color) of the product, in any order. Note that the choice group is inside the sequence group, allowing you to combine the power of both kinds of model groups.

Example 12–23. Multiple nested groups

```
<xs:complexType name="ProductType">
  <xs:sequence>
    <xs:element name="number" type="xs:integer"/>
    <xs:element name="name" type="xs:string"/>
    <xs:choice minOccurs="0" maxOccurs="unbounded">
      <xs:element name="size" type="SizeType"/>
      <xs:element name="color" type="ColorType"/>
    </xs:choice>
  </xs:sequence>
</xs:complexType>
```

12.5.4 all *groups*

An all group is used to indicate that elements can appear in any order. This is accomplished by using an all element, whose syntax is shown in Table 12–6.

An all group follows rules that are different from choice and sequence groups:

- In version 1.0, it can only contain element declarations and references, not other groups or wildcards. In version 1.1, this constraint has been relaxed, and an all group can contain wildcards and group references, as long as those groups also use all.
- In version 1.0, for each element it contains, maxOccurs must be 1, and minOccurs may only be 0 or 1. In version 1.1, this constraint has been eliminated; both minOccurs and maxOccurs can be greater than 1, and maxOccurs can be unbounded.

Table 12–6   XSD Syntax: `all` group

Name		
`all`		

Parents		
`complexType, restriction, extension, group`		

Attribute name	*Type*	*Description*
`id`	`ID`	Unique ID.
`minOccurs`	`"0"	"1" : 1`	Whether the entire group is optional.
`maxOccurs`	`"0"	"1" : 1`	Indicates that the `all` group cannot repeat.

Content		
`annotation?, (element | `any | `group)*`		

- It cannot occur multiple times. For the `all` element itself, `maxOccurs` must be 1, and `minOccurs` may only be 0 or 1.
- It cannot appear in other model groups. An `all` group must be at the top level of the complex type.

Example 12–24 uses an `all` group to represent the same basic structure for `product` elements, with no specific order for the children.

Example 12–24. An `all` group

```
<xs:complexType name="ProductType">
  <xs:all>
    <xs:element name="number" type="xs:integer"/>
    <xs:element name="name" type="xs:string"/>
    <xs:element name="size" type="SizeType" minOccurs="0"/>
    <xs:element name="color" type="ColorType" minOccurs="0"/>
  </xs:all>
</xs:complexType>
```

Example 12–25 shows some valid instances of `ProductType`, according to the new definition. The `name` and `number` elements are still required, but now they may appear in any order.

As mentioned above, an `all` group cannot appear inside another model group. Example 12–26 is illegal because the `all` group is inside a `sequence` group.

Example 12–25. Valid instances of `ProductType` using an `all` group

```
<product>
  <color value="blue"/>
  <size system="US-DRESS">10</size>
  <number>557</number>
  <name>Short-Sleeved Linen Blouse</name>
</product>

<product>
  <name>Short-Sleeved Linen Blouse</name>
  <number>557</number>
</product>
```

Example 12–26. An illegal `all` group

```
<xs:complexType name="ProductType">
  <xs:sequence>
    <xs:element name="number" type="xs:integer"/>
    <xs:element name="name" type="xs:string"/>
    <xs:all>
      <xs:element name="size" type="SizeType" minOccurs="0"/>
      <xs:element name="color" type="ColorType" minOccurs="0"/>
    </xs:all>
  </xs:sequence>
</xs:complexType>
```

12.5.5 *Named model group references*

Named model groups may be referenced in complex type definitions, in order to make use of predefined content model fragments. Named model groups are described in detail in Section 15.2 on p. 386. Example 12–27 shows a reference to a named model group in a complex type definition.

Example 12–27. Complex type with a named model group reference

```
<xs:complexType name="ProductType">
  <xs:sequence>
    <xs:group ref="DescriptionGroup"/>
    <xs:element name="number" type="xs:integer"/>
    <xs:element name="name" type="xs:string"/>
  </xs:sequence>
</xs:complexType>
```

12.5.6 *Deterministic content models*

Like XML DTDs, XML Schema requires that content models be deterministic. In XML Schema, this is known as the Unique Particle Attribution (UPA) constraint. A schema processor, as it makes its way through the children of an instance element, must be able to find only one branch of the content model that is applicable, without having to look ahead to the rest of the children. The classic example is Example 12–28. It is intended to represent a choice among a, b, and a followed by b.

Example 12–28. Illegal nondeterministic content model

```
<xs:complexType name="AOrBOrBothType">
  <xs:choice>
    <xs:element name="a" type="xs:string"/>
    <xs:element name="b" type="xs:string"/>
    <xs:sequence>
      <xs:element name="a" type="xs:string"/>
      <xs:element name="b" type="xs:string"/>
    </xs:sequence>
  </xs:choice>
</xs:complexType>
```

This content model is nondeterministic because the processor, if it first encounters a, will not know whether it should validate it against the first declaration of a or the second declaration of a without looking ahead to see if there is also a child b. It may seem that it should not matter which a declaration we are talking about; they both have the same type. However, they may have other properties that are different, such as default values, identity constraints, or annotations.

Example 12–29 represents the same desired content model in a deterministic way. There is only one declaration of a. There are two declarations of b, but distinguishing between them does not require looking ahead. If the processor encounters b as the first child, it knows to use the second declaration of b. If it encounters b after a, it uses the first declaration of b.

In this example, the conflict is between two element declarations with the same name. However, there are also more subtle conflicts, such as those between

- Two element wildcards whose valid values overlap
- An element declaration and a wildcard for which it is a valid replacement[1]
- An element declaration and the head of its substitution group

Example 12–29. Deterministic content model

```
<xs:complexType name="AOrBOrBothType">
  <xs:choice>
    <xs:sequence>
      <xs:element name="a" type="xs:string"/>
      <xs:element name="b" type="xs:string" minOccurs="0"/>
    </xs:sequence>
    <xs:element name="b" type="xs:string"/>
  </xs:choice>
</xs:complexType>
```

---

1.   This is a conflict in version 1.0 only. In version 1.1, the element declaration has precedence over the wildcard.

12.6 | Using attribute declarations

As with elements, attributes can be included in complex types as local declarations, as references to global declarations, or via attribute group references.

Within complex type definitions, attributes must be specified after the content model. The local attribute declarations, attribute references, and attribute group references may appear in any order, intermixed with each other. There is no significance to the ordering of attributes in XML.

It is illegal to define a complex type that contains two attribute declarations with the same qualified name. This is understandable, since XML forbids this. However, if two attribute declarations have the same local name but different namespace names, they may both appear in the same complex type.

12.6.1 *Local attribute declarations*

Complex type definitions can contain local attribute declarations. This means that the attributes are declared (that is, given a name, a type, and other properties) within the complex type. The scope of that attribute declaration is limited to the complex type within which it appears. Local attribute declarations are described in detail in Section 7.2.2 on p. 117.

Example 12–30 shows adding a local attribute declaration to `ProductType`. Note that the attribute declaration appears after the sequence group that represents the content model.

Example 12–30. Local attribute declaration

```
<xs:complexType name="ProductType">
  <xs:sequence>
    <!--...-->
  </xs:sequence>
  <xs:attribute name="effDate" type="xs:date"
                default="1900-01-01"/>
</xs:complexType>
```

12.6.2 *Attribute references*

Complex type definitions can also contain references to global attribute declarations. Global attribute declarations themselves are covered in detail in Section 7.2.1 on p. 115. The syntax used to reference a global attribute declaration is shown in Table 12–7.

Table 12–7   XSD Syntax: attribute reference

Name
attribute

Parents
complexType, restriction, extension, attributeGroup

Attribute name	Type	Description
id	ID	Unique ID.
ref	QName	Name of the attribute being referenced.
use	"optional" | "prohibited" | "required" : *optional*	Whether the attribute is required.
default	string	Default value for the attribute, see Section 7.5.1.
fixed	string	Fixed value for the attribute, see Section 7.5.2.
▪inheritable	boolean	Whether the value can be inherited by descendant elements, see Section 7.6.

Content
annotation?

The `use` attribute may be used to indicate whether the attribute is required or optional. The value `prohibited` is used only when restricting complex types. If `required` is chosen, then a default or fixed value in the global attribute declaration are ignored.

The `default` attribute may be used to add a default value, or to override the `default` attribute in the global attribute declaration. This is true for attribute references only; an element reference cannot override the default value in a global element declaration.

The `fixed` attribute may be used to add a fixed value, but it cannot override or remove a fixed value specified in the global attribute declaration. Only one of `default` and `fixed` may appear; they are mutually exclusive.

The `inheritable` attribute may be used to indicate that the attribute is inheritable, as described in Section 7.6 on p. 126. If it is not specified, it defaults to the `inheritable` value of the global attribute declaration, which itself defaults to `false`.

Example 12–31 shows a complex type definition with a reference to a global attribute declaration. Note that the `type` attribute is in the global attribute declaration. In this case, the `default` attribute in the attribute reference overrides the `default` attribute in the global attribute declaration.

For a detailed discussion of local or global attribute declarations see Section 7.2.3 on p. 119.

Example 12–31. Attribute reference

```
<xs:schema xmlns:xs="http://www.w3.org/2001/XMLSchema">
  <xs:attribute name="effDate" type="xs:date"
                default="1900-01-01"/>

  <xs:complexType name="ProductType">
    <xs:sequence>
      <!--...-->
    </xs:sequence>
    <xs:attribute ref="effDate" default="2000-12-31"/>
  </xs:complexType>
</xs:schema>
```

12.6.3 *Attribute group references*

Attribute groups may be referenced in complex type definitions, in order to make use of predefined groups of attributes. Attribute groups are described in detail in Section 15.3 on p. 392. Example 12–32 shows a complex type definition that references the attribute group `IdentifierGroup`.

Example 12–32. Complex type with attribute group reference

```
<xs:complexType name="ProductType">
  <xs:sequence>
    <!--...-->
  </xs:sequence>
  <xs:attributeGroup ref="IdentifierGroup"/>
  <xs:attribute name="effDate" type="xs:date"/>
</xs:complexType>
```

12.6.4 *Default attributes*

In version 1.1, it is possible to indicate that an attribute group is the default attribute group by specifying its name in the `defaultAttributes` attribute on the `schema` element. If such a default attribute group is defined, those attributes will automatically be allowed for every complex type in the schema document, unless you specifically disallow it. To disallow it, use the attribute `defaultAttributesApply="false"` to your complex type. Default attribute groups are described further in Section 15.3.3 on p. 399.

12.7 | Using wildcards

Wildcards allow for more flexibility in the content models and attributes defined in a complex type. There are two kinds of wildcards: element wildcards, which use the `any` element, and attribute wildcards, which use the `anyAttribute` element.

12.7.1 *Element wildcards*

Element wildcards provide flexibility in which child elements may appear. Element wildcards are represented by `any` elements, whose syntax is shown in Table 12–8. The elements in an instance that match the wildcard are referred to as *replacement elements* in this book.

Table 12–8   XSD Syntax: element wildcard

Name		
`any`		

Parents		
`choice, sequence, `▪`all, `▪`openContent, `▪`defaultOpenContent`		

Attribute name	*Type*	*Description*
`id`	`ID`	Unique ID.
`minOccurs`	`nonNegativeInteger: 1`	Minimum number of replacement elements that may appear.
`maxOccurs`	`nonNegativeInteger | "unbounded" : 1`	Maximum number of replacement elements that may appear.
`namespace`	`"##any" | "##other" | `list of `(anyURI | "##targetNamespace" | "##local")`	Which namespace(s) the replacement elements may be in.
`processContents`	`"lax" | "skip" | "strict" : strict`	How strictly to validate the replacement elements.
▪`notNamespace`	list of `(anyURI | "##targetNamespace" | "##local")`	Which namespace(s) the replacement elements may *not* be in.
▪`notQName`	list of `(QName | "##defined" | "##definedSibling")`	Which elements may not be used as replacement elements.

Content		
`annotation?`		

The `minOccurs` and `maxOccurs` attributes control the number of replacement elements. This number represents how many total replacement elements may appear, not how many of a particular type or how many types. The number does not include child elements of the replacement elements.

Example 12–33 shows a complex type definition for `ProductType` that includes an element wildcard allowing any number of replacement elements at the end of the content model.

Example 12–33. Using an element wildcard

```
<xs:element name="product" type="ProductType"/>
<xs:complexType name="ProductType">
  <xs:sequence>
    <xs:element name="number" type="xs:integer"/>
    <xs:element name="name" type="xs:string"/>
    <xs:any minOccurs="0" maxOccurs="unbounded"/>
  </xs:sequence>
</xs:complexType>
<xs:element name="color" type="xs:string"/>
<xs:element name="desc" type="xs:string"/>
<xs:element name="size" type="xs:integer"/>
```

Example 12–34 is a valid `product` instance. It has three replacement elements: two `color` elements and a `size` element, which can appear in any numbers and in any order.

Example 12–34. Instance with replacement elements

```
<product>
  <number>557</number>
  <name>Short-Sleeved Linen Blouse</name>
  <color>blue</color>
  <size>12</size>
  <color>red</color>
</product>
```

12.7.1.1 Controlling the namespace of replacement elements

The `namespace` attribute allows you to specify what namespaces the replacement elements may belong to. It may have the value `##any`, `##other`, or a list of values.

If it is `##any`, the replacement elements can be in any namespace whatsoever, or in no namespace. This is the default setting if neither the `namespace` nor the `notNamespace` attribute have been specified.

If it is `##other`, the replacement elements can be in any namespace other than the target namespace of the schema document, but they must be in a namespace. If the schema document has no target namespace, the replacement elements can have any namespace, but they must have one.

Otherwise, the value of the `namespace` attribute can be a whitespace-separated list of values that may include any or all of the following items:

- `##targetNamespace` to indicate that the replacement elements may be in the target namespace of the schema document
- `##local` to indicate that the replacement elements may be in no namespace
- Specific namespace names for the replacement elements

The namespace constraint applies only to the replacement elements. The children of each replacement element, if they exist, are then validated according to the type of the replacement element.

12.7.1.2 Controlling the strictness of validation

The `processContents` attribute controls how much validation takes place on the replacement elements. It may have one of three values:

- If it is `skip`, the schema processor performs no validation whatsoever, and does not attempt to find a schema document associated with the wildcard's namespace. The replacement elements must, however, be well-formed XML and must be in one of the namespaces allowed by the wildcard.

- If it is `lax`, the schema processor will validate replacement elements for which it can find declarations and raise errors if they are invalid. It will not, however, report errors on the elements for which it does not find declarations.

- If it is `strict`, the schema processor will attempt to find a schema document associated with the namespace, and validate all of the replacement elements. If it cannot find the schema document, or the elements are invalid, it will raise errors. This is the default value.

Suppose our `product` element can also contain an extended textual description that may run several paragraphs. This description is going to appear on the company's website, and we want the text to be formatted using XHTML. Example 12–35 shows an element wildcard that will allow `DescriptionType` to contain any elements that are part of the XHTML namespace.

Example 12–35. **Complex type with element wildcard**

```
<xs:complexType name="DescriptionType" mixed="true">
  <xs:sequence>
    <xs:any namespace="http://www.w3.org/1999/xhtml"
            minOccurs="0" maxOccurs="unbounded"
            processContents="skip"/>
  </xs:sequence>
</xs:complexType>
```

Example 12–36 shows a `description` element which has the type `DescriptionType`.

Since the `processContents` attribute is set to `skip`, it is not necessary to provide any information about where to find the schema to validate the replacement elements. It is only necessary that the elements in the instance have names that are qualified with the XHTML namespace. In our example, we accomplish this by associating the

Example 12–36. Instance with `processContents` of `skip`

```
<catalog xmlns:xhtml="http://www.w3.org/1999/xhtml">

  <description>
    This shirt is the <xhtml:b>best-selling</xhtml:b> shirt in
    our catalog! <xhtml:br/> Note: runs large.
  </description>
  <!--...-->
</catalog>
```

`xhtml` prefix with the XHTML namespace, and by prefixing all of the XHTML element names.

If we had chosen `strict` for the value of `processContents`, we would have to go further and tell the processor where to find the XHTML schema. We could do this by importing the XHTML namespace and schema into our schema, as described in Section 4.3.2 on p. 66.

12.7.1.3 Negative wildcards

Version 1.1 provides two additional attributes for wildcards that allow you to specify namespaces and names that are disallowed for replacement elements.

The `notNamespace` attribute allows you to specify the namespaces that the replacement elements may *not* belong to. It is a whitespace-separated list of values that may include any or all of the following items:

- `##targetNamespace` to indicate that the replacement elements may not be in the target namespace of the schema document.

- `##local` to indicate that the replacement elements must be in a namespace.

- Specific disallowed namespace names for the replacement elements.

The notNamespace and the namespace attributes on wildcards are mutually exclusive. They cannot both be specified. If neither is specified, the replacement elements can be in any namespace.

The notQName attribute allows you to disallow certain elements from being replacement elements. It is a whitespace-separated list of values that may include any or all of the following items:

- ##defined, to disallow replacement elements whose names match global element declarations in the schema.

- ##definedSibling, to disallow replacement elements whose names match declarations (local element declarations or element references) in the same complex type, i.e. that could be siblings of the replacement element.

- Specific names for the disallowed replacement elements, which may or may not actually be declared in the schema; if these names are in a namespace, they must be prefixed appropriately or use in-scope default namespace declarations to assign the namespace.

Example 12–37 shows the use of the notNamespace and notQName attributes, which can be used together or individually.

Example 12–37. Negative wildcards

```
<xs:element name="product" type="ProductType"/>
<xs:complexType name="ProductType">
  <xs:sequence>
    <xs:element name="number" type="xs:integer"/>
    <xs:element name="name" type="xs:string"/>
    <xs:any minOccurs="0" maxOccurs="unbounded"
            notNamespace="http://www.w3.org/1999/xhtml"
            notQName="##definedSibling desc size"
            processContents="lax"/>
  </xs:sequence>
</xs:complexType>
<xs:element name="color" type="xs:string"/>
<xs:element name="size" type="xs:integer"/>
```

Example 12–38 is a valid `product` instance. It has three replacement elements: two `color` elements and a `random` element. Neither `color` nor `random` is in the prohibited namespace or in the list of prohibited names. The `random` element is allowed even though it is not declared in the schema, because `processContents` is set to `lax`.

***Example 12–38.** Instance conforming to the schema with negative wildcards*

```
<product>
  <number>557</number>
  <name>Short-Sleeved Linen Blouse</name>
  <color>blue</color>
  <random>not declared in the schema</random>
  <color>red</color>
</product>
```

Example 12–39 is a `product` instance where every replacement element shown is invalid. A `size` element is disallowed from being a replacement element because it is listed in `notQName`, as is `desc`, even though there is no declaration for `desc` in the schema. Also disallowed as replacement elements are `number` and `name`, since `##definedSibling` is specified. Finally, there can be no replacement elements from the XHTML namespace because that namespace is listed in `notNamespace`.

***Example 12–39.** Invalid instance with disallowed namespaces and names*

```
<product xmlns:xhtml="http://www.w3.org/1999/xhtml">
  <number>557</number>
  <name>Short-Sleeved Linen Blouse</name>
  <size>12</size>
  <desc>Our best-selling shirt</desc>
  <number>12345</number>
  <xhtml:p>Our best-selling shirt</xhtml:p>
</product>
```

12.7.2 *Open content models*

Some XML vocabularies need to be very flexible about where they allow extension elements. To this end, version 1.1 allows you to specify an *open content model*, which is essentially an element wildcard that allows replacement elements to appear interleaved with other elements, without forcing the schema author to explicitly specify wildcards between every element declaration in a content model. An open content model can apply to a single complex type, or be declared as the default for complex types in a schema document.

12.7.2.1 Open content in a complex type

An open content model for a single complex type is defined using an openContent element, whose syntax is shown in Table 12–9. The openContent element always appears before the content model. It contains a standard any wildcard as defined in Section 12.7.1 on p. 285. The one difference is that the wildcard inside the openContent

Table 12–9   XSD Syntax: open content

Name		
openContent		

Parent		
complexType, extension, restriction		

Attribute name	Type	Description
id	ID	Unique ID.
mode	"none" | "interleave" | "suffix" : *interleave*	Where replacement elements are allowed to appear.

Content		
annotation?, any?		

cannot have `minOccurs` and `maxOccurs` specified; it is implied that any number of replacement elements can appear.

The `openContent` element has a `mode` attribute that indicates where the replacement elements can appear.

- If it is `interleave` (the default), the replacement elements can appear intermingled with the elements explicitly declared in the content model.

- If it is `suffix`, the replacement elements can only appear at the end of the content.

- If it is `none`, no any child appears within `openContent` and the content model is not open (this is primarily used to override a default open content model).

The complex type in Example 12–40 contains an `openContent` element that allows any element from any other namespace to appear interleaved in the instance.

Example 12–40. Defining an interleaved open content model

```
<xs:element name="product" type="OpenProductType"/>
<xs:complexType name="OpenProductType">
  <xs:openContent>
    <xs:any namespace="##other" processContents="lax"/>
  </xs:openContent>
  <xs:sequence>
    <xs:element name="number" type="xs:integer"/>
    <xs:element name="name" type="xs:string"/>
  </xs:sequence>
</xs:complexType>
```

Example 12–41 shows a valid instance, where the `product` element contains elements from an extension namespace interleaved with the declared `number` and `name` elements. The `number` and `name` elements must still conform to the content model specified in the `sequence` group.

Example 12–41. Instance of an interleaved open content model

```
<product xmlns:ext="http://datypic.com/extension">
  <ext:something>an extension element</ext:something>
  <number>557</number>
  <ext:something_else>another extension element</ext:something_else>
  <name>Short-Sleeved Linen Blouse</name>
  <ext:something_else>another extension element</ext:something_else>
  <ext:something>an extension element</ext:something>
</product>
```

To allow extension elements only at the end, simply add `mode="suffix"` to the `openContent` element, as shown in Example 12–42. This example also has different settings for the wildcard, namely that the replacement elements are being strictly validated and must not be in a namespace.

Example 12–42. Defining a suffix open content model

```
<xs:element name="product" type="OpenProductType"/>
<xs:complexType name="OpenProductType">
  <xs:openContent mode="suffix">
    <xs:any namespace="##local" processContents="strict"/>
  </xs:openContent>
  <xs:sequence>
    <xs:element name="number" type="xs:integer"/>
    <xs:element name="name" type="xs:string"/>
  </xs:sequence>
</xs:complexType>
<xs:element name="something" type="xs:string"/>
```

Example 12–43 is a valid instance, with the replacement elements now at the end. As with the previous example, multiple replacement elements may appear.

This example may not appear to be any different from simply including the wildcard at the end of the sequence group instead of in `openContent`. However, it is subtly different in that extensions of this type will expect the replacement elements to appear at the end of the extended type, not right after the `name` element. This is described further in Section 13.4.2.3 on p. 311.

Example 12–43. Instance of a suffix open content model

```
<product>
  <number>557</number>
  <name>Short-Sleeved Linen Blouse</name>
  <something>an extension element</something>
  <something>an extension element</something>
</product>
```

12.7.2.2 Default open content

It is also possible in version 1.1 to specify a default open content model that can apply to any complex type in the schema that allows children (that is, any one with element-only or mixed content). This is accomplished using a `defaultOpenContent` element, whose syntax shown in Table 12–10.

Table 12–10   XSD Syntax: default open content

Name		
defaultOpenContent		

Parent		
schema		

Attribute name	*Type*	*Description*
id	ID	Unique ID.
appliesToEmpty	boolean : *false*	Whether the open content applies to empty content types.
mode	"interleave" | "suffix" : *interleave*	Where replacement elements are allowed to appear.

Content
annotation?, any

The `defaultOpenContent` element works the same way as the `openContent` element, containing an element wildcard and specifying a `mode` attribute to indicate where the replacement elements can appear. However, since it applies to multiple complex types in a schema document, it appears at the top level of the schema, after any includes, imports, and overrides but before any component definitions. Example 12–44 is a schema that contains a `defaultOpenContent` and two complex types to which it applies.

Example 12–44. Defining a default open content model

```
<xs:schema xmlns:xs="http://www.w3.org/2001/XMLSchema">

  <xs:defaultOpenContent mode="suffix">
   <xs:any namespace="##local"/>
  </xs:defaultOpenContent>

  <xs:element name="catalog" type="CatalogType"/>

  <xs:complexType name="CatalogType">
    <xs:sequence>
      <xs:element name="product" type="ProductType"
                  maxOccurs="unbounded"/>
    </xs:sequence>
  </xs:complexType>

  <xs:complexType name="ProductType">
    <xs:sequence>
      <xs:element name="number" type="xs:integer"/>
      <xs:element name="name" type="xs:string"/>
    </xs:sequence>
  </xs:complexType>

  <xs:element name="something" type="xs:string"/>
</xs:schema>
```

A valid instance is shown in Example 12–45, where both the `catalog` and `product` elements can contain replacement elements. In this case, they must appear at the end, since the `mode` is set to `suffix`.

Example 12–45. Instance using default open content model

```
<catalog>
  <product>
    <number>557</number>
    <name>Short-Sleeved Linen Blouse</name>
    <something>an extension element</something>
    <something>an extension element</something>
  </product>
  <something>an extension element</something>
  <something>an extension element</something>
</catalog>
```

If a default open content model is defined, it is possible to override it in an individual complex type using the openContent element with a mode="none" attribute. In Example 12–46, CatalogType will not have open content because it overrides the default, but ProductType will.

Example 12–46. Overriding a default open content model

```
<xs:schema xmlns:xs="http://www.w3.org/2001/XMLSchema">
  <xs:defaultOpenContent mode="suffix">
    <xs:any namespace="##local"/>
  </xs:defaultOpenContent>

  <xs:element name="catalog" type="CatalogType"/>
  <xs:complexType name="CatalogType">
    <xs:openContent mode="none"/>
    <xs:sequence>
      <xs:element name="product" type="ProductType"
                  maxOccurs="unbounded"/>
    </xs:sequence>
  </xs:complexType>

  <xs:complexType name="ProductType">
    <xs:sequence>
      <xs:element name="number" type="xs:integer"/>
      <xs:element name="name" type="xs:string"/>
    </xs:sequence>
  </xs:complexType>
</xs:schema>
```

Note that the default open content model does not apply to complex types with simple content, since they do not allow children. By default, it does not apply to complex types with empty content, either. However, you can use an `appliesToEmpty="true"` attribute on `defaultOpenContent` to indicate that the default open content model *should* apply to complex types with empty content.

12.7.3 *Attribute wildcards*

Attribute wildcards are used to allow flexibility as to what attributes may appear on elements of a particular complex type. Attribute wildcards are represented by `anyAttribute` elements, whose syntax is shown in Table 12–11.

The `namespace`, `processContents`, `notNamespace`, and `notQName` attributes for attribute wildcards work exactly the same as for element wildcards described in Section 12.7.1 on p. 285. The only difference between attribute wildcards and element wildcards is that attribute wildcards cannot have `minOccurs` and `maxOccurs` specified. If an attribute wildcard is present, it is assumed that there may be zero, one, or many replacement attributes present.

Attribute wildcards in a complex type must appear after all of the attribute declarations, attribute references, and attribute group references. There can only be one attribute wildcard in each complex type definition.

Example 12–47 shows the definition of a type that allows any number of replacement attributes from any namespace other than the target namespace of the schema document.

Example 12–47. Complex type with attribute wildcard

```
<xs:complexType name="ProductType">
  <xs:sequence>
    <!--...-->
  </xs:sequence>
  <xs:anyAttribute namespace="##other" processContents="lax"/>
</xs:complexType>
```

Table 12–11   XSD Syntax: attribute wildcard

Name
anyAttribute

Parents
complexType, restriction, extension, attributeGroup

Attribute name	Type	Description
id	ID	Unique ID.
namespace	"##any" | "##other" | list of (anyURI | "##targetNamespace" | "##local")	Which namespace(s) the replacement attributes may be in.
processContents	"lax" | "skip" | "strict" : *strict*	How strictly to validate the replacement attributes.
▣notNamespace	list of (anyURI | "##targetNamespace" | "##local")	Which namespace(s) the replacement attributes may *not* be in.
▣notQName	list of (QName | "##defined")	Which attributes may not be used as replacement attributes.

Content
annotation?

Deriving complex types

Chapter

13

I n the previous chapter, we saw how to define new complex types that are not specifically derived from another type. This chapter covers the complexities of deriving complex types from other types, both complex and simple.

13.1 | Why derive types?

XML Schema allows you to derive a new complex type from an existing simple or complex type. While it is always possible to make a copy of an existing type and modify it to suit your needs, using type derivation has a number of advantages:

- *Subsetting*. If you want to define a more restrictive subset of a schema, the best way to do this is using restriction. Your schema processor will validate that you have in fact defined a legal subset. It also allows future modifications to the original types to be reflected in your derived types automatically.

- *Safe extensions.* If you want to add to existing schema compo-nents, XML Schema's extension mechanism ensures that you do that in such a way that an application can still handle the original definition.

- *Type substitution.* Derived types can substitute for their ancestor types in instances, which is a very flexible way to support variations in content.

- *Reuse.* If several types share the same basic structure but have minor differences, it makes sense to reuse the similar parts. This makes maintenance easier and ensures consistency. Type derivation is one way to reuse content model fragments and attributes.

- *Convenience in a type-aware language.* Languages such as XSLT 2.0 and XQuery are type-aware, which allows you to define processes on base types that may be passed down to their derived types. For example, XSLT 2.0 lets you apply a specific template to "anything of type `AddressType` or any type derived from it."

13.2 | Restriction and extension

Complex types are derived from other types either by restriction or extension.

- *Restriction*, as the name suggests, restricts the valid contents of a type. The values for the new type are a subset of those for the base type. All values of the restricted type are also valid according to the base type.

- *Extension* allows for adding children and/or attributes to a type. Values of the base type are not necessarily valid for the extended type, since required elements or attributes may be added.

It is not possible to restrict and extend a complex type at the same time, but it is possible to do this in two steps, first extending a type, and then restricting the extension, or vice versa. However, when doing this, it is not legal to remove something in a restriction and then use extension to add it back in an incompatible way; for example, you cannot re-add an element declaration with a different type.

13.3 | Simple content and complex content

A complex type always has either simple content or complex content. Simple content means that it has only character data content, with no children. Complex content encompasses the other three content types (mixed, element-only, and empty) that were covered in Section 12.3 on p. 262. A complex type is derived from another type using either a `simpleContent` element or a `complexContent` element.

13.3.1 `simpleContent` *elements*

A `simpleContent` element is used when deriving a complex type from a simple type, or from another complex type with simple content. This can be done to add or remove attribute declarations, or to further restrict the simple type of the character content. If a complex type has simple content, all types derived from it, directly or indirectly, must also have simple content. It is impossible to switch from simple content to complex content by deriving a type with child elements. Table 13–1 shows the syntax for a `simpleContent` element. It contains either an `extension` or a `restriction` child element. These elements are discussed in Sections 13.4.1 on p. 306 and 13.5.1 on p. 317, respectively.

Table 13–1   XSD Syntax: simple content definition

Name		
simpleContent		

Parents		
complexType		

Attribute name	*Type*	*Description*
id	ID	Unique ID.

Content		
annotation?, (extension | restriction)		

13.3.2 complexContent *elements*

A complexContent element is used when deriving a complex type from another complex type which itself has complex content. This includes mixed, element-only, and empty content types. This can be done to add or remove parts of the content model as well as attribute declarations. Table 13–2 shows the syntax for a complexContent

Table 13–2   XSD Syntax: complex content definition

Name		
complexContent		

Parents		
complexType		

Attribute name	*Type*	*Description*
id	ID	Unique ID.
mixed	boolean	Whether the complex type allows mixed content; defaults to mixed value of complexType.

Content		
annotation?, (extension | restriction)		

element. It too must contain either an `extension` or a `restriction`, but with definitions different from their counterparts in `simpleContent`. These elements are discussed in Sections 13.4.2 on p. 307 and 13.5.2 on p. 318, respectively.

If `complexContent` has a `mixed` attribute, that value is used. If it has no `mixed` attribute, the `mixed` attribute of `complexType` is used. If neither element has a `mixed` attribute, the default for `mixed` is `false`.

13.4 | Complex type extensions

Complex types may be extended by adding to the content model and to the attribute declarations. Table 13–3 shows the legal extensions for each content type.

Table 13–3 Legal extensions by content type

		BASE TYPE				
		Simple type	*Complex type*			
			Simple content	*Element-only*	*Mixed*	*Empty*
DERIVED TYPE	*Simple type*	no	no	no	no	no
Complex type	*Simple content*	yes, see 13.4.1	yes, see 13.4.1	no	no	no
	Element-only	no	no	yes, see 13.4.2	no	yes, see 13.4.4
	Mixed	no	no	no	yes, see 13.4.3	yes, see 13.4.4
	Empty	no	no	no	no	yes, see 13.4.4

13.4.1 *Simple content extensions*

The only purpose of simple content extensions is to add attribute declarations. It is not possible to extend the value space of the simple content, just as it is not possible to extend the value space of a simple type. Table 13–4 shows the syntax for an `extension` element that is the child of a `simpleContent` element.

Table 13–4   XSD Syntax: simple content extension

Name		
`extension`		

Parents		
`simpleContent`		

Attribute name	Type	Description
`id`	`ID`	Unique ID.
base	`QName`	Base type being extended.

Content		
`annotation?, (attribute | attributeGroup)*, anyAttribute?,` ▣`assert*`		

Example 13–1. Simple content extension

Schema:

```
<xs:complexType name="SizeType">
  <xs:simpleContent>
    <xs:extension base="xs:integer">
      <xs:attribute name="system" type="xs:token"/>
    </xs:extension>
  </xs:simpleContent>
</xs:complexType>
```

Instance:

```
<size system="US-DRESS">10</size>
```

Example 13–1 shows the definition of a complex type SizeType that has simple content. It has a content type of integer, and it has been extended to add the system attribute declaration. A valid instance is also shown.

13.4.2 *Complex content extensions*

Complex content extensions allow you to add to the end of the content model of the base type. You can also add attribute declarations, but you cannot modify or remove the base type's attribute declarations. Table 13–5 shows the syntax for an extension element that is the child of a complexContent element.

Table 13–5   XSD Syntax: complex content extension

Name
extension

Parents
complexContent

Attribute name	Type	Description
id	ID	Unique ID.
base	QName	Base type being extended.

Content
annotation?, ▣openContent?, (group | all | choice | sequence)?, (attribute | attributeGroup)*, anyAttribute?, ▣assert*

When defining a complex content extension, you do not need to copy the content model from the base type. The processor handles complex content extensions by appending the new content model after the base type's content model, as if they were together in a sequence group.

Example 13–2 shows a complex content extension. The complex type `ProductType` has two children: `number` and `name`. The type `ShirtType` extends `ProductType` by adding a `choice` group containing two additional children: `size` and `color`.

The effective content model of `ShirtType` is shown in Example 13–3. It is as if there were a `sequence` group at the top level of the

Example 13–2. Complex content extension

```
<xs:complexType name="ProductType">
  <xs:sequence>
    <xs:element name="number" type="xs:integer"/>
    <xs:element name="name" type="xs:string"/>
  </xs:sequence>
</xs:complexType>

<xs:complexType name="ShirtType">
  <xs:complexContent>
    <xs:extension base="ProductType">
      <xs:choice maxOccurs="unbounded">
        <xs:element name="size" type="xs:integer"/>
        <xs:element name="color" type="xs:string"/>
      </xs:choice>
    </xs:extension>
  </xs:complexContent>
</xs:complexType>
```

Example 13–3. Effective content model of `ShirtType`

```
<xs:complexType name="ShirtType">
  <xs:sequence>
    <xs:sequence>
      <xs:element name="number" type="xs:integer"/>
      <xs:element name="name" type="xs:string"/>
    </xs:sequence>
    <xs:choice maxOccurs="unbounded">
      <xs:element name="size" type="xs:integer"/>
      <xs:element name="color" type="xs:string"/>
    </xs:choice>
  </xs:sequence>
</xs:complexType>
```

complex type, which contains the content model of ProductType, followed by the content model extensions specified in the ShirtType definition itself.

13.4.2.1 Extending choice groups

Since extending requires the addition of an "artificial" sequence group, extension does not work well as a way to add elements to choice groups. Example 13–4 shows a type ExpandedItemsType that extends ItemsType to add new product types. Intuitively, you may think that the two additional element references, sweater and suit, are added to the choice group, allowing a choice among the five element declarations. In fact, the effective content model of ExpandedItemsType is a sequence group that contains two choice groups. As a result, ExpandedItemsType will require any of the shirt, hat, and umbrella elements to appear before any of the sweater or suit elements.

Example 13–4. choice **group extension**

```
<xs:complexType name="ItemsType">
  <xs:choice maxOccurs="unbounded">
    <xs:element ref="shirt"/>
    <xs:element ref="hat"/>
    <xs:element ref="umbrella"/>
  </xs:choice>
</xs:complexType>

<xs:complexType name="ExpandedItemsType">
  <xs:complexContent>
    <xs:extension base="ItemsType">
      <xs:choice maxOccurs="unbounded">
        <xs:element ref="sweater"/>
        <xs:element ref="suit"/>
      </xs:choice>
    </xs:extension>
  </xs:complexContent>
</xs:complexType>
```

A better way to extend a `choice` group is through substitution groups. See Section 22.2.4 on p. 607 for more information.

13.4.2.2 Extending `all` groups

In version 1.0, extension is not allowed for `all` groups. In version 1.1, this constraint has been relaxed, and complex types that contain `all` groups can be extended, provided that the derived type also uses an `all` group, as shown in Example 13–5.

Example 13–5. `all` group extension

```
<xs:complexType name="ProductType">
  <xs:all>
    <xs:element name="number" type="xs:integer"/>
    <xs:element name="name" type="xs:string"/>
  </xs:all>
</xs:complexType>

<xs:complexType name="ShirtType">
  <xs:complexContent>
    <xs:extension base="ProductType">
      <xs:all>
        <xs:element name="size" type="xs:integer"/>
        <xs:element name="color" type="xs:string"/>
      </xs:all>
    </xs:extension>
  </xs:complexContent>
</xs:complexType>
```

The effective content model in this case is one big `all` group, shown in Example 13–6, not two `all` groups inside a `sequence`.

When extending an `all` group with another `all` group, both groups must have the same value for `minOccurs` (if any). The `minOccurs` of the effective resulting group is the `minOccurs` of both groups. In Example 13–5, the value for both groups defaults to 1, so the group shown in Example 13–6 does also. Alternatively, both of the `all` groups could have, for example, `minOccurs="0"`, in which case the effective `minOccurs` is 0.

Example 13–6. **Effective content model of** `ShirtType` **with** `all` **groups combined**

```
<xs:complexType name="ShirtType">
  <xs:all>
    <xs:element name="number" type="xs:integer"/>
    <xs:element name="name" type="xs:string"/>
    <xs:element name="size" type="xs:integer"/>
    <xs:element name="color" type="xs:string"/>
  </xs:all>
</xs:complexType>
```

13.4.2.3 Extending open content

It is possible to extend a type that has open content, or to add open content in an extension. There are several possible scenarios:

- If `openContent` is specified for the base type but not the derived type, the `openContent` is inherited as is from the base type.
- If `openContent` is specified for the derived type but not the base type, it is considered to be added in the derived type.
- If it is specified in both the base type and the derived type, it must be the same or less restrictive in the derived type. For example, if `mode` is `suffix` in the base type but `interleave` in the derived type, this is legal because it is less constraining. The opposite is not legal; attempting to turn `interleave` mode into `suffix` mode means creating a more restrictive type. In addition, the namespace allowances on the derived type must be the same as, or a superset of, those allowed for the base type.

Example 13–7 shows the case where `openContent` appears in both types. This example is legal because the mode is equally constraining and the list of allowed namespaces is less constraining.

Note that since the `mode` is `suffix`, in an instance of `ShirtType` the replacement elements for the wildcard will go at the very end, after the `color` element. Even though `openContent` is defined for the base type, it is not possible to include replacement elements directly after name, where they would appear in an instance of ProductType.

Example 13–7. Extending open content

```
<xs:complexType name="ProductType">
  <xs:openContent mode="suffix">
    <xs:any namespace="##other" processContents="lax"/>
  </xs:openContent>
  <xs:sequence>
    <xs:element name="number" type="xs:integer"/>
    <xs:element name="name" type="xs:string"/>
  </xs:sequence>
</xs:complexType>

<xs:complexType name="ShirtType">
  <xs:complexContent>
    <xs:extension base="ProductType">
      <xs:openContent mode="suffix">
        <xs:any namespace="##any" processContents="lax"/>
      </xs:openContent>
      <xs:sequence>
        <xs:element name="size" type="xs:integer"/>
        <xs:element name="color" type="xs:string"/>
      </xs:sequence>
    </xs:extension>
  </xs:complexContent>
</xs:complexType>
```

13.4.3 *Mixed content extensions*

Complex types with mixed content can be extended, but the derived type must also have mixed content. The extension is treated the same way as it is for element-only complex types described in the previous section. It is illegal to extend a mixed content type to result in an element-only content type. The reverse is also true; it is illegal to extend an element-only content type to result in a mixed content type.

When extending a mixed content type, you must also specify the `mixed` attribute for the derived type. Example 13–8 shows a mixed complex type `LetterType` that is extended to derive another mixed complex type, `ExtendedLetterType`.

Example 13–8. Mixed content extension

```
<xs:complexType name="LetterType" mixed="true">
  <xs:sequence>
    <xs:element name="custName" type="xs:string"/>
    <xs:element name="prodName" type="xs:string"/>
    <xs:element name="prodSize" type="xs:integer"/>
  </xs:sequence>
</xs:complexType>

<xs:complexType name="ExtendedLetterType" mixed="true">
  <xs:complexContent>
    <xs:extension base="LetterType">
      <xs:sequence>
        <xs:element name="prodNum" type="xs:string"/>
      </xs:sequence>
    </xs:extension>
  </xs:complexContent>
</xs:complexType>
```

13.4.4 *Empty content extensions*

Complex types with empty content can be extended to add a content model and/or attribute declarations. Example 13–9 shows an empty complex type named `ItemType`, which is extended by `ProductType` to add a `sequence` group containing two element declarations.

Example 13–9. Empty content extension

```
<xs:complexType name="ItemType">
  <xs:attribute name="routingNum" type="xs:integer"/>
</xs:complexType>
```

(Continues)

Example 13–9.   (Continued)

```
<xs:complexType name="ProductType">
  <xs:complexContent>
    <xs:extension base="ItemType">
      <xs:sequence>
        <xs:element name="number" type="xs:integer"/>
        <xs:element name="name" type="xs:string"/>
      </xs:sequence>
    </xs:extension>
  </xs:complexContent>
</xs:complexType>
```

13.4.5 *Attribute extensions*

When defining an extension, you may specify additional attribute declarations in the derived type's definition. When extending complex types, attributes are always passed down from the base type to the new type. It is not necessary (or even legal) to repeat any attribute declarations from the base type or any other ancestors in the new type definition. It is not possible to modify or remove any attribute declarations from the base type in an extension.

Example 13–10 shows the definition of ProductType, which extends ItemType. It adds two attribute declarations: effDate and lang. It may be surprising that lang is legal, since it appears in the base type definition. This is because the new lang is in a different namespace, so it is allowed. The lang in the base type definition must be prefixed when it appears in the instance, as shown in the instance example.

Example 13–10. Attribute extension

Schema:

```
<xs:complexType name="ItemType">
  <xs:attribute name="id" type="xs:ID" use="required"/>
  <xs:attribute ref="xml:lang"/>
</xs:complexType>
```

(Continues)

Example 13–10.   (Continued)

```
<xs:complexType name="ProductType">
  <xs:complexContent>
    <xs:extension base="ItemType">
      <xs:attribute name="effDate" type="xs:date"/>
      <xs:attribute name="lang" type="xs:language"/>
    </xs:extension>
  </xs:complexContent>
</xs:complexType>
```

Instance:

```
<product id="prod557"
  xml:lang="en"
  lang="en"
  effDate="2001-04-12"/>
```

13.4.6 *Attribute wildcard extensions*

If an attribute wildcard is specified in an extension, and there is no attribute wildcard specified in the definition of its base type or any of its ancestors, it is a straightforward matter of using the one attribute wildcard. If, however, one or more of the ancestor types have an attribute wildcard, the effective wildcard is the union of the new wildcard and all ancestor wildcards. The value for processContents is taken from the new derived type, and the union of the namespace constraints of the attribute wildcards is used. A simple rule of thumb is that if an attribute is an allowed replacement attribute for at least one of the attribute wildcards, it can be used.

Example 13–11 shows the definition of DerivedType that extends BaseType. Both DerivedType and BaseType have attribute wildcards specified, with different values for processContents and namespace.

Example 13–12 shows the effective definition of DerivedType, after taking the union of the two attribute wildcards. Note that the value of processContents is taken from the derived type, and the namespace list is the union of those of the two types.

Example 13–11. Attribute wildcard extension

```
<xs:complexType name="BaseType">
  <xs:anyAttribute processContents="lax"
                   namespace="##local
                              http://datypic.com/prod"/>
</xs:complexType>

<xs:complexType name="DerivedType">
  <xs:complexContent>
    <xs:extension base="BaseType">
      <xs:anyAttribute processContents="strict"
                       namespace="##targetNamespace
                                  http://www.w3.org/1999/xhtml"/>
    </xs:extension>
  </xs:complexContent>
</xs:complexType>
```

Example 13–12. Effective attribute wildcard

```
<xs:complexType name="DerivedType">
  <xs:anyAttribute processContents="strict"
                   namespace="##local
                              http://datypic.com/prod
                              ##targetNamespace
                              http://www.w3.org/1999/xhtml"/>
</xs:complexType>
```

13.5 | Complex type restrictions

Complex types may be restricted by eliminating or restricting attribute declarations as well as by subsetting content models. When restriction is used, instances of the derived type will always be valid for the base type as well. Table 13–6 shows the legal restrictions for each content type.

Table 13–6   Legal restrictions by content type

| | | | Simple type | Complex type | | | |
				Simple content	Element-only	Mixed	Empty
D E R I V E D	Simple type		yes, see 8.3.1	no	no	no	no
	Complex type	Simple content	no	yes, see 13.5.1	no	yes,[†] see 13.5.3	no
D T Y P E		Element-only	no	no	yes, see 13.5.2	yes, see 13.5.3	no
		Mixed	no	no	no	yes, see 13.5.3	no
		Empty	no	no	yes,[†] see 13.5.2	yes,[†] see 13.5.3	yes, see 13.5.4

BASE TYPE

[†] If all children are optional

13.5.1 *Simple content restrictions*

The purpose of a simple content restriction is to restrict the simple content and/or attribute declarations of a complex type. Table 13–7 shows the syntax of a `restriction` element that is the child of a `simpleContent` element. The base attribute must refer to a complex type with simple content, not a simple type. This is because a restriction of a simple type is another simple type, not a complex type.

In Example 13–1 we defined a complex type `SizeType` that had simple content, and declared a `system` attribute. Example 13–13 shows a new type, `SmallSizeType`, which restricts `SizeType`. It restricts both the content, by applying the `minInclusive` and `maxInclusive` facets, and the `system` attribute declaration, by making it required. See Section 13.5.5 on p. 333 for more information on restricting attribute declarations.

Table 13–7   XSD Syntax: simple content restriction

Name
restriction

Parents
simpleContent

Attribute name	Type	Description
id	ID	Unique ID.
base	QName	Base type being restricted.

Content

annotation?, simpleType?, (enumeration | length | maxExclusive
| maxInclusive | maxLength | minExclusive | minInclusive |
minLength | pattern | totalDigits | fractionDigits |
whiteSpace| pattern | ▣assertion | ▣explicitTimezone |
▣*{any element in another namespace}*)*, (attribute |
attributeGroup)*, anyAttribute?

Example 13–13. Simple content restriction

```
<xs:complexType name="SmallSizeType">
  <xs:simpleContent>
    <xs:restriction base="SizeType">
      <xs:minInclusive value="2"/>
      <xs:maxInclusive value="6"/>
      <xs:attribute name="system" type="xs:token"
                    use="required"/>
    </xs:restriction>
  </xs:simpleContent>
</xs:complexType>
```

13.5.2 *Complex content restrictions*

Complex content restrictions allow you to restrict the content model
and/or attribute declarations of a complex type. Table 13–8 shows

Table 13–8   XSD Syntax: complex content restriction

Name		
restriction		

Parents		
complexContent		

Attribute name	*Type*	*Description*
id	ID	Unique ID.
base	QName	Base type being restricted.

Content

annotation?, ▪openContent?, (group | all | choice |
sequence)?, (attribute | attributeGroup)*, anyAttribute?,
▪assert*

the syntax of a `restriction` element that is the child of a
`complexContent` element.

When restricting complex content, it is necessary to repeat all of
the content model that is desired. The full content model specified
in the restriction becomes the content model of the derived type. This
content model must be a restriction of the content model of the base
type. This means that all instances of the new restricted type must also
be valid for the base type.

Example 13–14 shows the definition of a complex type `Restricted-
ProductType` that restricts the complex type `ProductType` by elimi-
nating the `size` and `color` child elements. This is legal because all
instances of `RestrictedProductType` are also valid according to
`ProductType`. However, if the `size` element declaration had a
`minOccurs` value of 1 in `ProductType`, the restriction would not be
legal, because values of `RestrictedProductType` would not be valid
according to `ProductType`; they would be missing a required element.

Example 13–14. Complex content restriction

```
<xs:complexType name="ProductType">
  <xs:sequence>
    <xs:element name="number" type="xs:integer"/>
    <xs:element name="name" type="xs:string"/>
    <xs:element name="size" type="xs:integer" minOccurs="0"/>
    <xs:element name="color" type="xs:string" minOccurs="0"/>
  </xs:sequence>
</xs:complexType>

<xs:complexType name="RestrictedProductType">
  <xs:complexContent>
    <xs:restriction base="ProductType">
      <xs:sequence>
        <xs:element name="number" type="xs:integer"/>
        <xs:element name="name" type="xs:string"/>
      </xs:sequence>
    </xs:restriction>
  </xs:complexContent>
</xs:complexType>
```

In most cases, you can use common sense to determine whether a restriction is legal. If you can think of a valid instance of the derived type that is not valid for the base type, there is a problem with your restriction. In case you want to do a more thorough analysis, the rest of this section describes the rules for legal content model restrictions that are detailed in version 1.0.

In version 1.1, these specific rules have been replaced with a general statement that the derived type must be more restrictive than the base type. However, the following sections may still be useful as a guideline for the types of restrictions that can be defined.

13.5.2.1 Eliminating meaningless groups

Any meaningless groups may be eliminated. This includes:

- Groups with no children
- Groups that have minOccurs and maxOccurs equal to 1, and only have one child

- sequence groups that have `minOccurs` and `maxOccurs` equal to 1 and are contained in another `sequence` group (this is illustrated in Example 13–15)
- `choice` groups that have `minOccurs` and `maxOccurs` equal to 1 and are contained in another `choice` group

Example 13–15. Eliminating meaningless groups

Base group:

```
<xs:sequence>
  <xs:sequence>
    <xs:element name="a"/>
    <xs:element name="b"/>
  </xs:sequence>
</xs:sequence>
```

Legal restriction:

```
<xs:sequence>
  <xs:element name="a"/>
  <xs:element name="b"/>
</xs:sequence>
```

13.5.2.2 Restricting element declarations

When restricting a specific element declaration, several rules apply.

- The occurrence constraints in the derived element declaration must be equal or more restrictive. This is illustrated by `a` in Example 13–16.
- The type in the derived element declaration must be a restriction of the type in the base element declaration (or they must have the same type). This is illustrated by `c` in Example 13–16.
- If the base element declaration specified a fixed value, the derived element declaration must specify the same fixed value. This is illustrated by `b` in Example 13–16.

- The identity constraints (key, keyref, unique) in the derived element declaration must be more restrictive than those of the base element declaration.

- The contents of the block attribute of the derived element declaration must be a subset of that of the base element declaration.

- If the base element declaration had nillable set to false, the derived element declaration cannot reverse that property.

Example 13–16. Restricting element declarations

Base group:

```
<xs:sequence>
  <xs:element name="a" maxOccurs="3"/>
  <xs:element name="b" fixed="bValue"/>
  <xs:element name="c" type="xs:string"/>
</xs:sequence>
```

Legal restriction:

```
<xs:sequence>
  <xs:element name="a" maxOccurs="2"/>
  <xs:element name="b" fixed="bValue"/>
  <xs:element name="c" type="xs:token"/>
</xs:sequence>
```

Illegal restriction:

```
<xs:sequence>
  <xs:element name="a" maxOccurs="4"/>
  <xs:element name="b" fixed="newValue"/>
  <xs:element name="c" type="xs:integer"/>
</xs:sequence>
```

13.5.2.3 Restricting wildcards

When replacing an element wildcard with specific element declarations or a group of element declarations, these derived declarations must yield valid replacement elements for the wildcard, in terms of their namespace and occurrence constraints. This is illustrated in Example 13–17 which shows a restriction that is illegal for two reasons. First, b is illegal because it is in the same namespace as the other elements (while the wildcard says `##other`). Second, two replacement elements are declared, but the wildcard has a `maxOccurs` of `1`.

Example 13–17. Replacing a wildcard with element declarations

Base group:

```
<xs:sequence>
  <xs:element name="a"/>
  <xs:any namespace="##other" maxOccurs="1"/>
</xs:sequence>
```

Legal restriction:

```
<xs:sequence>
  <xs:element name="a"/>
  <xs:element ref="otherns:b"/>
</xs:sequence>
```

Illegal restriction:

```
<xs:sequence>
  <xs:element name="a"/>
  <xs:element ref="b"/>
  <xs:element name="c"/>
</xs:sequence>
```

When replacing an element wildcard with another element wildcard, the derived wildcard's namespace constraint must be a subset of the base wildcard's namespace constraint, as described in Section 13.5.6 on p. 335. Also, the occurrence constraints must be a subset. This is illustrated in Example 13–18, which shows a restriction that is illegal because neither the namespace constraint nor the occurrence constraint specifies a subset of what is allowed by the base wildcard.

Example 13–18. Replacing a wildcard with another wildcard

Base wildcard:

```
<xs:any namespace="urn:a:1 urn:a:2" maxOccurs="2"/>
```

Legal restriction:

```
<xs:any namespace="urn:a:1" maxOccurs="1"/>
```

Illegal restriction:

```
<xs:any namespace="##other" maxOccurs="3"/>
```

13.5.2.4 Restricting groups

When replacing a group with an element declaration, it must be valid for an instance of that group to just have that one element child. For example, a `choice` group that contains that element declaration, or a `sequence` group declaring all other elements optional, would work as base groups in this case. This is illustrated in Example 13–19.

When replacing a group with another group, the occurrence constraints must become more restrictive. For example, if the `maxOccurs` value for a group in the base type is 5, the group in the derived type cannot have a `maxOccurs` that is greater than 5. This is illustrated in Example 13–20.

Example 13–19. Replacing a group with an element declaration

Base group:

```
<xs:sequence>
  <xs:element name="a"/>
  <xs:element name="b" minOccurs="0"/>
</xs:sequence>
```

Legal restriction:

```
<xs:element name="a"/>
```

Example 13–20. Restricting occurrence constraints of a group

Base group:

```
<xs:sequence minOccurs="2" maxOccurs="5">
  <xs:element name="a"/>
  <xs:element name="b"/>
</xs:sequence>
```

Legal restriction:

```
<xs:sequence minOccurs="3" maxOccurs="4">
  <xs:element name="a"/>
  <xs:element name="b"/>
</xs:sequence>
```

Illegal restriction:

```
<xs:sequence minOccurs="0" maxOccurs="6">
  <xs:element name="a"/>
  <xs:element name="b"/>
</xs:sequence>
```

When replacing a group with a group of the same kind (`all`, `choice`, or `sequence`), the order of the children (element declarations and groups) must be preserved. This is true even for `all` and `choice` groups, when the order is not significant for validation. This is illustrated in Example 13–21.

Example 13–21. Maintaining the order of the children in an `all` group

Base group:

```
<xs:all>
  <xs:element name="a"/>
  <xs:element name="b" minOccurs="0"/>
  <xs:element name="c"/>
</xs:all>
```

(Continues)

Example 13–21.   (Continued)

Legal restriction:

```
<xs:all>
  <xs:element name="a"/>
  <xs:element name="c"/>
</xs:all>
```

Illegal restriction:

```
<xs:all>
  <xs:element name="c"/>
  <xs:element name="a"/>
</xs:all>
```

When restricting an `all` or `sequence` group, if any child element declarations or groups are not included in the derived group, they must be optional in the base group. This is illustrated in Example 13–22.

Example 13–22. Restricting an `all` group

Base group:

```
<xs:all>
  <xs:element name="a"/>
  <xs:element name="b" minOccurs="0"/>
  <xs:element name="c"/>
</xs:all>
```

Legal restriction:

```
<xs:all>
  <xs:element name="a"/>
  <xs:element name="c"/>
</xs:all>
```

(Continues)

Example 13–22.   (Continued)

Illegal restriction:

```
<xs:all>
  <xs:element name="a"/>
  <xs:element name="b"/>
</xs:all>
```

When replacing a `choice` group with another `choice` group, the child element declarations of the derived group must be a subset of those in the base group. This is illustrated in Example 13–23.

Example 13–23. Restricting a `choice` group

Base group:

```
<xs:choice>
  <xs:element name="a"/>
  <xs:element name="b"/>
  <xs:element name="c"/>
</xs:choice>
```

Legal restriction:

```
<xs:choice>
  <xs:element name="a"/>
  <xs:element name="c"/>
</xs:choice>
```

Illegal restriction:

```
<xs:choice>
  <xs:element name="a"/>
  <xs:element name="d"/>
</xs:choice>
```

When replacing an `all` group with a `sequence` group, each element declaration in the `all` group cannot appear more than once in the `sequence` group, or appear with `maxOccurs` greater than 1. This is illustrated in Example 13–24.

Example 13–24. Replacing an `all` group with a `sequence` group

Base group:

```
<xs:all>
  <xs:element name="a"/>
  <xs:element name="b" minOccurs="0"/>
  <xs:element name="c"/>
</xs:all>
```

Legal restriction:

```
<xs:sequence>
  <xs:element name="a"/>
  <xs:element name="c"/>
</xs:sequence>
```

Illegal restriction:

```
<xs:sequence>
  <xs:element name="a"/>
  <xs:element name="b"/>
  <xs:element name="c" minOccurs="2"/>
</xs:sequence>
```

When replacing a `choice` group with a `sequence` group, the `maxOccurs` of the `choice` group must be enough to cover the number of elements that the `sequence` group will yield. This is illustrated in Example 13–25.

Example 13–25. Replacing a `choice` group with a `sequence` group

Base group:

```
<xs:choice maxOccurs="2">
  <xs:element name="a"/>
  <xs:element name="b"/>
  <xs:element name="c"/>
</xs:choice>
```

Legal restriction:

```
<xs:sequence>
  <xs:element name="a"/>
  <xs:element name="c"/>
</xs:sequence>
```

Illegal restriction:

```
<xs:sequence>
  <xs:element name="a"/>
  <xs:element name="b"/>
  <xs:element name="c"/>
</xs:sequence>
```

13.5.2.5 Restricting open content

It is possible to restrict a type that has open content, but as with the rest of the content model, it is not inherited automatically. If open content is desired in the restricted type, it is necessary to respecify it. In order to be a legal restriction, the open content in the restricted type should not be more permissive than the base type, in terms of both the mode and the namespace constraint.

Example 13–26 shows the two examples of restricting open content. The first, `LegalDerivedType`, is legal because `suffix` mode is as permissive as the base type, and the namespace constraint is more restrictive in the derived type (one choice instead of two). The second example, `IllegalDerivedType`, is illegal because `interleave` mode is *more* permissive than the base type, and the namespace constraint of `##any` is also more permissive.

Example 13–26. Restricting open content

Base group:

```
<xs:complexType name="BaseType">
  <xs:openContent mode="suffix">
    <xs:any namespace="http://datypic.com/prod
                       http://datypic.com/ord"/>
  </xs:openContent>
  <xs:sequence>
    <xs:element name="a" type="xs:string" minOccurs="0"/>
  </xs:sequence>
</xs:complexType>
```

Legal restriction:

```
<xs:complexType name="LegalDerivedType">
  <xs:complexContent>
    <xs:restriction base="BaseType">
      <xs:openContent mode="suffix">
        <xs:any namespace="http://datypic.com/prod"/>
      </xs:openContent>
      <xs:sequence>
        <xs:element name="a" type="xs:string" minOccurs="0"/>
      </xs:sequence>
    </xs:restriction>
  </xs:complexContent>
</xs:complexType>
```

Illegal restriction:

```
<xs:complexType name="IllegalDerivedType">
  <xs:complexContent>
    <xs:restriction base="BaseType">
      <xs:openContent mode="interleave">
        <xs:any namespace="##any"/>
      </xs:openContent>
      <xs:sequence>
        <xs:element name="a" type="xs:string" minOccurs="0"/>
      </xs:sequence>
    </xs:restriction>
  </xs:complexContent>
</xs:complexType>
```

It is also legal to remove the openContent element completely in a restriction, since that is less permissive. As you would expect, it is not legal to add one unless the mode is none.

13.5.3 *Mixed content restrictions*

Complex types with mixed content may be restricted to derive other complex types with mixed content or with element-only content. The reverse is not true: It is not possible to restrict an element-only complex type to result in a complex type with mixed content.

If you want the derived type to be mixed, you must specify the mixed attribute for the derived type, since the quality of being mixed is not inherited from the base type. Example 13–27 shows a mixed complex type LetterType that is restricted to derive another mixed complex type, RestrictedLetterType.

Example 13–27. Mixed content restriction

```
<xs:complexType name="LetterType" mixed="true">
  <xs:sequence>
    <xs:element name="custName" type="xs:string"/>
    <xs:element name="prodName" type="xs:string"/>
    <xs:element name="prodSize" type="xs:integer" minOccurs="0"/>
  </xs:sequence>
</xs:complexType>

<xs:complexType name="RestrictedLetterType" mixed="true">
  <xs:complexContent>
    <xs:restriction base="LetterType">
      <xs:sequence>
        <xs:element name="custName" type="xs:string"/>
        <xs:element name="prodName" type="xs:string"/>
      </xs:sequence>
    </xs:restriction>
  </xs:complexContent>
</xs:complexType>
```

It is also possible to restrict a mixed content type to derive an empty content type, or even a complex type with simple content. This is only legal if all of the children in the content model of the base type are optional. Example 13–28 shows a slightly different `LetterType` definition where the sequence group is optional. The derived type `RestrictedLetterType` will allow only character data content of type `string`, with no children. Note that this is the only case where a `restriction` element must have both a `base` attribute and a `simpleType` child.

Example 13–28. Mixed content restricted to simple content

```
<xs:complexType name="LetterType" mixed="true">
  <xs:sequence minOccurs="0">
    <xs:element name="custName" type="xs:string"/>
    <xs:element name="prodName" type="xs:string"/>
    <xs:element name="prodSize" type="xs:integer"/>
  </xs:sequence>
</xs:complexType>

<xs:complexType name="RestrictedLetterType">
  <xs:simpleContent>
    <xs:restriction base="LetterType">
      <xs:simpleType>
        <xs:restriction base="xs:string"/>
      </xs:simpleType>
    </xs:restriction>
  </xs:simpleContent>
</xs:complexType>
```

13.5.4 *Empty content restrictions*

Complex types with empty content may be restricted, but the restriction applies only to the attributes. The derived type must also have empty content. Example 13–29 shows a restriction of the empty complex type `ItemType`. The only restriction is applied to the type of the `routingNum` attribute.

Example 13–29. Empty content restriction

```
<xs:complexType name="ItemType">
  <xs:attribute name="routingNum" type="xs:integer"/>
</xs:complexType>

<xs:complexType name="RestrictedItemType">
  <xs:complexContent>
    <xs:restriction base="ItemType">
      <xs:attribute name="routingNum" type="xs:short"/>
    </xs:restriction>
  </xs:complexContent>
</xs:complexType>
```

13.5.5 *Attribute restrictions*

When defining a restriction, you may restrict or eliminate attribute declarations of the base type. All attribute declarations are passed down from the base type to the derived type, so the only attribute declarations that need to appear in the derived type definition are those you want to restrict or remove. The legal ways to restrict an attribute declaration are as follows:

- Change the type, as long as the new type is a restriction (or a restriction of a restriction, etc.) of the original type
- Add, change, or remove a default value
- Add a fixed value if none is present in the base type
- Make optional attributes required
- Make optional attributes prohibited

It is *not* legal in a restriction to

- Change the type to one that is not a restriction of the original type
- Change or remove a fixed value
- Make required attributes optional
- Make required attributes prohibited

Example 13–30 shows a definition of DerivedType which legally restricts BaseType. The declarations of attributes a, b, c, d, e, f, and g represent, respectively, changing the type, adding a default, changing a default, adding a fixed value, keeping the fixed value the same, making an optional attribute required, and prohibiting an optional attribute. Instances of DerivedType can also have the attribute x, although it is not mentioned in the definition. This is because all of the attributes of BaseType are passed down to DerivedType.

Example 13–30. Legal restrictions of attributes

```
<xs:complexType name="BaseType">
     <xs:attribute name="a" type="xs:integer"/>
     <xs:attribute name="b" type="xs:string"/>
     <xs:attribute name="c" type="xs:string" default="c"/>
     <xs:attribute name="d" type="xs:string"/>
     <xs:attribute name="e" type="xs:string" fixed="e"/>
     <xs:attribute name="f" type="xs:string"/>
     <xs:attribute name="g" type="xs:string"/>
     <xs:attribute name="x" type="xs:string"/>
</xs:complexType>

<xs:complexType name="DerivedType">
  <xs:complexContent>
    <xs:restriction base="BaseType">
      <xs:attribute name="a" type="xs:positiveInteger"/>
      <xs:attribute name="b" type="xs:string" default="b"/>
      <xs:attribute name="c" type="xs:string" default="c2"/>
      <xs:attribute name="d" type="xs:string" fixed="d"/>
      <xs:attribute name="e" type="xs:string" fixed="e"/>
      <xs:attribute name="f" type="xs:string" use="required"/>
      <xs:attribute name="g" type="xs:string" use="prohibited"/>
    </xs:restriction>
  </xs:complexContent>
</xs:complexType>
```

Example 13–31 shows a definition of IllegalDerivedType, which illegally restricts the complex type BaseType2. Attribute h is illegal because decimal is not a restriction of integer. Attribute i is illegal because the fixed value is changed. Attribute j is illegal because the fixed value is removed and replaced by a default value. Attribute k is illegal because a required attribute is made optional. Attribute l is illegal because a required attribute is made prohibited. Attributes pref:l and m are illegal because they do not appear in the definition of BaseType2.

Example 13–31. Illegal attribute restrictions

```
<xs:complexType name="BaseType2">
    <xs:attribute name="h" type="xs:integer"/>
    <xs:attribute name="i" type="xs:string" fixed="i"/>
    <xs:attribute name="j" type="xs:string" fixed="j"/>
    <xs:attribute name="k" type="xs:string" use="required"/>
    <xs:attribute name="l" type="xs:string" use="required"/>
</xs:complexType>

<xs:complexType name="IllegalDerivedType">
  <xs:complexContent>
    <xs:restriction base="BaseType2">
    <xs:attribute name="h" type="xs:decimal"/>
    <xs:attribute name="i" type="xs:string" fixed="i2"/>
    <xs:attribute name="j" type="xs:string" default="j"/>
    <xs:attribute name="k" type="xs:string"/>
    <xs:attribute name="l" type="xs:string" use="prohibited"/>
    <xs:attribute ref="pref:l"/>
    <xs:attribute name="m" type="xs:string"/>
    </xs:restriction>
  </xs:complexContent>
</xs:complexType>
```

13.5.6 *Attribute wildcard restrictions*

Unlike attribute declarations, attribute wildcards are not automatically passed down from the base type to the restricted type. If you want to use an attribute wildcard for the restricted type, you must specify it inside the restriction element.

When an attribute wildcard is specified in a restriction, that wildcard becomes the effective wildcard of the type, overriding any attribute wildcards of the base type or its ancestors. However, if any ancestor has an attribute wildcard, the namespace constraint of the new wildcard must be a subset of the ancestor wildcard's namespace constraint. Table 13–9 shows the legal subsets of namespace constraints.

Table 13–9   Wildcard namespace subsets

Base type	Derived type
`##any`	Any value or list of values
Any list of values (including `##targetNamespace` and `##local`)	Any list of values that is the same or a subset of the base type's list
`##other`	`##other` (if the target namespaces of the base type and of the derived type are the same) or any list of values that does not include the target namespace of the base type or `##local`

Example 13–32 shows a definition of `DerivedType` that restricts `BaseType`. Both `DerivedType` and `BaseType` have attribute wildcards specified, with different values for `processContents` and `namespace`. This definition is legal because `DerivedType`'s wildcard is a subset of `BaseType`'s wildcard.

Example 13–32. Restricting an attribute wildcard

```
<xs:complexType name="BaseType">
  <xs:anyAttribute processContents="lax" namespace="##any"/>
</xs:complexType>

<xs:complexType name="DerivedType">
  <xs:complexContent>
    <xs:restriction base="BaseType">
      <xs:anyAttribute processContents="strict"
                    namespace="##targetNamespace
                               http://www.w3.org/1999/xhtml"/>
    </xs:restriction>
  </xs:complexContent>
</xs:complexType>
```

It is also possible to restrict an attribute wildcard by replacing it with declarations for attributes that are valid according to that wildcard. This is illustrated in Example 13–33.

Example 13–33. Replacing an attribute wildcard with attributes

```
<xs:complexType name="BaseType">
  <xs:anyAttribute processContents="lax" namespace="##any"/>
</xs:complexType>

<xs:complexType name="DerivedType">
  <xs:complexContent>
    <xs:restriction base="BaseType">
      <xs:attribute name="id" type="xs:ID" use="required"/>
      <xs:attribute name="name" type="xs:string"/>
    </xs:restriction>
  </xs:complexContent>
</xs:complexType>
```

13.5.7 *Restricting types from another namespace*

Sometimes it is useful to define complex types in your schema that are restrictions of base types defined in another target namespace. It may be that you are embedding elements from another XML vocabulary in your elements, and you only want to allow a restricted subset of the other vocabulary. Example 13–34 shows this case where the base type, `ProductType`, is in a schema document with `http://datypic.com/prod` as the target namespace. `RestrictedProductType` is a derived type, but it is defined in a schema document whose target namespace is `http://datypic.com/ord`.

This example shows a legal restriction because the complex type contains references to global element declarations. All of the element names in the restricted type are still in the `http://datypic.com/prod` namespace, as evidenced by the use of the `prod` prefix.

Example 13–34. Restricting a type from another namespace with global declarations

---

prod.xsd

```
<xs:schema xmlns:xs="http://www.w3.org/2001/XMLSchema"
           targetNamespace="http://datypic.com/prod"
           xmlns:prod="http://datypic.com/prod"
           elementFormDefault="qualified"
           attributeFormDefault="qualified">
  <xs:complexType name="ProductType">
    <xs:sequence>
      <xs:element ref="prod:number"/>
      <xs:element ref="prod:name"/>
      <xs:element ref="prod:size" minOccurs="0"/>
    </xs:sequence>
    <xs:attribute ref="prod:dept"/>
  </xs:complexType>
  <xs:element name="number" type="xs:integer"/>
  <xs:element name="name" type="xs:string"/>
  <xs:element name="size" type="xs:integer"/>
  <xs:attribute name="dept" type="xs:string"/>
</xs:schema>
```

ord.xsd

```
<xs:schema xmlns:xs="http://www.w3.org/2001/XMLSchema"
           targetNamespace="http://datypic.com/ord"
           xmlns:prod="http://datypic.com/prod">
  <xs:import namespace="http://datypic.com/prod"
             schemaLocation="prod.xsd"/>
  <xs:complexType name="RestrictedProductType">
    <xs:complexContent>
      <xs:restriction base="prod:ProductType">
        <xs:sequence>
          <xs:element ref="prod:number"/>
          <xs:element ref="prod:name"/>
        </xs:sequence>
        <xs:attribute ref="prod:dept" use="required"/>
      </xs:restriction>
    </xs:complexContent>
  </xs:complexType>
</xs:schema>
```

A problem arises, however, if local element declarations are used and they are qualified with a namespace name (either via a `form` attribute on the element declaration, or an `elementFormDefault` attribute on the schema). In that case, the `name` attribute is used instead of `ref`, and it is not legal to use a namespace prefix in the `name` attribute; all of the values of `name` take on the target namespace of the schema document. If Example 13–34 were modified to use local element declarations, the elements in `RestrictedProductType` would take on the `http://datypic.com/ord` namespace, and no longer be a valid restriction of the base type since the element names have changed. The same problem arises for attributes as well as elements, but this occurs less frequently since qualified local attribute declarations are less common.

In version 1.0, this problem is typically avoided by creating a new schema document in the `http://datypic.com/prod` namespace whose sole purpose is to restrict the original schema document. That new schema document is the one that is imported into the `http://datypic.com/ord` schema document, which can then reference the restricted types.

13.5.7.1 Using `targetNamespace` on element and attribute declarations

Starting in version 1.1, it *is* possible to restrict a type that has a different target namespace, even if it uses qualified local declarations. This is addressed by the use of a `targetNamespace` attribute, which can appear on a local element declaration or local attribute declaration.

This is shown in Example 13–35, which is similar to Example 13–34 but with local declarations instead of global ones. The `targetNamespace` attribute is used on the two element declarations and one attribute declaration in the restricted type to indicate that these names still refer to the `http://datypic.com/prod` namespace.

Example 13–35. Using `targetNamespace` on element and attribute declarations

prod.xsd

```
<xs:schema xmlns:xs="http://www.w3.org/2001/XMLSchema"
           targetNamespace="http://datypic.com/prod"
           elementFormDefault="qualified"
           attributeFormDefault="qualified">
  <xs:complexType name="ProductType">
    <xs:sequence>
      <xs:element name="number" type="xs:integer"/>
      <xs:element name="name" type="xs:string"/>
      <xs:element name="size" type="xs:integer" minOccurs="0"/>
    </xs:sequence>
    <xs:attribute name="dept" type="xs:string"/>
  </xs:complexType>
</xs:schema>
```

ord.xsd

```
<xs:schema xmlns:xs="http://www.w3.org/2001/XMLSchema"
           targetNamespace="http://datypic.com/ord"
           xmlns:prod="http://datypic.com/prod"
           elementFormDefault="qualified"
           attributeFormDefault="qualified">
  <xs:import namespace="http://datypic.com/prod"
             schemaLocation="prod.xsd"/>
  <xs:complexType name="RestrictedProductType">
    <xs:complexContent>
      <xs:restriction base="prod:ProductType">
        <xs:sequence>
          <xs:element name="number" type="xs:string"
                      targetNamespace="http://datypic.com/prod"/>
          <xs:element name="name" type="xs:string"
                      targetNamespace="http://datypic.com/prod"/>
        </xs:sequence>
        <xs:attribute name="dept" type="xs:string" use="required"
                      targetNamespace="http://datypic.com/prod"/>
      </xs:restriction>
    </xs:complexContent>
  </xs:complexType>
</xs:schema>
```

Without the `targetNamespace` attributes, this example would not be a legal restriction because it would be trying to change the namespaces of the elements and the attribute from `http://datypic.com/prod` to `http://datypic.com/ord`.

Note that this technique is only allowed when restricting a type from another namespace. It is not possible to use the `targetNamespace` attribute generally to declare elements and attributes in a target namespace other than that of the schema document.

13.6 | Type substitution

One of the elegant features of derived types is that they can substitute for their ancestor types in instances. In an instance, an element declared to be of one type can actually have any type that either extends or restricts it. Suppose we have a section of a purchase order that lists products of various kinds. We want repeating `product` elements, but we also want to allow different content models for each kind of product. For example, a shirt may have a color and a size, in addition to the normal product information.

Example 13–36 shows a definition of `ShirtType` that extends `ProductType`. It adds the children `size` and `color` to the end of the content model.

Example 13–36. A derived type

```
<xs:complexType name="ProductType">
  <xs:sequence>
    <xs:element name="number" type="xs:integer"/>
    <xs:element name="name" type="xs:string"/>
  </xs:sequence>
</xs:complexType>
<xs:element name="product" type="ProductType"/>
```

(Continues)

Example 13–36. (Continued)

```
<xs:complexType name="ShirtType">
  <xs:complexContent>
    <xs:extension base="ProductType">
      <xs:choice maxOccurs="unbounded">
        <xs:element name="size" type="xs:integer"/>
        <xs:element name="color" type="xs:string"/>
      </xs:choice>
    </xs:extension>
  </xs:complexContent>
</xs:complexType>
```

Example 13–37 shows a valid instance of `product`. Instead of `ProductType`, it has the type `ShirtType` which allows it to contain the `color` element. It uses the `xsi:type` attribute to indicate the type substitution. We could define an additional type for every kind of product, each with a different content model.

Example 13–37. Substitution of `ShirtType` for `ProductType`

```
<items xmlns:xsi="http://www.w3.org/2001/XMLSchema-instance">

  <product xsi:type="ShirtType">
    <number>557</number>
    <name>Short-Sleeved Linen Blouse</name>
    <color>blue</color>
  </product>

  <!--...-->
</items>
```

The `xsi:type` attribute is part of the XML Schema Instance Namespace, which must be declared in the instance. This attribute does not, however, need to be declared in the type definition for `product`; a schema processor recognizes `xsi:type` as a special attribute that may appear on any element.

13.7 | Controlling type derivation and substitution

Type derivation is a powerful tool, but in some cases, you may want to control the creation or substitution of derived types. Three properties of complex types control their derivation:

- The `final` property limits the definition of derived types in schemas.
- The `block` property limits the substitution of derived types in instances.
- The `abstract` property forces the definition of derived types.

This section describes each of these three properties in detail.

13.7.1 `final`: *Preventing complex type derivation*

You may want to prevent the derivation of other complex types from your type. This is accomplished using the `final` attribute, which may have one of the following values:

- `#all` prevents any other types from extending or restricting your type.
- `extension` prevents any other types from extending your type.
- `restriction` prevents any other types from restricting your type.
- `extension restriction` and `restriction extension` have the same effect as `#all`.
- `" "` (an empty string) means that there are no restrictions. This value is useful for overriding the value of `finalDefault`, as described below.

- If no `final` attribute is specified, it takes its value from the `finalDefault` attribute of the `schema` element.[1] If neither `final` nor `finalDefault` is specified, there are no restrictions on derivation of that complex type.

Example 13–38 shows the definition of a complex type that cannot be restricted or extended by any other type.

Example 13–38. Preventing derivation

```
<xs:complexType name="ProductType" final="#all">
  <xs:sequence>
    <xs:element name="number" type="xs:integer"/>
    <xs:element name="name" type="xs:string"/>
  </xs:sequence>
</xs:complexType>
```

13.7.2 `block`: *Blocking substitution of derived types*

As we saw in Section 13.6 on p. 341, derived types may substitute for their ancestor types in an instance. While this is a valuable feature, there are times when you only want to allow the original type to be used. This is accomplished using the `block` attribute, which may have one of the following values:

- `#all` prevents any derived types from substituting for your type in instances.
- `extension` prevents any extensions of your type from substituting for your type in instances.
- `restriction` prevents any restrictions of your type from substituting for your type in instances.

---

1. The `finalDefault` attribute can contain the values `list` and `union` which are not applicable to complex types. If these values are present, they are ignored in this context.

- extension restriction and restriction extension have the same effect as #all.

- "" (an empty string) means that there are no restrictions. This value is useful for overriding the value of blockDefault, as described below.

- If no block attribute is specified, it takes its value from the blockDefault attribute of the schema element. If neither block nor blockDefault is specified, there are no restrictions.

Example 13–39 shows a definition of ProductType that does not allow extensions of the type to be used in its place.

Example 13–39. Preventing substitution of derived types

```
<xs:complexType name="ProductType" block="extension">
  <xs:sequence>
    <xs:element name="number" type="xs:integer"/>
    <xs:element name="name" type="xs:string"/>
  </xs:sequence>
</xs:complexType>
<xs:element name="product" type="ProductType"/>

<xs:complexType name="ShirtType">
  <xs:complexContent>
    <xs:extension base="ProductType">
      <xs:choice maxOccurs="unbounded">
        <xs:element name="size" type="xs:integer"/>
        <xs:element name="color" type="xs:string"/>
      </xs:choice>
    </xs:extension>
  </xs:complexContent>
</xs:complexType>
<xs:element name="shirt" type="ShirtType"/>
```

The definition of ShirtType in this example is completely legal. The block attribute does not prohibit extensions of ProductType, just the substitution of the extensions in place of the original type in the instance. Example 13–40 shows an illegal instance where the element product is attempting to substitute ShirtType for

ProductType. This example would have been legal if the block attribute had not been used.

Example 13–40. Illegal substitution of ShirtType

```
<product xsi:type="ShirtType">
  <number>557</number>
  <name>Short-Sleeved Linen Blouse</name>
  <color>blue</color>
</product>
```

13.7.3 *Blocking type substitution in element declarations*

You can also block type substitution for an element declaration that uses the type, rather than the type itself. An element element can also have the block attribute, with the same valid values as for complexType.[1] If, in Example 13–39, the block="extension" attribute had appeared in the product element declaration rather than in the ProductType definition, the effect would have been the same as far as the product instance elements are concerned. Other elements using ProductType would then be free to substitute derived types.

13.7.4 abstract: *Forcing derivation*

Abstract complex types are types that cannot be used in instances. They exist solely as placeholders for their derived types. Example 13–41 shows our ProductType example as an abstract type.

---

1. The block attribute of element may also contain the value substitution, as described in Section 16.7.2 on p. 419.

Example 13–41. An abstract type

```
<xs:complexType name="ProductType" abstract="true">
  <xs:sequence>
    <xs:element name="number" type="xs:integer"/>
    <xs:element name="name" type="xs:string"/>
  </xs:sequence>
</xs:complexType>
<xs:element name="product" type="ProductType"/>

<xs:complexType name="ShirtType">
  <xs:complexContent>
    <xs:extension base="ProductType">
      <xs:choice maxOccurs="unbounded">
        <xs:element name="size" type="xs:integer"/>
        <xs:element name="color" type="xs:string"/>
      </xs:choice>
    </xs:extension>
  </xs:complexContent>
</xs:complexType>
<xs:element name="shirt" type="ShirtType"/>
```

Note that `product` is declared to be of the type `ProductType`. This is legal, but if a `product` element appears in an instance, it must use the `xsi:type` attribute to indicate a type that is derived from `ProductType`, as shown in Example 13–42.

Example 13–42. Legal instances of `product` and `shirt`

```
<product xsi:type="ShirtType">
  <number>557</number>
  <name>Short-Sleeved Linen Blouse</name>
  <color>blue</color>
</product>

<shirt>
  <number>557</number>
  <name>Short-Sleeved Linen Blouse</name>
  <color>blue</color>
</shirt>
```

Example 13–43 shows two illegal `product` elements that attempt to use the type `ProductType`.

***Example 13–43.** Illegal uses of the abstract `ProductType`*

```
<product>
  <number>557</number>
  <name>Short-Sleeved Linen Blouse</name>
</product>

<product xsi:type="ProductType">
  <number>557</number>
  <name>Short-Sleeved Linen Blouse</name>
</product>
```

Assertions

A ssertions are a powerful new feature in 1.1 that allows you to specify additional constraints using XPath 2.0. This addresses a significant limitation in XML Schema 1.0 that prevented the definition of co-constraints, where one data item affects the validity of another. It also generally allows for much more complex validation criteria to be expressed.

This chapter covers assertions, as well as conditional type assignment which allows the type of an element to be determined by an XPath expression on its attributes. Conditional type assignment is also new in version 1.1. Although this feature is separate from assertions, it has similar syntax and some overlapping use cases.

14.1 | Assertions

Assertions are defined on types, rather than element or attribute declarations, so they are shared across all elements or attributes that have a particular type. Example 14–1 shows two types, one simple and one complex, that have assertions. For `SizeType`, it is testing to make sure that the value is not equal to zero. For `ProductType`, it is testing the validity of the product number, based on the department.

Example 14–1. Assertions on simple and complex types

```
<xs:simpleType name="SizeType">
  <xs:restriction base="xs:integer">
    <xs:assertion test="$value != 0"/>
  </xs:restriction>
</xs:simpleType>
<xs:complexType name="ProductType">
  <xs:sequence>
    <xs:element name="number" type="xs:integer"/>
    <xs:element name="name" type="xs:string"/>
    <xs:element name="size" type="SizeType"/>
  </xs:sequence>
  <xs:attribute name="dept" type="xs:string"/>
  <xs:assert test="(@dept = 'ACC' and number > 500) or
                   (number &lt; 300)"/>
</xs:complexType>
```

As you can see, two different elements are used: `assertion` is used in simple types (and in simple content), and `assert` is used in complex types. Both `assertion` and `assert` have a `test` attribute that specifies an XPath expression. The XPath returns a Boolean (true/false) value. If the expression is true, the element or attribute is valid with respect to the assertion. If it is false, it is invalid.

Assertions are specified using XPath 2.0, which is a powerful language that includes over a hundred built-in functions and many operators. This chapter describes some of the XPath 2.0 functions, operators, and expression syntax that are most useful for assertions, but it is by no means complete. For a complete explanation of all XPath operators and syntax, you can refer to the *XML Path Language (XPath) 2.0* recommendation at www.w3.org/TR/xpath20.

Syntactically, any XPath 2.0 is allowed in an assertion. However, one limitation of assertions is that your XPath expression has to stay within the scope of the type itself. It can only access attributes, content, and descendants of the element that has that type. It cannot access the parent or other ancestor elements, siblings, separate XML documents, or any other nondescendant elements. This means that for cross-element validation, the assertion needs to be specified on an ancestor type that contains all of the elements or attributes mentioned in the assertion.

14.1.1 *Assertions for simple types*

Assertions in simple types are facets, and as such they appear alongside all the other facets inside a `restriction` element. That facet is called `assertion`, and its syntax is shown in Table 14–1.

Table 14–1   XSD Syntax: simple type assertion

Name		
assertion		

Parents		
restriction		

Attribute name	Type	Description
id	ID	Unique ID.
test	XPath expression	Assertion test.
xpathDefaultNamespace	anyURI | "##defaultNamespace" | "##targetNamespace" | "##local"	The default namespace for XPath expressions.

Content		
annotation?		

Example 14–2 shows an assertion on a simple type. Simple type assertions are generally less complicated than those for complex types

because there are no descendants, only a value to test. A special built-in variable is used to access that value, called $value. There is no context item for a simple type assertion, so you cannot use a period (.) to represent the current element or value[1] like you might in some XPath expressions.

Example 14–2. An assertion on a simple type

```
<xs:simpleType name="SizeType">
  <xs:restriction base="xs:integer">
    <xs:assertion test="$value != 0"/>
  </xs:restriction>
</xs:simpleType>
```

The assertion facet can also be used inside the restriction element for complex types with simple content, just like any other facet. Example 14–3 shows two complex types with simple content, one restricting the other by adding an assertion. However, if you need to access the attributes of that type in the assertion, you should use an assert instead, as shown later in Example 14–17.

Example 14–3. An assertion on the simple content of a complex type

```
<xs:complexType name="SizeType">
  <xs:simpleContent>
    <xs:extension base="xs:integer">
      <xs:attribute name="system" type="xs:string"/>
    </xs:extension>
  </xs:simpleContent>
</xs:complexType>
<xs:complexType name="RestrictedSizeType">
  <xs:simpleContent>
    <xs:restriction base="SizeType">
      <xs:assertion test="$value != 0"/>
    </xs:restriction>
  </xs:simpleContent>
</xs:complexType>
```

---

1.   Except inside subexpressions, such as predicates.

You can specify multiple assertions on the same simple type, in which case they must all return true for the element or attribute to be valid. Values of type DepartmentCodeType in Example 14–4 must be valid with respect to both specified assertions. Assertions can be combined with other facets, in any order. In fact, it is recommended that you continue to use other facets if they can express the constraint. For example, use the length facet as shown rather than an assertion with a test of string-length($value) = 3.

Example 14–4. A simple type with more than one assertion

```
<xs:simpleType name="DepartmentCodeType">
  <xs:restriction base="xs:token">
    <xs:assertion test="not(contains($value,'X'))"/>
    <xs:assertion test="substring($value,2,2) != '00'"/>
    <xs:length value="3"/>
  </xs:restriction>
</xs:simpleType>
```

14.1.1.1 Using XPath 2.0 operators

The XPath 2.0 language allows a number of operators in its syntax, for example for performing comparisons and arithmetic operations. Table 14–2 shows some of the operators that are likely to be used in simple type assertions, along with examples.

Parentheses can be used in XPath to change the evaluation order of these operators. For example, by default, and takes precedence over or. The assertion in Example 14–5 uses parentheses around the first two comparisons to change the evaluation order. Without the parentheses, the second and third comparisons would have been combined by and before evaluating the or.

Parentheses can also be used to create a sequence of multiple values to test, as shown in the assertion in Example 14–6. The expression evaluates to true if the value is any of the three strings listed.

Table 14–2   Common XPath 2.0 operators

Operator	Description	Example
=	equals	$value = 'ABC'
!=	not equals	$value != 'ABC'
>, >=, <, <=	comparison	$value > 12 $value <= 50
and	Boolean "and"	$value > 12 and $value <= 50
or	Boolean "or"	$value <= 12 or $value > 50
+	addition	$value + 2 > 12
-	subtraction	$value - 2 > 12
*	multiplication	$value * 2 > 12
div	division	$value div 2 > 12
mod	modulus (remainder after division)	$value mod 2 = 0

Example 14–5. Using parentheses to change evaluation order

```
<xs:simpleType name="SizeType">
  <xs:restriction base="xs:integer">
    <xs:assertion test="($value &lt; 12 or $value > 50)
                    and $value != 0"/>
  </xs:restriction>
</xs:simpleType>
```

Example 14–6. Using parentheses to create sequences

```
<xs:simpleType name="DepartmentCodeType">
  <xs:restriction base="xs:token">
    <xs:assertion test="$value = ('ACC','WMN','MEN')"/>
  </xs:restriction>
</xs:simpleType>
```

14.1.1.2 Using XPath 2.0 functions

XPath 2.0 includes over 100 built-in functions. Functions in XPath are called using a syntax that is probably familiar from other programming languages: the function name, followed by parentheses that contain the arguments to the function separated by commas. Table 14–3 provides a sample of built-in functions that would commonly be used in simple type assertions. For a complete list, refer to the *XQuery 1.0 and XPath 2.0 Functions and Operators* recommendation at www.w3.org/TR/xpath-functions.

Table 14–3   Common XPath 2.0 functions on single values

Function name	Returns
String-related	
`string-length($arg)`	The number of characters in the string.
`substring($sourceString, $startingLoc, $length)`	A substring of the `$sourceString`, based on a starting location and optional length.
`substring-before($arg1, $arg2)`	A substring of `$arg1` that appears before the first occurrence of `$arg2`.
`substring-after($arg1, $arg2)`	A substring of `$arg1` that appears after the first occurrence of `$arg2`.
`upper-case($arg)`	`$arg` converted to upper case.
`lower-case($arg)`	`$arg` converted to lower case.
`normalize-space($arg)`	`$arg` with whitespace normalized as if it were a `token` value.
`contains($arg1, $arg2)`	Whether `$arg1` contains the string `$arg2`.
`starts-with($arg1, $arg2)`	Whether `$arg1` starts with the string `$arg2`.

(Continues)

Table 14–3   (Continued)

Function name	Returns
ends-with($arg1, $arg2)	Whether $arg1 ends with the string $arg2.
matches($input, $pattern, $flags)	Whether $input matches a regular expression pattern, with an optional set of flags controlling how to interpret the regular expression.
Number-related	
round($arg)	$arg rounded to the nearest integer.
round-half-to-even($arg, $precision)	$arg rounded with the specified precision.
Boolean-related	
not($arg)	True if $arg is false, false if $arg is true.
true()	A Boolean true value.
false()	A Boolean false value.
exists($arg)	True if $arg is not the empty sequence.
empty($arg)	True if $arg is the empty sequence.

These functions are all built in, and you do not need to use namespace prefixes on their names. Your schema processor may support additional implementation-defined functions that are in other namespaces. Typically, in simple type assertions, you will be passing $value as one of the arguments. Table 14–4 shows some example values for simple type assertions that use common XPath functions.

Note that the matches function interprets regular expressions slightly differently from the pattern facet. The value of a pattern facet is the regular expression for the whole string, with implied anchors at the beginning and the end. The matches function, on the other hand, tests whether a string contains any substring that matches the pattern. To indicate that a pattern should match the start and/or end

Table 14–4   Examples of XPath 2.0 function calls

Example	Explanation
`not($value = ('ABC','DEF','GHI'))`	Value is not one of ABC, DEF, or GHI.
`substring($value,2,2) != 'XX'`	Value does not have XX in the second position.
`not(upper-case($value) = 'ABC')`	Value is not ABC in upper, lower, or mixed case.
`not(starts-with($value,'ABC'))`	Value does not start with ABC.
`not(matches($value,'^ABC'))`	Value does not match the regular expression ^ABC.
`matches($value,'^ABC', 'i')`	Value matches the *case-insensitive* regular expression ^ABC.
`normalize-space($value) != ''`	Value is not all whitespace characters.

of the entire string, anchors ^ (for the start of a string) and $ (for the end of the string) must be used.

The examples in the table focus on assertions that cannot be expressed with other facets. For example, to simply test whether a value starts with ABC, you could use a pattern, as in `<xs:pattern value="ABC.*"/>`. However, it usually requires an assertion to express that a value must *not* match a pattern or an enumeration, or to indicate that processing should be case-sensitive.

14.1.1.3 Types and assertions

XPath 2.0 is a type-aware language, meaning that the processor pays attention to the types of values when performing operations on them. It is not valid in XPath 2.0 to compare an integer to a string, at least not with converting one value to the other's type. Likewise, the built-in functions require arguments to be of a specific type. For example, the `substring` function will not accept an integer as the first argument, because it is expecting a string.

The processor is getting the information about the type of the value from the simple type definition itself. For example, if the simple type is a restriction of `integer`, then the value will be treated like an integer. Example 14–7 shows three simple types that have type errors in their assertions.

1. `SizeType` is in error because the value is an integer and it is being passed to the `string-length` function which expects a string.

2. `DepartmentCodeType` is in error because the value is a string but it is being compared to a number.

3. `EffectiveDateTimeType` is in error because the value is a date/time but it is being compared to a string.

Example 14–7. Assertions with type errors

```
<xs:simpleType name="SizeType">
  <xs:restriction base="xs:integer">
    <xs:assertion test="string-length($value) &lt; 2"/>
  </xs:restriction>
</xs:simpleType>
<xs:simpleType name="DepartmentCodeType">
  <xs:restriction base="xs:string">
    <xs:assertion test="$value != 001"/>
  </xs:restriction>
</xs:simpleType>
<xs:simpleType name="EffectiveDateTimeType">
  <xs:restriction base="xs:dateTime">
    <xs:assertion test="$value > '2000-01-01T12:00:00'"/>
  </xs:restriction>
</xs:simpleType>
```

Some processors will treat these type errors like dynamic errors, meaning that they are not reported as errors in the schema. Instead, dynamic errors simply cause the assertion to return false, rendering the element or attribute in question invalid. Most processors will issue

warnings in these cases, though. XPath syntax errors and other static errors, on the other hand, will be flagged as errors in the schema by your processor.

To correct type errors like these, one should consider whether the simple types are being derived from the correct primitive types to start with. If you are performing arithmetic operations on a value, perhaps it should have a numeric type rather than a string type. For these examples, let's assume that the primitive types were chosen correctly.

SizeType is really trying to limit the size of the integer. In this case, it makes sense to change it to use one of the bounds facets to limit the value of the integer, instead of trying to constrain its string representation.

For DepartmentCodeType, both operands in the comparison need to have the same type (or have types derived from each other). You could convert the $value to a numeric type, but the best approach here is to put quotes around the 001 to make it a string. Comparing them as strings takes into account the leading zeroes, which may be significant in a string-based department code.

For EffectiveDateType, as with the previous example, the operands need to be of comparable types. We could convert $value to a string, but then it would compare the values as strings instead of date/time values, which would mean that time zones may not be taken into account correctly. Instead, it is preferable to convert the second operand to a date/time type. This is done in XPath 2.0 using a *type constructor*, which is a special kind of function whose name is the appropriate built-in type name. It accepts a single argument, the value to be converted. For example, xs:dateTime('2000-01-01T12:00:00') converts the string to a date/time.

Example 14–8 shows our three examples, corrected to reflect the types of the values.

In addition to the type constructor functions, there is a string function that converts a value to a string, and a number function that converts a value to a floating-point number (double). Both of these functions also take a single argument, the value to be converted.

Example 14–8. Assertions with corrected type errors

```
<xs:simpleType name="SizeType">
  <xs:restriction base="xs:integer">
    <xs:maxExclusive value="100"/>
  </xs:restriction>
</xs:simpleType>
<xs:simpleType name="DepartmentCodeType">
  <xs:restriction base="xs:string">
    <xs:assertion test="$value != '001'"/>
  </xs:restriction>
</xs:simpleType>
<xs:simpleType name="EffectiveDateTimeType">
  <xs:restriction base="xs:dateTime">
    <xs:assertion test="$value >
                        xs:dateTime('2000-01-01T12:00:00')"/>
  </xs:restriction>
</xs:simpleType>
```

14.1.1.4 Inheriting simple type assertions

Like other facets, assertions are inherited when a simple type restricts another simple type. Any assertions that are specified in the restriction are added to the constraints on that value. In other words, a value must conform to the assertions on its simple type and on any other simple types it restricts, directly or indirectly. Values of type `NonOverheadDepartmentCodeType` in Example 14–9 must conform both to the assertion in that type and to the one specified in `DepartmentCodeType`.

Example 14–9. A simple type with inherited assertions

```
<xs:simpleType name="DepartmentCodeType">
  <xs:restriction base="xs:token">
    <xs:assertion test="not(contains($value,'X'))"/>
    <xs:length value="3"/>
  </xs:restriction>
</xs:simpleType>
<xs:simpleType name="NonOverheadDepartmentCodeType">
  <xs:restriction base="DepartmentCodeType">
    <xs:assertion test="substring($value,2,2) != '00'"/>
  </xs:restriction>
</xs:simpleType>
```

14.1.1.5 Assertions on list types

In most cases, $value evaluates to a single atomic value. However, when the value has a list type and consists of multiple items, $value is a sequence of multiple atomic values. You can still do a comparison, such as $value > 2, but that will return true if *at least one* of the values in the list is greater than 2. You can refer to specific values in the list using numeric predicates—for example, $value[1] to get the first value in the list. Example 14–10 shows an assertion on a list type stating that the first item in the list must be 0.

When working with multiitem sequences, there are a number of additional XPath functions that are useful. They are listed in Table 14–5. As we will see later, these functions are also useful on complex type assertions when there are repeating children—another example of multiitem sequences.

Example 14–10. An assertion on a list type

```
<xs:simpleType name="SizeListType">
  <xs:restriction>
    <xs:simpleType>
      <xs:list itemType="xs:integer"/>
    </xs:simpleType>
    <xs:assertion test="$value[1] = 0"/>
  </xs:restriction>
</xs:simpleType>
```

Table 14–5 Common XPath 2.0 functions on multiitem sequences

Function name	*Returns*
count($arg)	The number of items in $arg.
distinct-values($arg)	A sequence of the unique values in $arg.
avg($arg)	The average of the values in $arg.
max($arg)	The maximum of the values in $arg.
min($arg)	The minimum of the values in $arg.

(Continues)

Table 14–5   (Continued)

Function name	Returns
`sum($arg)`	The sum of the values in `$arg`.
`position()`	The position of the current item in the current context (typically used inside a predicate).
`last()`	The number of items in the current context (typically used inside a predicate to obtain the last item).

Table 14–6 shows some additional examples of XPath tests that are appropriate for list types.

Table 14–6   Examples of assertion tests on list types

Example	Explanation
`count($value) > 2`	There are more than two items in the list.
`$value > 12`	At least one of the values is greater than 12.
`not($value > 12)`	None of the values is greater than 12.
`sum($value) < 20`	The sum of the values in the list is less than 20.
`$value[1] = 'ABC'`	The first value in the list is equal to ABC.
`$value[last()] = 'ABC'`	The last value in the list is equal to ABC.
`$value[position() > 1] = 'ABC'`	At least one of the values after the first one in the list is equal to ABC.
`count($value) =` `count(distinct-values($value))`	No values in the list are repeated.

The assertions in Table 14–6 apply to the list as a whole. If you want to constrain every value in the list, it makes more sense to put the assertion on the item type instead. Example 14–11 is a simple type `SizeType` that has one assertion on the item type of the list (testing that the value is less than 12) and one assertion on the list itself (testing the number of items in the list).

Example 14–11. Assertions on a list type and its item type

```
<xs:simpleType name="SizeListType">
  <xs:restriction>
    <xs:simpleType>
      <xs:list>
        <xs:simpleType>
          <xs:restriction base="xs:integer">
            <xs:assertion test="$value &lt; 12"/>
          </xs:restriction>
        </xs:simpleType>
      </xs:list>
    </xs:simpleType>
    <xs:assertion test="count($value) > 2"/>
  </xs:restriction>
</xs:simpleType>
```

14.1.2 *Assertions for complex types*

For assertions on complex types, the `assert` element is used instead of `assertion`. The `assert` element, whose syntax is shown in Table 14–7, can appear in a complex type `extension` or `restriction`, or can appear directly as a child of `complexType` if neither `simpleContent` nor `complexContent` is used.

Example 14–12 shows a constraint where the valid values of a child element (`number`) depend on the value of an attribute (`dept`). Constraints that cross multiple elements or attributes are sometimes called co-constraints and are a common use case for complex type assertions. If it were just a constraint on the `number` child individually, for example that it must be greater than 500 or less than 300, the assertion could have been put on the simple type of the `number` element. However, an assertion on the `number` element's simple type would not have access to the `dept` attribute since it is out of scope, so the assertion must be moved up to the `product` parent.

Table 14–7   XSD Syntax: complex type assertion

Name
assert

Parents
complexType, extension, restriction

Attribute name	Type	Description
id	ID	Unique ID.
test	XPath expression	Assertion test.
xpathDefaultNamespace	anyURI | "##defaultNamespace" | "##targetNamespace" | "##local"	The default namespace for XPath expressions.

Content
annotation?

Example 14–12. An assertion on a complex type

```
<xs:element name="product" type="ProductType"/>
<xs:complexType name="ProductType">
  <xs:sequence>
    <xs:element name="number" type="xs:integer"/>
    <xs:element name="name" type="xs:string"/>
    <xs:element name="size" type="xs:integer"/>
  </xs:sequence>
  <xs:attribute name="dept" type="xs:string"/>
  <xs:assert test="(@dept = 'ACC' and number > 500) or
                   (number &lt; 300)"/>
</xs:complexType>
```

The same XPath operators and functions described in Sections 14.1.1.1 on p. 355 and 14.1.1.2 on p. 357 can be used in these complex type assertions. One difference is that in complex content assertions, you do not use the $value variable (since there is no simple value) but instead use element and attribute names to indicate the values to be tested. Attribute names are preceded by an at sign (@) in XPath, as shown in the reference to @dept.

14.1.2.1 Path expressions

When element or attribute names are used, they are known as *path expressions*, and they are evaluated relative to the element being validated. In Example 14–12, it is looking for a dept that is an attribute of product (or any other element of type ProductType), and a number element that is a direct child of product.

Path expressions can also have multiple steps, separated by forward slashes, that access elements and attributes further down in the element content. Example 14–13 shows a complex type CatalogType that is one level up from ProductType. To access the number child of product from there, it uses the multistep path product/number. Relative to catalog, product/number brings back multiple number elements and passes them all as a sequence to the max function, then compares that maximum to the maxNumber attribute of catalog.

As an alternative to specifying the exact path down to a descendant element, you can use the shortcut .// before an element name to indicate a descendant. For example, .//number, relative to catalog, will bring back all number elements that are descendants anywhere within the catalog, at any level.

Path expressions often involve predicates, which are Boolean expressions in square brackets that filter the elements and attributes returned by the expression. An element to which a predicate is applied is only returned if the Boolean expression returns true. For example, product[number > 500] will test for products whose number is greater than 500. Table 14–8 shows some examples of assertions using predicates that could apply to CatalogType from Example 14–13.

Example 14–13. An assertion with a multistep path

```
<xs:element name="catalog" type="CatalogType"/>
<xs:complexType name="CatalogType">
  <xs:sequence>
    <xs:element name="product" type="ProductType"
                maxOccurs="unbounded"/>
  </xs:sequence>
  <xs:attribute name="maxNumber" type="xs:integer"/>
  <xs:assert test="not(max(product/number) > @maxNumber)"/>
</xs:complexType>
<xs:complexType name="ProductType">
  <xs:sequence>
    <xs:element name="number" type="xs:integer"/>
    <xs:element name="name" type="xs:string"/>
    <xs:element name="size" type="xs:integer"/>
  </xs:sequence>
  <xs:attribute name="dept" type="xs:string"/>
</xs:complexType>
```

Table 14–8 Examples of assertion with predicates

Example	Explanation
`product[number < 500]`	There is at least one product whose number is less than 500.
`not(product[number < 500])`	There is no product whose number is less than 500.
`product[number < 500 and @dept='ACC']`	There is at least one product whose number is less than 500 and whose department is ACC.
`product[2][number < 500]`	The second product has a number that is less than 500.
`product[2][number]`	The second product has a number child (regardless of value).
`product[last()][number < 500]`	The last product has a number that is less than 500.

For the second example in Table 14–8, you might think that you can use product[number > 500] to test that product numbers are greater than 500. However, that will return true if there is at least one product number greater than 500; it does not ensure that *all* of the products have a number greater than 500. Using the not function, as shown in the table, works because it tests that there aren't any that are less than 500.

You may have noticed that most of the examples in the table actually return product elements rather than a Boolean true/false value. The results of XPaths used in assertions are automatically converted to a Boolean value. A sequence of one or more elements or attributes is treated as a "true" value, and an empty sequence (no elements or attributes) is treated as a "false" value.

14.1.2.2 Conditional expressions

The XPath 2.0 language also includes an if-then-else construct, known as a *conditional expression*, that is very useful for co-constraints. It uses if, then, and else keywords and the else clause is always required. The other syntactic requirement is that the if expression has to be in parentheses. Conditional expressions can be nested so that one conditional expression is embedded inside the then or else clause of another conditional expression.

Example 14–14 shows such an assertion which tests for different values of the dept attribute to determine the valid range of the number child. Since the else clause is always required, it simply calls the false function in the last clause, which means that if the department was not one of the three specified departments, the product is not valid, regardless of the number child.

Example 14–14. An assertion using conditional expressions

```
<xs:complexType name="ProductType">
  <xs:sequence>
    <xs:element name="number" type="xs:integer"/>
    <xs:element name="name" type="xs:string"/>
    <xs:element name="size" type="xs:integer"/>
  </xs:sequence>
  <xs:attribute name="dept" type="xs:string"/>
  <xs:assert test="if (@dept = 'ACC')
                   then number > 500
                   else if (@dept = 'WMN')
                   then number &lt;= 300 and number > 200
                   else if (@dept = 'MEN')
                   then number &lt; 200
                   else false()"/>
</xs:complexType>
```

14.1.2.3 Assertions in derived complex types

Assertions are inherited by derived complex types. Any assertions that are specified in an extension or restriction are added to the constraints on that type. In other words, an element must conform to the assertions on its complex type and on any other complex types from which its type is derived. Elements of type `ExtendedProductType` in Example 14–15 must conform both to the assertion in that type and the one specified in `ProductType`.

Example 14–15. Assertions in complex type extension

```
<xs:complexType name="ProductType">
  <xs:sequence>
    <xs:element name="number" type="xs:integer"/>
    <xs:element name="name" type="xs:string"/>
  </xs:sequence>
  <xs:attribute name="dept" type="xs:string"/>
  <xs:assert test="(@dept = 'ACC' and number > 500) or
                   (number &lt; 300)"/>
</xs:complexType>
```

(Continues)

Example 14–15.   (Continued)

```
<xs:complexType name="ExtendedProductType">
  <xs:complexContent>
    <xs:extension base="ProductType">
      <xs:sequence>
        <xs:element name="size" type="xs:integer" minOccurs="0"/>
      </xs:sequence>
      <xs:assert test="if (@dept = 'ACC')
                       then not(size)
                       else true()"/>
    </xs:extension>
  </xs:complexContent>
</xs:complexType>
```

Assertions are also inherited in restrictions. Elements of type `RestrictedProductType` in Example 14–16 must conform both to the assertion in that type and the one specified in `ProductType`. Unlike the content model, which needs to be respecified in the restricted type definition, assertions are inherited automatically.

Example 14–16. Assertions in complex type restriction

```
<xs:complexType name="ProductType">
  <xs:sequence>
    <xs:element name="number" type="xs:integer"/>
    <xs:element name="name" type="xs:string" minOccurs="0"/>
    <xs:element name="size" type="xs:integer" minOccurs="0"/>
  </xs:sequence>
  <xs:attribute name="dept" type="xs:string"/>
  <xs:assert test="(@dept = 'ACC' and number > 500) or
                   (number &lt; 300)"/>
</xs:complexType>
<xs:complexType name="RestrictedProductType">
  <xs:complexContent>
    <xs:restriction base="ProductType">
      <xs:sequence>
        <xs:element name="number" type="xs:integer"/>
        <xs:element name="name" type="xs:string"/>
        <xs:element name="size" type="xs:integer" minOccurs="0"/>
      </xs:sequence>
```

(Continues)

Example 14–16. (Continued)

```
        <xs:attribute name="dept" type="xs:string"
                       use="required"/>
        <xs:assert test="if (@dept = 'ACC')
                         then not(size)
                         else true()"/>
    </xs:restriction>
  </xs:complexContent>
</xs:complexType>
```

When a complex type with simple content extends a simple type, it can use `assert` to add assertions to the simple type. This is useful as an alternative to using `assertion` to restrict the content type, because the `assert` allows access to the attributes while the `assertion` doesn't. The `$value` variable can be used in this case; just like with simple types, `$value` will contain the content of the element, with an appropriate data type. Example 14–17 shows an assertion that tests both the `system` attribute and the value of the element.

Example 14–17. An assertion on a complex type with simple content

```
<xs:complexType name="SizeType">
  <xs:simpleContent>
    <xs:extension base="xs:integer">
      <xs:attribute name="system" type="xs:string"/>
      <xs:assert test="if (@system='US')
                       then $value &lt; 20
                       else $value >= 20"/>
    </xs:extension>
  </xs:simpleContent>
</xs:complexType>
```

14.1.3 *Assertions and namespaces*

If your schema has a target namespace, it is necessary to correctly prefix the element and attribute names used in XPath expressions. Example 14–18 shows a schema with a target namespace as well as a namespace declaration that maps that namespace to the prefix `prod`. The element names used in the assertion XPaths are then prefixed with `prod` to indicate that they are in that namespace. Otherwise, the processor would be looking for those elements in no namespace.

Example 14–18. Assertions using prefixed element names

```
<xs:schema xmlns:xs="http://www.w3.org/2001/XMLSchema"
           targetNamespace="http://datypic.com/prod"
           xmlns:prod="http://datypic.com/prod"
           elementFormDefault="qualified">
  <xs:element name="product" type="ProductType"/>
  <xs:complexType name="ProductType">
    <xs:sequence>
      <xs:element name="number" type="xs:integer"/>
      <xs:element name="name" type="xs:string"/>
      <xs:element name="size" type="xs:string" minOccurs="0"/>
    </xs:sequence>
    <xs:attribute name="dept" type="xs:string"/>
    <xs:assert test="(@dept = 'ACC' and prod:number > 500) or
                      (prod:number &lt; 300)"/>
    <xs:assert test="if (@dept = 'ACC')
                     then not(prod:size)
                     else true()"/>
  </xs:complexType>
</xs:schema>
```

Note the fact that `elementFormDefault` is set to `qualified`, which is what puts the locally declared `number` and `size` in the target namespace. Otherwise, you wouldn't need to prefix their names in the XPath, since they would be unqualified. For more information on qualified and unqualified element names, see Section 6.3 on p. 98.

14.1.3.1 Using `xpathDefaultNamespace`

You might expect to be able to declare a default namespace, such as `xmlns="http://datypic.com/prod"`, to avoid having to prefix the element names. However, regular default namespace declarations do not apply to XPath expressions. You can, however, use an `xpathDefaultNamespace` attribute to designate the default namespace for all unprefixed element names that are used in the XPath. As with regular default namespace declarations, `xpathDefaultNamespace` does not affect attribute names.

Example 14–19 uses the `xpathDefaultNamespace` attribute on the `schema` element. This means that the element names `number` and `size` in the XPaths are interpreted as being in the `http://datypic.com/prod` namespace. It is not looking for the `dept` attribute in that namespace. This is appropriate since the `attributeFormDefault` is defaulting to `unqualified`, meaning that locally declared attributes are in no namespace.

Example 14–19. Assertions using `xpathDefaultNamespace`

```
<xs:schema xmlns:xs="http://www.w3.org/2001/XMLSchema"
           targetNamespace="http://datypic.com/prod"
           xmlns:prod="http://datypic.com/prod"
           elementFormDefault="qualified"
           xpathDefaultNamespace="http://datypic.com/prod">
  <xs:element name="product" type="prod:ProductType"/>
  <xs:complexType name="ProductType">
    <xs:sequence>
      <xs:element name="number" type="xs:integer"/>
      <xs:element name="name" type="xs:string"/>
      <xs:element name="size" type="xs:string" minOccurs="0"/>
    </xs:sequence>
    <xs:attribute name="dept" type="xs:string"/>
    <xs:assert test="(@dept = 'ACC' and number > 500) or
                     (number &lt; 300)"/>
    <xs:assert test="if (@dept = 'ACC')
                     then not(size)
                     else true()"/>
  </xs:complexType>
</xs:schema>
```

Instead of containing a specific namespace name, the `xpathDefaultNamespace` attribute can contain one of three special keywords:

- `##targetNamespace`, indicating that the default XPath namespace is the same as the target namespace

- `##defaultNamespace`, indicating that the default XPath namespace is the namespace that is declared as the default (with an `xmlns=` attribute)
- `##local`, indicating that there is no default XPath namespace

In Example 14–19, changing the value to `##targetNamespace` would have the same meaning, since `http://datypic.com/prod` is the target namespace.

It is most convenient to specify `xpathDefaultNamespace` on the `schema` element, in which case it applies to all XPath expressions in the schema document. It can also be specified on (and is relevant to) the following elements:

- The `assert` and `assertion` elements, where it affects the `test` attribute
- The `alternative` element, where it affects the `test` attribute
- The `selector` and `field` elements, where it affects the `xpath` attribute

If `xpathDefaultNamespace` does not appear on one of these elements, the value is taken from the schema. If no value is provided for the schema, the default value is no namespace, meaning that unprefixed element names are interpreted as not being in a namespace.

14.2 | Conditional type assignment

Another new feature in XML Schema 1.1 is *conditional type assignment*, which allows for the type of an element to be assigned based on the values and/or presence of its attributes. A set of *type alternatives* are specified using `alternative` elements, which appear as children of the element declaration.

14.2.1 *The* alternative *element*

The syntax of an alternative element is shown in Table 14–9. It has a test attribute that specifies the condition under which that type is selected, in the form of an XPath 2.0 expression. It also indicates the type if this condition is true, which is signified either by a type attribute or an anonymous simpleType or complexType child.

Table 14–9   XSD Syntax: type alternative

Name		
alternative		

Parents		
element		

Attribute name	*Type*	*Description*
id	ID	Unique ID.
test	limited XPath 2.0 expression	The condition under which this alternative applies.
type	QName	The designated type. Either a type attribute or a simpleType or complexType child is required.
xpathDefaultNamespace	anyURI | "##defaultNamespace" | "##targetNamespace" | "##local"	The default namespace for XPath expressions, see Section 14.1.3.1.

Content
annotation?, (simpleType | complexType)?

14.2.2 *Specifying conditional type assignment*

Example 14–20 shows an example of conditional type assignment where there are three type alternatives:

1. The first alternative indicates that if the value of the dept attribute is ACC, the type assigned to the element declaration is AccessoryType.

2. The second alternative indicates that if the value of the dept attribute is either WMN or MEN, the type assigned is ClothingType.

3. The third alternative has no test attribute, indicating that ProductType is the default type if neither of the two other alternatives apply.

Example 14–20. Conditional type assignment with default type

```
<xs:element name="product">
  <xs:alternative test="@dept='ACC'" type="AccessoryType"/>
  <xs:alternative test="@dept='WMN' or @dept='MEN'"
                  type="ClothingType"/>
  <xs:alternative type="ProductType"/>
</xs:element>
```

The processor will run through the alternatives and choose the first one in order whose test returns true. If none of the tests return true, and there is a default type specified by an alternative with no test attribute, as there is in Example 14–20, that alternative indicates the type.

It is also possible to use type alternatives even though you have already declared a type in the usual way, giving element a type attribute or a simpleType or complexType child. An example is shown in Example 14–21, where the type attribute is used on element to assign the type ProductType to the element.

This is saying that ProductType is the type for product unless one of the alternatives applies. It is similar to the previous example, but defining it this way comes with the additional constraint that the type

Example 14–21. Conditional type assignment with declared type

```
<xs:element name="product" type="ProductType">
  <xs:alternative test="@dept='ACC'" type="AccessoryType"/>
  <xs:alternative test="@dept='WMN' or @dept='MEN'"
                  type="ClothingType"/>
</xs:element>
```

alternatives must be derived from the declared type. In this case, `AccessoryType` and `ClothingType` must be derived (directly or indirectly) from `ProductType`.

A third possibility is that neither a declared type nor a default type is specified, as in Example 14–22. In that case, if no alternatives apply, a `product` element can contain any well-formed XML; its type is `anyType`.

Example 14–22. Conditional type assignment with no default

```
<xs:element name="product">
  <xs:alternative test="@dept='ACC'" type="AccessoryType"/>
  <xs:alternative test="@dept='WMN' or @dept='MEN'"
                  type="ClothingType"/>
</xs:element>
```

14.2.3 *Using XPath in the* `test` *attribute*

Only a very small subset of the XPath 2.0 syntax is allowed in the `test` attribute by default, although some implementations may choose to support a more complete subset. The only XPath functions and operators that are allowed are:

- and and or Boolean operators
- Comparison operators (=, !=, <, <=, >, >=)
- The not function
- The type constructor functions

In addition, the XPath expression can only access the *attributes* of the element being validated. It cannot access its parent or ancestors, and it cannot even access its children or descendants like assertions can.

Additional example values for the `test` attribute are shown in Table 14–10.

Table 14–10   Examples of type alternative tests

Example	Explanation
`@foo`	The `foo` attribute exists.
`not(@foo)`	The `foo` attribute does not exist.
`@foo = 'yes'`	The `foo` attribute exists and contains a value equal to `yes`.
`@foo != 'yes'`	The `foo` attribute exists and contains a value equal to something other than `yes`.
`not(@foo = 'yes')`	The `foo` attribute exists and contains a value equal to something other than `yes`, *or* the `foo` attribute does not exist.
`@foo = 'yes' and @bar = 'A'`	The `foo` attribute exists and contains a value equal to `yes`, and the `bar` attribute exists and contains a value equal to `A`.
`@foo = 'yes' or @bar = 'A'`	The `foo` attribute exists and contains a value equal to `yes`, *or* the `bar` attribute exists and contains a value equal to `A`.
`@foo != @bar`	The `foo` and `bar` attributes both exist and contain different values.
`@num > 12`	The `num` attribute exists and contains a value greater than 12.
`xs:integer(@num) > xs:integer(@maxNum)`	The `num` attribute contains a value that is greater than the value of the `maxNum` attribute, when they are compared as integers.

The last example in the table makes use of the `integer` type constructor function to ensure that the two values are being compared as
numbers. Otherwise, they would be compared as strings, and a string
`100` is considered to be less than a string `99`.

This highlights an important difference between assertions and
conditional type assignment with regard to types in XPath. In assertions,
type information is used in the XPath expressions because there is only
one type to consider. In the case of conditional type assignment, the
type has not even been assigned yet, so it is impossible to determine
the types of the attributes. When `num` is compared to a literal integer,
as in the second-to-last example, it is automatically converted to an
integer. But when `num` and `maxNum` are compared to each other, and
neither has a type, they need to be converted to integers to ensure that
they are compared appropriately.

14.2.4 *The* `error` *type*

A special built-in simple type named `error` (in the XML Schema
namespace) is defined for use in conditional type assignment.[1] It is
used to indicate that a validation error should be raised under certain
conditions.

Example 14–23 uses the `error` type to raise an error if the `dept`
attribute is equal to anything other than `ACC`, `WMN`, or `MEN`.

Example 14–23. Using the `error` type as the default

```
<xs:element name="product">
  <xs:alternative test="@dept='ACC'" type="AccessoryType"/>
  <xs:alternative test="@dept='WMN' or @dept='MEN'"
                  type="ClothingType"/>
  <xs:alternative type="xs:error"/>
</xs:element>
```

---

1.   Technically, it can be used anywhere a type is normally used, but it is only
      practically useful in conditional type assignment.

It doesn't have to just be the last alternative, with no test, that uses the `error` type. It can be used with a test, and as an earlier alternative, as shown in Example 14–24. This example will raise an error if the product does not have a `dept` attribute.

Example 14–24. Using the `error` type with a test

```
<xs:element name="product">
  <xs:alternative test="not(@dept)" type="xs:error"/>
  <xs:alternative test="@dept='ACC'" type="AccessoryType"/>
  <xs:alternative test="@dept='WMN' or @dept='MEN'"
                  type="ClothingType"/>
</xs:element>
```

14.2.5 *Conditional type assignment and namespaces*

As with assertions, if the schema has a target namespace, you may need to pay attention to namespace prefixes in your XPath. It is less likely to be an issue because you are only using attribute names and it is less common for attributes to be in the target namespace of the schema. However, if an attribute is in a namespace, for example because it is globally declared or because `attributeFormDefault` is set to `qualified`, its name does need to be prefixed.

Example 14–25 shows a revised example where `dept` is globally declared, which means that it is in the target namespace. The XPath must now reflect the target namespace, so a `prod` prefix is added to `dept` wherever it appears in the XPaths.

As with assertions, the `xpathDefaultNamespace` attribute affects the XPaths in type alternatives. However, since it does not affect attribute names, it is unlikely to be useful in conditional type assignment.

Example 14–25. Conditional type assignment with globally declared attribute

```
<xs:schema xmlns:xs="http://www.w3.org/2001/XMLSchema"
           targetNamespace="http://datypic.com/prod"
           xmlns:prod="http://datypic.com/prod"
           elementFormDefault="qualified">
  <xs:element name="product" type="prod:ProductType">
    <xs:alternative test="@prod:dept='ACC'"
                     type="prod:AccessoryType"/>
    <xs:alternative test="@prod:dept='WMN' or @prod:dept='MEN'"
                     type="prod:ClothingType"/>
  </xs:element>
  <xs:complexType name="ProductType">
    <xs:sequence>
      <xs:element name="number" type="xs:integer"/>
      <xs:element name="name" type="xs:string"/>
    </xs:sequence>
    <xs:attribute ref="prod:dept"/>
  </xs:complexType>
  <xs:attribute name="dept" type="xs:string"/>
  <!--...-->
</xs:schema>
```

14.2.6 *Using inherited attributes in conditional type assignment*

Section 7.6 on p. 126 introduced the concept of inherited attributes, which are relevant not just to an element but also to its descendant elements. Example 14–26 shows an instance example where a `language` attribute is intended to be inherited by the first `title` element from its parent `workTitles`.

Example 14–26. Instance with an inherited attribute

```
<workTitles language="en">
  <title>Time Transfixed</title>
  <title language="fr">La Durée poignardée</title>
</workTitles>
```

Example 14–27 is a schema that defines a type alternative for the title element. It says that if the language is English, it has the type EnglishTitleType, meaning that the contents can only contain basic Latin characters (which is admittedly very simplified). Otherwise, the title element has the less restrictive type TitleType that allows any string.

Example 14–27. Assertions on inherited attribute

```
<xs:element name="workTitles" type="WorkTitlesType"/>
<xs:complexType name="WorkTitlesType">
  <xs:sequence>
    <xs:element name="title" maxOccurs="unbounded"
                type="TitleType">
      <xs:alternative test="@language='en'"
                      type="EnglishTitleType"/>
    </xs:element>
  </xs:sequence>
  <xs:attribute name="language" type="xs:language"
                inheritable="true"/>
</xs:complexType>
<xs:complexType name="EnglishTitleType">
  <xs:simpleContent>
    <xs:restriction base="TitleType">
      <xs:pattern value="\p{IsBasicLatin}+"/>
    </xs:restriction>
  </xs:simpleContent>
</xs:complexType>
<xs:complexType name="TitleType">
  <xs:simpleContent>
    <xs:extension base="xs:string">
      <xs:attribute name="language" type="xs:language"/>
    </xs:extension>
  </xs:simpleContent>
</xs:complexType>
```

The interesting thing about this example is that although the first title element does not have a language attribute in its start tag in the instance, in the XPath expressions it is treated as if it does, because the attribute is inherited. The instance in Example 14–26 is valid according to this schema.

Named groups

Chapter 15

X ML Schema provides the ability to define groups of element and attribute declarations that are reusable by many complex types. Named model groups are fragments of content models, and attribute groups are bundles of attribute declarations that are commonly used together. This chapter explains how to define and reference named model groups and attribute groups.

15.1 | Why named groups?

Defining a group and reusing it many times has the advantages of

- Encouraging consistency across schema components
- Allowing the schema author to change multiple content models in only one place
- Making it obvious that certain complex types share similar children or attributes
- In many cases, making the schema less verbose

15.2 | Named model groups

Named model groups are reusable fragments of content models. For example, if there are many type definitions in your schema that specify a description, optionally followed by a comment, you could define a group that represents this content model fragment. The group could then be used by many complex type definitions. Named model groups cannot contain attribute declarations; that is the purpose of attribute groups, which are described in Section 15.3 on p. 392.

A note on terminology: XML Schema formally uses the term "model group definition" for group elements, and "model group" for all, choice, and sequence groups. In this book, group elements are referred to as "named model groups" to reduce confusion associated with the two similar terms.

15.2.1 *Defining named model groups*

Named model groups are represented by group elements whose syntax is shown in Table 15–1. Named model groups are required to have a name, and that name must be unique among all the named model groups in the schema. Named model groups are always defined globally, meaning that their parent is always schema.[1]

Named model groups may contain any content model. However, a group cannot contain an element directly. Instead, group must have one and only one model group (choice, sequence, or all) as a child. There is an additional constraint that this one model group child cannot have occurrence constraints (minOccurs and maxOccurs) like other model groups. If you wish to indicate that the contents of the group appear multiple times, you may put occurrence constraints on the group reference, as described in Section 15.2.2.1 on p. 388.

Example 15–1 shows the definition of a named model group that contains a description optionally followed by a comment. Note

---

1.   Except in the case of a redefine or override.

Table 15–1   XSD Syntax: named model group definition

Name
group

Parents
schema, redefine, ▣override

Attribute name	Type	Description
id	ID	Unique ID.
name	NCName	Name of the named model group.

Content
annotation?, (all | choice | sequence)

Example 15–1. Named model group with local element declarations

```
<xs:schema xmlns:xs="http://www.w3.org/2001/XMLSchema">
  <xs:group name="DescriptionGroup">
    <xs:sequence>
      <xs:element name="description" type="xs:string"/>
      <xs:element name="comment" type="xs:string" minOccurs="0"/>
    </xs:sequence>
  </xs:group>
</xs:schema>
```

that the group has one child, a sequence, which has no occurrence constraints on it.

In Example 15–1, the element declarations are local in the group, as evidenced by the appearance of a name attribute instead of a ref attribute. It is also possible to use global element declarations, and then reference them from the named model group, as shown in Example 15–2.

Note that the type attribute is now in the global element declaration, while minOccurs stays in the reference to the element declaration. This is the same syntax as that used in complex types to reference global element declarations. In fact, when a complex type references a

Example 15–2. Named model group with element references

```
<xs:schema xmlns:xs="http://www.w3.org/2001/XMLSchema">

  <xs:element name="description" type="xs:string"/>
  <xs:element name="comment" type="xs:string"/>

  <xs:group name="DescriptionGroup">
    <xs:sequence>
      <xs:element ref="description"/>
      <xs:element ref="comment" minOccurs="0"/>
    </xs:sequence>
  </xs:group>
</xs:schema>
```

named model group, it is as if the schema author cut and pasted the contents of the group element into the complex type definition. All local element declarations in the group become local to that complex type.

Whether to use local element declarations in the group depends on whether you want these element declarations to be local to the complex type. For a complete discussion of global versus local element declarations, see Section 6.1.3 on p. 95.

15.2.2 *Referencing named model groups*

Named model groups may be referenced in complex types and in other groups. Since they are named global schema components, they may be referenced not only from within the same schema document, but also from other schema documents.

15.2.2.1 Group references

The syntax to reference a named model group is shown in Table 15–2. Named model groups are referenced through the ref attribute, just like other global schema components.

Table 15–2   XSD Syntax: named model group reference

Name
group

Parents
complexType, restriction, extension, sequence, choice, ▦all

Attribute name	Type	Description
id	ID	Unique ID.
ref	QName	Name of the group being referenced.
minOccurs	nonNegativeInteger: *1*	Minimum number of times the group may appear.
maxOccurs	nonNegativeInteger | "unbounded" : *1*	Maximum number of times the group may appear.

Content
annotation?

15.2.2.2 Referencing a named model group in a complex type

Example 15–3 shows the definition of the complex type PurchaseOrderType that references DescriptionGroup.

Example 15–3. Referencing a group from a complex type definition

```
<xs:complexType name="PurchaseOrderType">
  <xs:sequence>
    <xs:group ref="DescriptionGroup" minOccurs="0"/>
    <xs:element ref="items"/>
    <!--...-->
  </xs:sequence>
</xs:complexType>
```

Note that when referencing a group, `minOccurs` and `maxOccurs` may be specified to indicate how many times the contents of the group may appear. If `minOccurs` and `maxOccurs` are not specified, the default for both values is 1. The value for `minOccurs` must be less than or equal to the value for `maxOccurs`. This means that if a `minOccurs` value is specified that is more than 1, `maxOccurs` must also appear, with a value greater than or equal to `minOccurs`.

To illustrate how named model group references are handled, Example 15–4 shows a content model equivalent to Example 15–3 (assuming it was referencing `DescriptionGroup` from Example 15–1) but without a named model group being used. Note that the `minOccurs="0"` constraint that appeared in the group reference now appears in the `sequence` tag.

Example 15–4. Equivalent content model without a named model group reference

```
<xs:complexType name="PurchaseOrderType">
  <xs:sequence>
    <xs:sequence minOccurs="0">
      <xs:element name="description" type="xs:string"/>
      <xs:element name="comment" type="xs:string" minOccurs="0"/>
    </xs:sequence>
    <xs:element ref="items"/>
    <!--...-->
  </xs:sequence>
</xs:complexType>
```

In Example 15–3, the group is referenced within a `sequence` group. Named model groups may be referenced anywhere in the content model, and multiple named model group references (even to the same group) are allowed.

A named model group may also be referenced at the top level of a `complexType`, if the group contains the entire content model of the type. A complex type may only directly contain either one named model group (`group`) or one model group (`all`, `sequence`, or choice). Example 15–5 shows the definition of `DescriptionType` that references `DescriptionGroup` at the top level.

Example 15–5. Group reference at the top level of the content model

```
<xs:complexType name="DescriptionType">
  <xs:group ref="DescriptionGroup"/>
  <xs:attribute ref="xml:lang"/>
</xs:complexType>
```

15.2.2.3 Using `all` in named model groups

An `all` group may appear in named model groups, but the additional constraints on `all` groups still apply. Example 15–6 shows a legal use of an `all` group within a named model group. In version 1.0, an `all` group may only contain element declarations or references, not other groups.

Example 15–6. Group with an `all` model group

```
<xs:schema xmlns:xs="http://www.w3.org/2001/XMLSchema">
  <xs:group name="DescriptionGroup">
    <xs:all>
      <xs:element name="description" type="xs:string"/>
      <xs:element name="comment" type="xs:string" minOccurs="0"/>
    </xs:all>
  </xs:group>
</xs:schema>
```

In version 1.0, since `all` groups can only appear at the top level of a complex type, the only way to reference a named model group that contains an `all` group is at the top level, as shown in Example 15–5. Version 1.1 has relaxed this constraint, and it is possible to reference a named model group that contains `all` from another `all` group, provided that `minOccurs` and `maxOccurs` are 1 on the group reference. However, it is still not legal to reference such a group from within a `choice` or `sequence`.

15.2.2.4 Named model groups referencing named model groups

Named model groups may reference other named model groups. This is shown in Example 15–7, where `ProductPropertyGroup` references `DescriptionGroup`.

Example 15–7. Group reference from a group

```
<xs:schema xmlns:xs="http://www.w3.org/2001/XMLSchema">
  <xs:group name="ProductPropertyGroup">
    <xs:sequence>
      <xs:group ref="DescriptionGroup"/>
      <xs:element name="number" type="xs:integer"/>
      <xs:element name="name" type="xs:string"/>
    </xs:sequence>
  </xs:group>

  <xs:group name="DescriptionGroup">
    <xs:sequence>
      <xs:element name="description" type="xs:string"/>
      <xs:element name="comment" type="xs:string" minOccurs="0"/>
    </xs:sequence>
  </xs:group>
</xs:schema>
```

The group references cannot be circular. That is, group a cannot reference itself, and group a cannot reference group b if the latter references group a, or another group c which references a, and so on. In addition, groups may only contain *references* to other groups; they cannot actually contain the definitions of groups, since all groups are defined globally.

15.3 | Attribute groups

Attribute groups are used to represent groups of related attributes that appear in many different complex types. For example, if the attributes id, name, and version are used in multiple complex types in your schema, it may be useful to define an attribute group that contains declarations for these three attributes, and then reference the attribute group in various complex type definitions.

15.3.1 *Defining attribute groups*

Attribute groups are represented by `attributeGroup` elements, whose syntax is shown in Table 15–3. Attribute groups are required to have a `name`, and that name must be unique among all the attribute groups in the schema. Attribute groups are always defined globally, meaning that their parent is always `schema`.[1]

Table 15–3   XSD Syntax: attribute group definition

Name		
`attributeGroup`		

Parents		
`schema, redefine,` ▥ `override`		

Attribute name	*Type*	*Description*
`id`	`ID`	Unique ID.
`name`	`NCName`	Attribute group name.

Content		
`annotation?, (attribute | attributeGroup)*, anyAttribute?`		

Attribute groups may contain any number of attribute declarations and references to other attribute groups, plus one optional attribute wildcard. An attribute group cannot contain more than one attribute declaration with the same qualified name. In version 1.0, there is

---

1.   Except in the case of a redefine or override.

an additional constraint that an attribute group cannot contain more than one attribute declaration of type ID.

For example, if many complex type definitions will use the attributes id and version, you could define an attribute group that contains declarations for these two attributes, as shown in Example 15–8.

Example 15–8. Attribute group with local attribute declarations

```
<xs:schema xmlns:xs="http://www.w3.org/2001/XMLSchema">
  <xs:attributeGroup name="IdentifierGroup">
    <xs:attribute name="id" type="xs:ID" use="required"/>
    <xs:attribute name="version" type="xs:decimal"/>
  </xs:attributeGroup>
</xs:schema>
```

In Example 15–8, the attributes are declared locally in the attribute group, as evidenced by the appearance of a name attribute instead of a ref attribute. It is also possible to use global attribute declarations and reference them from the attribute group, as shown in Example 15–9.

Example 15–9. Attribute group with attribute references

```
<xs:schema xmlns:xs="http://www.w3.org/2001/XMLSchema">
  <xs:attribute name="id" type="xs:ID"/>
  <xs:attribute name="version" type="xs:decimal"/>

  <xs:attributeGroup name="IdentifierGroup">
    <xs:attribute ref="id" use="required"/>
    <xs:attribute ref="version"/>
  </xs:attributeGroup>
</xs:schema>
```

Note that the type attribute is now in the global attribute declaration, while the use attribute stays in the reference to the attribute declaration. This is the same way that complex types reference global attribute declarations. In fact, when a complex type references an attribute group, it is as if the schema author cut and pasted the contents of the attribute group definition into the complex type definition. All attributes that are declared locally in the attribute group become local to that complex type.

Whether to declare attributes locally in the attribute group depends on whether you want the attributes to be local to the complex type. For a complete discussion of global versus local attribute declarations, see Section 7.2.3 on p. 119.

Attribute groups may reference other attribute groups, as described in the next section. Attribute groups may also contain one attribute wildcard at the very end, as shown in Example 15–10. Attribute groups are limited to one attribute wildcard because a complex type cannot contain more than one attribute wildcard. See Section 12.7.3 on p. 298 for more information.

Example 15–10. Attribute group with a wildcard

```
<xs:schema xmlns:xs="http://www.w3.org/2001/XMLSchema">
  <xs:attributeGroup name="IdentifierGroup">
    <xs:attribute name="id" type="xs:ID" use="required"/>
    <xs:attribute name="version" type="xs:decimal"/>
    <xs:anyAttribute namespace="##other"/>
  </xs:attributeGroup>
</xs:schema>
```

15.3.2 *Referencing attribute groups*

Attribute groups may be referenced in complex types and in other attribute groups. Since they are named global schema components, they may be referenced not only from within the same schema document, but also from other schema documents.

15.3.2.1 Attribute group references

The syntax to reference an attribute group is shown in Table 15–4. Attribute groups are referenced using the `ref` attribute, just like other global schema components.

Table 15–4   XSD Syntax: attribute group reference

Name

`attributeGroup`

Parents

`complexType, restriction, extension, attributeGroup`

Attribute name	Type	Description
`id`	ID	Unique ID.
`ref`	QName	Name of the attribute group being referenced.

Content

`annotation?`

15.3.2.2 Referencing attribute groups in complex types

Example 15–11 shows the definition of the complex type `ProductType` that references the attribute group `IdentifierGroup`.

Example 15–11. Referencing an attribute group from a complex type definition

```
<xs:complexType name="ProductType">
  <xs:sequence>
    <!--...-->
  </xs:sequence>
  <xs:attributeGroup ref="IdentifierGroup"/>
  <xs:attribute name="effDate" type="xs:date"/>
</xs:complexType>
```

As shown in the example, references to attribute groups must appear after the content model (a `sequence` group in this example). They may appear before, after, or in between attribute declarations. The order of attribute groups (and attributes) in a complex type is insignificant.

To illustrate how XML Schema handles attribute group references, Example 15–12 shows a complex type definition that is equivalent to Example 15–11 (assuming it was referencing `IdentifierGroup` from Example 15–8) but without an attribute group being used. It is as if the schema author cut and pasted the attribute declarations from the attribute group.

Example 15–12. Equivalent complex type without an attribute group

```
<xs:complexType name="ProductType">
  <!--...-->
  <xs:attribute name="id" type="xs:ID" use="required"/>
  <xs:attribute name="version" type="xs:decimal"/>
  <xs:attribute name="effDate" type="xs:date"/>
</xs:complexType>
```

15.3.2.3 Duplicate attribute names

It is illegal to declare two attributes with the same qualified name in the same complex type. When using attribute groups, be sure that the referenced attribute group does not declare an attribute that is already declared directly in your complex type definition. Also, when referencing more than one attribute group in a complex type definition, be sure that the two attribute groups do not contain attribute declarations with identical names.

In Example 15–13, each of the attribute groups `IdentifierGroup` and `VersionGroup` contain a declaration of `version`, and the definition of `ProductType` references both attribute groups. This results in an illegal duplication of the `version` attribute for `ProductType`.

Example 15–13. Illegal duplication of attributes

```
<xs:schema xmlns:xs="http://www.w3.org/2001/XMLSchema">
  <xs:attributeGroup name="IdentifierGroup">
    <xs:attribute name="id" type="xs:ID" use="required"/>
    <xs:attribute name="version" type="xs:decimal"/>
  </xs:attributeGroup>
```

(Continues)

Example 15–13.   (Continued)

```
<xs:attributeGroup name="VersionGroup">
  <xs:attribute name="version" type="xs:decimal"/>
</xs:attributeGroup>

<xs:complexType name="ProductType">
  <xs:attributeGroup ref="IdentifierGroup"/>
  <xs:attributeGroup ref="VersionGroup"/>
</xs:complexType>
</xs:schema>
```

15.3.2.4 Duplicate attribute wildcard handling

Each attribute group definition may only contain one attribute wildcard. However, it is possible for a complex type definition to reference two attribute groups, each of which contains an attribute wildcard. The complex type definition may also have a "local" wildcard, that is, an anyAttribute child.

In such a case, an effective attribute wildcard is determined by taking the intersection of the constraints of all of the wildcards, including the local wildcard and any that were included from attribute groups. A simple rule of thumb is that any replacement attribute must conform to all of the attribute wildcards for that complex type.

The value of processContents for this effective wildcard is the value of processContents for the local wildcard, if it is present. If it is not, the schema processor takes the value of processContents from the first attribute wildcard among the attributeGroup children.

For more information on attribute wildcards, see Section 12.7.3 on p. 298.

15.3.2.5 Attribute groups referencing attribute groups

Definitions of attribute groups may also reference other attribute groups. This is shown in Example 15–14, where HeaderGroup references

IdentifierGroup. Attribute groups may only contain *references* to other attribute groups; they cannot actually contain the definitions of attribute groups, since all attribute groups are defined globally.

Example 15–14. Attribute group referencing an attribute group

```
<xs:schema xmlns:xs="http://www.w3.org/2001/XMLSchema">
  <xs:attributeGroup name="HeaderGroup">
    <xs:attributeGroup ref="IdentifierGroup"/>
    <xs:attribute ref="xml:lang"/>
  </xs:attributeGroup>

  <xs:attributeGroup name="IdentifierGroup">
    <xs:attribute name="id" type="xs:ID" use="required"/>
    <xs:attribute name="version" type="xs:decimal"/>
  </xs:attributeGroup>

</xs:schema>
```

In version 1.0, attribute group references cannot be circular. That is, HeaderGroup cannot reference IdentifierGroup if IdentifierGroup also has a reference back to HeaderGroup (either directly or through a chain of attribute group references). In version 1.1, circular references are permitted, and the effect is that all of the attributes of both HeaderGroup and IdentifierGroup are included.

15.3.3 *The default attribute group*

In version 1.1, you can indicate that an attribute group is the default attribute group by specifying its name in the defaultAttributes attribute on the schema element. If such a default attribute group is defined, the attributes declared in that group will automatically be allowed for every complex type in the schema document, unless you specifically disallow it.

Example 15–15 shows a schema that defines a default attribute group. The `defaultAttributes` attribute on the `schema` names `prod:IdentifierGroup` as the default attribute group. It uses the `prod` prefix because the namespace must be taken into account when referencing any other schema component.

Example 15–15. Default attribute group

```
<xs:schema xmlns:xs="http://www.w3.org/2001/XMLSchema"
          xmlns:prod="http://datypic.com/prod"
          targetNamespace="http://datypic.com/prod"
          defaultAttributes="prod:IdentifierGroup">

  <xs:attributeGroup name="IdentifierGroup">
    <xs:attribute name="id" type="xs:ID" use="required"/>
    <xs:attribute name="version" type="xs:decimal"/>
  </xs:attributeGroup>

  <xs:complexType name="ProductType">
    <xs:sequence>
      <!--...-->
    </xs:sequence>
    <xs:attribute name="dept" type="xs:string"/>
  </xs:complexType>

  <xs:complexType name="CatalogType" defaultAttributesApply="false">
    <xs:sequence>
      <!--...-->
    </xs:sequence>
    <xs:attribute name="catalogNumber" type="xs:integer"/>
  </xs:complexType>
</xs:schema>
```

The effect of declaring the default attribute group is as if `ProductType` had included a reference to the attribute group; `id` and `version` attributes can appear on instances of this type. `ProductType` can also contain other attribute declarations or attribute group references. `CatalogType`, however, does not use the default attribute group, because it specifically disallows it using the attribute `defaultAttributesApply="false"`.

15.4 | Named groups and namespaces

Like most global components, named groups take on the target namespace of the schema document, so they need to be referenced with their qualified names. Example 15–16 works because the target namespace is the same as the default namespace, so that when the groups are referenced using the ref attribute, it is looking for their names in the target namespace.

Example 15–16. Named groups with a target namespace

```
<xs:schema xmlns:xs="http://www.w3.org/2001/XMLSchema"
           elementFormDefault="qualified"
           xmlns="http://datypic.com/prod"
           targetNamespace="http://datypic.com/prod">
  <xs:group name="DescriptionGroup">
    <xs:sequence>
      <xs:element name="description" type="xs:string"/>
      <xs:element name="comment" type="xs:string" minOccurs="0"/>
    </xs:sequence>
  </xs:group>
  <xs:attributeGroup name="IdentifierGroup">
    <xs:attribute name="id" type="xs:ID" use="required"/>
    <xs:attribute name="version" type="xs:decimal"/>
    <xs:anyAttribute namespace="##other"/>
  </xs:attributeGroup>
  <xs:complexType name="PurchaseOrderType">
    <xs:sequence>
      <xs:group ref="DescriptionGroup" minOccurs="0"/>
      <xs:element ref="items"/>
      <!--...-->
    </xs:sequence>
    <xs:attributeGroup ref="IdentifierGroup"/>
  </xs:complexType>
</xs:schema>
```

When referencing named groups that are defined in a different namespace, the names need to be appropriately prefixed. This is shown in Example 15–17 where the values of the ref attribute use prefixed names prod:DescriptionGroup and prod:IdentifierGroup because that namespace is not the default in ord.xsd.

Example 15–17. Named groups across namespaces

ord.xsd

```
<xs:schema xmlns:xs="http://www.w3.org/2001/XMLSchema"
           elementFormDefault="qualified"
           xmlns="http://datypic.com/ord"
           xmlns:prod="http://datypic.com/prod"
           targetNamespace="http://datypic.com/ord">
  <xs:import namespace="http://datypic.com/prod"
             schemaLocation="prod.xsd"/>
  <xs:complexType name="PurchaseOrderType">
    <xs:sequence>
      <xs:group ref="prod:DescriptionGroup" minOccurs="0"/>
      <xs:element ref="items"/>
      <!--...-->
    </xs:sequence>
    <xs:attributeGroup ref="prod:IdentifierGroup"/>
  </xs:complexType>
</xs:schema>
```

prod.xsd

```
<xs:schema xmlns:xs="http://www.w3.org/2001/XMLSchema"
           elementFormDefault="qualified"
           xmlns="http://datypic.com/prod"
           targetNamespace="http://datypic.com/prod">
  <xs:group name="DescriptionGroup">
    <xs:sequence>
      <xs:element name="description" type="xs:string"/>
      <xs:element name="comment" type="xs:string" minOccurs="0"/>
    </xs:sequence>
  </xs:group>
  <xs:attributeGroup name="IdentifierGroup">
    <xs:attribute name="id" type="xs:ID" use="required"/>
    <xs:attribute name="version" type="xs:decimal"/>
    <xs:anyAttribute namespace="##other"/>
  </xs:attributeGroup>
</xs:schema>
```

The locally declared elements have qualified names, that is, they are in a namespace and `elementFormDefault` is set to `qualified`. Note that the names of those elements declared in `prod.xsd` will retain the target namespace of that schema document, `http://datypic.com/prod`. Being referenced as a group from a schema document with a different target namespace does not change their namespace, even though they are locally declared.

15.5 | Design hint: Named groups or complex type derivations?

There may be cases where it is unclear when to define a named group and when to use complex type derivation. Complex type derivation, like named groups, serves the purpose of allowing reuse of content models and attributes.

For example, if there are several places in your purchase order where you allow a `description` optionally followed by a `comment`, you could define a named model group to represent this. You could then reuse this group in the content model of several, possibly dissimilar complex types.

However, it is also possible to represent this differently. You can define a base complex type that has the descriptive element declarations, and several complex types that extend the base type to specify additional children. Example 15–18 illustrates this approach.

The same dilemma can apply to attributes, which can be reused both through attribute groups and through complex type extensions.

Either of these two methods is legal, but each has its advantages and disadvantages. Use a named model group if:

- The fragment you want to reuse does not appear first in some of the types' content models. This is because extension adds a derived type's content model after its base type's content model as if they were in a `sequence` group. In the above example, if the descriptive information did not come first, it would have been impossible to use extension.

Example 15–18. Reusing content model fragments through derivation

```
<xs:complexType name="DescribedType">
  <xs:sequence>
    <xs:element name="description" type="xs:string"/>
    <xs:element name="comment" type="xs:string" minOccurs="0"/>
  </xs:sequence>
</xs:complexType>

<xs:complexType name="PurchaseOrderType">
  <xs:complexContent>
    <xs:extension base="DescribedType">
      <xs:sequence>
        <xs:element ref="items"/>
        <!--...-->
      </xs:sequence>
    </xs:extension>
  </xs:complexContent>
</xs:complexType>

<xs:complexType name="ItemsType">
  <xs:complexContent>
    <xs:extension base="DescribedType">
      <xs:sequence>
        <xs:element ref="product" maxOccurs="unbounded"/>
        <!--...-->
      </xs:sequence>
    </xs:extension>
  </xs:complexContent>
</xs:complexType>
```

- The types are dissimilar concepts that just happen to share a small content model fragment. It may not be intuitive to derive them from the same base type.

On the other hand, use a complex type derivation if:

- The reusable content model fragments appear at the beginning of the content model.
- The types have mostly the same content model with just a few differing element or attribute declarations.

Substitution groups

Chapter 6

S ubstitution groups are a flexible way to designate element declarations as substitutes for other element declarations in content models. You can easily designate new element declarations as substitutes, from other schema documents and even other namespaces, without changing the original content model. This chapter describes how to define and use substitution groups.

16.1 | Why substitution groups?

Substitution groups are useful for simplifying content models and making them more extensible and flexible. Suppose you have a section of a purchase order that lists products of various kinds. You could use repeating product elements, each having an attribute or child element to indicate what kind of a product it is. However, you may also want to allow different content models for different kinds of products. For example, shirts have a mandatory size, while umbrellas are not allowed to have a size specified. Also, you may want to use descriptive element names that indicate the kind of product. Lastly, you may want the definition to be flexible enough to accept new kinds of products without altering the original schema. This is a perfect application for substitution groups.

16.2 | The substitution group hierarchy

Each substitution group consists of a head and one or more members. Wherever the head element declaration is referenced in a content model, one of the member element declarations may be substituted in place of the head. For example, the head of your substitution group might be `product`, with the members being the different kinds of products such as `shirt`, `hat`, and `umbrella`. This hierarchy is depicted in Figure 16–1.

This means that anywhere `product` appears in a content model, any of `product`, `shirt`, `hat`, or `umbrella` may appear in the instance. The members themselves cannot be substituted for each other. For example, if `shirt` appears in a content model, `umbrella` cannot be substituted in its place.

Substitution groups form a hierarchy. There can be multiple levels of substitution, and a member of one group may be the head of another group. Other element declarations might have `shirt` as their substitution group head, as shown in Figure 16–2. In this case, `tShirt` and `blouse` may substitute for either `product` or `shirt`.

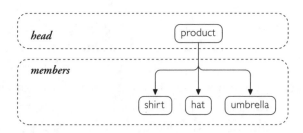

Figure 16–1   Substitution group hierarchy

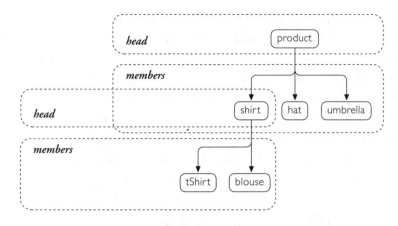

Figure 16–2   Multilevel substitution group hierarchy

16.3 | Declaring a substitution group

Example 16–1 shows the ItemsType complex type that contains a product element declaration. The product element declaration will

Example 16–1. The head of a substitution group

```
<xs:schema xmlns:xs="http://www.w3.org/2001/XMLSchema">
  <xs:element name="items" type="ItemsType"/>
  <xs:complexType name="ItemsType">
    <xs:sequence>
      <xs:element ref="product" maxOccurs="unbounded"/>
    </xs:sequence>
  </xs:complexType>

  <xs:element name="product" type="ProductType"/>
  <xs:complexType name="ProductType">
    <xs:sequence>
      <xs:element name="number" type="xs:integer"/>
      <xs:element name="name" type="xs:string"/>
    </xs:sequence>
  </xs:complexType>
</xs:schema>
```

be the head of the substitution group, although there is nothing special about the `product` declaration to indicate this. It is significant, however, that it is a global declaration, since only a global element declaration can be the head of a substitution group.

Example 16–2 shows the three element declarations that are members of the substitution group. The `product`, `shirt`, `hat`, and `umbrella` element declarations can be used interchangeably wherever `product` appears in any content model. Each of the declarations uses the `substitutionGroup` attribute to indicate that it is substitutable for

Example 16–2. Members of a substitution group

```
<xs:schema xmlns:xs="http://www.w3.org/2001/XMLSchema">

  <xs:element name="shirt" type="ShirtType"
              substitutionGroup="product"/>
  <xs:complexType name="ShirtType">
    <xs:complexContent>
      <xs:extension base="ProductType">
        <xs:sequence>
          <xs:element name="size" type="ShirtSizeType"/>
          <xs:element name="color" type="ColorType"/>
        </xs:sequence>
      </xs:extension>
    </xs:complexContent>
  </xs:complexType>

  <xs:element name="hat" substitutionGroup="product">
    <xs:complexType>
      <xs:complexContent>
        <xs:extension base="ProductType">
          <xs:sequence>
            <xs:element name="size" type="HatSizeType"/>
          </xs:sequence>
        </xs:extension>
      </xs:complexContent>
    </xs:complexType>
  </xs:element>

  <xs:element name="umbrella" substitutionGroup="product"/>

  <!--...-->
</xs:schema>
```

product. Members of a substitution group must be globally declared; it is not legal to use the `substitutionGroup` attribute in local element declarations or element references.

Example 16–3 shows a valid instance. Since `items` can contain an unlimited number of `product` elements, any combination of `product`, `shirt`, `hat`, and `umbrella` may appear in `items`, in any order. Keep in mind that everywhere a reference to the global `product` element declaration appears in a content model, it can be replaced by these other element declarations because the substitution group is in effect. If there is a content model where you only want `product` elements to be valid, with no substitution, you can get around this by supplying a local `product` element declaration in that content model.

Example 16–3. Instance of `items`

```
<items>
  <product>
    <number>999</number>
    <name>Special Seasonal</name>
  </product>
  <shirt>
    <number>557</number>
    <name>Short-Sleeved Linen Blouse</name>
    <size>10</size>
    <color value="blue"/>
  </shirt>
  <hat>
    <number>563</number>
    <name>Ten-Gallon Hat</name>
    <size>L</size>
  </hat>
  <umbrella>
    <number>443</number>
    <name>Deluxe Golf Umbrella</name>
  </umbrella>
</items>
```

The `substitutionGroup` attribute takes a `QName` as its value. This means that if the head's element name is in a namespace (i.e., the schema document in which it is declared has a target namespace), you must prefix the element name you specify in the `substitutionGroup` attribute. You can have an element declaration from a different namespace as the head of your substitution group, provided that the namespace of that element declaration has been imported into your schema document.

16.4 | Type constraints for substitution groups

In Example 16–2, the complex types of `shirt` and `hat` are both derived from the type of `product`. This is a requirement; members of a substitution group must have types that are either the same as the type of the head, or derived from it by either extension or restriction. They can be directly derived from it, or derived indirectly through multiple levels of restriction and/or extension.

In our example, `shirt` is assigned a named type, `ShirtType`, which extends `ProductType`, while `hat` has an anonymous type, also an extension of `ProductType`. The third element declaration, `umbrella`, does not specify a type. If a substitution group member is specified without a type, it automatically takes on the type of the head of its substitution group. Therefore, in this case, `umbrella` has the type `ProductType`.

This type constraint on the members of a substitution group is not as restrictive as it seems. You can make the type of the head very generic, allowing almost anything to be derived from it. In fact, you do not have to specify a type in the head element declaration at all, which gives it the generic `anyType`. Since all types are derived (directly or indirectly) from `anyType`, the members of the substitution group in this case can have any types, including simple types.

The previous examples in this chapter use complex types, but substitution groups may also be used for element declarations with simple types. If a member of a substitution group has a simple type, it must be a restriction of (or the same as) the simple type of the head.

Example 16–4 shows a substitution group of element declarations with simple types. Note that the head element declaration, `number`, does not specify a type, meaning that the members of the substitution group may have any type.

Example 16–4. Substitution group with simple types

```
<xs:schema xmlns:xs="http://www.w3.org/2001/XMLSchema">
  <xs:element name="number"/>
  <xs:element name="skuNumber" type="xs:string"
              substitutionGroup="number"/>
  <xs:element name="productID" type="xs:integer"
              substitutionGroup="number"/>
</xs:schema>
```

16.5 | Members in multiple groups

In version 1.0, each element declaration can only be a member of one substitution group. In version 1.1, it is possible for an element declaration to be a member of many substitution groups. This is done by specifying a space-separated list of names as the value of the `substitutionGroup` attribute, as shown in Example 16–5.

Example 16–5. A member of two substitution groups

```
<xs:schema xmlns:xs="http://www.w3.org/2001/XMLSchema">
  <xs:element name="product" type="ProductType"/>
  <xs:element name="discontinuedProduct" type="ProductType"/>
  <xs:element name="hat" type="HatType"
              substitutionGroup="product"/>
  <xs:element name="shirt" type="ShirtType"
              substitutionGroup="product"/>
  <xs:element name="umbrella" type="UmbrellaType"
              substitutionGroup="product discontinuedProduct"/>
  <!--...-->
</xs:schema>
```

In this example, there are two head element declarations: `product` and `discontinuedProduct`. The `hat` and `shirt` declarations are in just the `product` substitution group, but `umbrella` is in both. This means that `umbrella` can appear anywhere either of these two elements can appear. The type restrictions described in the previous section still apply, so it is generally necessary for the two head element declarations to use same type (which can be `anyType`) or types that are related to each other by derivation.

16.6 | Alternatives to substitution groups

Substitution groups are very useful, but as you may have guessed, there are other methods of achieving similar goals. This section will take a closer look at two of these methods.

16.6.1 *Reusable* `choice` *groups*

The behavior of substitution groups is similar to that of named `choice` groups. In the previous examples, we said that wherever `product` can appear, it can really be `product`, `shirt`, `hat`, or `umbrella`. This choice can also be represented by a named `choice` group that lists the relevant element declarations. Example 16–6 shows the definition of a named model group that allows a choice of `product` or `shirt` or `hat` or `umbrella`. This named model group is then referenced in the `ItemsType` definition.

It is easy to see the list of elements that are allowed, because they are all declared within the named model group. This can be an advantage if the list of member element declarations will not change. On the other hand, if you want to be able to add new element declarations as needed, from a variety of schema documents, using substitution groups

Example 16–6. Using a `choice` group

```
<xs:schema xmlns:xs="http://www.w3.org/2001/XMLSchema">

  <xs:element name="items" type="ItemsType"/>
  <xs:complexType name="ItemsType">
    <xs:group ref="ProductGroup" maxOccurs="unbounded"/>
  </xs:complexType>

  <xs:group name="ProductGroup">
    <xs:choice>
      <xs:element name="product" type="ProductType"/>
      <xs:element name="shirt" type="ShirtType"/>
      <xs:element name="hat" type="HatType"/>
      <xs:element name="umbrella" type="ProductType"/>
    </xs:choice>
  </xs:group>

  <!--...-->
</xs:schema>
```

is a much better approach. This is because named `choice` groups are more rigid. While you can use redefining or overriding to extend a named `choice` group, it is more cumbersome and can only be done in schema documents with the same target namespace.

16.6.2 *Substituting a derived type in the instance*

Another alternative to using substitution groups is to repeat the same element name for all of the items (in this case `product`), and use `xsi:type` attributes to distinguish between the different types of products. Using this approach, we would not declare `shirt`, `hat`, or `umbrella` elements at all, just their types, as shown in Example 16–7. Remember, it is acceptable to substitute a derived type in an instance if you specify the `xsi:type` attribute. This is described in more detail in Section 13.6 on p. 341.

Example 16–7. Defining derived types

```
<xs:schema xmlns:xs="http://www.w3.org/2001/XMLSchema">
  <xs:complexType name="ShirtType">
    <xs:complexContent>
      <xs:extension base="ProductType">
        <xs:sequence>
          <xs:element name="size" type="ShirtSizeType"/>
          <xs:element name="color" type="ColorType"/>
        </xs:sequence>
      </xs:extension>
    </xs:complexContent>
  </xs:complexType>

  <xs:complexType name="HatType">
    <xs:complexContent>
      <xs:extension base="ProductType">
        <xs:sequence>
          <xs:element name="size" type="HatSizeType"/>
        </xs:sequence>
      </xs:extension>
    </xs:complexContent>
  </xs:complexType>

  <xs:complexType name="UmbrellaType">
    <xs:complexContent>
      <xs:extension base="ProductType"/>
    </xs:complexContent>
  </xs:complexType>

  <!--...-->
</xs:schema>
```

Example 16–8 shows a valid instance for this approach. The `product` element is repeated many times, with the `xsi:type` attribute distinguishing between the different product types.

The advantage of this approach is that the instance may be easier to process. A Java program or XSLT stylesheet that handles this instance can treat all product types the same based on their element name, but also distinguish between them using the value of `xsi:type` if necessary.

Example 16–8. Valid instance using derived types

```
<items xmlns:xsi="http://www.w3.org/2001/XMLSchema-instance">
  <product>
    <number>999</number>
    <name>Special Seasonal</name>
  </product>
  <product xsi:type="ShirtType">
    <number>557</number>
    <name>Short-Sleeved Linen Blouse</name>
    <size>10</size>
    <color value="blue"/>
  </product>
  <product xsi:type="HatType">
    <number>563</number>
    <name>Ten-Gallon Hat</name>
    <size>L</size>
  </product>
  <product xsi:type="UmbrellaType">
    <number>443</number>
    <name>Deluxe Golf Umbrella</name>
  </product>
</items>
```

Using substitution groups, with some XML technologies, if one wanted to retrieve all the products, it would be necessary to select them based on their position in the instance (e.g., all children of `items`) rather than their element name (`product`), which could be less reliable. This distinction is not as important with schema-aware technologies like XSLT 2.0, with which you can refer generically to `schema-element(product)` which means "`product` or any of its substitutes."

Type substitution also has some disadvantages. It works fine for schema validation, but it is impossible to write a DTD that would validate this instance to the same degree. Also, it looks slightly more complicated and requires a declaration of the XML Schema Instance Namespace, which adds an extra dependency.

16.7 | Controlling substitution groups

Substitution groups are a powerful tool, and you may want to control their use. Three attributes of element declarations control the creation and use of substitutions.

- The `final` attribute limits the declaration of substitution groups in schemas.
- The `block` attribute limits the use of substituted elements in instances.
- The `abstract` attribute forces element substitution in instances.

These three attributes only apply to global element declarations, since local element declarations can never serve as heads of substitution groups.

16.7.1 `final`: *Preventing substitution group declarations*

You may want to prevent other people from defining schemas that use your element declaration as the head of a substitution group. This is accomplished using the `final` attribute in the element declaration, which may have one of the following values:

- `#all`, in version 1.0, prevents any other element declaration from using your element declaration as a substitution group head. In version 1.1, it only prevents element declarations whose types are extensions or restrictions from being in the substitution group, but allows element declarations that have the same type as the head.
- `extension` prevents extension in substitution group members. An element declaration that uses your element declaration as its substitution group head must have a type that is either the

same as, or derived by restriction from, the type of your element declaration.

- `restriction` prevents restriction in substitution group members. An element declaration that uses your element declaration as its substitution group head must have a type that is either the same as, or derived by extension from, the type of your element declaration.

- `extension restriction` and `restriction extension` are values that have the same effect as `#all`.

- `""` (an empty string) means that there are no restrictions. This value is useful for overriding the value of `finalDefault`, as described below.

- If no `final` attribute is specified, it takes its value from the `finalDefault` attribute of the `schema` element. If neither `final` nor `finalDefault` is specified, there are no restrictions on substitutions for that element declaration.

Example 16–9 shows four element declarations that control the use of substitution groups. With this declaration of `product`, the schema shown in Example 16–2 would have been illegal, since it attempts to use the `product` element declaration as the head of a substitution group.

Example 16–9. Using `final` to control substitution group declaration

```
<xs:element name="product" type="ProductType" final="#all"/>
<xs:element name="items" type="ItemsType" final="extension"/>
<xs:element name="color" type="ColorType" final="restriction"/>
<xs:element name="size" type="SizeType" final=""/>
```

16.7.2 `block`: *Blocking substitution in instances*

In the previous section, we saw how to prevent a schema from containing an element declaration that uses your element declaration as its substitution group head. There is another way to control element substitutions, this time in the instance. This is accomplished by using the `block` attribute, and assigning the value `substitution` (or `#all`) to it. Example 16–10 shows element declarations that use the `block` attribute.

With this declaration of `product`, the schema shown in Example 16–2 would have been *legal,* but the instance in Example 16–3 would have been illegal. This is the extremely subtle difference between the `final` and `block` attributes as they relate to substitution groups.

The `block` attribute also accepts the values `extension` and `restriction`, as described in Section 13.7.3 on p. 346. These values can also affect substitution groups, in that they can block members whose types are derived by either extension or restriction. For example, if Example 16–2 were changed to add `block="extension"` to the `product` declaration, that would make substituting `shirt` or `hat` invalid in the instance, because their types are derived by extension from the type of `product`.

Example 16–10. Using `block` to prevent substitution group use

```
<xs:element name="product" type="ProductType" block="#all"/>
<xs:element name="hat" type="HatType" block="substitution"/>
```

16.7.3 `abstract`: *Forcing substitution*

An element declaration may be abstract, meaning that its sole purpose is to serve as the head of a substitution group. Elements declared as abstract can never appear in instance documents. This is indicated by the `abstract` attribute in the element declaration. Example 16–11 shows an abstract element declaration for `product`. With this declaration, Example 16–3 would be invalid because a `product` element appears in the instance. Instead, only `shirt`, `hat`, and `umbrella` would be able to appear in `items`.

Example 16–11. An abstract element declaration

```
<xs:element name="product" type="ProductType" abstract="true"/>
```

Identity
constraints

Chapter 7

I dentity constraints allow you to uniquely identify nodes in a document and ensure the integrity of references between them. This chapter explains how to define and use identity constraints.

17.1 | Identity constraint categories

There are three categories of identity constraints.

- *Uniqueness constraints* enforce that a value (or combination of values) is unique within a specified scope. For example, all product numbers must be unique within a catalog.
- *Key constraints* also enforce uniqueness, and additionally require that all values be present. For example, every product must have a number and it must be unique within a catalog.
- *Key references* enforce that a value (or combination of values) corresponds to a value represented by a key or uniqueness

constraint. For example, for every product number that appears as an item in a purchase order, there must be a corresponding product number in the product description section.

17.2 | Design hint: Should I use `ID` / `IDREF` or `key` / `keyref`?

The identity constraints described in this chapter are much more powerful than using attributes of types `ID` and `IDREF`. Limitations of `ID` and `IDREF` include:

- They are recommended for use only for attributes, not elements.
- They are scoped to the entire document only.
- They are based on one value, as opposed to multifield keys.
- They require `ID` or `IDREF` to be the type of the attribute, precluding data validation of that attribute.
- They are based on string equality, as opposed to value equality.
- They require that the values be based on XML names, meaning they must start with a letter and can only contain letters, digits, and a few punctuation marks.

However, if `ID` and `IDREF` fulfill your requirements, there is no reason not to use them, particularly when representing simple cross-references in narrative documents or converting DTDs that are already in use.

17.3 | Structure of an identity constraint

The three categories of identity constraints are similar in their definitions and associated rules. This section describes the basic structure of identity constraints. Example 17–1 shows an instance that contains product catalog information.

Example 17–1. Product catalog information

```
<catalog>
  <department number="021">
    <product>
      <number>557</number>
      <name>Short-Sleeved Linen Blouse</name>
      <price currency="USD">29.99</price>
    </product>
    <product>
      <number>563</number>
      <name>Ten-Gallon Hat</name>
      <price currency="USD">69.99</price>
    </product>
    <product>
      <number>443</number>
      <name>Deluxe Golf Umbrella</name>
      <price currency="USD">49.99</price>
    </product>
  </department>
</catalog>
```

Example 17–2 shows the definition of a uniqueness constraint that might be applied to the instance in Example 17–1.

Example 17–2. A uniqueness constraint

```
<xs:element name="catalog" type="CatalogType">
  <xs:unique name="prodNumKey">
    <xs:selector xpath="*/product"/>
    <xs:field xpath="number"/>
  </xs:unique>
</xs:element>
```

All three categories of identity constraints are defined entirely within an element declaration. It can be either a global or local element declaration, but it cannot be an element reference. Identity constraints must be defined at the end of the element declaration, after any `simpleType` or `complexType` child. There can be multiple identity constraints in a single element declaration.

Every identity constraint has a name, which takes on the target namespace of the schema document. The qualified name must be unique among all identity constraints of all categories within the entire schema. For example, it would be illegal to have a key constraint named `customerNumber` and a uniqueness constraint named `customerNumber` in the same schema, even if they were scoped to different elements.

There are three parts to an identity constraint definition.

1. The *scope* is an element whose declaration contains the constraint. In our example, a `catalog` element is the scope. It is perfectly valid to have two products with the same number if they are contained in two different `catalog` elements.

2. The *selector* serves to select all the nodes to which the constraint applies. In our example, the selector value is `*/product`, which selects all the `product` grandchildren of `catalog`.

3. The one or more *fields* are the element and attribute values whose combination must be unique among the selected nodes. There can be only one instance of the field per selected node. In our example, there is one field specified: the `number` child of each `product` element.

17.4 | Uniqueness constraints

A uniqueness constraint is used to validate that the values of certain elements or attributes are unique within a particular scope. This is represented by a `unique` element, whose syntax is shown in Table 17–1.

In Example 17–2, we used a uniqueness constraint to ensure that all the product numbers in the catalog are unique. It is also possible to ensure uniqueness of a combination of multiple fields. In the instance shown in Example 17–3, each product may have an effective date.

Table 17–1   XSD Syntax: uniqueness constraint

Name		
unique		

Parents		
element		

Attribute name	Type	Description
id	ID	Unique ID.
name	NCName	Unique name.

Content		
annotation?, selector, field+		

Example 17–3. Product catalog information, revisited

```
<catalog>
  <department number="021">
    <product effDate="2000-02-27">
      <number>557</number>
      <name>Short-Sleeved Linen Blouse</name>
      <price currency="USD">29.99</price>
    </product>
    <product effDate="2001-04-12">
      <number>557</number>
      <name>Short-Sleeved Linen Blouse</name>
      <price currency="USD">39.99</price>
    </product>
    <product effDate="2001-04-12">
      <number>563</number>
      <name>Ten-Gallon Hat</name>
      <price currency="USD">69.99</price>
    </product>
    <product>
      <number>443</number>
      <name>Deluxe Golf Umbrella</name>
      <price currency="USD">49.99</price>
    </product>
  </department>
</catalog>
```

It is valid for two products to have the same number, as long as they have different effective dates. In other words, we want to validate that the combinations of number and effDate are unique. Example 17–4 shows the uniqueness constraint that accomplishes this.

Example 17–4. Constraining uniqueness of two combined fields

```
<xs:element name="catalog" type="CatalogType">
  <xs:unique name="dateAndProdNumKey">
    <xs:selector xpath="department/product"/>
    <xs:field xpath="number"/>
    <xs:field xpath="@effDate"/>
  </xs:unique>
</xs:element>
```

Note that this example works because both number and effDate are subordinate to the product elements. Using the instance in Example 17–3, it would be invalid to define a multifield uniqueness constraint on the department number and the product number. If you defined the selector to select all departments, the product/number field would yield more than one field node per selected node, which is not permitted. If you defined the selector to select all products, you would have to access an ancestor node to get the department number, which is not permitted.

You can get around this by defining two uniqueness constraints: one in the scope of catalog to ensure that all department numbers are unique within a catalog, and another in the scope of department to ensure that all product numbers are unique within a department.

17.5 | Key constraints

A key constraint is similar to a uniqueness constraint in that the combined fields in the key must be unique. Key constraints have an additional requirement that all of the field values must be present in the document. Therefore, you should not define keys on elements or attributes that are optional. In addition, the fields on which the key is defined cannot be nillable.

Key constraints are represented by key elements, whose syntax is shown in Table 17–2. It is identical to that of the unique elements.

Table 17–2   XSD Syntax: key constraint

Name		
key		

Parents		
element		

Attribute name	Type	Description
id	ID	Unique ID.
name	NCName	Unique name.

Content		
annotation?, selector, field+		

Example 17–5 changes Example 17–2 to be a key constraint instead of a uniqueness constraint. In this case, every product element in the instance would be required to have a number child, regardless of whether the complex type of product requires it. The values of those number children have to be unique within the scope of catalog.

Example 17–5. Defining a key on product number

```
<xs:element name="catalog" type="CatalogType">
  <xs:key name="prodNumKey">
    <xs:selector xpath="*/product"/>
    <xs:field xpath="number"/>
  </xs:key>
</xs:element>
```

17.6 | Key references

Key references are used to ensure that there is a match between two sets of values in an instance. They are similar to foreign keys in databases. Key references are represented by `keyref` elements, whose syntax is shown in Table 17–3.

Table 17–3   XSD Syntax: key reference

Name		
`keyref`		

Parents		
`element`		

Attribute name	Type	Description
`id`	`ID`	Unique ID.
`name`	`NCName`	Unique name.
`refer`	`QName`	Name of the key/uniqueness constraint being referenced.

Content		
`annotation?, selector, field+`		

The `refer` attribute is used to reference a key or uniqueness constraint by its qualified name. If the constraint is defined in a schema document with a target namespace, the `refer` attribute must reference a name that is either prefixed or in the scope of a default namespace declaration.

Suppose we have an order for three items: two shirts and one sweater, as shown in Example 17–6. The two shirts are the same except for their color, so they both have the same product number. All the descriptive product information appears at the end of the order. We want a way to ensure that every item in the order has a corresponding product description in the document.

Example 17–6. Key references

```
<order>
  <number>123ABBCC123</number>
  <items>
    <shirt number="557">
      <quantity>1</quantity>
      <color value="blue"/>
    </shirt>
    <shirt number="557">
      <quantity>1</quantity>
      <color value="sage"/>
    </shirt>
    <hat number="563">
      <quantity>1</quantity>
    </hat>
  </items>
  <products>
    <product>
      <number>557</number>
      <name>Short-Sleeved Linen Blouse</name>
      <price currency="USD">29.99</price>
    </product>
    <product>
      <number>563</number>
      <name>Ten-Gallon Hat</name>
      <price currency="USD">69.99</price>
    </product>
  </products>
</order>
```

Example 17–7 shows the definition of a key reference and its associated key. In this example, the number attribute of any child of items must match a number child of a product element. The meaning of the XPath syntax will be described in detail later in this chapter.

Note that the key reference field values are not required to be unique; that is not their purpose. It is valid to have duplicate shirt numbers in the items section.

As with key and uniqueness constraints, key references can be on multiple fields. There must be an equal number of fields in the key reference as there are in the key or uniqueness constraint that it

Example 17–7. Defining a key reference on product number

```
<xs:element name="order" type="OrderType">
  <xs:keyref name="prodNumKeyRef" refer="prodNumKey">
    <xs:selector xpath="items/*"/>
    <xs:field xpath="@number"/>
  </xs:keyref>
  <xs:key name="prodNumKey">
    <xs:selector xpath=".//product"/>
    <xs:field xpath="number"/>
  </xs:key>
</xs:element>
```

references. The fields are matched in the same order, and they must have related types.

17.6.1 *Key references and scope*

There is an additional constraint on the scope of key references and key constraints. The `key` referenced by a `keyref` must be defined in the same element declaration or in a declaration of one of its descendants. It is not possible for a `keyref` to reference a `key` that is defined in a sibling or ancestor element declaration. In our example, the `key` and `keyref` were both defined in the declaration of `order`. It would also have been valid if the `key` had been defined in the `products` declaration. However, it would have been invalid if the `keyref` had been defined in the `items` declaration, because `items` is a child of `order`.

17.6.2 *Key references and type equality*

When defining key references, it is important to understand XML Schema's concept of equality. When determining whether two values are equal, their type is taken into account. Values with unrelated types will never be considered equal. For example, a value 2 of type `string` is not equal to a value 2 of type `integer`. However, if two types are related by restriction, such as `integer` and `positiveInteger`, they can have equal values. When you define a key reference, make sure that the types of its fields are related to the types of the fields in the referenced key or uniqueness constraint. In Example 17–7, if the `number` attribute of `shirt` were declared as an `integer` and the `number` child of `product` were declared as a `string`, there would have been no matches. For more information on type equality, see Section 11.7 on p. 253.

17.7 | Selectors and fields

All three categories of identity constraints are specified in terms of a selector and one or more fields. This section explains selectors and fields in more detail.

17.7.1 *Selectors*

The purpose of a selector is to identify the set of nodes to which the constraint applies. The selector is relative to the scoping element. In Example 17–2, our selector was `*/product`. This selects all the `product` grandchildren of `catalog`. There may be other grandchildren of `catalog`, or other `product` elements elsewhere in the document, but the constraint does not apply to them.

   The selector is represented by a `selector` element, whose syntax is shown in Table 17–4.

Table 17–4   XSD Syntax: constraint selector

Name
`selector`

Parents
`unique, key, keyref`

(Continues)

Table 17–4   (Continued)

Attribute name	Type	Description
id	ID	Unique ID.
xpath	XPath subset	XPath to the selected nodes.
[1.1]xpathDefault-Namespace	anyURI | "##defaultNamespace" | "##targetNamespace" | "##local"	The default namespace for XPath expressions.

Content

annotation?

17.7.2 *Fields*

Each field must identify a single node relative to each node selected by the selector. The key reference in Example 17–7 works because there can only ever be one number attribute per selected node. In the instance in Example 17–6, the selector selects three nodes (the three children of items), and there is only one number attribute per node.

You might have been tempted to define a uniqueness constraint as shown in Example 17–8. This would not work because the selector would select one node (the single department element) and there would be three product/number nodes relative to it.

Example 17–8. Illegal uniqueness constraint

```
<xs:element name="catalog" type="CatalogType">
  <xs:unique name="prodNumKey">
    <xs:selector xpath="department"/>
    <xs:field xpath="product/number"/>
  </xs:unique>
</xs:element>
```

The elements or attributes that are used as fields must have simple content and cannot be declared nillable.

Fields are represented by `field` elements, whose syntax is shown in Table 17–5.

Table 17–5 XSD Syntax: constraint field

Name		
`field`		

Parents		
`unique, key, keyref`		

Attribute name	Type	Description
`id`	`ID`	Unique ID.
`xpath`	XPath subset	XPath to the key field.

`xpathDefault-`
`Namespace`
	`anyURI |`
	`"##defaultNamespace" |`
	`"##targetNamespace" |`
	`"##local"`
		The default namespace for XPath expressions.

Content		
`annotation?`		

17.8 | XPath subset for identity constraints

All values of the `xpath` attribute in the `selector` and `field` tags must be legal XPath expressions. However, they must also conform to a subset of XPath that is defined specifically for identity constraints.

XPath expressions are made up of paths, separated by vertical bars. For example, the XPath expression `department/product/name|` `department/product/price` uses two paths to select all the nodes that are either `name` or `price` children of `product` elements whose parent is `department`.

Each path may begin with the `.//` literal, which means that the matching nodes may appear anywhere among the descendants of the current scoping element. If it is not included, it is assumed that matching nodes may appear only as direct children of the scoping element.

Each path is made up of steps, separated by forward slashes. For example, the path `department/product/name` is made up of three steps: `department`, `product`, and `name`. Table 17–6 lists the types of steps that may appear in the identity constraint XPath subset.

The context node of the selector expression is the element in whose declaration the identity constraint is defined. The context node of the field expression is the result of evaluating the selector expression.

Table 17–7 shows some legal XPath expressions for selectors and fields. They assume that the scope of the identity constraint is the `catalog` element, as shown in Example 17–3.

Table 17–6   XPath subset steps

Step	Description	Example
Qualified element name	A child element name, which must be prefixed if it is in a namespace.	`department,` `prod:department`
Period (.)	The current element.	`.`
Asterisk (*)	A wildcard representing any element.	`*`
Prefix plus an asterisk	A wildcard representing any element in the namespace mapped to that prefix.	`prod:*`
@ plus a qualified attribute name	An attribute name, which must be prefixed if the attribute name is in a namespace (legal for `field` only).	`@number,` `@prod:number`

Table 17–7   XPath subset expressions in the scope of `catalog`

XPath	*Nodes selected*
`.`	`catalog` itself.
`*`	All direct children of `catalog`.
`.//*`	All elements appearing anywhere in `catalog`.
`department` or `./department`	All `department` elements that are direct children of `catalog`.
`./*/*`	All grandchildren of `catalog` (regardless of their or their parents' element names).
`.//product`	All `product` elements appearing anywhere in `catalog`.
`./*/product`	All `product` elements that are grandchildren of `catalog` (regardless of their parent).
`.//product/name`	All `name` elements whose parent is `product` appearing anywhere in `catalog`.
`./department/product/name`	All `name` elements whose parent is a `product` whose parent is a `department` whose parent is `catalog`.
`.//department | .//product`	All `department` elements and `product` elements appearing anywhere in `catalog`.
`@effDate`	The `effDate` attribute (legal only for `field`, not `selector`).
`product/@effDate`	The `effDate` attributes of all `product` children (legal only for `field`, not `selector`).
`/prod:product/prod:*`	All grandchildren whose parent is `product` in the namespace mapped to the `prod` prefix.

Technically, any of the XPath expressions in Table 17–7 is legal for a field. However, since the field XPath can only identify a node that appears once relative to the selected node, most of the expressions that contain wildcards to select multiple nodes are inappropriate for fields. The field XPath will usually consist of a single child element or a single attribute.

Table 17–8 shows some expressions that, while they are legal XPath, are not in the identity constraint XPath subset.

Table 17–8   Illegal XPath subset expressions

XPath(s)	Comments	Workaround
`../department` or `ancestor::department` or `parent::department`	Ancestors cannot be accessed.	Move the constraint up one level to the parent element (this does not always work if the fields appear at multiple levels).
`descendant::product`	The `descendant` keyword is not supported.	`.//product`
`text()`	You only need to specify the element name; `text()` is implied.	Use a single period (`.`) if it is the current node, otherwise simply leave off the `text()`.
`department//name`	All steps must contain something; double slash is not allowed except for "`.//`" at the beginning of path.	`department/*/name | department/*/*/name | ...` or move the constraint down one level to the `department` element.
`//product`	The document root cannot be accessed.	Move the constraint up to the level of the root (`catalog`) element, then use `.//product`.

(Continues)

Table 17–8   (Continued)

XPath(s)	Comments	Workaround
`/catalog/product`	The document root cannot be accessed.	Move the constraint up to the level of the root (`catalog`) element, then use `product`.

17.9 | Identity constraints and namespaces

Special consideration must be given to namespaces when defining identity constraints. By default, qualified element names and attribute names used in the XPath expressions must be prefixed in order to be legal. Let's take another look at our uniqueness constraint from Example 17–4. That definition assumed that the schema document had no target namespace. If we add a target namespace, it looks like Example 17–9.

Each of the element names in the XPath is prefixed with `prod`, mapping it to the `http://datypic.com/prod` namespace. In our

Example 17–9. Prefixing names in the XPath expression

```
<xs:schema xmlns:xs="http://www.w3.org/2001/XMLSchema"
           xmlns:prod="http://datypic.com/prod"
           targetNamespace="http://datypic.com/prod">
  <xs:element name="catalog" type="prod:CatalogType">
    <xs:unique name="dateAndProdNumKey">
      <xs:selector xpath="prod:department/prod:product"/>
      <xs:field xpath="prod:number"/>
      <xs:field xpath="@effDate"/>
    </xs:unique>
  </xs:element>
  <xs:element name="department" type="prod:DepartmentType"/>
  <xs:element name="product" type="prod:ProductType"/>
  <xs:element name="number" type="xs:integer"/>
  <!--...-->
</xs:schema>
```

example, all element declarations (department, product, and number) are global, and therefore their names must be prefixed. Let's assume that the attribute effDate is locally declared and unqualified, so its name is not prefixed in the XPath expression.

The names that must be qualified in an XPath expression are those that must be qualified in an instance, namely:

- All element names and attribute names in global declarations
- Element names and attribute names in local declarations whose form is qualified, either directly, using the form attribute, or indirectly through elementFormDefault or attributeFormDefault

Note that the target namespace is mapped to a prefix, rather than being the default namespace. This is because XPath expressions are not affected by default namespace declarations. Unprefixed names in XPath expressions are assumed to be in no namespace, even if a default namespace declaration is in scope.

Therefore, if you want to use identity constraints in a schema document that has a target namespace, you must map the target namespace to a prefix. Example 17–10 uses unprefixed names in the XPath

Example 17–10. Illegal attempt to apply default namespace to XPath

```
<xs:schema xmlns:xs="http://www.w3.org/2001/XMLSchema"
           xmlns="http://datypic.com/prod"
           targetNamespace="http://datypic.com/prod">
  <xs:element name="catalog" type="CatalogType">
    <xs:unique name="dateAndProdNumKey">
      <xs:selector xpath="department/product"/>
      <xs:field xpath="number"/>
      <xs:field xpath="@effDate"/>
    </xs:unique>
  </xs:element>
  <xs:element name="department" type="DepartmentType"/>
  <xs:element name="product" type="ProductType"/>
  <xs:element name="number" type="xs:integer"/>
  <!--...-->
</xs:schema>
```

expressions, assuming that these names take on the default namespace. This is not the case; in fact, these elements will not be found because the processor will be looking for elements with unqualified names when evaluating the XPath expressions.

17.9.1 *Using* `xpathDefaultNamespace`

In version 1.1, this problem is alleviated somewhat because you can specify an `xpathDefaultNamespace` attribute, which designates the default namespace for all unprefixed element names that are used in the XPath. It does not affect attribute names.

Example 17–11 uses the `xpathDefaultNamespace` attribute on the `schema` element. This means that the element names `department`, `product`, and `number` used in the selector and field XPaths are interpreted as being in the `http://datypic.com/prod` namespace.

Instead of specifying a namespace name, the `xpathDefault-Namespace` attribute can contain one of three special keywords: `##targetNamespace`, `##defaultNamespace`, or `##local`. These are described in detail in Section 14.1.3.1 on p. 373.

Example 17–11. Using `xpathDefaultNamespace`

```
<xs:schema xmlns:xs="http://www.w3.org/2001/XMLSchema"
           xmlns="http://datypic.com/prod"
           targetNamespace="http://datypic.com/prod"
           xpathDefaultNamespace="http://datypic.com/prod">
  <xs:element name="catalog" type="CatalogType">
    <xs:unique name="dateAndProdNumKey">
      <xs:selector xpath="department/product"/>
      <xs:field xpath="number"/>
      <xs:field xpath="@effDate"/>
    </xs:unique>
  </xs:element>
  <xs:element name="department" type="DepartmentType"/>
  <xs:element name="product" type="ProductType"/>
  <xs:element name="number" type="xs:integer"/>
  <!--...-->
</xs:schema>
```

17.10 | Referencing identity constraints

In version 1.1, identity constraints can be defined once and referenced from multiple elements. This is true for all three kinds of identity constraints: uniqueness constraints, key constraints, and key references. This is useful if you have the same constraints in multiple scopes and want to reuse the code.

The syntax for referencing an identity constraint is shown in Table 17–9. It is the same for all three kinds of identity constraints. Instead of a `name` attribute, it has a `ref` attribute that references the identity constraint by its qualified name. References to identity constraints do not contain `selector` or `field` elements; they take their definition from the constraint they reference.

Table 17–9   XSD Syntax: identity constraint reference

Name		
unique, key, keyref		
Parents		
element		
Attribute name	*Type*	*Description*
id	ID	Unique ID.
ref	QName	Name of the identity constraint being referenced.
Content		
annotation?		

Example 17–12 shows a new element declaration `discontinued-ProductList` that has the same uniqueness constraint as `catalog`. To indicate this, it contains a `unique` element, but with a `ref` attribute

instead of a `name`. Note that the two element declarations specify the same type; this is not a requirement, but it is common since most identity constraints would only be shared among elements that contain a similar structure.

Example 17–12. Referencing an identity constraint

```
<xs:schema xmlns:xs="http://www.w3.org/2001/XMLSchema"
           xmlns="http://datypic.com/prod"
           targetNamespace="http://datypic.com/prod"
           xpathDefaultNamespace="http://datypic.com/prod">
  <xs:element name="catalog" type="CatalogType">
    <xs:unique name="dateAndProdNumKey">
      <xs:selector xpath="department/product"/>
      <xs:field xpath="number"/>
      <xs:field xpath="@effDate"/>
    </xs:unique>
  </xs:element>

  <xs:element name="discontinuedProductList" type="CatalogType">
    <xs:unique ref="dateAndProdNumKey"/>
  </xs:element>

  <!--...-->
</xs:schema>
```

Being able to reference identity constraints is also useful when restricting types. In version 1.0, if you used a local element declaration that contained an identity constraint, it was impossible to restrict the complex type that contained it because there was no formal definition of a valid restriction of an identity constraint. Now that it can be named and referenced, there is a formal way of indicating that an identity constraint is the same as the identity constraint in the base type. This is shown in Example 17–13, where the `catalog` element declaration in the base type has an identity constraint, and the `catalog` element declaration in the derived type references that identity constraint.

Example 17–13. Referencing an identity constraint in a restriction

```
<xs:schema xmlns:xs="http://www.w3.org/2001/XMLSchema"
           targetNamespace="http://datypic.com/prod"
           xmlns="http://datypic.com/prod"
           xpathDefaultNamespace="http://datypic.com/prod">
  <xs:complexType name="CatalogListType">
    <xs:sequence>
      <xs:element name="catalog" type="CatalogType"
                  maxOccurs="unbounded">
        <xs:unique name="dateAndProdNumKey">
          <xs:selector xpath="department/product"/>
          <xs:field xpath="number"/>
          <xs:field xpath="@effDate"/>
        </xs:unique>
      </xs:element>
    </xs:sequence>
  </xs:complexType>

  <xs:complexType name="RestrictedCatalogListType">
    <xs:complexContent>
      <xs:restriction base="CatalogListType">
        <xs:sequence>
          <xs:element name="catalog" type="CatalogType"
                      maxOccurs="1">
            <xs:unique ref="dateAndProdNumKey"/>
          </xs:element>
        </xs:sequence>
      </xs:restriction>
    </xs:complexContent>
  </xs:complexType>

  <!--...-->
</xs:schema>
```

Redefining and overriding schema components

Chapter 8

T here are two methods of including a schema document into a schema while modifying or overriding certain parts of it: *redefine* and *override*. Redefinition—a version 1.0 feature—allows you to extend or restrict certain components (namely types and groups), replacing the original definitions, but only in certain constrained ways. Because of the limitations of redefinition and its inconsistent implementation among processors, redefinition was deprecated in version 1.1 and replaced with a new override feature which is more flexible and better defined.

For the sake of completeness, redefinition is covered in the first half of this chapter. However, it being deprecated, in version 1.1 you are strongly encouraged to use the override feature instead if you require this kind of functionality. Overrides are described in the second half of this chapter.[1]

---

1. The override section contains information that is redundant with the redefine section; this is to allow readers who are implementing one or the other to skip the section that does not interest them.

447

18.1 | Redefinition

Redefinition is a way to extend and modify schemas over time while still reusing the original definitions. It involves defining a new version of a schema component, with the same name, that replaces the original definition throughout the schema. This is useful for extending and/or creating a subset of an existing schema.

18.1.1 *Redefinition basics*

A `redefine` is similar to an `include`, with the additional option of specifying new definitions of some or all of the components in the redefined schema document. This is depicted in Figure 18–1. Like included schema documents, redefined schema documents must have the same target namespace as the redefining schema document, or none at all.

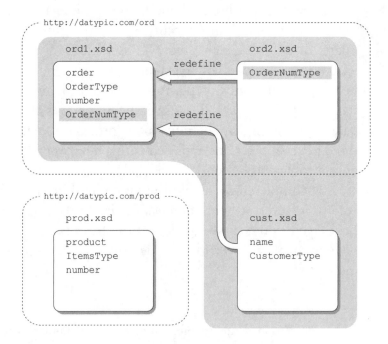

Figure 18–1   Redefine

Only certain types of schema components can be redefined, namely complex types, simple types, named model groups, and attribute groups. The new definitions must be based on the original definitions. For types, this means that the new type must restrict or extend the original type. For attribute groups and named model groups, it means that the new group must either be a subset or a superset of the original group.

Example 18–1 shows a simple redefinition where the schema document `prod2.xsd` redefines `prod1.xsd`. The simple type `DressSizeType` is redefined in `prod2.xsd`.

Example 18–1. A simple redefinition

prod1.xsd:

```
<xs:schema xmlns:xs="http://www.w3.org/2001/XMLSchema">
  <xs:simpleType name="DressSizeType">
    <xs:restriction base="xs:integer"/>
  </xs:simpleType>

  <xs:element name="size" type="DressSizeType"/>

  <xs:element name="color" type="xs:string"/>
</xs:schema>
```

prod2.xsd:

```
<xs:schema xmlns:xs="http://www.w3.org/2001/XMLSchema"
           xmlns="http://datypic.com/prod"
           targetNamespace="http://datypic.com/prod">

  <xs:redefine schemaLocation="prod1.xsd">
    <xs:simpleType name="DressSizeType">
      <xs:restriction base="DressSizeType">
        <xs:minInclusive value="2"/>
        <xs:maxInclusive value="16"/>
      </xs:restriction>
    </xs:simpleType>
  </xs:redefine>

  <xs:element name="newSize" type="DressSizeType"/>
</xs:schema>
```

18.1.1.1 Include plus redefine

When a schema document is redefined, *all* of its components are included in the redefining schema document, regardless of whether they are specifically mentioned in the redefinition. In this way, the redefine feature is similar to the include feature. In our example, the resulting schema document includes *all* of the components defined and declared in both `prod2.xsd` and `prod1.xsd`. Even though `color` is not mentioned in `prod2.xsd`, it will be included in the resulting schema document.

18.1.1.2 Redefine and namespaces

The target namespace of the redefined schema document must be the same as that of the redefining schema document, or nonexistent. If the redefined schema document does not have a target namespace, all of its components become chameleon components and will take on the target namespace of the redefining schema document. For example, since `prod1.xsd` does not have a target namespace, all of its components will take on the target namespace of `prod2.xsd`. This includes `color`, which is not specifically mentioned in the redefinition. It is not a problem that the `size` element declaration in `prod1.xsd` references `DressSizeType` without a prefix; the processor will correctly interpret the references between components.

18.1.1.3 Pervasive impact

Once a schema is redefined, the new definitions completely replace the original definitions—not just for components in the new (redefining) schema document, but also for components that reference them in the original (redefined) schema document. In Example 18–1, the `size` element declaration now uses the new `DressSizeType`. If there had been types derived from `DressSizeType` in `prod1.xsd`, they would now become derived from the new `DressSizeType`.

Redefinition of a component has a ripple effect on all the other components that depend on it. For a type, that includes all other types that are derived from it at any level. For a group, that includes all complex types that reference it, as well as the types derived from those types. While this is generally intentional and desirable, there is no guarantee that you will not break these dependent components, and schema processors are not required to warn you if you do. Specific risks associated with redefinition are described in Section 18.3 on p. 468.

For a comparison of redefinition, type derivation, and other methods of extending schemas see Section 22.2 on p. 599.

18.1.2 *The mechanics of redefinition*

A `redefine` element is used to contain redefined schema components. A `redefine` element may only occur at the top level of a schema document (with `schema` as its parent), and all `redefine` children must be at the beginning of the schema document, along with the `include`, `import`, and `override` elements. The syntax for a `redefine` element is shown in Table 18–1.

Table 18–1   XSD Syntax: redefinition

Name		
redefine		

Parents		
schema		

Attribute name	Type	Description
id	ID	Unique ID.
schemaLocation	anyURI	Location of the schema document with the components being redefined.

Content		
(annotation | attributeGroup | complexType | group | simpleType) *		

A schema document can contain multiple redefinitions of various other schema documents. The schemaLocation attribute indicates the location of the schema document to be redefined. It must reference a complete schema document with schema as its root element. As mentioned above, the redefined schema document must have the same target namespace as the redefining schema document, or none at all.

The redefine element contains the new definitions of the schema components, in any order. For every definition that appears in a redefine element, there must be a corresponding definition (with the same qualified name) in the redefined schema document. Only the components that need to be modified should appear in the redefine element. All other components of the redefined schema document will be included in the new schema as is. In fact, a redefine element is not required to have any children at all, in which case it acts exactly like an include element.

18.1.3 *Redefining simple types*

When redefining a simple type, the new definition must restrict the original simple type. Example 18–2 shows how you would redefine DressSizeType to change minInclusive to be 2. The restricted DressSizeType uses itself as the base type. Redefinition is the only case where a simple type can restrict itself.

The redefinition of DressSizeType affects not only the newSize element declaration in prod2.xsd, but also the size element declaration in prod1.xsd. Because of the redefinition, size instances that conform to prod2.xsd cannot have the value 0. This illustrates the effect redefinition has on components in the original schema.

Example 18–2. Redefining a simple type

prod1.xsd:

```
<xs:schema xmlns:xs="http://www.w3.org/2001/XMLSchema">
  <xs:simpleType name="DressSizeType">
    <xs:restriction base="xs:integer">
      <xs:minInclusive value="0"/>
      <xs:maxInclusive value="18"/>
    </xs:restriction>
  </xs:simpleType>
  <xs:element name="size" type="DressSizeType"/>
</xs:schema>
```

prod2.xsd:

```
<xs:schema xmlns:xs="http://www.w3.org/2001/XMLSchema">
  <xs:redefine schemaLocation="prod1.xsd">
    <xs:simpleType name="DressSizeType">
      <xs:restriction base="DressSizeType">
        <xs:minInclusive value="2"/>
      </xs:restriction>
    </xs:simpleType>
  </xs:redefine>
  <xs:element name="newSize" type="DressSizeType"/>
</xs:schema>
```

18.1.4 *Redefining complex types*

Complex types can also be redefined, provided that the new definition of the complex type either extends or restricts the original complex type. Example 18–3 shows how you would redefine ProductType to add a new element declaration and a new attribute declaration. Like a simple type, a complex type can be based on itself when it is part of a redefinition.

Example 18–3. Redefining a complex type

prod1.xsd:

```
<xs:schema xmlns:xs="http://www.w3.org/2001/XMLSchema">
  <xs:complexType name="ProductType">
    <xs:sequence>
      <xs:element name="number" type="xs:integer"/>
      <xs:element name="name" type="xs:string"/>
      <xs:element name="size" type="xs:integer"/>
    </xs:sequence>
  </xs:complexType>
</xs:schema>
```

prod2.xsd:

```
<xs:schema xmlns:xs="http://www.w3.org/2001/XMLSchema">
  <xs:redefine schemaLocation="prod1.xsd">
    <xs:complexType name="ProductType">
      <xs:complexContent>
        <xs:extension base="ProductType">
          <xs:sequence>
            <xs:element name="color" type="xs:string"/>
          </xs:sequence>
          <xs:attribute name="effDate" type="xs:date"/>
        </xs:extension>
      </xs:complexContent>
    </xs:complexType>
  </xs:redefine>
</xs:schema>
```

18.1.5 *Redefining named model groups*

When redefining named model groups, the new definition must be either a subset or a superset of the original group.

18.1.5.1 Defining a subset

Example 18–4 shows the redefinition of `DescriptionGroup` to disallow the `comment` element.

Example 18–4. Redefining a named model group as a subset

prod1.xsd:

```
<xs:schema xmlns:xs="http://www.w3.org/2001/XMLSchema">
  <xs:group name="DescriptionGroup">
    <xs:sequence>
      <xs:element name="description" type="xs:string"/>
      <xs:element name="comment" type="xs:string" minOccurs="0"/>
    </xs:sequence>
  </xs:group>
</xs:schema>
```

prod2.xsd:

```
<xs:schema xmlns:xs="http://www.w3.org/2001/XMLSchema">
  <xs:redefine schemaLocation="prod1.xsd">
    <xs:group name="DescriptionGroup">
      <xs:sequence>
        <xs:element name="description" type="xs:string"/>
      </xs:sequence>
    </xs:group>
  </xs:redefine>
</xs:schema>
```

Our example is legal because the comment elements are optional per the original definition. The exact definition of a legal subset is the same as that used for complex type restriction. In other words, if a content model is considered a legal restriction of another content model (in complex type derivation), it is also a legal subset in the redefinition of a named model group. See Section 13.5 on p. 316 for the rules of complex type restriction.

18.1.5.2 Defining a superset

On the other hand, suppose you want to extend the definition of DescriptionGroup to include more children. Example 18–5 shows the redefinition of DescriptionGroup to add new element declarations. In this case, you are saying that you want all of the original

Example 18–5. Redefining a named model group as a superset

prod1.xsd:

```
<xs:schema xmlns:xs="http://www.w3.org/2001/XMLSchema">
  <xs:group name="DescriptionGroup">
    <xs:sequence>
      <xs:element name="description" type="xs:string"/>
      <xs:element name="comment" type="xs:string" minOccurs="0"/>
    </xs:sequence>
  </xs:group>
</xs:schema>
```

prod2.xsd:

```
<xs:schema xmlns:xs="http://www.w3.org/2001/XMLSchema">
  <xs:redefine schemaLocation="prod1.xsd">
    <xs:group name="DescriptionGroup">
      <xs:sequence>
        <xs:group ref="DescriptionGroup"/>
        <xs:element name="notes" type="xs:string"/>
      </xs:sequence>
    </xs:group>
  </xs:redefine>
</xs:schema>
```

element declarations of `DescriptionGroup`, followed by the new `notes` element declaration.

The group refers to itself the way it would refer to any other group. Redefinition is the only case where a group reference can be circular, but there are two constraints.

- The group may only reference itself once.
- `maxOccurs` and `minOccurs` of that self-reference must be 1 (or not present, in which case they default to 1).

18.1.6 *Redefining attribute groups*

Like a named model group, an attribute group can be redefined to be a subset or superset of its original definition.

18.1.6.1 Defining a subset

Example 18–6 shows how you would redefine the `IdentifierGroup` as a subset. The new definition disallows the `xml:lang` attribute and changes the type of the `version` attribute from `decimal` to `integer`.

Example 18–6. Redefining an attribute group as a subset

prod1.xsd:

```
<xs:schema xmlns:xs="http://www.w3.org/2001/XMLSchema">
  <xs:import namespace="http://www.w3.org/XML/1998/namespace"/>
  <xs:attributeGroup name="IdentifierGroup">
    <xs:attribute name="id" type="xs:ID" use="required"/>
    <xs:attribute name="version" type="xs:decimal"/>
    <xs:attribute ref="xml:lang"/>
  </xs:attributeGroup>
</xs:schema>
```

prod2.xsd:

```
<xs:schema xmlns:xs="http://www.w3.org/2001/XMLSchema">
  <xs:redefine schemaLocation="prod1.xsd">
    <xs:attributeGroup name="IdentifierGroup">
      <xs:attribute name="id" type="xs:ID" use="required"/>
      <xs:attribute name="version" type="xs:integer"/>
    </xs:attributeGroup>
  </xs:redefine>
</xs:schema>
```

The rules used to define a subset of an attribute group are the same as those used for attribute restriction in complex type derivation. This means that you can eliminate optional attributes, make attributes required, add a fixed value, change default values, or change types to be more restrictive. Eliminating the `xml:lang` attribute in Example 18–6 is legal because it is optional (by default) in the original attribute group. Changing the type of `version` is legal because `integer` is a restriction of `decimal`. See Section 13.5.5 on p. 333 for more information on attribute restrictions.

Unlike complex type derivation, however, you must redeclare all attributes you want to appear in the new definition. The attribute declarations will not automatically be copied from the original definition to the new definition.

If the original definition contains an attribute wildcard, you may repeat or further restrict the wildcard. Subsetting of attribute wildcards also follows the rules used in complex type derivation. See Section 13.5.6 on p. 335 for more information on attribute wildcard restrictions.

18.1.6.2 Defining a superset

On the other hand, suppose you want to extend the definition of `IdentifierGroup` to include more attributes. Example 18–7 shows how you would redefine `IdentifierGroup` to add attributes. You

Example 18–7. Redefining an attribute group as a superset

---

prod1.xsd:

```
<xs:schema xmlns:xs="http://www.w3.org/2001/XMLSchema">
  <xs:import namespace="http://www.w3.org/XML/1998/namespace"/>
  <xs:attributeGroup name="IdentifierGroup">
    <xs:attribute name="id" type="xs:ID" use="required"/>
    <xs:attribute name="version" type="xs:decimal"/>
    <xs:attribute ref="xml:lang"/>
  </xs:attributeGroup>
</xs:schema>
```

prod2.xsd:

```
<xs:schema xmlns:xs="http://www.w3.org/2001/XMLSchema">
  <xs:redefine schemaLocation="prod1.xsd">
    <xs:attributeGroup name="IdentifierGroup">
      <xs:attributeGroup ref="IdentifierGroup"/>
      <xs:attribute name="effDate" type="xs:date"/>
    </xs:attributeGroup>
  </xs:redefine>
</xs:schema>
```

---

cannot alter the declarations of the attributes in the original group, only add new attributes. In this case, you are saying that you want all of the original attributes of `IdentifierGroup`, plus a new `effDate` attribute.

The attribute group refers to itself the way it would refer to any other attribute group. Redefinition is the only case where an attribute group reference can be circular in version 1.0.

18.2 | Overrides

The override feature is a convenient way to customize schemas. It involves defining a new version of a schema component, with the same name, that replaces the original definition throughout the schema. This is useful when you want to reuse a schema but you want to make some modifications (minor or major) to the components in that schema while still preserving the original definitions.

18.2.1 *Override basics*

An `override` is similar to an `include`, with the additional option of specifying new definitions for some or all of the components in the overridden schema document. This is depicted in Figure 18–2. Like included schema documents, overridden schema documents must have the same target namespace as the overriding schema document, or none at all.

You can override any top-level named schema component, namely complex types, simple types, global element declarations, global attribute declarations, named model groups, attribute groups, and notations. Unlike redefines, the new definitions do not have to be based on the original definitions. In fact, they cannot refer to the original definitions in the way that redefining components do.

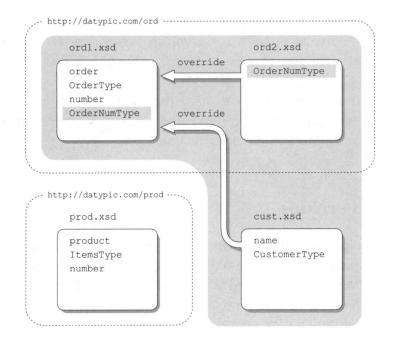

Figure 18–2 Override

Example 18–8 shows a simple override where the schema document `prod2.xsd` overrides `prod1.xsd`. The simple type `DressSizeType` is overridden in `prod2.xsd`.

Example 18–8. A simple override

prod1.xsd:

```
<xs:schema xmlns:xs="http://www.w3.org/2001/XMLSchema">
  <xs:simpleType name="DressSizeType">
    <xs:restriction base="xs:integer"/>
  </xs:simpleType>

  <xs:element name="size" type="DressSizeType"/>

  <xs:element name="color" type="xs:string"/>
</xs:schema>
```

(Continues)

Example 18–8.   (Continued)

prod2.xsd:

```
<xs:schema xmlns:xs="http://www.w3.org/2001/XMLSchema"
           xmlns="http://datypic.com/prod"
           targetNamespace="http://datypic.com/prod">

  <xs:override schemaLocation="prod1.xsd">
    <xs:simpleType name="DressSizeType">
      <xs:restriction base="xs:integer">
        <xs:minInclusive value="2"/>
        <xs:maxInclusive value="16"/>
      </xs:restriction>
    </xs:simpleType>
  </xs:override>

  <xs:element name="newSize" type="DressSizeType"/>
</xs:schema>
```

18.2.1.1 Include plus override

When a schema document is overridden, *all* of its components are included in the overriding schema document, regardless of whether they are specifically mentioned in the override. In this way, the override feature is similar to the include feature. In our example, the resulting schema document includes *all* of the components defined and declared in both `prod2.xsd` and `prod1.xsd`. Even though `color` is not mentioned in `prod2.xsd`, it will be included in the resulting schema document.

18.2.1.2 Override and namespaces

The target namespace of the overridden schema document must be the same as that of the overriding schema document, or nonexistent. If the overridden schema document does not have a target namespace, all of its components become chameleon components and will take on the target namespace of the overriding schema document. For example, since `prod1.xsd` does not have a target namespace, all of its components will take on the target namespace of `prod2.xsd`. This includes `color`, which is not specifically mentioned in the override. It is not a problem that the `size` element declaration in `prod1.xsd` references `DressSizeType` without a prefix; the processor will correctly interpret the references between components.

18.2.1.3 Pervasive impact

Once a schema is overridden, the new definitions completely replace the original definitions—not just for components in the new overriding schema document, but also for components that reference it in the original, overridden schema document. In Example 18–8, the `size` element declaration now uses the new `DressSizeType`. If there had been types derived from `DressSizeType` in `prod1.xsd`, they would now be derived from the new `DressSizeType`.

Overriding a component has a ripple effect on all the other components that depend on it. For a type, this includes all other types that are derived from it at any level. For a group, it includes all complex types that reference it, as well as the types derived from those types. While this is generally intentional and desirable, there is no guarantee that you will not break these dependent components, and schema processors are not required to warn you if you do. Specific risks associated with overrides are described in Section 18.3 on p. 468.

For a comparison of overriding, type derivation, and other methods of extending schemas, see Section 22.2 on p. 599.

18.2.2 *The mechanics of overriding components*

An `override` element is used to contain overridden schema components. An `override` element may only occur at the top level of a schema document (with `schema` as its parent), and all `override` children must be at the beginning of the schema document, along with the `include`, `import`, and `redefine` elements. The syntax for an `override` element is shown in Table 18–2.

Table 18–2 XSD Syntax: override

Name		
override		

Parents		
schema		

Attribute name	Type	Description
id	ID	Unique ID.
schemaLocation	anyURI	Location of the schema document with the components being overridden.

Content

```
(annotation | simpleType | complexType | group |
attributeGroup | element | attribute | notation)*
```

A schema document can contain multiple overrides of various other schema documents. The `schemaLocation` attribute indicates the location of the schema document to be overridden. It must reference a complete schema document with `schema` as its root element. As mentioned above, the overridden schema document must have the same target namespace as the overriding schema document, or none at all.

The `override` element contains the new definitions of the schema components, in any order. For every definition that appears in an `override` element, there must be a corresponding definition (with the same qualified name) in the overridden schema document. Only the components that need to be modified should appear in the `override` element. All other components of the overridden schema document will be included in the new schema as is. In fact, an `override` element is not required to have any children at all, in which case it acts exactly like an `include` element.

18.2.3 *Overriding simple types*

Example 18–9 shows how you would override a simple type DressSizeType to change minInclusive to be 2. Unlike redefinition, the overriding type DressSizeType in prod2.xsd is not derived from or in any way related to its counterpart in prod1.xsd. Even though the maxInclusive constraint didn't change, it needs to be respecified in the overriding type.

Example 18–9. Overriding a simple type

prod1.xsd:

```
<xs:schema xmlns:xs="http://www.w3.org/2001/XMLSchema">
  <xs:simpleType name="DressSizeType">
    <xs:restriction base="xs:integer">
      <xs:minInclusive value="0"/>
      <xs:maxInclusive value="18"/>
    </xs:restriction>
  </xs:simpleType>
  <xs:element name="size" type="DressSizeType"/>
</xs:schema>
```

prod2.xsd:

```
<xs:schema xmlns:xs="http://www.w3.org/2001/XMLSchema">
  <xs:override schemaLocation="prod1.xsd">
    <xs:simpleType name="DressSizeType">
      <xs:restriction base="xs:integer">
        <xs:minInclusive value="2"/>
        <xs:maxInclusive value="18"/>
      </xs:restriction>
    </xs:simpleType>
  </xs:override>
  <xs:element name="newSize" type="DressSizeType"/>
</xs:schema>
```

The override of DressSizeType affects not only the newSize element declaration in prod2.xsd, but also the size element declaration in prod1.xsd. Because of the override, size instances that conform to `prod2.xsd` cannot have the value 0. This illustrates the effect overriding has on components in the original schema.

In this example, `DressSizeType` didn't change much. It is still based on `integer` but with some additional constraints. However, you are not limited in the changes you can make when overriding, as long as the overriding definition is still a simple type. It would be possible to turn `DressSizeType` into a `string` value, for example. It is not possible to override a simple type with a complex type.

18.2.4 *Overriding complex types*

Complex types can also be overridden. Example 18–10 shows how you would override `ProductType` to change the type of `number`, delete

Example 18–10. Overriding a complex type

prod1.xsd:

```
<xs:schema xmlns:xs="http://www.w3.org/2001/XMLSchema">
  <xs:complexType name="ProductType">
    <xs:sequence>
      <xs:element name="number" type="xs:integer"/>
      <xs:element name="name" type="xs:string"/>
      <xs:element name="size" type="xs:string"/>
    </xs:sequence>
  </xs:complexType>
</xs:schema>
```

prod2.xsd:

```
<xs:schema xmlns:xs="http://www.w3.org/2001/XMLSchema">
  <xs:override schemaLocation="prod1.xsd">
    <xs:complexType name="ProductType">
      <xs:sequence>
        <xs:element name="number" type="xs:string"/>
        <xs:element name="name" type="xs:string"/>
        <xs:element name="color" type="xs:string"/>
      </xs:sequence>
    </xs:complexType>
  </xs:override>
</xs:schema>
```

size, and add color. As with simple types, the overriding definition can be similar to the overridden definition, as it is in this case, but it can also be completely different.

18.2.5 *Overriding element and attribute declarations*

Unlike redefines, overrides can apply to element and attribute declarations, as long as they are global. Example 18–11 shows the override of the description global element declaration and the version global attribute declaration. In this case, description changed significantly, from having a simple type to having a complex type with element-only content.

Example 18–11. Overriding element and attribute declarations

prod1.xsd:

```
<xs:schema xmlns:xs="http://www.w3.org/2001/XMLSchema">
  <xs:element name="description" type="xs:string"/>
  <xs:attribute name="version" type="xs:decimal"/>
</xs:schema>
```

prod2.xsd:

```
<xs:schema xmlns:xs="http://www.w3.org/2001/XMLSchema">
  <xs:override schemaLocation="prod1.xsd">
    <xs:element name="description" type="DescriptionType"/>
    <xs:attribute name="version" type="xs:string" default="1.0"/>
  </xs:override>
  <xs:complexType name="DescriptionType">
    <xs:sequence>
      <xs:element name="source" type="xs:string"/>
      <xs:element name="content" type="xs:string"/>
    </xs:sequence>
  </xs:complexType>
</xs:schema>
```

Local element and attribute declarations cannot be overridden directly, but the complex types that contain them can be.

18.2.6 *Overriding named groups*

It is also possible to override named model groups and attribute groups. Unlike a redefinition, the new definition of a group has no superset or subset relationship to the original group definition.

Example 18–12 shows an override of the DescriptionGroup named model group and the IdentifierGroup attribute group.

Example 18–12. Overriding named groups

prod1.xsd:

```
<xs:schema xmlns:xs="http://www.w3.org/2001/XMLSchema">
  <xs:group name="DescriptionGroup">
    <xs:sequence>
      <xs:element name="description" type="xs:string"/>
      <xs:element name="comment" type="xs:string" minOccurs="0"/>
    </xs:sequence>
  </xs:group>
  <xs:attributeGroup name="IdentifierGroup">
    <xs:attribute name="id" type="xs:ID" use="required"/>
    <xs:attribute name="version" type="xs:decimal"/>
  </xs:attributeGroup>
</xs:schema>
```

prod2.xsd:

```
<xs:schema xmlns:xs="http://www.w3.org/2001/XMLSchema">
  <xs:override schemaLocation="prod1.xsd">
    <xs:group name="DescriptionGroup">
      <xs:sequence>
        <xs:element name="description" type="xs:string"/>
      </xs:sequence>
    </xs:group>
    <xs:attributeGroup name="IdentifierGroup">
      <xs:attribute name="effDate" type="xs:date"/>
      <xs:attribute name="id" type="xs:ID"/>
    </xs:attributeGroup>
  </xs:override>
</xs:schema>
```

18.3 | Risks of redefines and overrides

As mentioned previously, redefines and overrides both have a pervasive impact on all components—not just in the overriding/redefining schema document, but also in the overridden/redefined schema document. When you use either of these techniques, if there are other components that depend on the original definitions, you run the risk of rendering these dependent components invalid by changing the original definitions.

18.3.1 *Risks of redefining or overriding types*

For a type, the risks pertain to all other types that are derived from it at any level.

Example 18–13 shows a new `prod1.xsd` where there are two complex types derived from `ProductType`: `ShirtType` (an extension) and `RestrictedProductType` (a restriction). All changes to `ProductType` during override or redefine are passed down to the derived types, which is probably your intention. However, in this case, both derived types have been rendered illegal.

Example 18–13. Risks of overriding types

prod1.xsd:

```
<xs:schema xmlns:xs="http://www.w3.org/2001/XMLSchema">
  <xs:complexType name="ProductType">
    <xs:sequence>
      <xs:element name="number" type="xs:integer" minOccurs="0"/>
      <xs:element name="name" type="xs:string" minOccurs="0"/>
      <xs:element name="size" type="xs:string" minOccurs="0"/>
    </xs:sequence>
  </xs:complexType>
```

(Continues)

Example 18–13. (Continued)

```xml
<xs:complexType name="ShirtType">
  <xs:complexContent>
    <xs:extension base="ProductType">
      <xs:sequence>
        <xs:element name="color" type="xs:integer"/>
      </xs:sequence>
    </xs:extension>
  </xs:complexContent>
</xs:complexType>
<xs:complexType name="RestrictedProductType">
  <xs:complexContent>
    <xs:restriction base="ProductType">
      <xs:sequence>
        <xs:element name="number" type="xs:integer"
                    minOccurs="0"/>
        <xs:element name="size" type="xs:string" minOccurs="0"/>
      </xs:sequence>
    </xs:restriction>
  </xs:complexContent>
</xs:complexType>
</xs:schema>
```

prod2.xsd:

```xml
<xs:schema xmlns:xs="http://www.w3.org/2001/XMLSchema">
  <xs:override schemaLocation="prod1.xsd">
    <xs:complexType name="ProductType">
      <xs:sequence>
        <xs:element name="number" type="xs:integer"/>
        <xs:element name="name" type="xs:string"/>
        <xs:element name="color" type="xs:string"/>
      </xs:sequence>
    </xs:complexType>
  </xs:override>
</xs:schema>
```

Some of the risks associated with redefining or overriding
ProductType when there are extensions of the original definition are:

- Adding an attribute that ShirtType already has, resulting in
  duplicate attributes for ShirtType.

- Adding an element declaration to the content model that `ShirtType` already has, but with a different type, as shown in Example 18–13 with `color`. It is illegal for a complex type to contain two element declarations with the same name and different types.

- Adding element declarations to the content model that render the content model of `ShirtType` nondeterministic.

Some of the risks associated with redefining or overriding `ProductType` when there are restrictions of the original definition are:

- Restricting a content model further, or in a way incompatibly different, than how `RestrictedProductType` restricted it, as shown in Example 18–13.

- Restricting an attribute further than `RestrictedProductType` restricted it, rendering `RestrictedProductType`'s restriction illegal.

- Making an attribute, which is then restricted by `Restricted-ProductType`, prohibited, resulting in an illegal attribute declaration in the definition of `RestrictedProductType`.

Simple type derivations can also be negatively affected by redefines and overrides. As with complex types, if there are dependent types in the original schema document that restrict an overridden simple type further or in incompatible ways, it can render them invalid.

18.3.2 *Risks of redefining or overriding named groups*

When redefining or overriding a named group, you should be aware of an impact to the complex types that reference it, as well as the types derived from those types. The risks include:

- Making a content model nondeterministic.
- Introducing duplicate attribute names.

- Making element declarations inconsistent by introducing two element declarations with the same name but different types.
- Rendering illegal the types derived by extension or restriction from the types that directly use the group, in the ways described in the previous section.

Topics for DTD users

19

This chapter provides a jump-start on XML Schema for readers who are familiar with DTDs. It offers a detailed comparison of DTD and schema syntax, which is useful both for understanding XML Schema and for converting existing DTDs to schemas. It also describes some of the features of XML Schema that require the use of DTDs, such as entities and notations.

19.1 | Element declarations

Table 19–1 shows examples of various DTD content models and matches them up with the corresponding XML Schema content types. Each of these content types is explained in the rest of this section.

Table 19–1   Content types

Example DTD content model	Simple type	Complex type		
		Simple content	Complex content	
			Element-only Mixed Empty	
(#PCDATA) with no attributes	Section 19.1.1			
(#PCDATA) with attributes		Section 19.1.2		
(a | b)*			Section 19.1.3	
(#PCDATA | a | b)*			Section 19.1.4	
EMPTY				Section 19.1.5
ANY			Section 19.1.6	

19.1.1 *Simple types*

Element types with (#PCDATA) content and no attributes in a DTD correspond to element declarations with simple types in schemas. Example 19–1 shows such an element declaration.

Note that the built-in type decimal is assigned to price. It is possible to assign all #PCDATA element types the built-in type string, which handles whitespace in the same way as DTD processors handle whitespace for any character data content of an element. However, it is advisable to be as specific as possible when choosing a type for an element declaration. Chapter 11 describes the built-in simple types in detail, and Chapter 8 describes how to define your own simple types.

Example 19–1. Simple type

DTD:

```
<!ELEMENT price (#PCDATA)>
```

Schema:

```
<xs:element name="price" type="xs:decimal"/>
```

19.1.2 *Complex types with simple content*

Element types with (#PCDATA) content that do have attributes correspond to element declarations using complex types with simple content in schemas. Example 19–2 shows such an element declaration. It extends the simple type decimal to add the attribute currency.

Example 19–2. Simple content (with attributes)

DTD:

```
<!ELEMENT price (#PCDATA)>
<!ATTLIST price currency NMTOKEN #IMPLIED>
```

Schema:

```
<xs:element name="price">
  <xs:complexType>
    <xs:simpleContent>
      <xs:extension base="xs:decimal">
        <xs:attribute name="currency" type="xs:NMTOKEN"/>
      </xs:extension>
    </xs:simpleContent>
  </xs:complexType>
</xs:element>
```

19.1.3 *Complex types with complex content*

Element types that may have children, regardless of whether they have attributes, correspond to element declarations using complex types with complex content in schemas. Example 19–3 shows such an element declaration.

***Example 19–3.** Complex content*

DTD:

```
<!ELEMENT product (number, name+, size?, color*)>
```

Schema:

```
<xs:element name="product">
  <xs:complexType>
    <xs:sequence>
      <xs:element ref="number"/>
      <xs:element ref="name"  maxOccurs="unbounded"/>
      <xs:element ref="size"  minOccurs="0"/>
      <xs:element ref="color" minOccurs="0" maxOccurs="unbounded"/>
    </xs:sequence>
  </xs:complexType>
</xs:element>
```

In Example 19–3, the content model was converted into a sequence. Groups, enclosed in parentheses in DTDs, are represented by one of the three model groups in a schema.

- sequence groups require that the elements appear in order.
- choice groups allow a choice from several elements.
- all groups allow the elements to appear in any order.

Table 19–2 shows the mapping between DTD groups and XML Schema model groups.

Table 19–2   Group compositors

DTD model	*XML Schema model group*
(a,b,c)	sequence
(a|b|c)	choice
no equivalent	all

As shown in Example 19–3, the occurrence constraints on element types and groups are represented by the minOccurs and maxOccurs attributes in schemas. Table 19–3 shows the mapping between occurrence constraints in DTDs and schemas.

Table 19–3   Occurrence constraints

DTD symbol	*Schema* minOccurs *value*	*Schema* maxOccurs *value*
(none)	1	1
*	0	unbounded
+	1	unbounded
?	0	1

The defaults for minOccurs and maxOccurs are both 1. XML Schema can provide more specific validation than DTDs, since any non-negative integer can be specified. For example, you can specify that the color element may appear a maximum of three times.

Groups may be nested in schemas just as they may in DTDs, as illustrated in Example 19–4. Note that minOccurs and maxOccurs may appear on groups as well as on element declarations.

Example 19–4. **Nested groups**

DTD:

```
<!ELEMENT el ((a | b)*, (c | d)?)>
```

Schema:

```
<xs:element name="el">
  <xs:complexType>
    <xs:sequence>
      <xs:choice minOccurs="0" maxOccurs="unbounded">
        <xs:element ref="a"/>
        <xs:element ref="b"/>
      </xs:choice>
      <xs:choice minOccurs="0" maxOccurs="1">
        <xs:element ref="c"/>
        <xs:element ref="d"/>
      </xs:choice>
    </xs:sequence>
  </xs:complexType>
</xs:element>
```

19.1.4 *Mixed content*

Element types that have both #PCDATA content and children are said to have mixed content.[1] In schemas, mixed content is indicated by a `mixed` attribute of a `complexType` element, as shown in Example 19–5.

With DTDs, you are limited to the choice operator (|) with mixed content element types. In schemas, any content model can be mixed, allowing more complex validation of the children. For example, in a DTD you cannot specify that `custName` must appear before `prodName`. In schemas, you can accomplish this using a `sequence` group instead of a `choice` group.

---

1.   Technically, in DTDs mixed content also refers to element types with just #PCDATA content, but this case is covered in Sections 19.1.1 on p. 474 and 19.1.2 on p. 475.

Example 19–5. Mixed content

DTD:

```
<!ELEMENT letter (#PCDATA | custName | prodName)*>
```

Schema:

```
<xs:element name="letter">
  <xs:complexType mixed="true">
    <xs:choice minOccurs="0" maxOccurs="unbounded">
      <xs:element ref="custName"/>
      <xs:element ref="prodName"/>
    </xs:choice>
  </xs:complexType>
</xs:element>
```

19.1.5 *Empty content*

Empty content, indicated by the keyword EMPTY in DTDs, is simply indicated by an absence of a content model in a schema. Example 19–6 shows an element declaration with empty content, containing only attribute declarations.

Example 19–6. Empty content

DTD:

```
<!ELEMENT color EMPTY>
<!ATTLIST color value NMTOKEN #IMPLIED>
```

Schema:

```
<xs:element name="color">
  <xs:complexType>
    <!-- no content model is specified here -->
    <xs:attribute name="value" type="xs:NMTOKEN"/>
  </xs:complexType>
</xs:element>
```

19.1.6 *Any content*

Any content, indicated by the keyword ANY in DTDs, is represented by an element wildcard any in a schema. This is illustrated in Example 19–7.

Example 19–7. Any content

DTD:

```
<!ELEMENT anything ANY>
```

Schema:

```
<xs:element name="anything">
  <xs:complexType mixed="true">
    <xs:sequence>
      <xs:any minOccurs="0" maxOccurs="unbounded"/>
    </xs:sequence>
  </xs:complexType>
</xs:element>
```

XML Schema offers much more sophisticated wildcard capabilities than DTDs. It is possible with XML Schema to put a wildcard anywhere in a content model, specify how many replacement elements may appear, restrict the namespace(s) of the replacement elements, and control how strictly they are validated. See Section 12.7.1 on p. 285 for more information on element wildcards.

19.2 | Attribute declarations

19.2.1 *Attribute types*

The DTD attribute types are represented in XML Schema as simple types, most of them with the same name. Table 19–4 lists the DTD attribute types and their equivalent types in XML Schema.

Table 19–4   DTD attribute types and equivalents

DTD attribute type	*XML schema equivalent*
CDATA	normalizedString
NMTOKEN, NMTOKENS	NMTOKEN, NMTOKENS
ID, IDREF, IDREFS	ID, IDREF, IDREFS
ENTITY, ENTITIES	ENTITY, ENTITIES
NOTATION	Simple type derived from NOTATION, see Section 19.2.3
Enumerated values	Simple type derivation with enumeration facets specified, see Section 19.2.2

19.2.2 *Enumerated attribute types*

In order to represent an enumerated attribute type in a schema, it is necessary to define a new simple type and apply enumeration facets to restrict the values to the desired set. This is illustrated in Example 19–8.

Example 19–8. Representing an enumerated attribute

DTD:

```
<!ATTLIST price currency (USD | CHF) "USD">
```

Schema:

```
<xs:attribute name="currency" default="USD">
  <xs:simpleType>
    <xs:restriction base="xs:token">
      <xs:enumeration value="USD"/>
      <xs:enumeration value="CHF"/>
    </xs:restriction>
  </xs:simpleType>
</xs:attribute>
```

The built-in type `token` is used as the base type for the restriction, which will result in whitespace handling identical to that of enumerated attribute types in DTDs.

19.2.3 *Notation attributes*

A NOTATION attribute type exists in XML Schema as it does in XML DTDs. However, the NOTATION type cannot be used directly by an attribute. Instead, you must define a new simple type that restricts NOTATION and apply enumeration facets to list the possible values for that notation. This is illustrated in Example 19–9.

Example 19–9. Representing a notation attribute

DTD:

```
<!ATTLIST picture fmt NOTATION (jpg | gif) "jpg">
```

Schema:

```
<xs:attribute name="fmt" default="jpg">
  <xs:simpleType>
    <xs:restriction base="xs:NOTATION">
      <xs:enumeration value="jpg"/>
      <xs:enumeration value="gif"/>
    </xs:restriction>
  </xs:simpleType>
</xs:attribute>
```

19.2.4 *Default values*

Attribute default values are handled by three attributes in schemas: the `use` attribute which indicates whether the attribute being declared is required or optional, the `default` attribute which specifies a default value, and the `fixed` attribute which specifies a fixed value. Table 19–5 shows how the DTD attribute default values correspond to schema attributes.

Table 19–5   DTD default values and their equivalents

DTD *default value*	*Schema equivalent*
#REQUIRED	use="required"
#IMPLIED	use="optional"
#FIXED "x"	fixed="x"
"x"	default="x"

Example 19–10 provides some examples of attribute declarations with various types and default values.

Example 19–10. Attribute declarations

DTD:

```
<!ATTLIST product
    id ID #REQUIRED
    name CDATA #IMPLIED
    type NMTOKEN "PR"
    version NMTOKEN #FIXED "A123">
```

Schema:

```
<xs:attribute name="id" type="xs:ID" use="required"/>
<xs:attribute name="name" type="xs:normalizedString"
              use="optional"/>
<xs:attribute name="type" type="xs:NMTOKEN" default="PR"/>
<xs:attribute name="version" type="xs:NMTOKEN" fixed="A123"/>
```

19.3 | Parameter entities for reuse

Internal parameter entities are often used in DTDs to reuse pieces of element or attribute declarations. Using schemas, reuse is handled by creating reusable types, named model groups, and attribute groups.

This section explains how to convert internal parameter entities into XML Schema components.

19.3.1 *Reusing content models*

In DTDs, a parameter entity may be used to define a content model once and reuse it for multiple element types. Using schemas, the best way to accomplish this is to define a named complex type which is then used by multiple element declarations. This is illustrated in Example 19–11, where the AOrB content model is used by two element declarations, x and y.

Example 19–11. Reusing entire content models

DTD:

```
<!ENTITY % AOrB "(a | b)">

<!ELEMENT x %AOrB;>
<!ELEMENT y %AOrB;>
```

Schema:

```
<xs:complexType name="AOrBType">
  <xs:choice>
    <xs:element ref="a"/>
    <xs:element ref="b"/>
  </xs:choice>
</xs:complexType>

<xs:element name="x" type="AOrBType"/>
<xs:element name="y" type="AOrBType"/>
```

A parameter entity may also be used to represent a fragment of a content model. In XML Schema, named model groups are designated for this purpose. Example 19–12 shows a content model fragment AOrB

that is used as part of the entire content model in the x element declaration. See Section 15.2 on p. 386 for more information on named
model groups.

Example 19–12. Reusing fragments of content models

DTD:

```
<!ENTITY % AOrB "a | b">

<!ELEMENT x ((%AOrB;), c)>
```

Schema:

```
<xs:group name="AOrBGroup">
  <xs:choice>
    <xs:element ref="a"/>
    <xs:element ref="b"/>
  </xs:choice>
</xs:group>

<xs:element name="x">
  <xs:complexType>
    <xs:sequence>
      <xs:group ref="AOrBGroup"/>
      <xs:element ref="c"/>
    </xs:sequence>
  </xs:complexType>
</xs:element>
```

19.3.2 *Reusing attributes*

In some cases, parameter entities are used in DTDs to reuse an attribute
or a set of attributes that are common to several element types. In XML
Schema, attribute groups are used for this purpose. Example 19–13
shows the definition of an attribute group `HeaderGroup` containing
two attributes, which is then referenced by the x element declaration.

Example 19–13. Reusing groups of attributes

DTD:

```
<!ENTITY % HeaderGroup "id ID #REQUIRED
                        variety NMTOKEN #IMPLIED">

<!ATTLIST x %HeaderGroup;>
```

Schema:

```
<xs:attributeGroup name="HeaderGroup">
  <xs:attribute name="id" type="xs:ID" use="required"/>
  <xs:attribute name="variety" type="xs:NMTOKEN"/>
</xs:attributeGroup>

<xs:element name="x">
  <xs:complexType>
    <xs:attributeGroup ref="HeaderGroup"/>
  </xs:complexType>
</xs:element>
```

19.4 | Parameter entities for extensibility

Parameter entities are sometimes used to make DTDs more flexible and future-proof. Empty entities are declared and placed in various parts of the DTD, most often in content models and attribute lists. This allows a parent (or internal) DTD to override the entity declaration, thus overriding the original DTD without having to completely rewrite it. Using schemas, this can be accomplished through several methods: type derivation, substitution groups, redefines, or overrides.

19.4.1 *Extensions for* sequence *groups*

In DTDs, you can place a reference to an empty parameter entity at the end of a content model, as shown in Example 19–14. In XML

Schema, this can be accomplished using the redefine or override mechanism.

Example 19–14. Allowing future extensions for sequence groups

DTD:

```
<!ENTITY % ext "" >
<!ELEMENT x (a, b %ext;)>
```

Schema:

```
<xs:group name="ext">
  <xs:sequence/>
</xs:group>
<xs:element name="x">
  <xs:complexType>
    <xs:sequence>
      <xs:element ref="a"/>
      <xs:element ref="b"/>
      <xs:group ref="ext"/>
    </xs:sequence>
  </xs:complexType>
</xs:element>
```

Example 19–15 shows how these extensions could be accomplished in a new parent DTD or in a new schema. In the schema, the redefine mechanism is used to extend the named model group to add to the end of the content model. Redefinition is covered in Chapter 18.

Example 19–15. Implementing extensions for sequence groups using redefine

DTD:

```
<!ENTITY % ext ", c, d" >
<!ENTITY % original SYSTEM "original.dtd">
%original;
```

(Continues)

Example 19–15.   (Continued)

Schema:

```
<xs:schema xmlns:xs="http://www.w3.org/2001/XMLSchema">
  <xs:redefine schemaLocation="original.xsd">
    <xs:group name="ext">
      <xs:sequence>
        <xs:group ref="ext"/>
        <xs:element ref="c"/>
        <xs:element ref="d"/>
      </xs:sequence>
    </xs:group>
  </xs:redefine>
</xs:schema>
```

In version 1.1 of XML Schema, a better choice is to use `override`, since `redefine` is deprecated. Example 19–16 shows a revised example that uses `override`. Overrides are also covered in Chapter 18.

Example 19–16. Implementing extensions for `sequence` groups using `override`

DTD:

```
<!ENTITY % ext ", c, d" >
<!ENTITY % original SYSTEM "original.dtd">
%original;
```

Schema:

```
<xs:schema xmlns:xs="http://www.w3.org/2001/XMLSchema">
  <xs:override schemaLocation="original.xsd">
    <xs:group name="ext">
      <xs:sequence>
        <xs:element ref="a"/>
        <xs:element ref="b"/>
        <xs:element ref="c"/>
        <xs:element ref="d"/>
      </xs:sequence>
    </xs:group>
  </xs:override>
</xs:schema>
```

19.4.2 *Extensions for* choice *groups*

On the other hand, if it is a choice group that you wish to leave open, extension will not meet your needs. This is because all extensions are added to the end of the content model as part of a sequence group. For a more detailed explanation of this, see Section 13.4.2.1 on p. 309.

The best approach to extending a choice group is by using a substitution group. Substitution groups allow an element declaration to be replaced by any of a group of designated element declarations. New element declarations can be added to the substitution group at any time. The schema fragment in Example 19–17 uses a choice group that contains a reference to the ext element declaration. Because it is abstract, ext can never be used in an instance.

Example 19–17. Allowing future extensions for choice groups

DTD:

```
<!ENTITY % ext "" >
<!ELEMENT x (a | b %ext;)*>
```

Schema:

```
<xs:element name="x">
  <xs:complexType>
    <xs:choice maxOccurs="unbounded">
      <xs:element ref="a"/>
      <xs:element ref="b"/>
      <xs:element ref="ext"/>
    </xs:choice>
  </xs:complexType>
</xs:element>
<xs:element name="ext" abstract="true" type="xs:string"/>
```

Example 19–18 shows how these extensions would be accomplished in a new parent DTD or in a new schema. In the schema, element declarations c and d are added to the substitution group headed by ext, allowing these element declarations to appear in the content model as part of the choice.

Example 19–18. Implementing extensions for `choice` groups

DTD:

```
<!ENTITY % ext "| c | d" >
<!ENTITY % original SYSTEM "original.dtd">
%original;
```

Schema:

```
<xs:schema xmlns:xs="http://www.w3.org/2001/XMLSchema">
  <xs:include schemaLocation="original.xsd"/>
  <xs:element name="c" substitutionGroup="ext"/>
  <xs:element name="d" substitutionGroup="ext"/>
</xs:schema>
```

19.4.3 *Attribute extensions*

Parameter entities may also be used in DTDs to leave attribute lists open to future additions. Using schemas, this can be handled through redefining or overriding attribute groups. Example 19–19 shows

Example 19–19. Allowing future extensions for attributes

DTD:

```
<!ENTITY % attExt "" >
<!ATTLIST x id ID #REQUIRED
        %attExt;>
```

Schema:

```
<xs:attributeGroup name="attExt"/>
<xs:element name="x">
  <xs:complexType>
    <!-- content model here -->
    <xs:attribute name="id" type="xs:ID" use="required"/>
    <xs:attributeGroup ref="attExt"/>
  </xs:complexType>
</xs:element>
```

a DTD that includes an empty parameter entity in an attribute list. The corresponding schema has an empty attribute group that serves the same purpose.

Example 19–20 shows how attribute extensions would be accomplished in a new parent DTD or in a new schema. In the schema, the redefine mechanism is used to extend the attribute group to add a new attribute.

Example 19–20. Implementing extensions for attributes using `redefine`

DTD:

```
<!ENTITY % attExt "myAttr NMTOKEN #IMPLIED" >
<!ENTITY % original SYSTEM "original.dtd">
%original;
```

Schema:

```
<xs:schema xmlns:xs="http://www.w3.org/2001/XMLSchema">
  <xs:redefine schemaLocation="original.xsd">
    <xs:attributeGroup name="attExt">
      <xs:attributeGroup ref="attExt"/>
      <xs:attribute name="myAttr" type="xs:NMTOKEN"/>
    </xs:attributeGroup>
  </xs:redefine>
</xs:schema>
```

This technique can also replace the declaration of multiple ATTLISTs for a single element type that is sometimes used to extend attribute lists.

In version 1.1 of XML Schema, a better choice is to use `override`, since `redefine` is deprecated. Example 19–21 shows a revised example that uses `override`.

Example 19–21. Implementing extensions for attributes using `override`

DTD:

```
<!ENTITY % attExt "myAttr NMTOKEN #IMPLIED" >
<!ENTITY % original SYSTEM "original.dtd">
%original;
```

Schema:

```
<xs:schema xmlns:xs="http://www.w3.org/2001/XMLSchema">
  <xs:override schemaLocation="original.xsd">
    <xs:attributeGroup name="attExt">
      <xs:attribute name="myAttr" type="xs:NMTOKEN"/>
    </xs:attributeGroup>
  </xs:override>
</xs:schema>
```

19.5 | External parameter entities

External parameter entities are used to include other DTDs (or fragments of DTDs) in a parent DTD. In a schema, this is accomplished using either `include` or `import`. An `include` can be used if both schema documents are in the same namespace (or in no namespace), while `import` is used if they are in different namespaces. Example 19–22 illustrates the use of `include` to combine schema documents. See Section 4.3.1 on p. 62 for more detailed information on the include mechanism.

Example 19–22. Including other DTDs or schema documents

DTD:

```
<!ENTITY % prodInfo SYSTEM "prod.dtd">
%prodInfo;
```

Schema:

```
<xs:include schemaLocation="prod.xsd"/>
```

19.6 | General entities

19.6.1 *Character and other parsed entities*

General entities are used in DTDs to represent characters or other repeated character data that appears in instances. Unfortunately, there
is no direct equivalent for general entities in XML Schema. It is still
possible to use an internal or external DTD to declare the entities
and use this DTD in conjunction with schemas, as explained in
Section 19.9 on p. 499.

19.6.2 *Unparsed entities*

Unparsed entities are used in conjunction with notations to reference
external data in non-XML formats, such as graphics files. A schema-
validated instance must be associated with a DTD (usually an internal
DTD subset) that declares the unparsed entities. This is described
further in Section 19.7.3 on p. 496.

19.7 | Notations

Notations are used to indicate the format of non-XML data. For example, notations can be declared to indicate whether certain binary
graphics data embedded in a `picture` element is in JPEG or GIF format. Notations may describe data embedded in an XML instance, or
data in external files that are linked to the instance through unparsed
entities.

A notation may have a `system` or `public` identifier. There are no
standard notation names or identifiers for well-known formats such as
JPEG. Sometimes the identifier points to an application that can be
used to process the format, for example `viewer.exe`, and other times
it points to documentation about that format. Sometimes it is simply
an abbreviation that can be interpreted by an application. Schema

processors do not resolve these identifiers; it is up to the consuming application to process the notations as desired.

To indicate that a `picture` element contains JPEG data, it will generally have a notation attribute (for example, `fmt`) that indicates which notation applies. An element should only have one notation attribute.

Example 19–23 shows an instance that uses a notation. The `fmt` attribute contains the name of the notation that applies to the contents of `picture`.

Example 19–23. Using a notation in an instance

```
<picture fmt="jpeg">47494638396132003200F7FF00FFFFFFFFFFCCFFFF99FF
FF66FFFF33FFFF00FF</picture>
```

19.7.1 *Declaring a notation*

Notations in XML Schema are declared using `notation` elements, whose syntax is shown in Table 19–6. Notations are always declared globally, with `schema` as their parent. Notations are named components whose qualified names must be unique among all notations in a schema. Like other named, global components, notations take on the target namespace of the schema document. However, for compatibility, it is recommended that notations only be declared in schemas that have no target namespace.

Table 19–6   XSD Syntax: notation

Name
notation

Parents
schema, **1.1**override

(Continues)

Table 19–6   (Continued)

Attribute name	Type	Description
id	ID	Unique ID.
name	NCName	Name of the notation.
public	token	Public identifier; at least one of the system and public attributes must be present.
system	anyURI	System identifier.

Content
annotation?

19.7.2 *Declaring a notation attribute*

As mentioned earlier, elements that contain data described by a notation have a notation attribute. This attribute has a type that restricts the type NOTATION by specifying one or more enumeration facets. Each of these enumeration values must match the name of a declared notation.

Example 19–24 shows two notation declarations that represent graphics formats. A simple type PictureNotationType is then defined, based on NOTATION, which enumerates the names of the notations. Next, an element declaration for picture is provided which declares an attribute fmt of type PictureNotationType.

Example 19–24. Declaring notations and notation attributes

```
<xs:notation name="jpeg" public="JPG"/>
<xs:notation name="gif" public="GIF"/>

<xs:simpleType name="PictureNotationType">
  <xs:restriction base="xs:NOTATION">
    <xs:enumeration value="jpeg"/>
    <xs:enumeration value="gif"/>
  </xs:restriction>
</xs:simpleType>
```

(Continues)

Example 19–24. (Continued)

```
<xs:element name="picture">
  <xs:complexType>
    <xs:simpleContent>
      <xs:extension base="xs:hexBinary">
        <xs:attribute name="fmt" type="PictureNotationType"/>
      </xs:extension>
    </xs:simpleContent>
  </xs:complexType>
</xs:element>
```

19.7.3 *Notations and unparsed entities*

Example 19–24 showed the graphics data embedded directly in the XML in binary format. Notations can also be used to indicate the format of an unparsed general entity. Example 19–25 shows an XML document that lists products and links to pictures of those products. In the schema, `picture` is declared to have an attribute `location` that is of type ENTITY. In the instance, each value of the `location` attribute (in this case, `prod557` and `prod563`) matches the name of an entity declared in the internal DTD subset for the instance. The entity, in turn, refers to the notation via the NDATA parameter. In this case, the notation must appear in the internal DTD subset of the instance in order for the entity to be able to reference it.

Example 19–25. A notation with an unparsed entity

Schema:

```
<xs:element name="picture">
  <xs:complexType>
    <xs:attribute name="location" type="xs:ENTITY"/>
  </xs:complexType>
</xs:element>
<!--...-->
```

(Continues)

Example 19–25.   (Continued)

Instance:

```
<!DOCTYPE catalog SYSTEM "catalog.dtd" [
<!NOTATION jpeg SYSTEM "JPG">
<!ENTITY prod557 SYSTEM "prod557.jpg" NDATA jpeg>
<!ENTITY prod563 SYSTEM "prod563.jpg" NDATA jpeg>
]>

<catalog>
  <product>
    <number>557</number>
    <picture location="prod557"/>
  </product>
  <product>
    <number>563</number>
    <picture location="prod563"/>
  </product>
</catalog>
```

19.8 | Comments

DTDs often use comments to further explain the declarations they contain. Schema documents, as XML, can also contain comments. However, XML Schema also offers an annotation facility that is designed to provide more structured, usable documentation of schema components. Example 19–26 shows a DTD fragment that has a comment describing a section (CUSTOMER INFORMATION) and two element declarations with element-specific comments appearing before each one.

The corresponding schema places each of these comments within an annotation element. The first annotation element, which describes the section, appears as a direct child of the schema. The element-specific annotations, on the other hand, are defined entirely within the element declarations to which they apply. In all three cases, documentation elements are used, which are designed for human-readable information. The schema is considerably more verbose than the DTD, but the descriptive information is much better structured. Section 21.8 on p. 580 covers schema documentation in detail.

Example 19–26. Comments

DTD:

```
<!-- ******************** -->
<!-- CUSTOMER INFORMATION -->
<!-- ******************** -->

<!-- billing address -->
<!ELEMENT billTo (%AddressType;)>
<!-- shipping address -->
<!ELEMENT shipTo (%AddressType;)>
```

Schema:

```
<xs:schema xmlns:xs="http://www.w3.org/2001/XMLSchema"
           xmlns:doc="http://datypic.com/doc">

  <xs:annotation>
    <xs:documentation>
      <doc:section>CUSTOMER INFORMATION</doc:section>
    </xs:documentation>
  </xs:annotation>

  <xs:element name="billTo" type="AddressType">
    <xs:annotation>
      <xs:documentation>
        <doc:description>billing address</doc:description>
      </xs:documentation>
    </xs:annotation>
  </xs:element>

  <xs:element name="shipTo" type="AddressType">
    <xs:annotation>
      <xs:documentation>
        <doc:description>shipping address</doc:description>
      </xs:documentation>
    </xs:annotation>
  </xs:element>
</xs:schema>
```

19.9 | Using DTDs and schemas together

There is nothing to prevent an instance from being validated against both a DTD and a schema. In fact, if you wish to use general entities, you must continue to use DTDs alongside schemas. Example 19–27 shows an instance that has both a DTD and a reference to a schema.

Example 19–27. Using a DTD and a schema

```
<!DOCTYPE catalog SYSTEM "catalog.dtd" [
<!NOTATION jpeg SYSTEM "JPG">
<!ENTITY prod557 SYSTEM "prod557.jpg" NDATA jpeg>
<!ENTITY prod563 SYSTEM "prod563.jpg" NDATA jpeg>]>

<catalog xmlns:xsi="http://www.w3.org/2001/XMLSchema-instance"
         xsi:noNamespaceSchemaLocation="prod.xsd">
  <product>
    <number>557</number>
    <picture location="prod557"/>
  </product>
  <product>
    <number>563</number>
    <picture location="prod563"/>
  </product>
</catalog>
```

Two separate validations can take place: one against the DTD and one against the schema. The DTD validity will be assessed first. This process will not only validate the instance, but also augment it by resolving the entities, filling in attributes' default values, and normalizing whitespace in attribute values. Validity according to the schema is then assessed on the augmented instance. None of the declarations in the DTD override the declarations in the schema. If there are declarations for the same element in both the DTD and the schema and these declarations are conflicting, an element may be DTD-valid but not schema-valid.

XML information modeling

Chapter 20

This chapter addresses some of the general modeling and design questions that come up when designing XML documents, and to a lesser extent the schemas that describe them. For developers who are accustomed to defining data as entity-relationship models, relational tables, UML, and object-oriented models and classes, there is a learning curve associated with the hierarchical model of XML.

This chapter will help you up that curve. It first compares XML modeling and design to other disciplines, such as relational models and object-oriented models, and shows how XML Schema features can be used to describe these models. It then provides some general design principles for modeling web services, dealing with document-oriented narrative content, and working with a hierarchical information model.

20.1 | Data modeling paradigms

If you are approaching the subject of XML Schema with some previous background in data design, you may be wondering how to represent in XML concepts from

- Relational models, such as entity-relationship data models or relational database design
- Object-oriented models, which may exist for example as UML class diagrams and/or object-oriented program code

You may continue to use these modeling paradigms along with your XML application. For example, you may be parsing XML and storing it in a relational database (this is sometimes known as "shredding"), in which case you still have a relational model for your data. You may be processing your XML documents with object-oriented code, so there still needs to be a correspondence between the XML and the object model.

Some schema designers choose to maintain these models, such as UML models, entity-relationship diagrams, and/or supplementary documentation, alongside the XML Schema. Others rely more heavily on the XML Schema to represent the entire model. This is convenient in that there is a one-to-one mapping to the actual XML documents that are in use. However, it does have some drawbacks in that XML Schema cannot express every constraint on the data and is somewhat technology-specific.

Some developers maintain a connection between the models using toolkits that generate program code or even databases. It is particularly common to use data binding toolkits to generate object-oriented classes from schemas. As appropriate, this chapter describes some of the considerations for designing XML documents to optimize the use of these toolkits.

20.2 | Relational models

Designing an XML message structure is different in some ways from traditional entity-relationship modeling and relational database design, where the data model is a persistent-storage representation of the data. When creating an entity-relationship model, great care is (hopefully) taken to define what an entity is, as opposed to how it is used in any particular context. For example, when you model a "customer" entity, you decide on your definition of a customer, its unique identifier, and all of its attributes. You also normalize all the relationships between customers and other entities: For example, a customer can have one or more addresses, and can be associated with zero or more purchases.

An XML message, on the other hand, often represents a particular usage or view of the data, useful at a particular time in a certain operation. Instead of being the definitive source for all information about that entity, it contains only the subset that is useful for the operation in question. For a purchase order, you probably do not need to include all of the information that can be known about a customer; perhaps you just need an identifier, name, and shipping address. For a line item in the purchase order, you may need to know a product's identifier, name, and price, but not its other attributes such as a long description or a list of features.

Relationships also differ in the two models. In an entity-relationship or relational model, there is no single starting point to the model; entities exist and can be accessed independently of each other. In an XML hierarchy, one element must be at the root of the structure, and there is an implied relationship between all of the elements within that hierarchy. Again, only the relationships that are relevant to the particular message are included, and their cardinality may differ in the message as compared to the relational data model. Representing relationships in XML is discussed later in this chapter.

In an ideal scenario, you will have a standardized canonical model that you will draw on for your XML message schemas. Just as in relational database design, in XML message design it makes sense to use the same element names, types, and relationships for the same data where possible. For example, if your corporate data model says that an `Address` entity has the properties `line1`, `line2`, `city`, `state`, and `zip`, it makes sense to use the same definitions and names (or the relevant subset of them) for the elements in your XML messages.

On the other hand, it is best to avoid tightly coupling your XML messages with any one relational database schema. You might use the same names and definitions if they are well-designed, but should not, for example, generate your XML schemas from relational databases or have your application automatically insert the contents of XML elements into relational columns of the same name. This would create too close a relationship between the XML message and the database, where the message schema would have to change if the database changes.

20.2.1 *Entities and attributes*

In a relational model, you will typically have entities, each with a set of attributes or properties. In a relational database, these would be implemented as tables and columns, with each instance represented as a row with multiple cells. In XML, this roughly translates into elements with complex content and elements with simple content. For the entity-relationship model shown in Figure 20–1, our first cut at representing

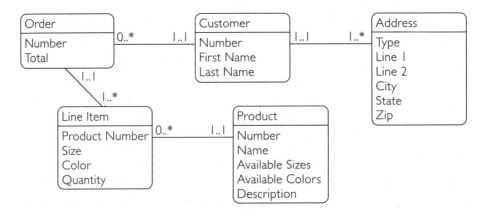

Figure 20–1   Entity-relationship diagram

that in XML (leaving aside the relationships for now) might be as shown in Example 20–1.

Example 20–1. A simple representation of relational entities in XML

```
<model>
  <order>
    <number>1234</number>
    <total>213.12</total>
  </order>
  <customer>
    <number>12345</number>
    <firstName>Priscilla</firstName>
    <lastName>Walmsley</lastName>
  </customer>
  <address>
    <type>Billing</type>
    <line1>123 Main Street</line1>
    <line2>Apartment 2B</line2>
    <city>Traverse City</city>
    <state>MI</state>
    <zip>49684</zip>
  </address>
  <address>
    <type>Shipping</type>
    <line1>PO Box 9999999</line1>
    <city>Traverse City</city>
    <state>MI</state>
    <zip>49686</zip>
  </address>
  <lineItem>
    <giftWrap>bday</giftWrap>
    <number>557</number>
    <size>12</size>
    <color>blue</color>
    <quantity>1</quantity>
  </lineItem>
  <lineItem>
    <number>443</number>
    <size>L</size>
    <color>tan</color>
    <quantity>2</quantity>
  </lineItem>
```

(Continues)

Example 20–1. (Continued)

```
<product>
  <number>557</number>
  <name>Short-Sleeved Linen Blouse</name>
  <availableSizes>2 4 6 8 10 12 14</availableSizes>
  <availableColors>blue red</availableColors>
  <desc>Our best-selling shirt!</desc>
</product>
<product>
  <number>563</number>
  <name>Ten-Gallon Hat</name>
  <availableSizes>S M L</availableSizes>
</product>
<product>
  <number>443</number>
  <name>Deluxe Golf Umbrella</name>
  <availableColors>tan black</availableColors>
  <desc>Protect yourself from the rain!</desc>
</product>
</model>
```

This representation adheres strictly to a structure where every child of `model` is an entity, and every grandchild is an attribute. However, there can be any number of hierarchical levels of elements in XML, which allows additional flexibility to add structure that is sometimes useful. For example, it may be useful to combine `firstName` and `lastName` into a parent `name` structure. This is described further in Section 20.6.1 on p. 527.

Another difference is that with XML, any attribute or property can repeat. With a relational database design, you would either need to define a finite number of occurrences of an attribute or create a separate table with repeating rows. In this example, instead of `line1` and `line2`, in XML it would be more natural to have a repeating `line` element. The order of elements is significant in XML, so the numeric designators are not required to indicate whether it is the first or second line of the address.

20.2.2 *Relationships*

An entity-relationship model allows entities to be independent of each other and have relationships to various other entities. Sometimes these relationships map naturally onto a hierarchical XML model, especially in the case of XML messages that represent a temporary view on the data. Sometimes it is more of a challenge to represent relationships in XML.

20.2.2.1 One-to-one and one-to-many relationships

Many relationships in XML are simply modeled as parent-child relationships, also known as containment relationships. For example, suppose each customer only has one address. In an entity-relationship model, there might be two separate entities: one for customer and one for address. This would be a good design if other entities (such as suppliers) also have addresses. In XML, this would be modeled as a parent-child relationship, where the `customer` element would contain a single `address` element.

A similar approach works if a customer can have more than one address. In an entity-relationship model, there would be a one-to-many relationship between the customer and the address. In XML, the `customer` element can simply contain more than one `address` element.

20.2.2.2 Many-to-many relationships

Many-to-many relationships are harder to represent directly in XML. In many cases, since an XML message represents a temporary view of the data, a one-to-many containment relationship is sufficient even if a many-to-many relationship exists in the real world. For example, a purchase order might represent orders for more than one product, and any one product can be ordered using many purchase orders, but for the purposes of the message you only need to follow the relationship in one direction: include all the products for the given purchase order.

Sometimes there is a many-to-many relationship that does need to be fully represented in one message. Suppose that instead of a single purchase order, our XML document represents a summary report that shows all the orders and the products that are ordered, over time. An order can be for multiple products, and a product can be part of multiple orders, and this many-to-many relationship needs to be represented in the XML. There are several ways to approach this, described in this section.

20.2.2.2.1 *Approach #1: Use containment with repetition*

In this approach, you choose one entity as the parent, for example `order`. Within each `order`, there is a repeating `product` child that contains all of the product information. This is shown in Example 20–2. This will result in some products being repeated, in their entirety, more than once in the message, as is the case for product number 557 in the example.

This is a perfectly acceptable solution for low volumes of information with low repetition. However, if there were a lot of other information in the message about each product, and a product could be repeated in dozens of orders, the message would quickly become unnecessarily large.

Example 20–2. Relationship with repetition

```
<report>
  <order>
    <number>1234</number>
    <total>213.12</total>
    <lineItem>
      <giftWrap>bday</giftWrap>
      <size>12</size>
      <color>blue</color>
      <quantity>1</quantity>
```

(Continues)

Example 20–2.   (Continued)

```
      <product>
        <number>557</number>
        <name>Short-Sleeved Linen Blouse</name>
        <availableColors>blue red</availableColors>
      </product>
    </lineItem>
    <lineItem>
      <size>L</size>
      <color>tan</color>
      <quantity>2</quantity>
      <product>
        <number>443</number>
        <name>Deluxe Golf Umbrella</name>
        <availableColors>tan black</availableColors>
      </product>
    </lineItem>
  </order>
  <order>
    <number>5678</number>
    <total>245.55</total>
    <lineItem>
      <giftWrap>bday</giftWrap>
      <size>12</size>
      <color>blue</color>
      <quantity>1</quantity>
      <product>
        <number>557</number>
        <name>Short-Sleeved Linen Blouse</name>
        <availableColors>blue red</availableColors>
      </product>
    </lineItem>
    <lineItem>
      <size>L</size>
      <quantity>1</quantity>
      <product>
        <number>563</number>
        <name>Ten-Gallon Hat</name>
        <availableSizes>S M L</availableSizes>
      </product>
    </lineItem>
  </order>
</report>
```

20.2.2.2.2 *Approach #2: Use containment with references*

Another option is to keep the orders and products separate and use unique identifiers to specify the relationships. This approach is similar to foreign keys in a database. An order might contain several reference elements that refer to unique keys of the products. An example is shown in Example 20–3.

Here, as in the previous approach, the relationship from order to product is represented, but not the relationship back from product to order. However, the relationship from product to order can be gleaned from the XML using program code.

Example 20–3. Relationship via reference

```
<report>
  <order>
    <number>1234</number>
    <total>213.12</total>
    <lineItem>
      <giftWrap>bday</giftWrap>
      <size>12</size>
      <color>blue</color>
      <quantity>1</quantity>
      <productRef ref="557"/>
    </lineItem>
    <lineItem>
      <size>L</size>
      <color>tan</color>
      <quantity>2</quantity>
      <productRef ref="443"/>
    </lineItem>
  </order>
  <order>
    <number>5678</number>
    <total>245.55</total>
    <lineItem>
      <giftWrap>bday</giftWrap>
      <size>12</size>
      <color>blue</color>
      <quantity>1</quantity>
      <productRef ref="557"/>
    </lineItem>
```

(Continues)

Example 20–3.   (Continued)

```
      <lineItem>
        <size>L</size>
        <quantity>1</quantity>
        <productRef ref="563"/>
      </lineItem>
    </order>
    <product>
      <number>443</number>
      <name>Deluxe Golf Umbrella</name>
      <availableColors>tan black</availableColors>
    </product>
    <product>
      <number>557</number>
      <name>Short-Sleeved Linen Blouse</name>
      <availableColors>blue red</availableColors>
    </product>
    <product>
      <number>563</number>
      <name>Ten-Gallon Hat</name>
      <availableSizes>S M L</availableSizes>
    </product>
</report>
```

In your schema, you can use either ID- and IDREF-typed attributes or identity constraints to validate the relationship. Identity constraints, described fully in Chapter 17, use the key and keyref elements. This is shown in Example 20–4, where the key element defines the unique identifier of each product. Within it, selector identifies the element that needs to be unique (the product), and field specifies the element that contains the unique identifier (the number child).

The keyref element is used to establish the foreign key relationship from the productRef's ref attribute to the product element's number child. It uses a syntax similar to the key element, except that it also includes a refer attribute that indicates the key to which it refers.

Compared to the first approach, this type of structure can be harder to process, either in XPath or in program code generated by data binding tools. Although the relationship can be expressed and validated

Example 20–4. Using identity constraints to validate references

```
<xs:element name="report" type="ReportType">
  <xs:key name="productKey">
    <xs:selector xpath=".//product"/>
    <xs:field xpath="number"/>
  </xs:key>
  <xs:keyref name="productKeyRef" refer="productKey">
    <xs:selector xpath=".//productRef"/>
    <xs:field xpath="@ref"/>
  </xs:keyref>
</xs:element>
```

using a schema, defining it via the schema identity constraints will not have any particular representation or meaning in generated class definitions. For example, for a generated `Order` class, it will not generate a `getProduct` method that will go out and get a related `Product` object, whereas with the first approach you can simply use a `getProduct` method. However, this approach has the advantage of being a lot less verbose if there is a lot of product information and/or it is repeated many times.

20.2.2.2.3 *Approach #3: Use relationship elements*

A third option is to use a separate relationship element (called, for example, `orderProductRelationship`) placed outside the contents of either the `order` or the `product` elements. This is shown in Example 20–5. This has the advantage of representing the relationship in both directions in a compact way. It also provides a container for information about that relationship, such as the quantity and color ordered in our example. The disadvantage is that this is even more difficult to process using generated classes. It compounds the issues with the previous method by requiring yet a third unrelated object (`orderProductRelationship`) that has to be retrieved.

Example 20–5. Using a separate relationship element

```
<report>
  <order>
    <number>1234</number>
    <total>213.12</total>
  </order>
  <order>
    <number>5678</number>
    <total>245.55</total>
  </order>
  <product>
    <number>443</number>
    <name>Deluxe Golf Umbrella</name>
    <availableColors>tan black</availableColors>
  </product>
  <product>
    <number>557</number>
    <name>Short-Sleeved Linen Blouse</name>
    <availableColors>blue red</availableColors>
  </product>
  <product>
    <number>563</number>
    <name>Ten-Gallon Hat</name>
    <availableSizes>S M L</availableSizes>
  </product>
  <orderProductRelationship>
    <orderRef ref="1234"/>
    <productRef ref="557"/>
    <giftWrap>bday</giftWrap>
    <size>12</size>
    <color>blue</color>
    <quantity>1</quantity>
  </orderProductRelationship>
  <orderProductRelationship>
    <orderRef ref="1234"/>
    <productRef ref="443"/>
    <size>L</size>
    <color>tan</color>
    <quantity>2</quantity>
  </orderProductRelationship>
```

(Continues)

Example 20–5. (Continued)

```
<orderProductRelationship>
  <orderRef ref="5678"/>
  <productRef ref="557"/>
  <giftWrap>bday</giftWrap>
  <size>12</size>
  <color>blue</color>
  <quantity>1</quantity>
</orderProductRelationship>
<orderProductRelationship>
  <orderRef ref="5678"/>
  <productRef ref="563"/>
  <size>L</size>
  <quantity>1</quantity>
</orderProductRelationship>
</report>
```

20.3 | Modeling object-oriented concepts

Object-oriented concepts fit nicely with XML Schema. Complex types in XML Schema are like classes, and element declarations are like instance variables that have those classes. Some of the considerations described in the previous section apply to object-oriented concepts as well. Objects are in some ways analogous to entities, and they can have associations (relationships) that can be represented using the three approaches described. Some additional object-oriented concepts are compared to XML in this section.

20.3.1 *Inheritance*

Object-oriented inheritance can be implemented using type derivation in XML Schema. For example, suppose we want to have separate elements for three different kinds of products: shirts, hats, and umbrellas. They have some information in common, such as product number, name, and description. The rest of their content is specific to their subclass: Shirts might have a choice of sizes and a fabric. A hat might also have a choice of sizes, with the values conforming to a different sizing scheme, as well as a different property like an SPF rating. This is depicted as an object model in Figure 20–2.

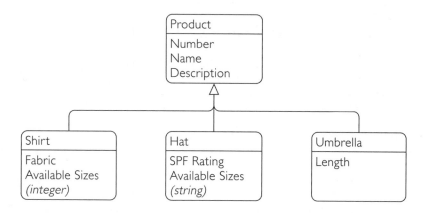

Figure 20–2   Class inheritance

In XML Schema, you can create a `ProductType` type, like the one shown in Example 20–6, that specifies the content common to all three types. The type can optionally be abstract, meaning that it cannot be used directly by an element declaration.

Example 20–6. An abstract product type

```
<xs:complexType name="ProductType" abstract="true">
  <xs:sequence>
    <xs:element name="number" type="xs:integer"/>
    <xs:element name="name" type="xs:string"/>
    <xs:element name="desc" type="xs:string"/>
  </xs:sequence>
</xs:complexType>
```

You can then derive three new types from `ProductType`, one for each kind of product. An example of `ShirtType` is shown in Example 20–7.

Example 20–7. A derived shirt type

```
<xs:element name="shirt" type="ShirtType"/>
<xs:complexType name="ShirtType">
  <xs:complexContent>
    <xs:extension base="ProductType">
      <xs:sequence>
        <xs:element name="fabric" type="xs:string"/>
        <xs:element name="availableSizes"
                    type="AvailableShirtSizesType"/>
      </xs:sequence>
    </xs:extension>
  </xs:complexContent>
</xs:complexType>
<xs:simpleType name="AvailableShirtSizesType">
  <xs:list>
    <xs:simpleType>
      <xs:restriction base="xs:integer">
        <xs:minInclusive value="2"/>
        <xs:maxInclusive value="18"/>
      </xs:restriction>
    </xs:simpleType>
  </xs:list>
</xs:simpleType>
```

As you can see, ShirtType is defined as an extension of ProductType. This means that it inherits the entire content model of ProductType and adds two new elements, fabric and availableSizes, which must appear at the end. A valid instance of ShirtType is shown in Example 20–8.

Example 20–8. Instance of the derived shirt type

```
<shirt>
  <number>557</number>
  <name>Short-Sleeved Linen Blouse</name>
  <desc>Our best-selling shirt!</desc>
  <fabric>linen</fabric>
  <availableSizes>2 4 6 8 10 12 14</availableSizes>
</shirt>
```

A different extension of ProductType could then be defined for the hat element, as shown in Example 20–9.

Example 20–9. A derived hat type

```
<xs:element name="hat" type="HatType"/>
<xs:complexType name="HatType">
  <xs:complexContent>
    <xs:extension base="ProductType">
      <xs:sequence>
        <xs:element name="spfRating" type="xs:integer"/>
        <xs:element name="availableSizes"
                    type="AvailableHatSizesType"/>
      </xs:sequence>
    </xs:extension>
  </xs:complexContent>
</xs:complexType>
<xs:simpleType name="AvailableHatSizesType">
  <xs:list>
    <xs:simpleType>
      <xs:restriction base="xs:string"/>
    </xs:simpleType>
  </xs:list>
</xs:simpleType>
```

HatType also adds an availableSizes element, but its type is different from that in ShirtType. Using locally declared elements, as we do here, allows the same element name to have different types in different contexts.

Data binding tools will generally treat complex type extensions as class inheritance. They will generate a class named ShirtType that extends the class named ProductType. ShirtType will inherit all methods from ProductType and add new ones. This can be beneficial for the same reasons it is beneficial in object-oriented programming. Defining the common components once ensures that they are consistent and makes it easier to write and maintain the code that manipulates the common data. In addition, objects can be treated in the application code either generically as products, or specifically as shirts or hats, depending on the needs of the application.

XML Schema offers several other ways of representing class hierarchies.

- Complex types can be derived by restriction (rather than extension) from other complex types. The derived type must allow only a subset of what the base type allows. This is of limited usefulness unless you are attempting to define a subset of another schema.

- Type substitution allows the same element name to be used for derived types (by extension or restriction). For example, I could declare a `product` element whose type is `ProductType`, and then in the message itself use the `xsi:type` attribute to indicate a derived type—for example, `<product xsi:type="ShirtType">`. It is essentially casting an individual product element to a subtype, `ShirtType`, at runtime. While this can be an elegant way to achieve flexibility, it is not well supported in tools. For more interoperable schemas, it is best to define separate elements (`shirt`, `hat`, `umbrella`) for each type (`ShirtType`, `HatType`, `UmbrellaType`), as shown earlier in this section.

- Substitution groups describe hierarchies of elements rather than types. They allow you to specify that one or more elements are substitutable for another element. For example, I could put the `shirt`, `hat`, and `umbrella` elements in the substitution group of the `product` element. Then, anywhere `product` appears in a content model, any of the other three elements could appear instead. It is a more extensible alternative to `choice` groups. However, the support of substitution groups in data binding tools is also somewhat limited. Data-oriented messages are usually fairly predictable, so unless you need this kind of flexibility, you are better off creating a hierarchy of types and explicitly stating where elements of each type can appear.

20.3.2 *Composition*

There is an alternative way to represent the fact that shirts, hats, and umbrellas have properties in common. Through the use of named model groups, XML Schema allows you to identify shared content model fragments. This distinction could be seen as composition rather than generalization in object-oriented terminology. A shirt definition is composed of product properties, plus has its own properties.

Named model groups are described in detail in Chapter 15. Example 20–10 shows a named model group, `ProductProperties`, with a content model fragment describing all the generic product information.

Example 20–10. Product property group

```
<xs:group name="ProductProperties">
  <xs:sequence>
    <xs:element name="number" type="xs:integer"/>
    <xs:element name="name" type="xs:string"/>
    <xs:element name="desc" type="xs:string"/>
  </xs:sequence>
</xs:group>
```

Example 20–11 shows how `ShirtType` references the `ProductProperties` group. It also uses a `group` element, but this time with a `ref` attribute instead of a `name` attribute. The effect of referencing a group is as if you cut and pasted the content of the group into the place where it is referenced.

`HatType` could similarly reference the group to reuse the definition of the product properties. The instances of `shirt` and `hat` will look exactly the same as if we used type extension; there will be no `ProductProperties` element in the message content.

The advantage of this approach is its flexibility. When using named model groups, the shared portion can appear anywhere in the content

Example 20–11. Shirt type that uses the product property group

```
<xs:complexType name="ShirtType">
  <xs:sequence>
    <xs:group ref="ProductProperties"/>
    <xs:element name="fabric" type="xs:string"/>
    <xs:element name="availableSizes"
                type="AvailableShirtSizesType"/>
  </xs:sequence>
</xs:complexType>
```

model, not just at the beginning. This might be a consideration if the order matters, although you should avoid giving any significance to the order of elements. It's also more flexible in that you can also include more than one group in a content model. With type derivation, there is only single inheritance.

The disadvantage is that although the generic product components are shared in the schema, most data binding toolkits do not generate shared code or interfaces for these components. They will typically generate a `ShirtType` class that has all the generic product properties, and a separate `HatType` class that has separate definitions of the generic product properties. No separate `ProductProperties` class or interface will be generated; it will be as if the group did not exist.

Use of named model groups is most appropriate when the types represent different concepts that happen to have a few of the same child elements. However, if the types are really subclasses of a more generic class, it is better to use type derivation because the generated code will be more useful and representative of the real model.

Another option for composition is to define a child element to contain the shared information. We could use the same `ProductType` complex type we defined before. Instead of deriving `ShirtType` from it, we could give `ShirtType` a child element named `productProperties` that has the type `ProductType`. This is shown in Example 20–12.

Example 20–12. Using a child element for composition

```
<xs:complexType name="ProductType">
  <xs:sequence>
    <xs:element name="number" type="xs:integer"/>
    <xs:element name="name" type="xs:string"/>
    <xs:element name="desc" type="xs:string"/>
  </xs:sequence>
</xs:complexType>
<xs:complexType name="ShirtType">
  <xs:sequence>
    <xs:element name="productProperties" type="ProductType"/>
    <xs:element name="fabric" type="xs:string"/>
    <xs:element name="availableSizes"
               type="AvailableShirtSizesType"/>
  </xs:sequence>
</xs:complexType>
```

In this case, the message instance will have an extra level of structure with the productProperties element, as shown in Example 20–13.

Example 20–13. Instance of shirt type using child element

```
<shirt>
  <productProperties>
    <number>557</number>
    <name>Short-Sleeved Linen Blouse</name>
    <desc>Our best-selling shirt!</desc>
  </productProperties>
  <fabric>linen</fabric>
  <availableSizes>2 4 6 8 10 12 14</availableSizes>
</shirt>
```

One advantage of this approach is that it clearly identifies the shared information and provides a hook to access it. This can make it easier for the consumer of the message, especially when using a tool like XSLT. Using toolkits, an advantage over using named model groups is that one class will be generated for productProperties, so the code to process and generate that part of the message can be shared for both shirts and hats.

The disadvantage of this approach is that it adds an additional layer, and therefore some additional complexity, to the messages. Compared to the type inheritance method, this can make the message more verbose and writing and maintaining the code that implements the service slightly more difficult.

20.4 | Modeling web services

Modeling web services has a lot in common with the concepts already described in this chapter. Typically the information being passed in web service messages consists of entities and/or objects. Some people equate designing a web service with designing an object-oriented API. There are some similarities: There are interfaces (services) that have methods (operations) that encapsulate the underlying functionality. For very fine-grained utility services, this comparison holds true. For example, you might have some data services that are used to put a wrapper around certain low-level database transactions, such as inserting and updating customer information. These services might roughly resemble an object-oriented interface, with methods/operations like `updateCustomerStatus` and `insertCustomerAddress`.

However, as you design more coarse-grained composite services, especially those that will be used across organizational boundaries, the messages passed to and from the service are likely to be broader in scope than any data values you would normally pass in a call to a method. It is desirable, for reasons of performance, scalability, and reliability, for a service to not be too "chatty." A chatty service is one to which multiple calls must be made, often synchronously, to get a useful result. Instead, all the information the service needs to give you in a result should be included in the same message. This means that information needed to accomplish several different actions may be included in the message itself.

For example, for a purchasing service, the message passed to the service might include security information such as logon parameters, the purchase order itself, the state of the purchase order, what action needs to be performed next with it, the format of the desired response or acknowledgement, and the location to send the response. Some of this information will appear in the header. As the message is passed from service to service, it might accumulate additional information, such as customer details and more detailed pricing and tax information, for each of the ordered items. Modeling all of this information as a single message to be passed to an operation may not be intuitive for the average object-oriented designer.

A complete discussion of designing service-oriented architectures and their contracts is outside the scope of this book, but it is useful to note several key points related to message design.

- As described above, the scope of a single message should be somewhat coarse-grained; it should provide all of the content needed for an entire operation. This means that the root element type should be broad enough to include a variety of information, not just a single entity.

- It is helpful to use specific root elements for individual operations. For example, if the operation is to submit a purchase order, it is helpful to have a root element name that specifically states this using a verb, for example `submitPurchaseOrder` rather than a generic `message` element or even a `purchaseOrder` element. If you are using WSDL, you specify the root element for the input and output of each operation in a service. Using more specific root element names improves validation and results in a more precise interface that makes it easier to develop code to process.

- Although individual operations may use different root elements, it is highly desirable for the contents of the various message types to have as much in common as possible. Reusing types at all levels is very important in a service-oriented environment to avoid thousands of point-to-point transformations between different representations of, for example, addresses or products.

Some organizations develop canonical models in XML Schema whose use is mandatory in all newly developed services, as a way of formalizing proper reuse.

20.5 | Considerations for narrative content

Narrative content—the kind you read in documents like books, articles, and web pages—is very different from what we have been discussing so far in this chapter. But that unpredictable human-written, human-readable stuff also occurs alongside data-oriented content in even (or especially) the best-managed documents.

This section first introduces a key distinguishing trait of narrative content, the relationship between semantics and style. It then discusses other considerations for modeling and schema design.

20.5.1 *Semantics vs. style*

It is desirable in designing a narrative XML vocabulary to focus on the semantics, or meaning, of the content, as opposed to its appearance. For example, a phrase might be italicized because it is a foreign phrase or a citation. It is helpful to have separate elements (for example, `foreign` and `citation`) to reflect the semantics, instead of a single element indicating the italicization (`i`). Presentation-only features, such as colors and fonts, are best left to a stylesheet, not embedded in an XML document itself.

20.5.1.1 Benefits of excluding styling

The separation of pure semantic content from presentation style allows you to

- Style content separately for different output devices such as smartphones, e-book readers, and alternative web browsers

- Implement interactive behavior associated with certain kinds of text—for example, hyperlinks for intra- or inter-document references or pop-up directions for addresses

- Generate derivative presentations of the content, such as tables of contents, indexes, and summary views

- Provide more focused searching based on names of elements in the content

- Ensure more consistent formatting across an entire body of content

- Improve verification of the content—for example, determine whether intra-document references in a legal document are valid

20.5.1.2 Rendition elements: "block" and "inline"

Formatting an XML document occurs conceptually in two steps:

1. **Rendition,** which produces an abstract layout of the document, not yet particularized for a specific output device. It contains such elements as "page," "frame," "block," and "inline."

2. **Presentation,** which applies precise styling to produce a layout that is coded for the specific output device.

The mapping from elements in the document to rendition elements occurs in the stylesheet, along with the presentation styling. Usually, an element with characters at the top level of its content is rendered as either a "block" or an "inline" element. When presented, the content of a block element occupies its own vertical space in a page or frame, and the content of its inline elements occurs within that space. Examples of block elements are p in HTML and block in XSL-FO.

Elements rendered inline are generally used for identifying text within a paragraph for distinctive formatting and/or special processing (such as getting its content from a database). In HTML, b (bold) and a (anchor) are examples of inline elements. Substitution groups are often used to represent inline elements, since they can appear interchangeably in many different content models.

20.5.2 *Considerations for schema design*

20.5.2.1 Flexibility

XML models for narrative content tend to be much more flexible than data-oriented models. While you can mandate that every product has a product number and name, you are unlikely to mandate that every paragraph must contain a URL and an emphasized phrase in bold. The order of the actual elements is important in a narrative model (it is important that Chapter 1 appears before Chapter 2) but the order of the kinds of elements is generally less important. You would not require, for example, that all tables must appear after all paragraphs in a section.

20.5.2.2 Reusing existing vocabularies

If you are writing schemas to model general narrative content, it is highly desirable to reuse existing vocabularies, such as XHTML, XSL-FO, DocBook, and NLM XML. Be sure to choose appropriate elements for the degree of semantic specificity of your schema. XHTML and XSL-FO, for example, include rendition elements.

Reusing parts of these vocabularies will save you time and ensure that your vocabulary is consistent with industry-accepted norms. You can either extend these standards using their formally defined methods, or pick and choose a subset of them that is useful to you.

20.5.2.3 Attributes are for metadata

Another characteristic of narrative XML models is that all of the "real" content of an element, such as visible content of a web page or a printed page, is contained in the element's syntactic content (i.e., between its start and end tags). Attributes are reserved for metadata about that content, for example the content's last revision date or its source.

20.5.2.4 Humans write the documents

Another consideration for designing narrative content models is that the corresponding XML document instances are far more likely to be hand-created by human users. Although they will be most likely using an editor to help them navigate the model, you should take their needs into consideration when designing the schemas:

- Pay special attention to consistency and clarity in the model.

- Do not offer multiple different ways to represent the same thing.

- Although flexibility is sometimes desirable, too many choices can be overwhelming. Instead of allowing an `article`, for example, to have too many child element choices, introduce an intermediate level comprising `front`, `body`, and `back` elements: `front` would allow elements such as `title`, `author`, etc.; the `body`, elements like `section`, `list`, `figure`, `table`, etc.; and the `back`, elements like `index` and `appendix`.

- Create separate authoring documentation that does not make use of XML Schema terminology.

20.6 | Considerations for a hierarchical model

XML modeling has more flexibility than other modeling paradigms in that you can have an unlimited number of levels of a hierarchy, and there are a variety of ways of organizing that hierarchy. This section describes some special considerations that allow you to take advantage of the flexibility of XML.

20.6.1 *Intermediate elements*

In XML, you can introduce intermediate elements anywhere in a model to make the document easier to process and understand. Using them as containers to group related elements together can be beneficial in promoting reuse, organizing the messages and generated code more logically, simplifying mapping to existing systems, and allowing more expressive content models.

Going back to our order example, you could define it using a fairly flat structure, depicted in Example 20–14. There are `lineItem` elements to group each line item together, but otherwise all of the data elements are at the same level of the purchase order. One possible schema to describe this document is shown in Example 20–15.

Example 20–14. A flat order example

```
<order>
  <number>12345</number>
  <date>2012-10-31</date>
  <customerNumber>12345</customerNumber>
  <customerName>Priscilla Walmsley</customerName>
  <billToAddressLine>123 Main Street</billToAddressLine>
  <billToCity>Traverse City</billToCity>
  <billToState>MI</billToState>
  <billToZip>49684</billToZip>
  <shipToAddressLine>5100 Garfield Road</shipToAddressLine>
  <shipToCity>Hillsborough</shipToCity>
  <shipToState>NJ</shipToState>
  <shipToZip>08876</shipToZip>
  <!--...-->
  <lineItem>
    <number>557</number>
    <!--...-->
  </lineItem>
  <lineItem>
    <number>443</number>
    <!--...-->
  </lineItem>
</order>
```

The `order` element shown in Example 20–14 contains all the required data, but its design has several weaknesses. The first is that it does not take advantage of reuse opportunities. The structure of the bill-to and ship-to addresses is the same, but it is defined twice in the design. The schema describing this document has to declare each city element twice, each state element twice, and so on. Since the

Example 20–15. A flat order schema

```
<xs:schema xmlns:xs="http://www.w3.org/2001/XMLSchema">
  <xs:element name="order" type="OrderType"/>
  <xs:complexType name="OrderType">
    <xs:sequence>
      <xs:element name="number" type="xs:integer"/>
      <xs:element name="date" type="xs:date"/>
      <xs:element name="customerNumber" type="xs:integer"/>
      <xs:element name="customerName" type="xs:string"/>
      <xs:element name="billToAddressLine" type="xs:string"
                  maxOccurs="unbounded"/>
      <xs:element name="billToCity" type="xs:string"/>
      <xs:element name="billToState" type="xs:string"/>
      <xs:element name="billToZip" type="xs:string"/>
      <xs:element name="shipToAddressLine" type="xs:string"
                  maxOccurs="unbounded"/>
      <xs:element name="shipToCity" type="xs:string"/>
      <xs:element name="shipToState" type="xs:string"/>
      <xs:element name="shipToZip" type="xs:string"/>
      <xs:element name="lineItem" type="LineItemType"
                  maxOccurs="unbounded"/>
    </xs:sequence>
  </xs:complexType>
  <xs:complexType name="LineItemType">
    <xs:sequence>
      <xs:element name="number" type="xs:integer"/>
      <!--...-->
    </xs:sequence>
  </xs:complexType>
</xs:schema>
```

element names are different, any code that handles address information (for example, to populate it or display it) also has to be written twice, once for each set of element names.

A better design is shown in Example 20–16, where two intermediate elements, billToAddress and shipToAddress, have been added to represent the bill-to and ship-to addresses. The two have identical children, which means that they can share the same complex type. It is named AddressType and is shown in Example 20–17 with the revised OrderType, whose elements reference it. AddressType is not only used twice in the revised schema for this message, but may also be reused in other schemas in other contexts.

Example 20–16. More structured address information

```
<order>
  <!--...-->
  <billToAddress>
    <addressLine>123 Main St.</addressLine>
    <city>Traverse City</city>
    <state>MI</state>
    <zip>49684</zip>
  </billToAddress>
  <shipToAddress>
    <addressLine>5100 Garfield Road</addressLine>
    <city>Hillsborough</city>
    <state>NJ</state>
    <zip>08876</zip>
  </shipToAddress>
  <!--...-->
</order>
```

Example 20–17. AddressType and revised OrderType definitions

```
<xs:complexType name="OrderType">
  <xs:sequence>
    <xs:element name="number" type="xs:integer"/>
    <xs:element name="date" type="xs:date"/>
    <xs:element name="customerNumber" type="xs:integer"/>
    <xs:element name="customerName" type="xs:string"/>
    <xs:element name="billToAddress" type="AddressType"/>
    <xs:element name="shipToAddress" type="AddressType"/>
    <xs:element name="lineItem" type="LineItemType"
                maxOccurs="unbounded"/>
  </xs:sequence>
</xs:complexType>
<xs:complexType name="AddressType">
  <xs:sequence>
    <xs:element name="addressLine" type="xs:string"/>
    <xs:element name="city" type="xs:string"/>
    <xs:element name="state" type="xs:string"/>
    <xs:element name="zip" type="xs:string"/>
  </xs:sequence>
</xs:complexType>
```

In addition to reuse, another benefit of the more detailed structure is that a code generation tool will generate a separate class to represent the address information. This tends to be more logical to the developer, and can make it easier to integrate existing systems if, for example, the party information is part of a different application or database than the purchase order information. This further promotes reuse, since the class written to handle address information can be reused as well as the complex type.

Intermediate elements can also allow more robust content models. In this case, if the ship-to address can be optional (for example, when it is the same as the bill-to address), you can make the entire shipToAddress element optional. You can then specify that if the shipToAddress does appear, it must have certain required children such as addressLine and zip. In the flat structure, the only option would be to make all of the shipTo*Xxx* elements optional, which would be a much less expressive content model. It would allow illogical or incomplete documents—for example, one containing a shipToAddressLine but not a shipToCity.

Finally, the use of intermediate elements can address extensibility and address versioning problems. If you later decide that there can be more than one ship-to address (for example, in the case of multi-shipment orders), you can simply increase the maxOccurs attribute on the shipToAddress element declaration without introducing a backward-incompatible change.

Example 20–17 shows an appropriate structure for the purchase order document. However, it is possible to have too many intermediate elements. Excessive levels of nesting in an XML message can make it difficult to understand and overly lengthy. It can also make the schema and program code more difficult to maintain.

20.6.2 *Wrapper lists*

A slightly different kind of intermediate element is a container element that is used to group lists of like elements together. In the flat order example shown in Example 20–14, all of the lineItem elements appear at the top level of the order. It is common practice to place repeating elements into a container element whose name is usually the plural of the name of the element being repeated. In our case, we would wrap our lineItem elements into a lineItems element, as shown in Example 20–18.

This has some of the same benefits described in the previous section, namely extensibility and more expressive content models. It is more extensible because, if you later decide to keep some other information about the list, or change the contents of the list, you do not need to make a backward-incompatible change to the outer complex type (OrderType). In version 1.0, it will also allow a more expressive content model if you choose to use all groups instead of sequence groups in the outer content model, because it will get around the problem of all groups not allowing repeating elements. Finally, documents with container elements can be easier to process using technologies like XSLT.

Example 20–18. A repeating container element lineItems

```
<order>
  <!--...-->
  <lineItems>
    <lineItem>
      <number>557</number>
      <!--...-->
    </lineItem>
    <lineItem>
      <number>443</number>
      <!--...-->
    </lineItem>
  </lineItems>
</order>
```

20.6.3 *Level of granularity*

Another factor to consider is how far down to take the hierarchy. Many data items have composite values, and it is sometimes unclear to what extent they should be broken down into separate elements. For example, suppose a product ID consists of two letters that represent its department, followed by a four-digit number. Should all six characters be modeled as one element, or should it be broken down into two subelements?

It depends on how that data item is to be used. The value should be split up if:

- The components are available separately, or can be separated by a known parsing algorithm. For example, if an address is always stored as a whole text block by an application that gathers this information, it may not be feasible to split it apart to put it in the XML document.
- The components will be processed separately, for example for display or for use in arithmetic operations.
- The objects will be sorted by one or more of the components separately.
- The components have different data types.
- The components should be validated separately.
- The components need to establish a higher level of constraint granularity.

It is easier to concatenate two data values back together than it is to parse them apart, especially if the logic for splitting them is complex.

On the other hand, if the value is always used as a whole by message consumers, it can be kept together. It comes down to the functional nature of the application. For example, a service that simply provides product information for display might offer the product ID as one value, while an order application that needs to treat departments separately may split it up.

20.6.4 *Generic vs. specific elements*

Another decision to make when modeling XML is how specific to make your element names. Using more generic element names allows for flexibility, but can limit validation specificity. One case where this comes into play is when you have several data items that represent a particular class of things, but each is a specialization. It is a design decision whether to use element names that represent the overall class or the specialized subclasses. Using the product example, each product has a number of features associated with it. Each feature has a name and a value. One way to represent this is by declaring a different specific element for each feature. To indicate whether a product is monogrammable, you might have a `monogrammable` element of type `boolean`. Example 20–19 shows some product features marked up with specific elements.

Example 20–19. Specific element names

```
<product>
  <!--...-->
  <availableColors>blue red</availableColors>
  <availableSizes>S M L</availableSizes>
  <monogrammable>true</monogrammable>
  <weight units="g">113</weight>
</product>
```

The downside of using these specific element names is that they are not very flexible. Every time a new feature comes along, which can be relatively often, a number of changes have to be made. The schema must be modified to add the new element declaration for the feature. Applications that use those documents, including any generated code, must also be changed to handle the new features.

On the other hand, you could use a more generic `feature` element that contains the value of the feature, and put the name of the feature in a `name` attribute, as shown in Example 20–20.

A product schema that uses a generic feature element is shown in Example 20–21. Certain fundamental features such as `number` and `name` still have specific elements, because they are common to all products and are important to validate. Both the value and the name of the feature are defined as strings.

Example 20–20. Generic element names

```
<product>
  <!--...-->
  <feature name="availableColors">blue red</feature>
  <feature name="availableSizes">S M L</feature>
  <feature name="monogrammable">true</feature>
  <feature name="weight">113</feature>
</product>
```

Example 20–21. ProductType with generic feature capability

```
<xs:complexType name="ProductType">
  <xs:sequence>
    <xs:element name="number" type="xs:integer"/>
    <xs:element name="name" type="xs:string"/>
    <xs:element name="desc" type="xs:string"/>
    <xs:element name="feature" maxOccurs="unbounded"
               type="FeatureType"/>
  </xs:sequence>
</xs:complexType>
<xs:complexType name="FeatureType">
  <xs:simpleContent>
    <xs:extension base="xs:string">
      <xs:attribute name="name" type="xs:string"/>
    </xs:extension>
  </xs:simpleContent>
</xs:complexType>
```

This is far more flexible, in that new features do not require changes to the schema or the basic structure of the service classes. The only modification that needs to be made is that the code that creates feature elements must add one for the new feature.

There is a downside to using generic elements, however. One is that you cannot specify data types for the values. There is no way in XML Schema to say "if a feature element's name attribute is weight, make the content integer, and if it's monogrammable, make it boolean." In version 1.0, this means that you cannot take advantage of XML Schema type validation to ensure that the values in the message conform to, for example, an enumerated list or range of values. This is not an issue when using specific elements because you simply create separate `weight` and `monogrammable` elements with different types.

Another downside to generic elements is that you have no control over their order or whether they are required or repeating. Using XML Schema 1.0, you cannot specify that there must be a `feature` element whose name is `weight`. You also cannot specify that there can only be one `feature` element whose name is `monogrammable`. For any `feature` name, there can be zero, one, or more values for it, and they can appear in any order. You could enforce this as part of the application, but then it would not be written into the service contract. Again, this is not a problem when you use specific elements for each feature because you can use `minOccurs` and `maxOccurs` on individual element declarations to control this.

Here are some considerations on whether to use generic versus specific elements.

- If there is little change (for example, if new features are rarely added), there is not much benefit to using generic elements.

- If the features are treated similarly (for example, if the consumer of the message is simply going to turn them into a "features" table on a web page for human consumption), it is easier to process them as generic elements.

- If the features are often treated differently, it can be easier to process them as specific elements. For example, if code is generated from the schema and the application needs to know the product's weight to determine shipping cost, it is more convenient to simply call a method like `product.getWeight()` than retrieve all the features through `product.getFeatures()` and loop through them until (possibly) finding one called `weight`.

- If the content is likely to be significantly different for each specialization (or example, if some features can have differing multipart or complex values), it is best to use specific elements so that you can adequately describe their structure in the schema.

- If it is important to validate the contents, or the order or appearance of the data items, it is best to use specific elements, because these constraints cannot be expressed in XML Schema 1.0 for generic elements.[1]

The decision whether to use generic versus specific elements can be made at any level, not just for low-level name-value pairs like features. One level higher, a decision must be made whether to use a generic `product` element versus separate `shirt` and `hat` elements. This can be taken all the way up to the root element of the document, where you could have a generic root element such as `message` with an attribute saying what type of message it is, or choose to use a specific root element for every kind of message. The same considerations described in this section apply, regardless of the level in the hierarchy.

---

1.   In version 1.1, you can use conditional type assignment or assertions to enforce certain constraints on generic elements, but it is not as straightforward as assigning types to specific elements.

Schema design and documentation

I t is fairly easy to create a schema once you know the syntax. It is harder to design one well. This chapter focuses on a strategy for designing schemas that are accurate, durable, and easy to implement. Carefully planning your schema design strategy is especially important when creating a complex set of schemas, or a standard schema that is designed to be used and extended by others.

21.1 | The importance of schema design

Schemas are a fundamental part of many XML-based applications, whether XML is being used in temporary messages for information sharing or as an enduring representation of content (e.g., in publishing). Enterprise architects, DBAs, and software developers often devote a lot of time to data design: They create enterprise data models, data dictionaries with strict naming, and documentation standards, and carefully design and optimize relational databases. Unfortunately, software designers and implementers often do not pay as much attention to good design when it comes to XML messages.

There are several reasons for this. Some people feel that with transitory XML messages, it is not important how they are structured. Some decide that it is easier to use whatever schema is generated for them by a toolkit. Others decide to use an industry-standard XML vocabulary, but fail to figure out how their data really fits into that standard, or to come up with a strategy for customizing it for their needs.

As with any data design, there are many ways to organize XML messages. For example, decisions must be made about how many levels of elements to include, whether the elements should represent generic or more specific concepts, how to represent relationships, and how far to break down data into separate elements. In addition, there are multiple ways to express the same XML structure in XML Schema. Decisions must be made about whether to use global versus local declarations, whether to use named versus anonymous types, whether to achieve reuse through type extension or through named model groups, and how schemas should be broken down into separate schema documents.

The choices you make when designing a schema can have a significant impact on the ease of implementation, ease of maintenance, and even the ongoing relevance of the system itself. Failure to take into account design goals such as reuse, graceful versioning, flexibility, and tool support can have serious financial impacts on software development projects.

21.2 | Uses for schemas

When designing a schema, it is first important to understand what it will be used for. Schemas actually play several roles.

- **Validation.** Validation is the purpose that is most often associated with schemas. Given an XML document, you can use a schema to automatically determine whether that document is valid or not. Are all of the required elements there, in the right order? Do they contain valid values according to their data types? Schema validation does a good job of checking the basic structure and content of elements.

- **A service contract.** A schema serves as part of the understanding between two parties. The document provider and the document consumer can both use the schema as a machine-enforceable set of rules describing an interface between two systems or services.

- **Documentation.** Schemas are used to document the XML structure for the developers and end users that will be implementing or using it. Narrative human-readable annotations can be added to schema components to further document them. Although schemas themselves are not particularly human-readable, they can be viewed by less technical users in a graphical XML editor tool. In addition, there are a number of tools that will generate HTML documentation from schemas, making them more easily understood.

- **Providing type information.** Schemas contain information about the data types that can affect how the information is processed. For example, if the schema tells an XSLT 2.0 stylesheet that a value is an integer, it will know to sort it and compare to other values as an integer instead of a string.

- **Assisted editing.** For documents that will be hand-modified by human users, a schema can be used by XML editing software to provide context-sensitive validation, help, and content completion.

- **Code generation.** Schemas are also commonly used, particularly in web services and other structured data interfaces, to generate classes and interfaces that read and write the XML message payloads. When a schema is designed first, classes can be generated automatically from the schema definitions, ensuring that they match. Other software artifacts can also be generated from schemas, for example, data entry forms.

- **Debugging.** Schemas can assist in the debugging and testing processes for applications that will process the XML. For example, importing a schema into a XSLT 2.0 stylesheet or an XQuery query can help identify invalid paths and type errors in the code that, otherwise, may not have been found during testing.

As you can see, schemas are an important part of an XML implementation, and can be involved at both design time and run time. Although it is certainly possible to use XML without schemas, valuable functionality would be lost. You would be forced to use a nonstandard method to validate your messages, document your system interfaces, and generate code for web services. You also would not be able to take advantage of the many schema-based tools that implement this functionality at low cost.

The various roles of schemas should be taken into account when designing them. For example, use of obscure schema features can make code generation difficult, and not adequately documenting schemas can impact the usefulness of generated documentation.

21.3 | Schema design goals

Designing schemas well is a matter of paying attention to certain important design considerations: flexibility and extensibility, reusability, clarity and simplicity, support for versioning, interoperability, and tool support. This section takes a closer look at each of these design goals.

21.3.1 *Flexibility and extensibility*

Schema design often requires a balancing act between flexibility, on the one hand, versus rigidity on the other. For example, suppose I am selling digital cameras that have a variety of features, such as resolution, battery type, and screen size. Each camera model has a different set of features, and the types of features change over time as new technology is developed. When designing a message that incorporates these camera descriptions, I want enough flexibility to handle variations in feature types, without having to redesign my message every time a new feature comes along. On the other hand, I want to be able to accurately and precisely specify these features.

To allow for total flexibility in the camera features, I could declare a `features` element whose type contains an element wildcard, which means that any well-formed XML is allowed. This would have the advantage of being extremely versatile and adaptable to change. The disadvantage is that the message structure is very poorly defined. A developer trying to write an application to process the message would have no idea what features to expect and what format they might have.

On the other hand, I can declare highly constrained elements for each feature, with no opportunity for variation. This has the benefit of making the features well defined, easy to validate, and much more predictable. Validation is more effective because certain features can be required and their values can be constrained by specific data types. However, the schema is brittle because it must be changed every time a new feature is introduced. When the schema changes, the applications that process the documents must also often change.

The ideal design is usually somewhere in the middle. A balanced approach in the case of the camera features might be to create a repeating `feature` element that contains the name of the feature as an attribute and the value of the feature as its content. This eliminates the brittleness while still providing a predictable structure for implementers.

21.3.2 *Reusability*

Reuse is an important goal in the design of any software. Schemas that reuse XML components across multiple kinds of documents are easier for developers and users to learn, are more consistent, and save development and maintenance time that could be spent writing redundant software components.

Using XML Schema, reuse can be achieved in a number of ways.

- **Reusing types.** It is highly desirable to reuse complex and simple types in multiple element and attribute declarations. For example, you can define a complex type named `AddressType` that represents a mailing address, and then use it for both `BillingAddress` and `ShippingAddress` elements. Only named, global types can be reused, so types in XML Schema should generally be named.

- **Type inheritance.** In XML Schema, complex types can be specialized from other types using type extensions. For example, I can create a more generic type `ProductType` and derive types named `CameraType` and `LensType` from it. This is a form of reuse because `CameraType` and `LensType` inherit a shared set of properties from `ProductType`.

- **Named model groups and attribute groups.** Through the use of named model groups, it is possible to define reusable pieces of content models. This is a useful alternative to type inheritance for types that are semantically different but just happen to share some properties with other types.

- **Reusing schema documents.** Entire schema documents can be reused by taking advantage of the include and import mechanisms of XML Schema. This is useful for defining components that might be used in several different contexts or services. In order to plan for reuse, schema documents should be broken down into logical components by subject area. Having schema documents that are too large and all-encompassing tends to inhibit reuse because it forces other schema documents to take all or nothing when importing them. It is also good practice to create a "core components" schema that has low-level building blocks, such as types for `Address` and `Quantity`, that are imported by all other schema documents.

21.3.3 *Clarity and simplicity*

When human users are creating and updating XML documents, clarity is of the utmost importance. If users have difficulty understanding the document structure, it will take far more time to edit a document, and the editing process will be much more prone to errors. Even when XML documents are both written and read by software applications, they still should be designed so that they are easy to conceptualize and process. Implementers on both sides—those who create XML documents and those who consume them—are writing and maintaining applications to process these messages, and they must understand them. Overly complex message designs lead to overly complex applications that create and process them, and both are hard to learn and maintain.

21.3.3.1 Naming and documentation

Properly and consistently naming schema components—elements, attributes, types, groups—can go a long way toward making the documents comprehensible. Using a common set of terms rather than multiple synonymous terms is good practice, as is the avoidance of obscure acronyms. In XML Schema, it is helpful to identify the kind of component in its name, for example by using the word "Type" at the end of type names. Namespaces should also be consistently and meaningfully named.

Of course, good documentation is very important to achieving clarity. XML Schema allows components to be documented using annotations. While you probably have other documentation that describes your system, having human-readable definitions of the components in your schema is very useful for people who maintain and use that schema. It also allows you to use tools that automatically generate schema documentation more effectively.

21.3.3.2 Clarity of structure

Consistent structure can also help improve clarity. For example, if many different types have child elements `Identifier` and `Name`, put them first and always in the same order. Reuse of components helps to ensure consistent structure.

It is often difficult to determine how many levels of elements to put in a message. Using intermediate elements that group together related properties can help with understanding. For example, embedding all address-related elements (`street`, `city`, etc.) inside an `Address` child element, not directly inside a `Customer` element, is an obvious choice. It makes the components of the address clearly contained and allows you to make the entire address optional or repeating.

It is also often useful to use intermediate elements to contain lists of list-like elements. For example, it is a good idea to embed a repeating sequence of `OrderedItem` elements inside an `OrderedItems` (plural) container, rather than directly inside a `PurchaseOrder` element. These container elements can make messages easier to process and often work better with code generation tools.

However, there is such a thing as excessive use of intermediate elements. XML messages that are a dozen levels deep can become unwieldy and difficult to process.

21.3.3.3 Simplicity

It is best to minimize the number of ways a particular type of data or content can be expressed. Having multiple ways to represent a particular kind of data or content in your XML documents may seem like a good idea because it is more flexible. However, allowing too many choices is confusing to users, puts more of a burden on applications that process the documents, and can lead to interoperability problems.

21.3.4 *Support for graceful versioning*

Systems will change over time. Schemas should be designed with a plan for how to handle changes in a way that causes minimum impact on the systems that create and process XML documents.

A typical schema versioning strategy differentiates between major versions and minor versions. Major versions, such as 1.0, 2.0, or 3.0, are by definition disruptive and not backward-compatible; at times this is an unavoidable part of software evolution. On the other hand, minor versions, such as 1.1, 1.2, or 1.3, are backward-compatible. They involve changes to schemas that will still allow old message instances to be valid according to the new schema. For example, a version 1.2 message can be valid according to a version 1.3 schema if the version 1.3 limits itself to backward-compatible changes.

21.3.5 *Interoperability and tool compatibility*

Schemas are used heavily by tools—not just for validation but also for the generation of code and documentation. In an ideal world, all schema parsers and toolkits would support the exact same schema language, and all schemas would be interoperable. The unfortunate reality is that tools, especially code generation tools, vary in their support for XML Schema, for several reasons.

- Some toolkits incorrectly implement features of XML Schema because the recommendation is complex and in some cases even ambiguous.
- Some web services toolkits deliberately do not support certain features of XML Schema because they do not find them to be relevant or useful to a particular use case, such as data binding.
- Some XML Schema concepts do not map cleanly onto object-oriented concepts. Even if a toolkit attempts to support these features, it may do so in a less than useful way.

In general, it is advisable to stick to a subset of the XML Schema language that is well supported by the kinds of toolkits you will be using in your environment. For example, features of XML Schema to avoid in a web services environment where data-binding toolkits are in use include

- Mixed content (elements that allow text content as well as children)
- `choice` and `all` model groups
- Complex content models with nested model groups
- Substitution groups
- Dynamic type substitution using the `xsi:type` attribute
- Default and fixed values for elements or attributes
- Redefinition of schema documents

It is advisable to test your schemas against a variety of toolkits to be sure that they can handle them gracefully.

21.4 | Developing a schema design strategy

Many organizations that are implementing medium- to large-scale XML vocabularies develop enterprise-wide guidelines for schema design, taking into account the considerations described in this chapter. Sometimes these guidelines are organized into documents that are referred to as Naming and Design Rules (NDR) documents.

Having a cohesive schema design strategy has a number of benefits.

- It promotes a standard approach to schema development that improves consistency and therefore clarity.
- It ensures that certain strategies, such as how to approach versioning, are well thought out before too much investment has been made in development.

- It allows the proposed approach to be tested with toolkits in use in the organization to see if they generate manageable code.

- It serves as a basis for design reviews, which are a useful way for centralized data architects to guide or even enforce design standards within an organization.

A schema design strategy should include the following topics:

- **Naming standards:** standard word separators, upper versus lower case names, a standard glossary of terms, special considerations for naming types and groups. Naming standards are discussed in Section 21.6 on p. 559.

- **Namespaces:** what they should be named, how many to have, how many schema documents to use per namespace, how they should be documented. See Section 21.7 on p. 564 for namespace guidelines.

- **Schema structure strategy:** how many schema documents to have, recommended folder structure, global versus local components. Section 21.5 on p. 550 covers these topics.

- **Documentation standards:** the types of documentation required for schema components, where they are to be documented. Schema documentation is covered in Section 21.8 on p. 580.

- **XML Schema features:** a list of allowed (or prohibited) XML Schema features, limited to promote simplicity, better tool support, and interoperability.

- **Versioning strategy:** whether to require forward compatibility (and if so how to accomplish it), rules for backward compatibility of releases, patterns for version numbering. All of Chapter 23 is devoted to versioning, with particular attention paid to developing a versioning strategy in Section 23.4.1 on p. 636.

- **Reuse strategy:** recommended methods of achieving reuse, an approach for a common component library. Reuse is covered in Section 22.1 on p. 596.

- **Extension strategy:** which external standards are approved for use, description of the correct way to incorporate or extend them, how other standards should extend yours and under what conditions. Section 22.2 on p. 599 compares and contrasts six methods for extending schemas.

These considerations are covered in the rest of this chapter and the next two chapters.

21.5 | Schema organization considerations

There are a number of design decisions that affect the way a schema is organized, without impacting validation of instances. They include whether to use global or local declarations and how to modularize your schemas.

21.5.1 *Global vs. local components*

Some schema components can be either global or local. Element and attribute declarations, for example, can be scoped entirely with a complex type (local) or at the top level of the schema document (global). Type definitions (both simple and complex) can be scoped to a particular element or attribute declaration, in which case they are anonymous, or at the top level of the schema document, in which case they are named. Sections 6.1.3 on p. 95, 7.2.3 on p. 119, and 8.2.3 on p. 133 cover the pros and cons of global versus local components.

It is possible to decide individually for each component whether it should be global or local, but it is better to have a consistent strategy that is planned in advance. Table 21–1 provides an overview of the four possible approaches to the global/local decision. The names associated with the approaches (with the exception of Garden of Eden) were developed as the result of a discussion on XML-DEV led by Roger Costello, who wrote them up as a set of best practices at www.xfront.com/GlobalVersusLocal.pdf.

Table 21–1   Schema structure patterns

		Element declarations	
		Local	*Global*
Type definitions	*Anonymous/Local*	Russian Doll	Salami Slice
	Named/Global	Venetian Blind	Garden of Eden

This section provides an overview of the advantages and disadvantages of each approach. All four of these approaches will validate the same instance, so the question is more one of schema design than XML document design.

In all four approaches, the attribute declarations are locally declared. This follows the recommended practice of allowing unqualified attribute names when the attributes are part of the vocabulary being defined by the schema.

21.5.1.1 Russian Doll

The Russian Doll approach is characterized by all local definitions, with the exception of the root element declaration. All types are anonymous, and all element and attribute declarations are local. Example 21–1 is a Russian Doll schema.

The main disadvantage of this approach is that neither the elements nor the types are reusable. This can result in code that is redundant and hard to maintain. It can also be cumbersome to read. With all the indenting it is easy to lose track of where you are in the hierarchy.

There are a few advantages of this approach but they are less compelling.

- Since the elements are locally declared, it is possible to have more than one element with the same name but a different type or other characteristics. For example, there can be a `number` child of `product` that has a format different from a `number` child of `order`.

Example 21–1. Schema for Russian Doll approach

```
<xs:schema xmlns:xs="http://www.w3.org/2001/XMLSchema"
           xmlns="http://datypic.com/prod"
           targetNamespace="http://datypic.com/prod"
           elementFormDefault="qualified">
  <xs:element name="catalog">
    <xs:complexType>
      <xs:sequence>
        <xs:element name="product" maxOccurs="unbounded">
          <xs:complexType>
            <xs:sequence>
              <xs:element name="number" type="xs:integer"/>
              <xs:element name="name" type="xs:string"/>
              <xs:element name="size">
                <xs:simpleType>
                  <xs:restriction base="xs:integer">
                    <xs:minInclusive value="2"/>
                    <xs:maxInclusive value="18"/>
                  </xs:restriction>
                </xs:simpleType>
              </xs:element>
            </xs:sequence>
            <xs:attribute name="dept" type="xs:string"/>
          </xs:complexType>
        </xs:element>
      </xs:sequence>
    </xs:complexType>
  </xs:element>
</xs:schema>
```

- Since the elements are locally declared, their names can be unqualified in the instance. However, this practice is not recommended, as described in Section 21.7.3.6 on p. 579.

- There is only one global element declaration, so it is obvious which one is the root.

- Since there is no reuse, it is easier to see the impact of a change: You simply look up the hierarchy.

21.5.1.2 Salami Slice

The Salami Slice uses global element declarations but anonymous (local) types. This places importance on the element as the unit of reuse. Example 21–2 is a Salami Slice schema.

Example 21–2. Schema for Salami Slice approach

```
<xs:schema xmlns:xs="http://www.w3.org/2001/XMLSchema"
           xmlns="http://datypic.com/prod"
           targetNamespace="http://datypic.com/prod"
           elementFormDefault="qualified">
  <xs:element name="catalog">
    <xs:complexType>
      <xs:sequence>
        <xs:element ref="product" maxOccurs="unbounded"/>
      </xs:sequence>
    </xs:complexType>
  </xs:element>
  <xs:element name="product">
    <xs:complexType>
      <xs:sequence>
        <xs:element ref="number"/>
        <xs:element ref="name"/>
        <xs:element ref="size"/>
      </xs:sequence>
      <xs:attribute name="dept" type="xs:string"/>
    </xs:complexType>
  </xs:element>
  <xs:element name="number" type="xs:integer"/>
  <xs:element name="name" type="xs:string"/>
  <xs:element name="size">
    <xs:simpleType>
      <xs:restriction base="xs:integer">
        <xs:minInclusive value="2"/>
        <xs:maxInclusive value="18"/>
      </xs:restriction>
    </xs:simpleType>
  </xs:element>
</xs:schema>
```

The disadvantage of this approach is that the types are not reusable by multiple element declarations. Often you will have multiple element names that have the same structure, such as `billingAddress` and `shippingAddress` with the same address structure. Using this model, the entire address structure would need to be respecified each time, or put into a named model group. Anonymous types also cannot be used in derivation—another form of reuse and sometimes an important expression of an information model. Although you can reuse the element declarations, this might mean watered-down element names, such as `address` instead of a more specific kind of address. Since elements are globally declared, it is not possible to have more than one element with the same name but a different type or other characteristics; all element names in the entire schema must be unique.

This approach does have some advantages over Russian Doll, namely that it is more readable and does allow some degree of reuse through element declarations. Unlike Russian Doll, it does allow the use of substitution groups, which require global element declarations.

21.5.1.3 Venetian Blind

The Venetian Blind approach has local element declarations but named global types. Example 21–3 is a Venetian Blind schema.

The significant advantage to this approach is that the types are reusable. The advantages of named types over anonymous types are compelling and make this approach more flexible and better defined than either of the previous two approaches. Since elements are locally declared, it is possible to have more than one element with the same name but a different type or other characteristics, which also improves flexibility.

The disadvantage of this approach is that element declarations are not reused, so if they have complex constraints such as type alternatives or identity constraints, these need to be respecified in multiple places. Also, element declarations cannot participate in substitution groups.

If substitution groups aren't needed, this is the author's preferred approach and is the style used in most of this book. It allows for full

Example 21–3. Schema for Venetian Blind approach

```
<xs:schema xmlns:xs="http://www.w3.org/2001/XMLSchema"
           xmlns="http://datypic.com/prod"
           targetNamespace="http://datypic.com/prod"
           elementFormDefault="qualified">
  <xs:element name="catalog" type="CatalogType"/>
  <xs:complexType name="CatalogType">
    <xs:sequence>
      <xs:element name="product" type="ProductType"
                  maxOccurs="unbounded"/>
    </xs:sequence>
  </xs:complexType>
  <xs:complexType name="ProductType">
    <xs:sequence>
      <xs:element name="number" type="xs:integer"/>
      <xs:element name="name" type="xs:string"/>
      <xs:element name="size" type="SizeType"/>
    </xs:sequence>
    <xs:attribute name="dept" type="xs:string"/>
  </xs:complexType>
  <xs:simpleType name="SizeType">
    <xs:restriction base="xs:integer">
      <xs:minInclusive value="2"/>
      <xs:maxInclusive value="18"/>
    </xs:restriction>
  </xs:simpleType>
</xs:schema>
```

reuse through types, but also allows the flexibility of varying element names. It maps very cleanly onto an object-oriented model, where the complex types are analogous to classes and the element declarations are analogous to instance variables that have that class.

21.5.1.4 Garden of Eden

The Garden of Eden approach has all global (named) types and global element declarations. Example 21–4 is a Garden of Eden schema.

The only disadvantage of this approach, other than its verbosity, is that since elements are globally declared, it is not possible to have more than one element with the same name but a different type or

Example 21–4. Schema for Garden of Eden approach

```
<xs:schema xmlns:xs="http://www.w3.org/2001/XMLSchema"
           xmlns="http://datypic.com/prod"
           targetNamespace="http://datypic.com/prod"
           elementFormDefault="qualified">
  <xs:element name="catalog" type="CatalogType"/>
  <xs:complexType name="CatalogType">
    <xs:sequence>
      <xs:element ref="product" maxOccurs="unbounded"/>
    </xs:sequence>
  </xs:complexType>
  <xs:element name="product" type="ProductType"/>
  <xs:complexType name="ProductType">
    <xs:sequence>
      <xs:element ref="number"/>
      <xs:element ref="name"/>
      <xs:element ref="size"/>
    </xs:sequence>
    <xs:attribute name="dept" type="xs:string"/>
  </xs:complexType>
  <xs:element name="number" type="xs:integer"/>
  <xs:element name="name" type="xs:string"/>
  <xs:element name="size" type="SizeType"/>
  <xs:simpleType name="SizeType">
    <xs:restriction base="xs:integer">
      <xs:minInclusive value="2"/>
      <xs:maxInclusive value="18"/>
    </xs:restriction>
  </xs:simpleType>
</xs:schema>
```

other characteristics. All element names in the entire schema must be unique. However, some would consider unique, meaningful element names to be an advantage, and indeed it can simplify processing of the document using technologies like XSLT and SAX.

Garden of Eden is a very viable approach to schema design. Its big advantage is that it allows both element declarations and types to be referenced from multiple components, maximizing their reuse potential. In addition, compared to Venetian Blind, it allows the use of substitution groups. If substitution groups are needed, and it is acceptable to force the uniqueness of element names, this approach is the right choice. Many standard XML vocabularies use this approach.

Overall, the Garden of Eden and Venetian Blind, depending on your requirements, are the recommended approaches. The Russian Doll approach has obvious limitations in terms of reuse, and the Salami Slice approach does not benefit from the very significant advantages of named types over anonymous types.

21.5.2 *Modularizing schema documents*

Another decision related to schema structure is how to modularize your schema documents. Consider a project that involves orders for retail products. The order will contain information from several different domains. It will contain general information that applies to the order itself, such as the order number and date. It may also contain customer information, such as customer name, number, and address. Finally, it may contain product information, such as product number, name, description, and size.

Do you want one big schema document, or three schema documents, one for each of the subject areas (order, customer, and product)? There are a number of advantages to composing your schema representation from multiple schema documents.

- **Easier reuse.** If schema documents are small and focused, they are more likely to be reused. For example, a product catalog application might want to reuse the definitions from the product schema. This is much more efficient if the product catalog application is not forced to include everything from the order application.

- **Ease of maintenance.** Smaller schema documents are more readable and manageable.

- **Reduced chance of name collisions.** If different namespaces are used for the different schema documents, name collisions are less likely.

- **Versioning granularity.** It is helpful to separate components that change more frequently, or change on a different schedule, into a separate schema document. This creates less disruption when a new version is released. Code lists (simple types with enumerations) are often placed into individual schema documents so they can be versioned separately.
- **Access control granularity.** Security can be managed per schema document, allowing more granular access control.

Dividing up your schema documents too much, though, can make them hard to manage. For example, having one element declaration or type definition per schema document would necessitate the use of dozens of imports or includes in your schema documents. If different namespaces are used in these schema documents, that compounds the complexity, because an instance document will have to declare dozens of namespaces.

There are several ways to distribute your components among schema documents, for example:

- **Subject area.** If your instance will contain application data, this could mean one schema document per application or per database. If the instances incorporate XML documents of different types, such as test reports and product specifications, and each is defined by its own root element declaration, it would be logical to use a separate schema document for each document type.
- **General/specific.** There may be a base set of components that can be extended for a variety of different purposes. For example, you may create a schema document that contains generic (possibly abstract) definitions for purchase orders and invoices, and separate schema documents for each set of industry-specific extensions.
- **Basic/advanced.** Suppose you have a core set of components that are used in all instances, plus a number of optional components. You may want to define these optional components in a

separate schema document. This allows an instance to be validated against just the core set of components or the enhanced set, depending on the application.

- **Governance.** Schemas should be divided so that a single schema document is not governed by more than one group of people.

- **Versioning Schedule.** As mentioned above, it is helpful to separate components that are versioned frequently or on different schedules, such as code lists.

Another issue when you break up schema documents is whether to use the same namespace for all of them, or break them up into separate namespaces. This issue is covered in detail in Section 21.7.2 on p. 565.

21.6 | Naming considerations

This section provides detailed recommendations for choosing and managing names for XML elements and attributes, as well as for other XML Schema components. It discusses naming guidelines, the use of qualified and unqualified names, and organizing a namespace.

Consistency in naming can be as important as the names themselves. Consistent names are easier to understand, remember, and maintain. This section provides guidelines for defining an XML naming standard to ensure the quality and consistency of names.

These guidelines apply primarily to the names that will appear in an instance—namely, element, attribute, and notation names. However, much of this section is also applicable to the names used within the schema, such as type, group, and identity constraint names.

21.6.1 *Rules for valid XML names*

Names in XML must start with a letter or underscore (_), and can contain only letters, digits, underscores (_), colons (:), hyphens (-), and periods (.). Colons should be reserved for use with namespace prefixes. In addition, an XML name cannot start with the letters `xml` in either upper or lower case.

Names in XML are always case-sensitive, so `accountNumber` and `AccountNumber` are two different element names.

Since schema components have XML names, these name restrictions apply not only to the element and attribute names that appear in instances, but also to the names of the types, named model groups, attribute groups, identity constraints, and notations you define in your schemas.

21.6.2 *Separators*

If a name is made up of several terms, such as "account number," you should decide on a standard way to separate the terms. It can be done through capitalization (e.g., `accountNumber`) or through punctuation (e.g., `account-number`).

Some programming languages, database management systems, and other technologies do not allow hyphens or other punctuation in the names they use. Therefore, if you want to directly match your element names, for example, with variable names or database column names, you should use capitalization to separate terms.

If you choose to use capitalization, the next question is whether to use mixed case (e.g., `AccountNumber`) or camel case (e.g., `accountNumber`). In some programming languages, it is a convention to use mixed case for class names and camel case for instance variables. In XML, this maps roughly to using mixed case for type names and camel case for element names. This is the convention used in this book.

Regardless of which approach you choose, the most important thing is being consistent.

21.6.3 *Name length*

There is no technical limit to the length of an XML name. However, the ideal length of a name is somewhere between four and twelve characters. Excessively long element names, such as `HazardousMaterialsHandlingFeeDomestic`, can, if used frequently, add dramatically to the size of the instance. They are also difficult to type, hard to distinguish from other long element names, and not very readable. On the other hand, very short element names, such as `b`, can be too cryptic for people who are not familiar with the vocabulary.

21.6.4 *Standard terms and abbreviations*

In order to encourage consistency, it is helpful to choose a standard set of terms that will be used in your names. Table 21–2 shows a sample list of standard terms. This term list is used in the examples in this book. Synonyms are included in the list to prevent new terms from being created that have the same meaning as other terms.

Table 21–2 Terms

Term	Abbreviation	Synonyms
color	color	
currency	curr	
customer	cust	client, purchaser, account holder
date	date	
description	desc	
effective	eff	begin, start
identifier	id	
name	name	
number	num	code
order	ord	purchase order
price	price	cost
product	prod	item
size	size	

These consistent terms are then combined to form element and attribute names. For example, "product number" might become `productNumber`.

In some cases, the name will be too long if all of the terms are concatenated together. Therefore, it is useful to have a standard abbreviation associated with each term. Instead of `productNumber`, `prodNumber` may be more manageable by being shorter.

21.6.5 *Use of object terms*

In some contexts, using an element name such as `prodNumber` may be redundant. In Example 21–5, it is obvious from the context that the number is a product number as opposed to some other kind of number.

Example 21–5. Repetition of terms

```
<product>
  <prodNumber>557</prodNumber>
  <prodName>Short-Sleeved Linen Blouse</prodName>
  <prodSize sizeSystem="US-DRESS">10</prodSize>
</product>
```

In this case, it may be clearer to leave off the `prod` term on the child elements, as shown in Example 21–6.

Example 21–6. No repetition of terms

```
<product>
  <number>557</number>
  <name>Short-Sleeved Linen Blouse</name>
  <size system="US-DRESS">10</size>
</product>
```

There may be other cases where the object is not so obvious. In Example 21–7, there are two names: a customer name and a product name. If we took out the terms `cust` and `prod`, we would not be able to distinguish between the two names. In this case, it should be left as shown.

Example 21–7. Less clear context

```
<letter>Dear <custName>Priscilla Walmsley</custName>,
Unfortunately, we are out of stock of the
<prodName>Short-Sleeved Linen Blouse</prodName> in size
<prodSize>10</prodSize> that you ordered...</letter>
```

When creating element and attribute names, it is helpful to list two names: one to be used when the object is obvious, and one to be used in other contexts. This is illustrated in Table 21–3.

Table 21–3 Element or attribute names

Logical name	Object	Name inside object context	Name outside object context
customer name	customer	name	custName
product name	product	name	prodName
customer number	customer	number	custNum
product number	product	number	prodNum
order number	order	number	ordNum
product size	product	size	prodSize
product color	product	color	prodColor

21.7 | Namespace considerations

21.7.1 *Whether to use namespaces*

Some designers of XML vocabularies wonder whether they should even use namespaces. In general, using namespaces has a lot of advantages:

- It indicates clear ownership of the definitions in that namespace.

- The namespace name, if it is a URL, provides a natural place to locate more information about that XML vocabulary.

- It allows the vocabulary to be combined with other XML vocabularies with a clear separation and without the risk of name collision.

- It is an indication to processing software what kind of document it is.

The downside of using namespaces is the complexity, or perceived complexity. You have to declare them in your schemas and your instances, and the code you write to process the documents has to pay attention to them. Another possible disadvantage is their limited support in DTDs. If you are writing both a DTD and a schema for your vocabulary, it requires special care to flexibly allow namespace declarations and prefixes in the DTD.[1]

Despite some negative perceptions about namespaces, it is fairly unusual for standard, reusable vocabularies not to use namespaces. If you are writing a one-off XML vocabulary that is internal to a single organization or application, it is probably fine not to use namespaces. However, if you are planning for your vocabulary to be used by a variety of organizations, or combined with other vocabularies, namespaces are highly recommended.

---

1.   For a demanding real-world example, see the DTD for XSD in Appendix A of www.w3.org/TR/2012/REC-xmlschema11-1-20120405/structures.html.

The complexity of namespaces can be somewhat mitigated by choosing a straightforward namespace strategy. For example, using fewer namespaces, using qualified local element names, and using conventional prefixes consistently can make namespaces seem less cumbersome.

21.7.2 *Organizing namespaces*

Consider a project that involves orders for retail products. An order will contain information from several different domains. It will contain general information that applies to the order itself, such as order number and date. It may also contain customer information, such as customer name, number, and address. Finally, it may contain product information, such as product number, name, description, and size. Is it best to use the same namespace for all of them, or break them up into separate namespaces? There are three approaches:

1. **Same namespace:** Use the same namespace for all of the schema documents.

2. **Different namespaces:** Use multiple namespaces, perhaps a different one for each schema document.

3. **Chameleon namespaces:** Use a namespace for the parent schema document, but no namespaces for the included schema documents.

21.7.2.1 Same namespace

It is possible to give all the schema documents the same target namespace and use `include` to assemble them to represent a schema with that namespace. This is depicted in Figure 21–1.

Example 21–8 shows our three schema documents using this approach. They all have the same target namespace, and `ord.xsd` includes the other two schema documents.

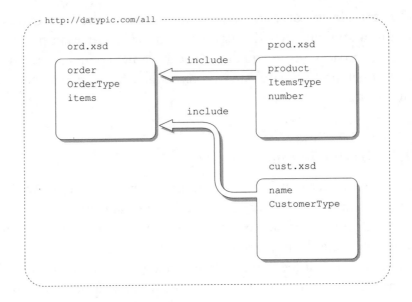

Figure 21–1   Same namespace

Example 21–8. Same namespace in a schema

ord.xsd:

```
<xs:schema xmlns:xs="http://www.w3.org/2001/XMLSchema"
           xmlns="http://datypic.com/all"
           targetNamespace="http://datypic.com/all"
           elementFormDefault="qualified">
  <xs:include schemaLocation="prod.xsd"/>
  <xs:include schemaLocation="cust.xsd"/>
  <xs:element name="order" type="OrderType"/>
  <xs:complexType name="OrderType">
    <xs:sequence>
      <xs:element name="customer" type="CustomerType"/>
      <xs:element name="items" type="ItemsType"/>
    </xs:sequence>
  </xs:complexType>
</xs:schema>
```

(Continues)

Example 21–8. (Continued)

prod.xsd:

```
<xs:schema xmlns:xs="http://www.w3.org/2001/XMLSchema"
           xmlns="http://datypic.com/all"
           targetNamespace="http://datypic.com/all"
           elementFormDefault="qualified">
  <xs:complexType name="ItemsType">
    <xs:sequence maxOccurs="unbounded">
      <xs:element name="product" type="ProductType"/>
    </xs:sequence>
  </xs:complexType>
  <xs:complexType name="ProductType">
    <xs:sequence>
      <xs:element name="number" type="xs:integer"/>
    </xs:sequence>
  </xs:complexType>
</xs:schema>
```

cust.xsd:

```
<xs:schema xmlns:xs="http://www.w3.org/2001/XMLSchema"
           xmlns="http://datypic.com/all"
           targetNamespace="http://datypic.com/all"
           elementFormDefault="qualified">
  <xs:complexType name="CustomerType">
    <xs:sequence>
      <xs:element name="name" type="xs:string"/>
    </xs:sequence>
  </xs:complexType>
</xs:schema>
```

Example 21–9 shows an instance that conforms to the schema. Since there is only one namespace for all of the elements, a default namespace declaration is used.

The advantages of this approach are that it is uncomplicated and the instance is not cluttered by prefixes. The disadvantage is that you cannot

Example 21–9. Same namespace in an instance

```
<order xmlns="http://datypic.com/all"
       xmlns:xsi="http://www.w3.org/2001/XMLSchema-instance"
       xsi:schemaLocation="http://datypic.com/all ord.xsd">
  <customer>
    <name>Priscilla Walmsley</name>
  </customer>
  <items>
    <product>
      <number>557</number>
    </product>
  </items>
</order>
```

have multiple global components with the same name in the same namespace, so you will have to be careful of name collisions.

This approach assumes that you have control over all the schema documents. If you are using elements from a namespace over which you have no control, such as the XHTML namespace, you should use the approach described in the next section.

This approach is best within a particular application where you have control over all the schema documents involved.

21.7.2.2 Different namespaces

It is also possible to give each schema document a different target namespace and use an `import` (or other method) to assemble the multiple schema documents. This is depicted in Figure 21–2.

Example 21–10 shows our three schema documents using this approach. They all have different target namespaces, and `ord.xsd` imports the other two schema documents.

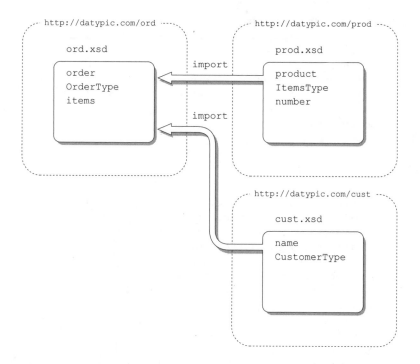

Figure 21–2   Different namespaces

Example 21–10. Different namespaces in a schema

ord.xsd:

```
<xs:schema xmlns:xs="http://www.w3.org/2001/XMLSchema"
           xmlns:prod="http://datypic.com/prod"
           xmlns:cust="http://datypic.com/cust"
           xmlns="http://datypic.com/ord"
           targetNamespace="http://datypic.com/ord"
           elementFormDefault="qualified">
  <xs:import schemaLocation="prod.xsd"
             namespace="http://datypic.com/prod"/>
  <xs:import schemaLocation="cust.xsd"
             namespace="http://datypic.com/cust"/>
  <xs:element name="order" type="OrderType"/>
```

(Continues)

Example 21–10. (Continued)

```
  <xs:complexType name="OrderType">
    <xs:sequence>
      <xs:element name="customer" type="cust:CustomerType"/>
      <xs:element name="items" type="prod:ItemsType"/>
    </xs:sequence>
  </xs:complexType>
</xs:schema>
```

prod.xsd:

```
<xs:schema xmlns:xs="http://www.w3.org/2001/XMLSchema"
           xmlns="http://datypic.com/prod"
           targetNamespace="http://datypic.com/prod"
           elementFormDefault="qualified">
  <xs:complexType name="ItemsType">
    <xs:sequence maxOccurs="unbounded">
      <xs:element name="product" type="ProductType"/>
    </xs:sequence>
  </xs:complexType>
  <xs:complexType name="ProductType">
    <xs:sequence>
      <xs:element name="number" type="xs:integer"/>
    </xs:sequence>
  </xs:complexType>
</xs:schema>
```

cust.xsd:

```
<xs:schema xmlns:xs="http://www.w3.org/2001/XMLSchema"
           xmlns="http://datypic.com/cust"
           targetNamespace="http://datypic.com/cust"
           elementFormDefault="qualified">
  <xs:complexType name="CustomerType">
    <xs:sequence>
      <xs:element name="name" type="xs:string"/>
    </xs:sequence>
  </xs:complexType>
</xs:schema>
```

Example 21–11 shows an instance that conforms to this schema. You are required to declare all three namespaces in the instance and to prefix the element names appropriately. However, since `ord.xsd` imports the other two schema documents, you are not required to specify xsi:schemaLocation pairs for all three schema documents, just the "main" one.

Example 21–11. Different namespaces in an instance

```
<order xmlns="http://datypic.com/ord"
       xmlns:prod="http://datypic.com/prod"
       xmlns:cust="http://datypic.com/cust"
       xmlns:xsi="http://www.w3.org/2001/XMLSchema-instance"
       xsi:schemaLocation="http://datypic.com/ord ord.xsd">
  <customer>
    <cust:name>Priscilla Walmsley</cust:name>
  </customer>
  <items>
    <prod:product>
      <prod:number>557</prod:number>
    </prod:product>
  </items>
</order>
```

To slightly simplify the instance, different default namespace declarations could appear at different levels of the document, resulting in the instance shown in Example 21–12. It could be simplified even further by the use of unqualified local element names, as discussed in Section 21.7.3.2 on p. 576.

Example 21–12. Different namespaces in an instance, with default namespaces

```
<order xmlns="http://datypic.com/ord"
       xmlns:xsi="http://www.w3.org/2001/XMLSchema-instance"
       xsi:schemaLocation="http://datypic.com/ord ord.xsd">
  <customer>
    <name xmlns="http://datypic.com/cust">Priscilla Walmsley</name>
  </customer>
  <items>
    <product xmlns="http://datypic.com/prod">
      <number>557</number>
    </product>
  </items>
</order>
```

This is an obvious approach when you are using namespaces over which you have no control—for example, if you want to include XHTML elements in your product description. There is no point trying to copy all the XHTML element declarations into a new namespace. This would create maintenance problems and would not be very clear to users. In addition, applications that process XHTML may require that the elements be in the XHTML namespace.

The advantage to this approach is that the source and context of an element are very clear. In addition, it allows different groups to be responsible for different namespaces. Finally, you can be less concerned about name collisions, because the names must only be unique within a namespace.

The disadvantage of this approach is that instances are more complex, requiring prefixes for multiple different namespaces. Also, you cannot use the `redefine` or `override` feature on these components, since they are in a different namespace.

21.7.2.3 Chameleon namespaces

The third possibility is to specify a target namespace only for the "main" schema document, not the included schema documents. The included components then take on the target namespace of the including document. In our example, all of the definitions and declarations in both `prod.xsd` and `cust.xsd` would take on the `http://datypic.com/ord` namespace once they are included in `ord.xsd`. This is depicted in Figure 21–3.

Example 21–13 shows our three schema documents using this approach. Neither `prod.xsd` nor `cust.xsd` has a target namespace, while `ord.xsd` does. `ord.xsd` includes the other two schema documents and changes their namespace as a result.

The instance in this case would look similar to that of the same-namespace approach shown in Example 21–9, since all the elements would be in the same namespace. The only difference is that in this case the namespace would be `http://datypic.com/ord` instead of `http://datypic.com/all`.

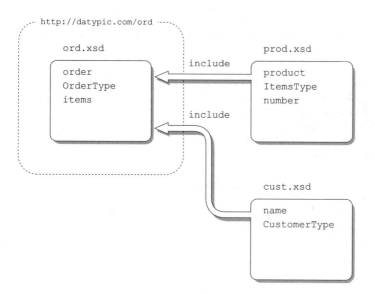

Figure 21–3   Chameleon namespaces

Example 21–13. Chameleon namespaces in a schema

ord.xsd:

```
<xs:schema xmlns:xs="http://www.w3.org/2001/XMLSchema"
           xmlns="http://datypic.com/ord"
           targetNamespace="http://datypic.com/ord"
           elementFormDefault="qualified">
  <xs:include schemaLocation="prod.xsd"/>
  <xs:include schemaLocation="cust.xsd"/>
  <xs:element name="order" type="OrderType"/>
  <xs:complexType name="OrderType">
    <xs:sequence>
      <xs:element name="customer" type="CustomerType"/>
      <xs:element name="items" type="ItemsType"/>
    </xs:sequence>
  </xs:complexType>
</xs:schema>
```

(Continues)

Example 21–13. (Continued)

prod.xsd:

```
<xs:schema xmlns:xs="http://www.w3.org/2001/XMLSchema"
           elementFormDefault="qualified">
  <xs:complexType name="ItemsType">
    <xs:sequence maxOccurs="unbounded">
      <xs:element name="product" type="ProductType"/>
    </xs:sequence>
  </xs:complexType>
  <xs:complexType name="ProductType">
    <xs:sequence>
      <xs:element name="number" type="xs:integer"/>
    </xs:sequence>
  </xs:complexType>
</xs:schema>
```

cust.xsd:

```
<xs:schema xmlns:xs="http://www.w3.org/2001/XMLSchema"
           elementFormDefault="qualified">
  <xs:complexType name="CustomerType">
    <xs:sequence>
      <xs:element name="name" type="xs:string"/>
    </xs:sequence>
  </xs:complexType>
</xs:schema>
```

The advantage of this approach is its flexibility. Components can be included in multiple namespaces, and redefined or overridden whenever desired.

The disadvantage is that the risk of name collisions is even more serious. If the non-namespace schema documents grow over time, the risk increases that there will be name collisions with the schema documents that include them. If they were in their own namespace, unexpected collisions would be far less likely.

Another disadvantage is that the chameleon components lack an identity. Namespaces can be well-defined containers that provide a recognizable context as well as specific semantics, documentation, and application code.

21.7.3 *Qualified vs. unqualified forms*

Many instances include elements from more than one namespace. This can potentially result in instances with a large number of different prefixes, one for each namespace. However, when an element declaration is local—that is, when it isn't at the top level of a schema document—you have the choice of using either qualified or unqualified element names in instances, a concept that was introduced in Section 6.3 on p. 98. Let's recap the two alternatives, this time looking at more complex multinamespace documents.

21.7.3.1 Qualified local names

Example 21–14 shows an instance where all element names are qualified. Every element name has a prefix that maps it to either the product namespace or the order namespace.

Example 21–14. Qualified local names

```
<ord:order xmlns:ord="http://datypic.com/ord"
           xmlns:prod="http://datypic.com/prod">
  <ord:number>123123</ord:number>
  <ord:items>
    <prod:product>
      <prod:number>557</prod:number>
    </prod:product>
  </ord:items>
</ord:order>
```

This instance is very explicit about which namespace each element is in. There will be no confusion about whether a particular number element is in the order namespace or in the product namespace. However, the application or person that generates this instance must be aware which elements are in the order namespace and which are in the product namespace.

21.7.3.2 Unqualified local names

Example 21–15, on the other hand, shows an instance where only the root element name, order, is qualified. The other element names have no prefix, and since there is no default namespace provided, they are not in any namespace.

This instance has the advantage of looking slightly less complicated and not requiring the instance author to care about what namespace each element belongs in. In fact, the instance author does not even need to know of the existence of the product namespace.

Example 21–15. **Unqualified local names**

```
<ord:order xmlns:ord="http://datypic.com/ord">
  <number>123123</number>
  <items>
    <product>
      <number>557</number>
    </product>
  </items>
</ord:order>
```

21.7.3.3 Using form in schemas

Let's look at the schemas that would describe these two instances. Example 21–16 shows how to represent the schema for the instance in Example 21–14, which has qualified element names. The representation is made up of two schema documents: ord.xsd, which defines components in the order namespace, and prod.xsd, which defines components in the product namespace.

Both schema documents have elementFormDefault set to qualified. As a result, locally declared elements must use qualified element names in the instance. In this example, the declaration for order is global and the declarations for product, items, and number are local.

Example 21–16. Schema for qualified local element names

ord.xsd:

```
<xs:schema xmlns:xs="http://www.w3.org/2001/XMLSchema"
           xmlns:prod="http://datypic.com/prod"
           xmlns="http://datypic.com/ord"
           targetNamespace="http://datypic.com/ord"
           elementFormDefault="qualified">
  <xs:import schemaLocation="prod.xsd"
             namespace="http://datypic.com/prod"/>
  <xs:element name="order" type="OrderType"/>
  <xs:complexType name="OrderType">
    <xs:sequence>
      <xs:element name="number" type="xs:integer"/>
      <xs:element name="items" type="prod:ItemsType"/>
    </xs:sequence>
  </xs:complexType>
</xs:schema>
```

prod.xsd:

```
<xs:schema xmlns:xs="http://www.w3.org/2001/XMLSchema"
           xmlns="http://datypic.com/prod"
           targetNamespace="http://datypic.com/prod"
           elementFormDefault="qualified">
  <xs:complexType name="ItemsType">
    <xs:sequence maxOccurs="unbounded">
      <xs:element name="product" type="ProductType"/>
    </xs:sequence>
  </xs:complexType>
  <xs:complexType name="ProductType">
    <xs:sequence>
      <xs:element name="number" type="xs:integer"/>
    </xs:sequence>
  </xs:complexType>
</xs:schema>
```

To create a schema for the instance in Example 21–15, which has unqualified names, you can simply change the value of `elementFormDefault` in both schema documents to `unqualified`. Since the default value is `unqualified`, you could alternatively simply omit the attribute. In this case, globally declared elements still must use qualified element names, hence the use of `ord:order` in the instance.

21.7.3.4 Form and global element declarations

An important thing to notice is that the choice between qualified and unqualified names applies only to local element declarations. All globally declared elements must have qualified element names in the instance; there is no way to override this. In our example, all of the element declarations except `order` are local. If the `product` declaration had been global, the `product` elements would have to use qualified element names, regardless of the value of `elementFormDefault`.

This can cause confusion if you choose to use unqualified local element names, and you want to mix global and local element declarations. Not only would an instance author be required to know what namespace each element is in, but he or she would also need to know whether it was globally or locally declared in the schema.

This can be avoided by making all element declarations local, except for the declaration for the root elements. However, you may not have this choice if you import element declarations from namespaces that are not under your control. Also, if you plan to use substitution groups, the participating element declarations must be global.

21.7.3.5 Default namespaces and unqualified names

Default namespaces do not mix well with unqualified element names. The instance in Example 21–17 declares the order namespace as the default namespace. However, this will not work with a schema document where `elementFormDefault` is set to `unqualified`, because it will be looking for the elements `items`, `product`, and `number` in the order namespace, in which they are not—they are not in any namespace.

Example 21–17. Invalid mixing of unqualified names and default namespace

```
<order xmlns="http://datypic.com/ord">
  <number>123ABBCC123</number>
  <items>
    <product>
      <number>557</number>
    </product>
  </items>
</order>
```

21.7.3.6 Qualified vs. unqualified element names

Whether to use qualified or unqualified local element names is a matter of style. The advantages of using qualified local element names are:

- You can tell by looking at the document which namespace a name is in. If you see that a b element is in the XHTML namespace, you can more quickly understand its meaning.

- There is no ambiguity to a person or application what namespace an element belongs in. In our example, there was a number element in each of the namespaces. In most cases, you can determine from its position in the instance whether it is an order number or a product number, but not always.

- Certain applications or processors, for example an XHTML processor, might be expecting the element names to be qualified with the appropriate namespace.

- You can mix global and local element declarations without affecting the instance authors. You may be forced to make some element declarations global because you are using substitution groups, or because you are importing a schema document over which you have no control. If you use unqualified local names, the instance author has to know which element declarations are global and which are local.

The advantages of using unqualified local element names are:

- The instance author does not have to be aware of which namespace each element name is in. If many namespaces are used in the instance, this can simplify creation of instances.

- The lack of prefixes and namespace declarations makes the instance look less cluttered.

In general, it is best to use qualified element names, for the reasons stated above. If consistent prefixes are used, they just become part of the name, and authors get used to writing `prod:number` rather than just `number`. Most XML editors assist instance authors in choosing the right element names, prefixed or not.

21.7.3.7 Qualified vs. unqualified attribute names

The decision about qualified versus unqualified forms is simpler for attributes than elements. Qualified attribute names should only be used for attributes that apply to a variety of elements in a variety of namespaces, such as `xml:lang` or `xsi:type`. Such attributes are almost always declared globally. For locally declared attributes, whose scope is the type definition in which they appear, prefixes add extra text without any additional meaning.

The best way to handle qualification of attribute names is to ignore the `form` and `attributeFormDefault` attributes completely. Then, globally declared attributes will have qualified names, and locally declared attributes will have unqualified names, which makes sense.

21.8 | Schema documentation

XML Schema is a full-featured language for describing the structure of XML documents. However, it cannot express everything there is to know about an instance or the data it contains. This section explains how you can extend XML Schema to include additional information for users and applications, using two methods: annotations and non-native attributes.

21.8.1 *Annotations*

Annotations are represented by `annotation` elements, whose syntax is shown in Table 21–4. An `annotation` may appear in almost any element in the schema, with the exception of `annotation` itself and its children, `appinfo` and `documentation`. The `schema`, `override`, and `redefine` elements can contain multiple `annotation` elements anywhere among their children. All other elements may only contain one `annotation`, and it must be their first child.

Table 21–4   XSD Syntax: annotation

Name
`annotation`

Parents
all elements except `annotation`, `appinfo`, and `documentation`

Attribute name	Type	Description
`id`	`ID`	Unique ID.

Content
`(documentation | appinfo)*`

The content model for `annotation` allows two types of children: `documentation` and `appinfo`. A `documentation` element is intended to be human-readable user documentation, and `appinfo` is machine-readable for applications. A single `annotation` may contain multiple `documentation` and `appinfo` elements, in any order, which may serve different purposes.

21.8.2 *User documentation*

User documentation is represented by the `documentation` element. Sometimes it will consist of simple text content used for a description of a component. However, as it can contain child elements, it can be used for a more complex structure. Often, it is preferable to store more detail than just a simple description. The types of user information that you might add to a schema include:

- Descriptive information about what the component means. The name and structure of a type definition or element declaration can explain a lot, but they cannot impart all the semantics of the schema component.

- An explanation of why a component is structured in a particular way, or why certain XML Schema mechanisms are used.

- Metadata such as copyright information, who is responsible for the schema component, its version, and when it was last changed.

- Internationalization and localization parameters, including language translations.

- Examples of valid instances.

21.8.2.1 Documentation syntax

The syntax for a `documentation` element is shown in Table 21–5. It uses an element wildcard for its content model, which specifies that it may contain any number of elements from any namespace (or no namespace), in any order. Its content is mixed, so it may contain character data as well as children.

The `source` attribute can contain a URI reference that points to further documentation. The schema processor does not dereference this URI during validation.

Example 21–18 shows the use of `documentation` to document the `product` element declaration.

Table 21–5   XSD Syntax: documentation

Name
`documentation`

Parents
`annotation`

Attribute name	Type	Description
`source`	`anyURI`	Source of further documentation.
`xml:lang`	`language`	Natural language of the documentation.

Content
any well-formed XML (any character data content and/or child elements)

Example 21–18. Documentation

```
<xs:schema xmlns:xs="http://www.w3.org/2001/XMLSchema"
           xmlns:doc="http://datypic.com/doc">
  <xs:element name="product" type="ProductType">
    <xs:annotation>
      <xs:documentation xml:lang="en"
                  source="http://datypic.com/prod.html#product">
        <doc:description>This element represents a product.
        </doc:description>
      </xs:documentation>
    </xs:annotation>
  </xs:element>
  <!--...-->
</xs:schema>
```

Although you can put character data content directly in
`documentation` or `appinfo`, it is preferable to structure it using at
least one child element. This allows the type of information (e.g.,
description) to be uniquely identified in the case of future additions.

Instead of (or in addition to) including the information in the annotation, you can also provide links to one or more external documents.
To do this, you can either use the `source` attribute or other

mechanisms, such as XLink. This allows reuse of documentation that may apply to more than one schema component.

21.8.2.2 Data element definitions

When creating reusable schema documents such as type libraries, it is helpful to have a complete definition of each component declared or defined in it. This ensures that schema authors are reusing the correct components, and allows you to automatically generate human-readable documentation about the components. Example 21–19 shows a schema document that includes a complete definition of a simple type CountryType in its documentation. The example is roughly based on ISO 11179, the ISO standard for the specification and standardization of data elements.

Example 21–19. ISO 11179-based type definition

```
<xs:schema xmlns:xs="http://www.w3.org/2001/XMLSchema"
           xmlns:doc="http://datypic.com/doc">

  <xs:simpleType name="CountryType">
    <xs:annotation>
      <xs:documentation>
        <doc:name>Country identifier</doc:name>
        <doc:identifier>3166</doc:identifier>
        <doc:version>1990</doc:version>
        <doc:registrationAuthority>ISO</doc:registrationAuthority>
        <doc:definition>A code for the names of countries of the
          world.</doc:definition>
        <doc:keyword>geopolitical entity</doc:keyword>
        <doc:keyword>country</doc:keyword>
        <!--...-->
      </xs:documentation>
    </xs:annotation>
    <xs:restriction base="xs:token">
      <!--...-->
    </xs:restriction>
  </xs:simpleType>

</xs:schema>
```

21.8.2.3 Code documentation

Another type of user documentation is code control information, such as when it was created and by whom, its version, and its dependencies. This is illustrated in Example 21–20. The element names used in the example are similar to the keywords in Javadoc.

Example 21–20. **Code documentation**

```
<xs:schema xmlns:xs="http://www.w3.org/2001/XMLSchema"
           xmlns:doc="http://datypic.com/doc">

  <xs:simpleType name="CountryType">
    <xs:annotation>
      <xs:documentation>
        <doc:author>Priscilla Walmsley</doc:author>
        <doc:version>1.1</doc:version>
        <doc:since>1.0</doc:since>
        <doc:see>
          <doc:label>Country Code Listings</doc:label>
          <doc:link>http://datypic.com/countries.html</doc:link>
        </doc:see>
        <doc:deprecated>false</doc:deprecated>
      </xs:documentation>
    </xs:annotation>
    <xs:restriction base="xs:token">
      <!--...-->
    </xs:restriction>
  </xs:simpleType>

</xs:schema>
```

21.8.2.4 Section comments

There is a reason that `schema`, `override`, and `redefine` elements can have multiple annotations anywhere in their content. These annotations can be used to break a schema document into sections and provide comments on each section. Example 21–21 shows annotations that serve as section comments. Although they are more verbose than regular XML comments (which are also permitted), they are more structured. This means that they can be used, for example, to generate XHTML documentation for the schema.

Example 21–21. Section identifiers

```
<xs:schema xmlns:xs="http://www.w3.org/2001/XMLSchema">

  <xs:annotation><xs:documentation><sectionHeader>
   ********* Product-Related Element Declarations ***************
  </sectionHeader></xs:documentation></xs:annotation>
  <xs:element name="product" type="ProductType"/>
  <xs:element name="size" type="SizeType"/>

  <xs:annotation><xs:documentation><sectionHeader>
   ********* Order-Related Element Declarations ****************
  </sectionHeader></xs:documentation></xs:annotation>
  <xs:element name="order" type="OrderType"/>
  <xs:element name="items" type="ItemsType"/>

  <!--...-->
</xs:schema>
```

21.8.3 *Application information*

There is a wide variety of use cases for adding application information to schemas. Some of the typical kinds of application information to include are:

- Extra validation rules, such as co-constraints. XML Schema alone cannot express every constraint you might want to impose on your instances.

- Mappings to other structures, such as databases or EDI messages. These mappings are a flexible way to tell an application where to store or extract individual elements.

- Mapping to XHTML forms or other user input mechanisms. The mappings can include special presentation information for each data element, such as translations of labels to other languages.

- Formatting information, such as a stylesheet fragment that can convert the instance element to XHTML, making it presentable to the user.

The syntax for `appinfo`, shown in Table 21–6, is identical to that of `documentation`, minus the `xml:lang` attribute.

Table 21–6   XSD Syntax: application information

Name		
appinfo		

Parents		
annotation		

Attribute name	*Type*	*Description*
source	anyURI	Source of further documentation.

Content		
any well-formed XML (any character data content and/or child elements)		

Example 21–22 shows the use of `appinfo` to map `product` to a database table.

Example 21–22. Application information

```
<xs:schema xmlns:xs="http://www.w3.org/2001/XMLSchema"
          xmlns:app="http://datypic.com/app">
  <xs:element name="product" type="ProductType">
    <xs:annotation>
      <xs:appinfo>
        <app:dbmapping>
          <app:tb>PRODUCT_MASTER</app:tb>
        </app:dbmapping>
      </xs:appinfo>
    </xs:annotation>
  </xs:element>
  <!--...-->
</xs:schema>
```

In this example, we declare a namespace `http://datypic.com/app` for the `dbmapping` and `tb` elements used in the annotation. This is not required; `appinfo` can contain elements with no namespace. However, it is preferable to use a namespace because it makes the extension easily distinguishable from other information that may be included for use by other applications.

21.8.4 *Non-native attributes*

In addition to annotations, all schema elements are permitted to have additional attributes. These attributes are known as non-native attributes, since they must be in a namespace other than the XML Schema Namespace. Example 21–23 shows an element declaration that has the non-native attribute `description`.

Example 21–23. Non-native attributes

```
<xs:schema xmlns:xs="http://www.w3.org/2001/XMLSchema"
           xmlns:doc="http://datypic.com/doc"
           xmlns:xsi="http://www.w3.org/2001/XMLSchema-instance"
           xsi:schemaLocation="http://datypic.com/doc doc.xsd">
  <xs:element name="product" type="ProductType"
           doc:description="This element represents a product."/>
  <!--...-->
</xs:schema>
```

As with `appinfo` and `documentation` contents, the non-native attributes are validated through a wildcard with lax validation. If attribute declarations can be found for the attributes, they will be validated, otherwise the processor will ignore them. In this case, the `xsi:schemaLocation` attribute points to a schema document for the additional attributes. Example 21–24 shows a schema that might be used to validate the non-native attributes.

The schema does not include new declarations for schema elements. Rather, it contains global declarations of any non-native attributes.

Example 21–24. A schema for non-native attributes

```
<xs:schema xmlns:xs="http://www.w3.org/2001/XMLSchema"
           xmlns="http://datypic.com/doc"
           targetNamespace="http://datypic.com/doc">
  <xs:attribute name="description" type="xs:string"/>
</xs:schema>
```

21.8.4.1 Design hint: Should I use annotations or non-native attributes?

This is roughly the same as the general question of whether to use elements or attributes. Both can convey additional information, and both are made available to the application by the schema processor. Non-native attributes are less verbose, and perhaps more clear because they are closer to the definitions to which they apply. However, they have drawbacks: they cannot be used more than once in a particular element, they cannot be extended in the future, and they cannot contain other elements. For example, if you decide that you want the descriptions to be expressed in XHTML, this cannot be done if the description is an attribute. For more information on attributes versus elements, see Section 7.1 on p. 113.

21.8.5 *Documenting namespaces*

It is generally a good idea to use URLs for namespace names and to put a resource at the location referenced by the URL. There are many reasons not to require your application to dereference a namespace name at runtime, including security, performance, and network availability. However, a person might want to dereference the namespace in order to find out more information about it.

It might seem logical to put a schema document at that location. Having a namespace name resolve to a schema document, though, is not ideal because:

- Many schemas may describe that namespace. Which one do you choose?

- A variety of documents in other formats may also describe that namespace, including DTDs, human-readable documentation, schemas written in other schema languages, and stylesheets. Each may be applicable in different circumstances.

- Schema documents are not particularly human-readable, even by humans who write them!

A better choice is a resource directory, which lists all the resources related to a namespace. Such a directory can be both human- and application-readable. It can also allow different resources to be used depending on the application or purpose.

One language that can be used to define a resource directory is RDDL (Resource Directory Description Language). RDDL is an extension of XHTML that is used to define a resource directory. It does not only apply to namespaces, but it is an excellent choice for documenting a namespace. Example 21–25 shows an RDDL document that might be placed at the location `http://datypic.com/prod`.

Example 21–25. RDDL for the product catalog namespace

```
<?xml version='1.0'?>
<!DOCTYPE html PUBLIC "-//XML-DEV//DTD XHTML RDDL 1.0//EN"
                      "rddl/rddl-xhtml.dtd">
<html xml:lang="en" xmlns="http://www.w3.org/1999/xhtml"
      xmlns:xlink="http://www.w3.org/1999/xlink"
      xmlns:rddl="http://www.rddl.org/">
<head><title>Product Catalog</title></head>
<body><h1>Product Catalog</h1>
  <div id="toc"><h2>Table of Contents</h2>
    <ol>
      <li><a href="#intro">Introduction</a></li>
      <li><a href="#related.resources">Resources</a></li>
    </ol>
  </div>
```

(Continues)

Example 21–25.   (Continued)

```
<div id="intro"><h2>Introduction</h2>
  <p>This document describes the <a href="#xmlschemap1">Product
    Catalog</a> namespace and contains a directory of links to
    related resources.</p>
</div>
<div id="related.resources">
  <h2>Related Resources for the Product Catalog Namespace</h2>
  <!-- start resource definitions -->

<div class="resource" id="DTD">
  <rddl:resource xlink:title="DTD for validation"
   xlink:arcrole="http://www.rddl.org/purposes#validation"
   xlink:role="http://www.isi.edu/in-
               notes/iana/assignments/media-types/text/xml-dtd"
   xlink:href="prod.dtd">
    <h3>DTD</h3>
    <p>A <a href="prod.dtd">DTD</a> for the Product Catalog.</p>
  </rddl:resource>
</div>

<div class="resource" id="xmlschema">
  <rddl:resource xlink:title="Products schema"
   xlink:role="http://www.w3.org/2001/XMLSchema"
   xlink:arcrole="http://www.rddl.org/purposes#schema-validation"
   xlink:href="prod.xsd">
    <h3>XML Schema</h3>
    <p>An <a href="prod.xsd">XML Schema</a> for the Product
       Catalog.</p>
  </rddl:resource>
</div>

<div class="resource" id="documentation">
  <rddl:resource xlink:title="Application Documentation"
   xlink:role="http://www.w3.org/TR/html4/"
   xlink:arcrole="http://www.rddl.org/purposes#reference"
   xlink:href="prod.html">
    <h3>Application Documentation</h3>
    <p><a href="prod.html">Application documentation</a> for
       the Product Catalog application.</p>
  </rddl:resource>
</div>
</div>
</body></html>
```

This document defines three related resources. Each resource has a *role*, which describes the nature of the resource (e.g., schema, DTD, stylesheet), and an *arcrole*, which indicates the purpose of the resource (e.g., validation, reference). An application that wants to do schema validation, for example, can read this document and extract the location of the schema document to be used for validation. A person could also read this document in a browser, as shown in Figure 21–4.

For more information on RDDL, see www.rddl.org.

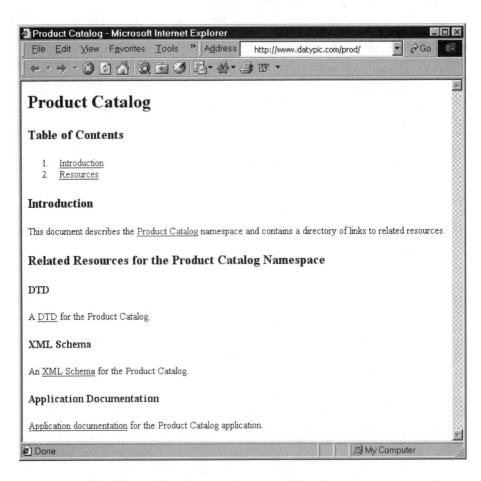

Figure 21–4   Viewing a RDDL document in a web browser

Extensibility and reuse

Chapter 22

S ometimes we forget that the "X" in XML stands for "eXtensible." One of the beauties of XML is that additional elements and attributes can appear in an instance without affecting the core information. Specialized requirements for particular applications, industries, or organizations can be addressed using extensions.

However, in order to make XML extensible, you need to leave avenues open to do that. If you write schemas and applications that require very strict validation of an instance, the major benefit of XML is not realized! This chapter provides detailed recommendations for developing schemas that will be reusable and extensible in the future. It also provides guidelines for extending existing schemas.

22.1 | Reuse

First, let's talk about reusing schema components exactly as they are. Later in this chapter, we will look at extending and restricting existing schema components. The benefits of reuse are numerous.

- It reduces development time, because schema developers are not reinventing the wheel. In addition, developers of stylesheets and program code to process instances can reuse their code, saving their time too.

- It reduces maintenance time, because changes only need to be made in one place. Again, this applies not just to schemas, but also to applications.

- It increases interoperability. If two systems are reusing some of the same schema components, it is easier for them to talk to each other.

- It results in better-designed schemas with fewer errors. Two heads are better than one, and reused components tend to be designed more carefully and reviewed more closely.

- It reduces the learning curve on schemas, because the reused components only need to be learned once. In addition, it encourages consistency, which also reduces learning curves.

22.1.1 *Reusing schema components*

When creating a schema, you should attempt to reuse components that have already been developed—either within your organization, by standards bodies, or by technology vendors. In addition, you should attempt to reuse as much within your schema as possible.

You do not have to reuse everything from a schema document that you import or include. If it was properly modularized, you should not have to include many components that you do not want to reuse. Components that can be reused include:

- Named types, both simple and complex
- Named model groups and attribute groups
- Global element and attribute declarations
- Notations

22.1.2 *Creating schemas that are highly reusable*

You should also consider the reusability of your components as you define them. To increase the reusability of your components:

- Use named types, because anonymous types cannot be reused.
- Use named model groups for fragments of content models that could be reused by multiple unrelated types.
- Use global element declarations, so they can participate in substitution groups.
- Use generic names when declaring elements and defining types. For example, if you are defining an address type for customers, call it `AddressType` rather than `CustomerAddressType`.
- Think about a broader applicability of your types. For example, when defining an address type, consider adding a `country` element declaration, even if you will only be using domestic addresses.
- Modularize your schemas into smaller documents, so that others reusing your components will not have to include or import them all.

22.1.3 *Developing a common components library*

When designing a complex vocabulary, it is advisable to create libraries of low-level components that can be used in many contexts. These components (usually types) are sometimes referred to as "common components" or "core components." Examples of good candidates for common components are:

- Identifiers (for example, product identifiers, customer identifiers, especially if they are made up of multiple parts)
- Code lists such as departments, product types, currencies, natural languages
- Measurement (i.e., an amount with a unit of measure)
- Price (a number with an associated currency)
- Person information, such as name, contact information, and mailing address

These are the kinds of data structures that tend to be rewritten over and over again if there is no plan in place to reuse them. Having one definition for these low-level components can save a lot of time in developing and maintaining not only the schema, but the code that processes and/or generates the messages.

If all of these common components are defined and placed in one or more separate schema documents, they are easier to reuse than if they are embedded in another context-specific schema document. Typically, they are defined as types rather than elements, so that they can be reused by many element declarations. Example 22–1 shows a simple common components library.

Example 22–1. Sample common components library

```
<xs:schema xmlns:xs="http://www.w3.org/2001/XMLSchema"
          targetNamespace="http://datypic.com/common"
          xmlns="http://datypic.com/common"
          elementFormDefault="qualified">
  <xs:simpleType name="ProductIDType">
    <xs:restriction base="xs:string">
      <xs:pattern value="[A-Z]{2}[0-9]{4}"/>
    </xs:restriction>
  </xs:simpleType>
```

(Continues)

Example 22–1.   (Continued)

```
<xs:complexType name="PriceType">
  <xs:simpleContent>
    <xs:extension base="xs:decimal">
      <xs:attribute name="currency" type="CurrencyCodeType"/>
    </xs:extension>
  </xs:simpleContent>
</xs:complexType>
<xs:complexType name="MeasurementType">
  <xs:simpleContent>
    <xs:extension base="xs:decimal">
      <xs:attribute name="units" type="UnitsCodeType"/>
    </xs:extension>
  </xs:simpleContent>
</xs:complexType>
<xs:complexType name="AddressType">
  <xs:sequence>
    <xs:element name="street" type="xs:string" maxOccurs="3"/>
    <xs:element name="city" type="xs:string"/>
    <xs:element name="state" type="xs:string"/>
    <xs:element name="postalCode" type="xs:string"/>
    <xs:element name="country" type="xs:string"/>
  </xs:sequence>
</xs:complexType>
<!--...-->
</xs:schema>
```

22.2 | Extending schemas

In some cases, you want to reuse existing schema components, but you have specific extensions you need to add to make them useful to you. Creating a completely new schema that copies the original definitions is tempting because it is easy and flexible. You do not have to worry about basing the new definitions on the original ones. However, there are some important drawbacks.

- Your new instances could be completely incompatible with the original ones.

- You will have duplicate definitions of the same components. This makes maintenance more difficult and discourages consistency.
- You do not have a record of the differences between the two definitions.

This section identifies several ways in which XML Schema allows extension. It describes both how to make your schemas extensible and how to extend others' schemas. The various extension mechanisms are summarized in Table 22–1.

Table 22–1   Comparison of extension mechanisms

	Wild-cards	[1]Open content	Type substi-tution	Substi-tution groups	Type redefi-nition	Named group redefi-nition	[1]Over-rides
Is an extended instance valid against original definition?	yes	yes	no	no	no	no	no
Does it require use of xsi:type in instance?	no	no	yes	no	no	no	no
Can it define extended types in a different namespace?	yes	yes	yes	yes	no	no	no
Must element extensions appear at the end of a content model?	no	no	yes[†]	no	yes	no	no

† Except when an `all` group is extended with another `all` group, which is only allowed in version 1.1.

Most of these extension methods take some planning, or at least require the use of certain design characteristics, such as global components, when the original schemas are being created. If you are designing an XML vocabulary, particularly a complex one or one that you intend for other organizations to use and extend, you should choose one or more of these extension methods and design your schemas accordingly. It is a good idea to document the extension method you have in mind, with examples, in your Naming and Design Rules document.

If you are in the position of extending another schema over which you have no control, you may not be able to use all of these methods, depending on how the original schema was designed.

22.2.1 *Wildcards*

Wildcards are the most straightforward way to define extensible types. They can be used to allow additional elements and attributes in your instances. Of the methods of extension discussed in this chapter, wildcards and open content are the only ones that allow an instance with extensions to validate against the original schema. All the other methods require defining a new schema for the extensions.

Example 22–2 shows a complex type definition that contains both an element wildcard (the `any` element) and an attribute wildcard

***Example 22–2.** Original type using wildcards*

```
<xs:complexType name="ProductType">
  <xs:sequence>
    <xs:element name="number" type="xs:integer"/>
    <xs:element name="name" type="xs:string"/>
    <xs:element name="size" type="xs:integer" minOccurs="0"/>
    <xs:any minOccurs="0" maxOccurs="unbounded"
           namespace="##other" processContents="lax"/>
  </xs:sequence>
  <xs:anyAttribute namespace="##other" processContents="skip"/>
</xs:complexType>
```

(the `anyAttribute` element). For a complete discussion of element and attribute wildcards, see Sections 12.7.1 on p. 285 and 12.7.3 on p. 298, respectively.

There are several things to note about the definition of `ProductType`.

- The namespace constraint is set to `##other`. This will avoid erroneous content from being validated, such as a product element that contains two `color` elements. It also avoids non-deterministic content models that violate the Unique Particle Attribute rule, as described at the end of this section.

- The value of `processContents` is `lax`. This allows the instance author to provide hints as to where to find the declarations for the additional elements or attributes. If they do not provide hints, or the particular processor ignores the hints, it is not a problem; no errors will be raised. However, if the declarations can be found, they will be validated.

- The values of `minOccurs` and `maxOccurs` are `0` and `unbounded`, respectively. This allows zero, one, or many replacement elements to appear. The values of these two attributes default to `1`, which is generally not the intention of the schema author.

- The wildcard appears at the end of the complex type definition. This allows replacement elements only after the defined content model. This is similar to the way extension works. You are permitted to put wildcards anywhere in the content model, but it might make processing the instance more difficult. With a wildcard at the end, the application can process what it is expecting and ignore the rest.

Suppose some additional features have been added to the ordering process, such as a points system to reward regular customers and a gift wrap capability. The instance shown in Example 22–3 takes advantage of the wildcards in the `ProductType` definition to add an `spc:giftWrap` element to the end of the content, as well as an `spc:points` attribute.

Example 22–3. Instance with extensions

```
<order xmlns="http://datypic.com/ord"
       xmlns:spc="http://datypic.com/spc">
  <product spc:points="100">
    <number>557</number>
    <name>Short-Sleeved Linen Blouse</name>
    <size>10</size>
    <spc:giftWrap>ADULT BDAY</spc:giftWrap>
  </product>
</order>
```

Since `processContents` was set to `lax`, the instance shown would be valid according to the original schema, without specifying any declarations for the new attribute and element. If you want to validate the new attribute and element, you can create a schema that contains their declarations, as shown in Example 22–4.

Example 22–4. Schema for extensions

```
<xs:schema xmlns:xs="http://www.w3.org/2001/XMLSchema"
           xmlns="http://datypic.com/spc"
           targetNamespace="http://datypic.com/spc">
  <xs:element name="giftWrap" type="xs:string"/>
  <xs:attribute name="points" type="xs:nonNegativeInteger"/>
</xs:schema>
```

Note that the element and attribute declarations are global. This is necessary so that the processor can find the declarations.

Another approach for "extending" complex types with wildcards is actually to restrict them. You could define a complex type that restricts `ProductType` and includes the declarations of `giftWrap` and `points`. For more information, see Section 13.5.2.3 on p. 322.

The advantage of using wildcards for making types extensible is that this is very flexible: The instance author is not required to have a schema that declares the replacement elements and attributes. However, in some cases this flexibility may be a little too forgiving, as it can obscure real errors.

One challenge of using wildcards in version 1.0 is that if the wildcards allow extensions in the same namespace, i.e. the target namespace of the schema, you can run into Unique Particle Attribution violations. If the wildcard is preceded by a declaration for an optional element, the processor does not know whether to use the element declaration or the wildcard to validate an element whose name matches the declaration. Fortunately, this is alleviated in version 1.1, and the processor will always choose the element declaration.

22.2.2 *Open content*

Open content is an even more flexible form of wildcards available starting in version 1.1. Complex types that have open content can allow replacement elements to appear anywhere within its content, not just in places designated by element wildcards.

Example 22–5 shows a complex type definition that has open content. Note that `openContent` doesn't apply to attributes, so it is necessary to include an attribute wildcard to support any attribute extensions. For a complete discussion of open content, see Section 12.7.2 on p. 292.

Example 22–5. Original type using open content

```
<xs:complexType name="ProductType">
  <xs:openContent>
    <xs:any namespace="##other" processContents="lax"/>
  </xs:openContent>
  <xs:sequence>
    <xs:element name="number" type="xs:integer"/>
    <xs:element name="name" type="xs:string"/>
    <xs:element name="size" type="xs:integer" minOccurs="0"/>
  </xs:sequence>
  <xs:anyAttribute namespace="##other" processContents="skip"/>
</xs:complexType>
```

The use of the openContent element means that the extension elements can appear interleaved anywhere in the content. To allow them to only appear at the end, you can use a mode="suffix" attribute on openContent. The instance shown in Example 22–6 takes advantage of the open content in the ProductType definition to add an spc:giftWrap element into the middle of the content.

Example 22–6. Instance with open content extensions

```
<order xmlns="http://datypic.com/ord"
       xmlns:spc="http://datypic.com/spc">
  <product spc:points="100">
    <number>557</number>
    <spc:giftWrap>ADULT BDAY</spc:giftWrap>
    <name>Short-Sleeved Linen Blouse</name>
    <size>10</size>
  </product>
</order>
```

As with the wildcard example, since processContents was set to lax, the instance shown would be valid according to the original schema, without specifying any declarations for the new attribute and element. If you want to validate the new attribute and element, you can create a schema that declares them globally, as was shown in Example 22–4.

22.2.3 *Type substitution*

Deriving new types from the existing types is another possibility. You can create a new schema whose types extend the original types. You would then have to indicate the new types in the instance, using the xsi:type attribute. Unlike the wildcard approach, instances that contain extensions would not be valid according to the original schema. If you want to use the extended instance as a replacement for the original instance, you should first check to make sure that your application can handle the new extended instance.

This approach is appropriate when you want to extend a schema over which you have no control. Example 22–7 shows a complex type that you might want to extend.

Example 22–7. Original type

```
<xs:complexType name="ProductType">
  <xs:sequence>
    <xs:element name="number" type="xs:integer"/>
    <xs:element name="name" type="xs:string"/>
    <xs:element name="size" type="xs:integer" minOccurs="0"/>
  </xs:sequence>
</xs:complexType>
```

There are several things to note about the definition of ProductType.

- It is a named complex type. Anonymous complex types cannot be extended.
- There are no block or final attributes to prohibit type derivation or substitution.
- A sequence group is used. Extension does not work well for choice groups, as described in the next section. For all groups, extension is forbidden in version 1.0 but permitted (and useful) in version 1.1.

Example 22–8 shows an extension of the original ProductType. For more information on complex content extension, see Section 13.4.2 on p. 307.

The instance shown in Example 22–9 conforms to the extended type definition, but not the base type definition. It is identical to the instance using wildcards shown in Example 22–3, except that the xsi:type attribute appears in the product tag. For more information on type substitution, see Section 13.6 on p. 341.

Example 22–8. Extended type

```
<xs:complexType name="ExtendedProductType">
  <xs:complexContent>
    <xs:extension base="ProductType">
      <xs:sequence>
        <xs:element ref="spc:giftWrap" minOccurs="0"/>
      </xs:sequence>
      <xs:attribute ref="spc:points"/>
    </xs:extension>
  </xs:complexContent>
</xs:complexType>
```

Example 22–9. Instance using extended type

```
<order xmlns="http://datypic.com/ord"
       xmlns:spc="http://datypic.com/spc"
       xmlns:xsi="http://www.w3.org/2001/XMLSchema-instance">
  <product spc:points="100" xsi:type="ExtendedProductType">
    <number>557</number>
    <name>Short-Sleeved Linen Blouse</name>
    <size>10</size>
    <spc:giftWrap>ADULT BDAY</spc:giftWrap>
  </product>
</order>
```

22.2.4 *Substitution groups*

As we saw in Section 13.4.2.1 on p. 309, extending a content model which contains a choice group can have unexpected results. Example 22–10 shows a type ExpandedItemsType that extends ItemsType to add new product types. Intuitively, you may think that the two additional element declarations, sweater and suit, are added to the choice group, allowing a choice among the five elements. In fact, the effective content model of ExpandedItemsType is a sequence group that contains two choice groups. As a result, ExpandedItemsType will require any of the shirt, hat, and umbrella elements to appear before any of the sweater or suit elements.

Example 22–10. `choice` **group extension**

```
<xs:complexType name="ItemsType">
  <xs:choice maxOccurs="unbounded">
    <xs:element ref="shirt"/>
    <xs:element ref="hat"/>
    <xs:element ref="umbrella"/>
  </xs:choice>
</xs:complexType>
<xs:complexType name="ExpandedItemsType">
  <xs:complexContent>
    <xs:extension base="ItemsType">
      <xs:choice maxOccurs="unbounded">
        <xs:element ref="sweater"/>
        <xs:element ref="suit"/>
      </xs:choice>
    </xs:extension>
  </xs:complexContent>
</xs:complexType>
```

Substitution groups are a better way to extend `choice` groups. If you add another element declaration, `otherProduct`, to the `choice` group in `ItemsType`, it can serve as the head of a substitution group. This makes extending the choice much easier. The element declarations for `sweater` and `suit` can be supplied in another schema document, even in another namespace.

In Example 22–11, the `otherProduct` element declaration is added to act as the head of the substitution group. It would also have been

Example 22–11. Original type with an abstract element declaration

```
<xs:complexType name="ItemsType">
  <xs:choice maxOccurs="unbounded">
    <xs:element ref="shirt"/>
    <xs:element ref="hat"/>
    <xs:element ref="umbrella"/>
    <xs:element ref="otherProduct"/>
  </xs:choice>
</xs:complexType>

<xs:element name="otherProduct" type="ProductType"
            abstract="true"/>
```

legal to simply make umbrella the head of the substitution group, but this would be less intuitive and would prevent you from ever allowing umbrella without also allowing sweater and suit in its place.

Example 22–12 shows the two element declarations that are substitutable for otherProduct.

Example 22–12. Extension using substitution groups

```
<xs:element name="sweater" substitutionGroup="otherProduct"/>
<xs:element name="suit" substitutionGroup="otherProduct"/>
```

Example 22–13 shows a valid instance. As you can see, the child elements can appear in any order. In this case, they are all in the same namespace. It is also possible for substitution element declarations to be in different namespaces.

Example 22–13. Instance using extension via substitution groups

```
<items>
  <shirt>...</shirt>
  <sweater>...</sweater>
  <shirt>...</shirt>
  <suit>...</suit>
</items>
```

It would have also been valid to put an element wildcard in the choice group. However, the substitution group approach is more controlled, because you can specifically designate the substitutable element declarations. For complete coverage of substitution groups, see Chapter 16.

22.2.5 *Type redefinition*

Redefinition, unlike type substitution, does not require the use of the xsi:type attribute in instances. The redefined components have the same name as they had in the original definition. However, redefinition can only be done within the same namespace, so it is not appropriate for altering schemas over which you have no control. In addition, redefinition has some risks associated with it, as detailed in Section 18.3 on p. 468.

The original type might look exactly like the one shown in Example 22–7, with similar constraints. It must be named, and it should use a sequence group. Example 22–14 shows a redefinition of ProductType to add a new element declaration and attribute declaration. It is similar to the definition of the derived type shown in Example 22–8, with two important differences.

1. It is defined entirely within the redefine element.
2. The extended type and the original type have the same name.

For more information on type redefinition, see Section 18.1.4 on p. 453.

Again, a valid instance would look like Example 22–3.

Example 22–14. Redefined type

```
<xs:schema xmlns:xs="http://www.w3.org/2001/XMLSchema"
           xmlns:spc="http://datypic.com/spc"
           xmlns="http://datypic.com/ord"
           targetNamespace="http://datypic.com/ord">
  <xs:import namespace="http://datypic.com/spc"/>
  <xs:redefine schemaLocation="original.xsd">
    <xs:complexType name="ProductType">
      <xs:complexContent>
        <xs:extension base="ProductType">
          <xs:sequence>
            <xs:element ref="spc:giftWrap" minOccurs="0"/>
          </xs:sequence>
          <xs:attribute ref="spc:points"/>
        </xs:extension>
      </xs:complexContent>
    </xs:complexType>
  </xs:redefine>
</xs:schema>
```

Although a redefinition of the type must take place in the same namespace, the extended element and attribute declarations are not required to be in that namespace. In our example, they are not.

22.2.6 *Named group redefinition*

Another alternative is to define named model groups and attribute groups, and redefine these groups. This is less rigid than redefining types because the extensions do not have to be at the end of the content models.

Example 22–15 shows the original `ProductType` definition, this time using a named model group and an attribute group. The entire content model of the type is contained in the group `ProductPropertyGroup`.

Example 22–15. Original type

```
<xs:complexType name="ProductType">
  <xs:group ref="ProductPropertyGroup"/>
  <xs:attributeGroup ref="ExtensionGroup"/>
</xs:complexType>

<xs:group name="ProductPropertyGroup">
  <xs:sequence>
    <xs:element name="number" type="xs:integer"/>
    <xs:element name="name" type="xs:string"/>
    <xs:element name="size" type="xs:integer" minOccurs="0"/>
  </xs:sequence>
</xs:group>

<xs:attributeGroup name="ExtensionGroup"/>
```

Example 22–16 shows a redefinition of the named model group and attribute group. Redefining the groups affects all the complex types that reference those groups.

Example 22–16. Redefined named model group and attribute group

```
<xs:schema xmlns:xs="http://www.w3.org/2001/XMLSchema"
           xmlns:spc="http://datypic.com/spc"
           xmlns="http://datypic.com/ord"
           targetNamespace="http://datypic.com/ord">
  <xs:import namespace="http://datypic.com/spc"/>
  <xs:redefine schemaLocation="original.xsd">
    <xs:group name="ProductPropertyGroup">
      <xs:sequence>
        <xs:element ref="spc:giftWrap"/>
        <xs:group ref="ProductPropertyGroup"/>
      </xs:sequence>
    </xs:group>
    <xs:attributeGroup name="ExtensionGroup">
      <xs:attributeGroup ref="ExtensionGroup"/>
      <xs:attribute ref="spc:points"/>
    </xs:attributeGroup>
  </xs:redefine>
</xs:schema>
```

A valid instance would look like the one shown in Example 22–17. In this case, `giftWrap` appears as the first child of `product`.

Example 22–17. Instance using redefined named model group and attribute group

```
<order xmlns="http://datypic.com/ord"
       xmlns:spc="http://datypic.com/spc">
  <product spc:points="100">
    <spc:giftWrap>ADULT BDAY</spc:giftWrap>
    <number>557</number>
    <name>Short-Sleeved Linen Blouse</name>
    <size>10</size>
  </product>
</order>
```

22.2.7 *Overrides*

Starting in version 1.1, overrides can be used instead of redefines. In fact, they are preferred because redefines are deprecated. Overrides work similarly to redefines, but have an advantage of being more flexible. The new definition does not have to relate to the original definition in any way.

Example 22–18 shows a schema similar to Example 22–14, but with an `override` instead of a `redefine`. In our case, we chose to modify it in a similar way: add the `spc:giftWrap` element declaration at the end and add the `spc:points` attribute. However, the `spc:giftWrap` element declaration could have appeared anywhere in the content model; in fact, the original element declarations could have been removed or reordered.

Example 22–18. Overridden type

```
<xs:schema xmlns:xs="http://www.w3.org/2001/XMLSchema"
           xmlns:spc="http://datypic.com/spc"
           xmlns="http://datypic.com/ord"
           targetNamespace="http://datypic.com/ord"
           elementFormDefault="qualified">
  <xs:import namespace="http://datypic.com/spc"/>
  <xs:override schemaLocation="original.xsd">
    <xs:complexType name="ProductType">
      <xs:sequence>
        <xs:element name="number" type="xs:integer"/>
        <xs:element name="name" type="xs:string"/>
        <xs:element name="size" type="xs:integer" minOccurs="0"/>
        <xs:element ref="spc:giftWrap" minOccurs="0"/>
      </xs:sequence>
      <xs:attribute ref="spc:points"/>
    </xs:complexType>
  </xs:override>
</xs:schema>
```

Overrides can also be used on named groups. Example 22–19 shows a schema similar to Example 22–16, again replacing the `redefine` with `override`.

A valid instance would look like the one shown in Example 22–20. In this case, `giftWrap` appears as the first child of `product`.

Example 22–19. Overridden named model group and attribute group

```
<xs:schema xmlns:xs="http://www.w3.org/2001/XMLSchema"
           xmlns:spc="http://datypic.com/spc"
           xmlns="http://datypic.com/ord"
           targetNamespace="http://datypic.com/ord"
           elementFormDefault="qualified">
  <xs:import namespace="http://datypic.com/spc"/>
  <xs:override schemaLocation="original.xsd">
    <xs:group name="ProductPropertyGroup">
      <xs:sequence>
        <xs:element ref="spc:giftWrap"/>
        <xs:element name="number" type="xs:integer"/>
        <xs:element name="name" type="xs:string"/>
        <xs:element name="size" type="xs:integer" minOccurs="0"/>
      </xs:sequence>
    </xs:group>
    <xs:attributeGroup name="ExtensionGroup">
      <xs:attribute ref="spc:points"/>
    </xs:attributeGroup>
  </xs:override>
</xs:schema>
```

Example 22–20. Instance using overridden named model group and attribute group

```
<order xmlns="http://datypic.com/ord"
       xmlns:spc="http://datypic.com/spc">
  <product spc:points="100">
    <spc:giftWrap>ADULT BDAY</spc:giftWrap>
    <number>557</number>
    <name>Short-Sleeved Linen Blouse</name>
    <size>10</size>
  </product>
</order>
```

Versioning

Chapter

23

A s business and technical requirements change over time, you will need to define new versions of your schemas. Defining new versions is a special case of extension and restriction. You may be both adding and removing components, with the intention of replacing the older version.

When you create a new version intended to replace a previous one, you should create a completely new schema rather than attempt to extend or restrict the existing one. Otherwise, as time goes on and additional versions are created, the definitions could become unnecessarily complicated and difficult to process. If you are not using the restriction and extension mechanisms of XML Schema, though, you need to take extra care to make the new definitions compatible with the old ones.

23.1 | Schema compatibility

In many cases, you will want to maintain some compatibility between versions. You might want to allow instances to be validated against either schema, or be processed by an application that supports either version. This is especially true if your instances persist for a period. If your instances are short-lived messages between applications, compatibility is less of an issue. However, you should still try to be as consistent as possible to reduce learning curves and minimize the changes in the applications that process the instances.

There are two kinds of compatibility:

1. *Backward compatibility*, where all instances that conform to the previous version of the schema are also valid according to the new version

2. *Forward compatibility*, where all instances that conform to the new version are also valid according to the previous version of the schema

23.1.1 *Backward compatibility*

Ideally, you should have backward compatibility of the schemas from one version to the next. That is, instances that were created to conform to version 2.0 of the schema should also be valid according to version 2.1.[1] This is possible if you are only adding optional new components and/or reducing restrictiveness. To accomplish this, the previous version must allow a subset of what is allowed by the new version.

The following changes to a schema are backward-compatible:

- Adding optional elements and attributes.
- Making required elements and attributes optional.
- Making occurrence constraints less restrictive—for example, allowing more than one `color` element where only one was allowed before.

---

1. Example version numbers start with 2.0 in this chapter to specify the version of the vocabulary being defined by the schema, to avoid confusion with the versions of the XML Schema language itself which are 1.0 and 1.1.

- Turning specific element declarations into `choice` groups. For example, where `color` was allowed, now it can be `color` or `size` or `weight`. Similarly, you can declare new substitution groups. For example, where the content model allowed `color`, now `size` and `weight` are valid substitutes.

- Making simple types less restrictive by making bounds facets and length facets less restrictive, adding enumeration values, or making patterns less restrictive.

- Turning a simple type into a union of that simple type and one or more other simple types.

- Turning a simple type into a list type that allows multiple values of the original type.

- Adding optional wildcards or open content.

- Replacing element or attribute declarations with wildcards.

- Turning a `sequence` group into an `all` group or a repeating `choice` group.

The following changes to a schema are *not* backward-compatible:

- Changing the order of elements or imposing an order where none was imposed previously.

- Changing the structure of elements, for example adding more levels of elements.

- Removing any element or attribute declarations.

- Removing wildcards or open content, or making them more restrictive in terms of what namespaces they allow or how strictly replacement elements are validated.

- Changing the names of any elements or attributes.

- Changing the target namespace of the schema.

- Adding any required elements or attributes.

- Making optional elements or attributes required.

- Making occurrence constraints more restrictive—for example, allowing only one `color` element where more than one was allowed before.

- Making simple types more restrictive by making bounds facets and length facets more restrictive, removing enumeration values, or making patterns more restrictive.

For example, suppose you have the complex type definition shown in Example 23–1. Its version number is 2.0.

Example 23–1. Version 2.0 of a complex type

```
<xs:schema xmlns:xs="http://www.w3.org/2001/XMLSchema"
          version="2.0">
  <xs:element name="product" type="ProductType"/>
  <xs:complexType name="ProductType">
    <xs:sequence>
      <xs:element name="number" type="xs:integer" minOccurs="0"/>
      <xs:element name="name" type="xs:string"/>
      <xs:element name="size" type="SizeType"
                  maxOccurs="unbounded"/>
    </xs:sequence>
  </xs:complexType>
  <xs:complexType name="SizeType">
    <xs:simpleContent>
      <xs:extension base="xs:integer">
        <xs:attribute name="system" type="xs:token"/>
      </xs:extension>
    </xs:simpleContent>
  </xs:complexType>
</xs:schema>
```

Example 23–2 shows a backward-incompatible definition for a new version, 2.1. It is backward-incompatible for a number of reasons.

- The order of the element declarations changed; `name` is now after `size`.

- The `number` element was removed, which is incompatible even though it was optional.

Example 23–2. Backward-incompatible definition

```
<xs:schema xmlns:xs="http://www.w3.org/2001/XMLSchema"
           version="2.1">
  <xs:element name="product" type="ProductType"/>
  <xs:complexType name="ProductType">
    <xs:sequence>
      <xs:element name="size" type="SizeType" maxOccurs="3"/>
      <xs:element name="name" type="xs:string"/>
      <xs:element name="description" type="xs:string"/>
    </xs:sequence>
  </xs:complexType>
  <xs:complexType name="SizeType">
    <xs:simpleContent>
      <xs:extension base="xs:positiveInteger">
        <xs:attribute name="system" type="xs:token"
                      use="required"/>
      </xs:extension>
    </xs:simpleContent>
  </xs:complexType>
</xs:schema>
```

- A required `description` element was added.
- The optional `system` attribute was made required.
- The occurrence constraints on `size` were made more restrictive.
- The contents of `SizeType` were made more restrictive, allowing only positive integers instead of all integers.

As a result of all these changes, an instance that conformed to version 2.0 may not be valid according to version 2.1. Example 23–3 shows such an instance. On the other hand, Example 23–4 shows a definition that *is* backward-compatible.

All of the changes in this example were backward-compatible because they do not affect the validity of version 2.0 instances. For example:

- No element or attribute declarations were removed or reordered.
- Only declarations for optional elements and attributes (`desc` and `units`) were added.
- The required `name` element was made optional.

Example 23–3. Backward-incompatible instance

```
<product>
  <number>557</number>
  <name>Short-Sleeved Linen Blouse</name>
  <size>0</size>
  <size>2</size>
  <size>4</size>
  <size>6</size>
</product>
```

Example 23–4. Backward-compatible definition

```
<xs:schema xmlns:xs="http://www.w3.org/2001/XMLSchema"
           version="2.1">
  <xs:element name="product" type="ProductType"/>
  <xs:complexType name="ProductType">
    <xs:sequence>
      <xs:element name="number" type="xs:integer"
                  minOccurs="0" maxOccurs="unbounded"/>
      <xs:element name="name" type="xs:string" minOccurs="0"/>
      <xs:element name="size" type="SizeType"
                  maxOccurs="unbounded"/>
      <xs:element name="desc" type="xs:string" minOccurs="0"/>
    </xs:sequence>
  </xs:complexType>
  <xs:complexType name="SizeType">
    <xs:simpleContent>
      <xs:extension base="xs:decimal">
        <xs:attribute name="system" type="xs:token"/>
        <xs:attribute name="units" type="xs:token"/>
      </xs:extension>
    </xs:simpleContent>
  </xs:complexType>
</xs:schema>
```

- The `number` element was made repeating, which is less restrictive.

- The contents of `SizeType` were made less restrictive, allowing any decimal number instead of only an integer.

23.1.2 *Forward compatibility*

Some schema designers take their versioning strategy a step further: They make their schemas forward-compatible, so that a version 2.1 instance is valid according to the version 2.0 schema. This requires some careful planning when developing the 2.0 schema. An area needs to be set aside for the elements that might be added in version 2.1. This area needs to be allowed to contain unspecified content in the 2.0 schema, but be more specifically defined (by adding new element declarations) in the 2.1 schema.

This is typically done by defining wildcards in the original schema. In Example 23–5, both element and attribute wildcards are used in the version 2.0 schema. The `processContents` option is set to `skip` so that the processor does not look for declarations that do not exist in this version of the schema.

Example 23–5. Version 2.0 of a forward-compatible complex type

```
<xs:schema xmlns:xs="http://www.w3.org/2001/XMLSchema"
           version="2.0">
  <xs:element name="product" type="ProductType"/>
  <xs:complexType name="ProductType">
    <xs:sequence>
      <xs:element name="number" type="xs:integer" minOccurs="0"/>
      <xs:element name="name" type="xs:string"/>
      <xs:element name="size" type="xs:integer"
                  maxOccurs="unbounded"/>
      <xs:any minOccurs="0" maxOccurs="unbounded"
              processContents="skip"/>
    </xs:sequence>
    <xs:anyAttribute processContents="skip"/>
  </xs:complexType>
</xs:schema>
```

Example 23–6 shows version 2.1 of the schema, with a new element `desc` and a new attribute `dept`. This version of the schema also includes element and attribute wildcards to allow it to be forward-compatible with version 2.2 of the schema.

Example 23–6. Version 2.1 of a forward-compatible complex type

```
<xs:schema xmlns:xs="http://www.w3.org/2001/XMLSchema"
           version="2.1">
  <xs:element name="product" type="ProductType"/>
  <xs:complexType name="ProductType">
    <xs:sequence>
      <xs:element name="number" type="xs:integer" minOccurs="0"/>
      <xs:element name="name" type="xs:string"/>
      <xs:element name="size" type="xs:integer"
                  maxOccurs="unbounded"/>
      <xs:element name="desc" type="xs:string"/>
      <xs:any minOccurs="0" maxOccurs="unbounded"
              processContents="skip"/>
    </xs:sequence>
    <xs:attribute name="dept" type="xs:token"/>
    <xs:anyAttribute processContents="skip"/>
  </xs:complexType>
</xs:schema>
```

Example 23–7 shows an instance that is valid according to version 2.1, but is also allowed by version 2.0 because of the wildcards.

Example 23–7. Forward-compatible instance

```
<product dept="WMN">
  <number>557</number>
  <name>Short-Sleeved Linen Blouse</name>
  <size>0</size>
  <desc>Our best-selling shirt</desc>
</product>
```

The method shown in Examples 23–5 and 23–6 works fine, but only because `size` is required. In version 1.0 of XML Schema, if `size` were optional, this complex type would violate the Unique Particle Attribution rule. A processor, upon encountering a `size` element, would not know whether to use the `size` element declaration or the wildcard to validate it. In version 1.1, this constraint has been eliminated, and the element declaration will always be used instead of the wildcard when both might apply.

In version 1.0, this problem can be avoided either by inserting a dummy required element at the end of the defined content model, or by putting the wildcard inside a child element, for example one called extension. Unfortunately, neither is a great option, because for every minor version there needs to be a new dummy element or extension child, cluttering up the content model. Instead, it is highly recommended that you upgrade to XML Schema 1.1 if you need forward compatibility.

One disadvantage of forward compatibility is that having an open-ended wildcard on every type makes the schemas very flexible. The wildcard in Example 23–6 will allow any replacement elements, including ones that are already declared in that version 2.1 schema. In version 1.1 of XML Schema, this can be mitigated by putting a notQName="##defined" attribute on the wildcard. This means that a replacement element cannot be one that is already declared in the schema.

In fact, version 1.1 offers a number of features to make forward compatibility easier, including:

- Open content, where wildcards can be automatically interleaved everywhere in a type. This removes the need to specify wildcards between each pair of adjacent elements when maximum future flexibility is needed. Open content is covered in Section 12.7.2 on p. 292.

- Negative wildcards, where you can specify names and namespaces that are *not* allowed as replacement elements, thus limiting excessive flexibility of wildcards. Negative wildcards are covered in Section 12.7.1.3 on p. 289.

- Looser restrictions on all groups, which means that it is easier to create types where the order of child elements doesn't matter. This makes it easier to insert elements that can be interleaved in future versions without requiring that all new content comes at the end. This is covered in Section 12.5.4 on p. 276.

Forward compatibility is harder to achieve and therefore less common. However, it is a worthy goal, especially in cases where it is likely that older application code (designed to process prior versions) is likely to persist unchanged for long periods of time.

Note that forward compatibility does not automatically include backward compatibility. It is possible to introduce backward-incompatible changes to a forward-compatible schema. In fact, Example 23–6 is not backward-compatible because the desc element is required. It is possible to have a 2.0 instance without a desc element, in which case it is invalid in version 2.1. If both forward compatibility and backward compatibility are desired, both must be considered when designing schemas.

23.2 | Using version numbers

23.2.1 *Major and minor versions*

The version numbers used in this chapter have the format of two numbers separated by a period, for example, 2.1. It is implied that "2" represents the major version number and "1" represents the minor version number. There is no requirement for version numbers to have this format in XML Schema. In fact, the version attribute will accept any string. However, it is common practice to use numeric version numbers because they make it easy to see the order over time.

It is also typical to use both major and minor version numbers. A change in the minor version number only indicates a minor release—one that has little impact in terms of the number or extensiveness of changes. A change in the major version number indicates a major release, which tends to be more disruptive and involve more changes. Many designers of XML vocabularies make this definition more formal: They use minor versions for releases that are backward-compatible and major versions for releases that are backward-incompatible.

Figure 23–1 depicts this approach. There is backward compatibility among the 2.x releases, and backward compatibility among the 3.x releases, but not between the two major releases. Within a particular major version, there is backward-compatibility from one release to the next. Version 2.1 is obviously designed to be backward-compatible with 2.0. Version 2.2 should be built on version 2.1, including all of the new (optional) elements and attributes and other changes made in version 2.1, so it is backward-compatible with *both* versions 2.1 and 2.0.

When version 3.0 is released, it doesn't have to be backward-compatible with version 2.3 or any of the 2.x versions. This is a chance to make significant changes. It may be useful during a major release to consider making some of the optional elements and attributes added in minor versions required. They may have been added as optional simply to achieve backward compatibility in minor releases, even though it was actually preferable to make them required. It is also an opportunity to remove any elements or attributes that were deprecated in previous releases.

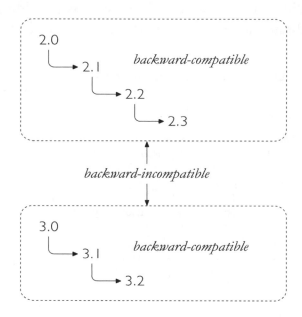

Figure 23–1 Major and minor versions

23.2.2 *Placement of version numbers*

Every schema should have an associated version number. There are at least four possible places to indicate the version number of a schema, none of which is actually required by XML Schema. They are discussed in this section.

23.2.2.1 Version numbers in schema documents

The version attribute of schema is an arbitrary string that represents the version of the vocabulary being described by the schema document. Note that it is not intended to convey whether you are using version 1.0 or 1.1 of the XML Schema language itself; there is no need to indicate this in your schema document. The version attribute is strictly for documentation; an XML Schema processor does not use it. It is optional, but its use is encouraged.

Example 23–8 shows a schema that uses the version attribute to indicate that it is version 2.1 of the schema, along with an instance that conforms to it. The instance in this example is not doing anything special to indicate the version of the schema to which it conforms.

Example 23–8. Using a version number in a schema

Schema (prod.xsd):

```
<xs:schema xmlns:xs="http://www.w3.org/2001/XMLSchema"
           elementFormDefault="qualified"
           xmlns="http://datypic.com/prod"
           targetNamespace="http://datypic.com/prod"
           version="2.1">
  <xs:element name="product" type="ProductType"/>
  <xs:complexType name="ProductType">
    <xs:sequence>
      <xs:element name="number" type="xs:integer" minOccurs="0"/>
      <xs:element name="name" type="xs:string"/>
    </xs:sequence>
  </xs:complexType>
</xs:schema>
```

(Continues)

Example 23–8.   (Continued)

Instance:

```
<product xmlns="http://datypic.com/prod"
         xmlns:xsi="http://www.w3.org/2001/XMLSchema-instance"
         xsi:schemaLocation="http://datypic.com/prod prod.xsd">
  <number>557</number>
  <name>Short-Sleeved Linen Blouse</name>
</product>
```

The version attribute is intended to apply to the schema document itself and all the components defined within it. It is also possible to use non-native attributes or annotations to indicate version numbers for individual components in a schema. Example 23–9 shows a schema document that uses non-native attributes to add a doc:version

Example 23–9. Using a version number on individual schema components

```
<xs:schema xmlns:xs="http://www.w3.org/2001/XMLSchema"
           elementFormDefault="qualified"
           xmlns="http://datypic.com/prod"
           targetNamespace="http://datypic.com/prod"
           xmlns:doc="http://datypic.com/doc"
           version="2.1">
  <xs:element name="product" type="ProductType" doc:version="2.0"/>
  <xs:complexType name="ProductType" doc:version="2.0">
    <xs:sequence>
      <xs:element name="number" type="xs:integer" minOccurs="0"/>
      <xs:element name="name" type="xs:string"/>
    </xs:sequence>
  </xs:complexType>
  <xs:element name="catalog" type="CatalogType" doc:version="2.1"/>
  <xs:complexType name="CatalogType" doc:version="2.1">
    <xs:sequence>
      <xs:element name="catalog_id" type="xs:string"/>
      <xs:element ref="product" maxOccurs="unbounded"/>
    </xs:sequence>
  </xs:complexType>
</xs:schema>
```

attribute to indicate that the `catalog` element declaration and its type are at version 2.1, while the `product` element declaration and its type are at version 2.0.

This may be useful as a way to clearly delineate which components have changed over multiple versions. However, it does require some extra management of the components.

23.2.2.2 Versions in schema locations

The filename or URL of the schema document can also contain the version number. For example, the new version may have a filename of `prod_2.1.xsd` or be located in a directory structure that indicates the version number, for example `2.1/prod.xsd` or `http://datypic.com/prod/2.1/prod.xsd`. Changing the URL makes it easier for other schema documents that may include or import your schema document to continue to use the previous version until they can upgrade. Example 23–10 shows a schema whose filename contains its version number.

Example 23–10. Using a version number in the schema location

Schema (prod_2.1.xsd):

```
<xs:schema xmlns:xs="http://www.w3.org/2001/XMLSchema"
           elementFormDefault="qualified"
           xmlns="http://datypic.com/prod"
           targetNamespace="http://datypic.com/prod">
  <xs:element name="product" type="ProductType"/>
  <xs:complexType name="ProductType">
    <xs:sequence>
      <xs:element name="number" type="xs:integer" minOccurs="0"/>
      <xs:element name="name" type="xs:string"/>
    </xs:sequence>
  </xs:complexType>
</xs:schema>
```

(Continues)

Example 23–10.   (Continued)

Instance:

```
<product xmlns="http://datypic.com/prod"
        xmlns:xsi="http://www.w3.org/2001/XMLSchema-instance"
        xsi:schemaLocation="http://datypic.com/prod prod_2.1.xsd">
  <number>557</number>
  <name>Short-Sleeved Linen Blouse</name>
</product>
```

23.2.2.3 Versions in instances

It may be worthwhile to have instances identify the schema version to which they conform. This will allow an application to process it accordingly. For example, in XSLT, the `stylesheet` element has a required attribute named `version`. This is a signal to processors that the stylesheet instance conforms to, for example, version 2.0 of XSLT.

Typically a version attribute in an instance appears on the root element. Example 23–11 shows a schema and related instance where the version number 2.1 is indicated on the root element. Note that the `version` attribute has to be declared in the schema; it is not a special attribute that can appear without a declaration.

Some schemas put a `fixed` value on the `version` declaration to ensure that an instance can only be validated by a particular version of a schema. For example, if `fixed="2.1"` were added to the attribute declaration in Example 23–11, the version number would have to be 2.1 (or the attribute would have to be absent) in the instance for it to be valid according to this schema. However, this is not recommended, at least for minor versions, because it breaks backward compatibility.

Example 23–11. Using a version number in the instance

Schema (prod.xsd):

```
<xs:schema xmlns:xs="http://www.w3.org/2001/XMLSchema"
           elementFormDefault="qualified"
           xmlns="http://datypic.com/prod"
           targetNamespace="http://datypic.com/prod">
  <xs:element name="product" type="ProductType"/>
  <xs:complexType name="ProductType">
    <xs:sequence>
      <xs:element name="number" type="xs:integer" minOccurs="0"/>
      <xs:element name="name" type="xs:string"/>
    </xs:sequence>
    <xs:attribute name="version"/>
  </xs:complexType>
</xs:schema>
```

Instance:

```
<product xmlns="http://datypic.com/prod"
         xmlns:xsi="http://www.w3.org/2001/XMLSchema-instance"
         xsi:schemaLocation="http://datypic.com/prod prod.xsd"
         version="2.1">
  <number>557</number>
  <name>Short-Sleeved Linen Blouse</name>
</product>
```

23.2.2.4 Versions in namespace names

Many vocabularies also indicate their version number in the namespace name. When you change a namespace name, it is as if you were completely renaming the components in that namespace. This instantly breaks backward compatibility between schema versions, as the names have essentially changed. It also frequently requires applications that process the instances to change, since many XML technologies (such as XPath, XQuery, and XSLT) are namespace-aware.

That may be desirable in the case of a major release where there is no intention of backward compatibility and the instances change so much that it is necessary for applications to change the way they process the instances. It is definitely not appropriate for minor releases intended to be backward-compatible. Therefore, when a version number is included in a namespace name, it is frequently only the major version number.

Example 23–12 shows a schema that uses the major version number ("2") in the namespace name.

Example 23–12. Using a version number in the namespace name

Schema (prod.xsd):

```
<xs:schema xmlns:xs="http://www.w3.org/2001/XMLSchema"
           elementFormDefault="qualified"
           xmlns="http://datypic.com/prod/2"
           targetNamespace="http://datypic.com/prod/2">
  <xs:element name="product" type="ProductType"/>
  <xs:complexType name="ProductType">
    <xs:sequence>
      <xs:element name="number" type="xs:integer" minOccurs="0"/>
      <xs:element name="name" type="xs:string"/>
    </xs:sequence>
  </xs:complexType>
</xs:schema>
```

Instance:

```
<product xmlns="http://datypic.com/prod/2"
         xmlns:xsi="http://www.w3.org/2001/XMLSchema-instance"
         xsi:schemaLocation="http://datypic.com/prod/2 prod.xsd">
  <number>557</number>
  <name>Short-Sleeved Linen Blouse</name>
</product>
```

23.2.2.5 A combination strategy

It is likely that you will use a combination of some, or all, of the four version number locations. Example 23–13 shows a schema that uses all four methods.

Example 23–13. Using multiple methods to indicate version number

Schema (schemas/prod/2.1/prod.xsd):

```
<xs:schema xmlns:xs="http://www.w3.org/2001/XMLSchema"
           elementFormDefault="qualified"
           xmlns="http://datypic.com/prod/2"
           targetNamespace="http://datypic.com/prod/2"
           version="2.1">
  <xs:element name="product" type="ProductType"/>
  <xs:complexType name="ProductType">
    <xs:sequence>
      <xs:element name="number" type="xs:integer" minOccurs="0"/>
      <xs:element name="name" type="xs:string"/>
    </xs:sequence>
    <xs:attribute name="version" type="xs:decimal"/>
  </xs:complexType>
</xs:schema>
```

Instance:

```
<product xmlns="http://datypic.com/prod/2"
         xmlns:xsi="http://www.w3.org/2001/XMLSchema-instance"
         xsi:schemaLocation="http://datypic.com/prod/2
                             schemas/prod/2.1/prod.xsd"
         version="2.1">
  <number>557</number>
  <name>Short-Sleeved Linen Blouse</name>
</product>
```

23.3 | Application compatibility

Whether or not you can achieve schema compatibility, it is also worthwhile to try to achieve application compatibility. Well-designed applications that were written to process the previous version should be able to process instances of the new version without crashing.

Likewise, applications that process the new version can be made to support both versions. If the new version only contains optional additions, the application can use the same logic for both versions of instances. Alternatively, the application can check the version number (as described in Section 23.2) and process each version differently.

It is impossible to predict how people will modify or extend a schema over time, but several simple practices can help handle changes more gracefully.

- *Ignore irrelevant elements or attributes.* The application should process the elements and attributes it is expecting, without generating errors if additional elements or attributes appear. This is especially true if they are in a different namespace. The application should treat every content model as if it had both attribute and element wildcards, even if it does not.

- *Avoid overdependence on the document structure.* Minimize the amount of structural checking you do in the application code. If you are using a SAX parser, process the element you are interested in by name, but do not necessarily keep track of its parent or grandparent. In XSLT, consider using more of a "push" model instead of "pull," creating templates for individual elements such as `product/number` rather than hard-coding entire paths like `catalog/product/number`. This will allow the XSLT to still work even if a `department` element is added between `catalog` and `product`.

- *Avoid overdependence on namespaces.* A change in a namespace name, for example to include a new version number, is disruptive to your code. While you may need to write entirely new code for the new version, it is ideal if you can reuse some of the code from the previous version. Avoiding the use of namespace names when referring to element names, or at least parameterizing the namespace names instead of hard-coding them throughout your code, can make the upgrade easier and promote reuse.

23.4 | Lessening the impact of versioning

A few best practices can ease the pain of versioning for the implementers of your XML vocabulary. They are discussed in this section.

23.4.1 *Define a versioning strategy*

If you are defining a complex vocabulary, one that changes frequently or one that is used by a variety of implementers, it is helpful to clearly define a versioning strategy. That way, implementers know what to expect when a new version is released. A versioning strategy should specify the following information:

- How will version numbers be formatted and ordered?
- Where will version numbers be indicated in the schemas? In the `version` attribute? In the schema document URL? In the instance? In the namespace? Using some combination of these?
- Are minor releases backward-compatible? Are they forward-compatible?
- Are major releases backward-compatible? Are they forward-compatible?
- How will deprecated components be indicated?
- How will changes be documented?
- Are implementers expected to support multiple versions?
- Are implementers expected to upgrade to the newest version in a particular time frame?

23.4.2 *Make only necessary changes*

When developing a new version that is not required to be backward-compatible, it is tempting to make small fixes—change names that are not as descriptive as they could be, reorder elements to be more intuitive, or change cardinalities to be slightly more constrained. Sometimes there are good reasons to make these changes, for example because the schema is not conformant to a particular NDR specification or is genuinely confusing. But if there is no good reason for that, don't give in to the temptation. The changes may seem small, but they can add up and cause confusion, software bugs, and incompatibilities, placing a significant burden on implementers.

23.4.3 *Document all changes*

All changes to a schema in a new version should be clearly documented in a set of release notes or a formal change log. Each entry in the change log should have the following information:

- Description of the change
- Reason for the change
- Whether the change is backward-compatible
- Notes on upgrading or downgrading—for example, if a required element is added, how should that value be determined when upgrading instances to the new version?

If there are a lot of changes, consider creating a side-by-side mapping document that shows all the differences, like the one shown in Table 23–1. The first two columns contain the element names used in new and old instances, indented to show the hierarchy of elements in each version. The third column describes the change, and the fourth column indicates whether the change is backward-compatible.

Table 23–1   Sample change log showing mapping

2.0 element	3.0 element	Change	BC?
catalog	catalog		
product	product	Max occurrences changed from 100 to unbounded	Y
name	name	Length now limited to 32 characters	N
number	number		
desc	description	Name change	N
size		Deleted element	N
	product_id	New required element	N
	price	New optional element	Y

23.4.4 *Deprecate components before deleting them*

To ease the transition from one version to the next, it is possible to indicate that certain components are deprecated—that is, they are still in the schema but are not recommended for use, and are likely to be deleted in a future version of the schema.

There is no formal way to deprecate components in XML Schema, but deprecation can be indicated in non-native attributes or annotations. If the deprecated element is intended to be replaced by another element, the two can be put together in a `choice` group or substitution group during the deprecation period, so that either is allowed. It is also useful to provide human-readable descriptive information that includes its replacement, if any.

Example 23–14 shows one approach to deprecation. A `deprecated` element with a value `true` is inserted into `appinfo` to formally indicate

Example 23–14. One approach to deprecation

```
<xs:schema xmlns:xs="http://www.w3.org/2001/XMLSchema"
           xmlns:doc="http://datypic.com/doc"
           version="2.1">
  <xs:element name="product" type="ProductType"/>
  <xs:complexType name="ProductType">
    <xs:sequence>
      <xs:element name="number" type="xs:integer"/>
      <xs:element name="name" type="xs:string"/>
      <xs:choice>
        <xs:element name="color" type="xs:NMTOKEN">
          <xs:annotation>
            <xs:documentation>Deprecated in
                favor of colorList.</xs:documentation>
            <xs:appinfo>
              <doc:deprecated>true</doc:deprecated>
            </xs:appinfo>
          </xs:annotation>
        </xs:element>
        <xs:element name="colorList" type="xs:NMTOKENS"/>
      </xs:choice>
    </xs:sequence>
  </xs:complexType>
</xs:schema>
```

that it is deprecated, and a human-readable description is also provided in `documentation`. The deprecated element, `color`, is placed in a `choice` group with its intended replacement, `colorList`. In the next version, `color` will be deleted, leaving `colorList` as the only choice.

23.4.5 *Provide a conversion capability*

If a new version is not backward-compatible, you should provide a clear upgrade path from the old version to the new version. A good way to do this is by providing an XSLT stylesheet to upgrade instances, which can be done automatically by an application.

Such a conversion needs to handle two changes carefully:

1. If required elements or attributes are added in the new version, the XSLT should insert them, ideally with a default value if one can be determined or calculated. Otherwise, an empty or nil value may be appropriate.

2. If elements or attributes are deleted, the XSLT should provide messages to the user that it is deleting information. It could also insert the deleted data as comments in the output, for a human user who may be reviewing the converted documents.

It may also be worthwhile to write an opposite conversion—one that downgrades instances from the newer version to the older one. This makes sense if older implementations that only support the previous version are likely to persist for some time, and there is no forward compatibility. The considerations listed above when adding and deleting components also apply to the downgrade conversion.

23.5 | Versions of the XML Schema language

In addition to having multiple versions of your XML vocabulary, you may be dealing with multiple versions of the XML Schema language itself. This book describes two different versions of XML Schema: 1.0 and 1.1. Depending on which processor you are using, you may be required to use one version or the other. Unlike some other XML vocabularies, there is no way to indicate in your schema which version of XML Schema you are using. Instead, this might be a setting that you pass to your XML Schema processor, or the processor may only support one of the versions.

23.5.1 *New features in version 1.1*

Version 1.1 of XML Schema introduces a number of useful new features, including:

- Assertions (XPath constraints) on types (Sections 14.1.1 on p. 353 and 14.1.2 on p. 365)
- Conditional type assignment for elements (Section 14.2 on p. 375)
- Open content for complex types (Section 12.7.2 on p. 292)
- Relaxed constraints on `all` groups (Section 12.5.4 on p. 276)
- More powerful namespace constraints for wildcards (Section 12.7.1.3 on p. 289)
- Multiple inheritance for substitution groups (Section 16.5 on p. 413)
- Default attributes (Section 15.3.3 on p. 399)
- Inheritable attributes (Section 7.6 on p. 126)
- Overrides, as a replacement for redefines (Section 18.2 on p. 459)
- A new `explicitTimezone` facet (Section 8.4.7 on p. 150)
- Three new built-in simple types: `yearMonthDuration` (Section 11.4.11 on p. 231), `dayTimeDuration` (Section 11.4.12 on p. 232), and `dateTimeStamp` (Section 11.4.4 on p. 224)

- Support for implementation-defined facets and types (Section 8.6 on p. 154)

- Simplification of restrictions through relaxed rules for valid restrictions (Section 13.5.2 on p. 318), the ability to reuse identity constraints (Section 17.10 on p. 442), and the ability to restrict element and attribute declarations in a different target namespace (Section 13.5.7.1 on p. 339)

These new features required the introduction of new elements and attributes into the XML Schema language. Version 1.1 of XML Schema is backward-compatible with version 1.0, so any 1.0 schema will also work with a 1.1 processor and have the same meaning. However, there is no forward compatibility between the two versions, so a 1.0 processor will not be able to handle a 1.1 schema if it uses any of the 1.1 elements or attributes.

23.5.2 *Forward compatibility of XML Schema 1.1*

Version 1.1 of XML Schema has some new capabilities to accommodate the fact that there may be new versions of the XML Schema language in the future. Specifically, it provides a mechanism for indicating that a particular XML Schema component applies only to certain versions of the XML Schema language. These constructs use the `minVersion` and/or `maxVersion` attributes, which are in the Version Control Namespace, `http://www.w3.org/2007/XMLSchema-versioning`.

In Example 23–15, the first declaration for `product` indicates that it should only be honored by processors using version 1.3 or higher. Presumably, it makes use of special version 1.3 constructs that are unknown to version 1.1. If an XML Schema 1.1 processor parses this schema, it will ignore the first declaration and all of its descendants. The second `product` declaration indicates that it should be honored by processors using versions from 1.1 up to, but not including, version 1.3. A processor will only be using one version of XML Schema during any given validation.

Example 23–15. Using `minVersion` and `maxVersion`

```
<xs:schema xmlns:xs="http://www.w3.org/2001/XMLSchema"
           xmlns:vc="http://www.w3.org/2007/XMLSchema-versioning">
  <xs:element name="product" vc:minVersion="1.3">
    <!-- a declaration that uses XML Schema 1.3 constructs -->
  </xs:element>
  <xs:element name="product" vc:minVersion="1.1"
                             vc:maxVersion="1.3">
    <!-- a declaration conformant to versions 1.1 and 1.2 -->
  </xs:element>
</xs:schema>
```

This example may seem to violate one of the basic rules of XML Schema—namely, it has two global element declarations with the same name. However, the version control attributes have a special power, signaling to the processor that it should preprocess the schema (using a process called *conditional inclusion*) to strip out all the declarations that don't apply to the version it is using. It is the output of this preprocessing that must follow all the rules of XML Schema. In Example 23–15, there will never be more than one `product` declaration in the schema after preprocessing. However, care must be taken not to use overlapping values for `minVersion` and/or `maxVersion`, lest duplicate declarations remain after preprocessing.

Unfortunately, this mechanism does not help with the transition from XML Schema 1.0 to 1.1, because a typical 1.0 processor will not honor or even know about the `minVersion` and/or `maxVersion` attributes.

23.5.3 *Portability of implementation-defined types and facets*

Another aspect of handling variations in the XML Schema language involves support for implementation-defined types and facets. Section 8.6 on p. 154 introduced the concept, providing examples of type definitions and element declarations that depend on type names and facets that may only be supported by specific implementations.

Example 23–16 provides a recap, showing a simple type definition based on a hypothetical implementation-defined type (`ext:ordinalDate`), as well as a simple type definition that uses an implementation-defined facet (`saxon:preprocess`) which is currently implemented in Saxon.

Example 23–16. Using implementation-defined types and facets

```
<xs:schema xmlns:xs="http://www.w3.org/2001/XMLSchema"
           xmlns:ext="http://example.org/extensions"
           xmlns:saxon="http://saxon.sf.net/">
  <xs:element name="anyOrdinalDate" type="ext:ordinalDate"/>
  <xs:element name="recentOrdinalDate" type="OrdinalDateIn2011"/>
  <xs:simpleType name="OrdinalDateIn2011">
    <xs:restriction base="ext:ordinalDate">
      <xs:minInclusive value="2011-001"/>
      <xs:maxInclusive value="2011-365"/>
    </xs:restriction>
  </xs:simpleType>

  <xs:element name="size" type="SMLXSizeType"/>
  <xs:simpleType name="SMLXSizeType">
    <xs:restriction base="xs:token">
      <saxon:preprocess action="upper-case($value)"/>
      <xs:enumeration value="SMALL"/>
      <xs:enumeration value="MEDIUM"/>
      <xs:enumeration value="LARGE"/>
      <xs:enumeration value="EXTRA LARGE"/>
    </xs:restriction>
  </xs:simpleType>
</xs:schema>
```

While implementation-defined types and facets can be useful, they do affect the portability of your schema. In fact, if a processor encounters a reference to any implementation-defined type or facet that it does not understand, the entire component, and any other components that depend on it, is considered "unknown" and excluded from the schema used for validation. It is not technically an error in the schema, but if one of these dependent elements or attributes is used in an instance it will fail validation. In Example 23–16, that means that a recentOrdinalDate or anyOrdinalDate element could never be valid if the processor does not understand ext:ordinalDate, and a size element could never be valid if the processor does not understand saxon:preprocess.

It is possible to take special measures to ensure that implementation-defined types and facets are only used by processors that can understand them. This is accomplished through four attributes in the Version Control Namespace: typeAvailable, typeUnavailable, facetAvailable, and facetUnavailable. These attributes can be used on any element in a schema document, and their value is a qualified name or a space-separated list of qualified names.

23.5.3.1 Using typeAvailable and typeUnavailable

The typeAvailable attribute is used to test whether the named type(s) are known to the processor. If any of the listed types is known, the schema element on which it appears is retained; if the types are not known, that element and all of its descendants are ignored. The typeUnavailable has the opposite effect, and the two are often used in conjunction with each other.

Example 23–17 shows a more portable schema that uses ordinalDate: There are two separate anyOrdinalDate declarations, one with the typeAvailable attribute and one with the typeUnavailable attribute. If ordinalDate is known to the processor, the first declaration is used, and if it is not, the second declaration is used.

Likewise, there are two separate definitions of the OrdinalDate-In2011 type. If ordinalDate is known to the processor, the first type definition is used, and if it is not, the second one is used. This means that while validation is less strict if a different processor is used, at least it will not fail unnecessarily.

Example 23–17. Using `vc:typeAvailable` and `vc:typeUnavailable`

```
<xs:schema xmlns:xs="http://www.w3.org/2001/XMLSchema"
           xmlns:ext="http://example.org/extensions"
           xmlns:vc="http://www.w3.org/2007/XMLSchema-versioning">
  <xs:element name="anyOrdinalDate" type="ext:ordinalDate"
              vc:typeAvailable="ext:ordinalDate"/>
  <xs:element name="anyOrdinalDate" type="xs:string"
              vc:typeUnavailable="ext:ordinalDate"/>

  <xs:element name="recentOrdinalDate" type="OrdinalDateIn2011"/>
  <xs:simpleType name="OrdinalDateIn2011"
                 vc:typeAvailable="ext:ordinalDate">
    <xs:restriction base="ext:ordinalDate">
      <xs:minInclusive value="2011-001"/>
      <xs:maxInclusive value="2011-365"/>
    </xs:restriction>
  </xs:simpleType>
  <xs:simpleType name="OrdinalDateIn2011"
                 vc:typeUnavailable="ext:ordinalDate">
    <xs:restriction base="xs:string">
      <xs:pattern value="2011-\d{3}"/>
    </xs:restriction>
  </xs:simpleType>
</xs:schema>
```

23.5.3.2 Using `facetAvailable` and `facetUnavailable`

The `facetAvailable` and `facetUnavailable` attributes work similarly. Example 23–18 is a schema that contains two type definitions: The first is used if the `saxon:preprocess` facet is known, and the second is used if it is unknown.

As with the `minVersion` and `maxVersion` attributes, these attributes do not have to be on top-level components; they can appear on any element in the schema to indicate that it should be included only under the specified conditions. Example 23–19 shows a schema that uses the `facetAvailable` attribute on the `ext:maxLength-WithoutWhitespace` facet itself to instruct the processor to not read it if it does not understand it.

Example 23–18. Using `vc:facetAvailable` and `vc:facetUnavailable`

```
<xs:schema xmlns:xs="http://www.w3.org/2001/XMLSchema"
           xmlns:saxon="http://saxon.sf.net/"
           xmlns:vc="http://www.w3.org/2007/XMLSchema-versioning">
  <xs:element name="size" type="SMLXSizeType"/>
  <xs:simpleType name="SMLXSizeType"
                 vc:facetAvailable="saxon:preprocess">
    <xs:restriction base="xs:token">
      <saxon:preprocess action="upper-case($value)"/>
      <xs:enumeration value="SMALL"/>
      <xs:enumeration value="MEDIUM"/>
      <xs:enumeration value="LARGE"/>
      <xs:enumeration value="EXTRA LARGE"/>
    </xs:restriction>
  </xs:simpleType>
  <xs:simpleType name="SMLXSizeType"
                 vc:facetUnavailable="saxon:preprocess">
    <xs:restriction base="xs:token"/>
  </xs:simpleType>
</xs:schema>
```

Example 23–19. Using `vc:facetAvailable`

```
<xs:schema xmlns:xs="http://www.w3.org/2001/XMLSchema"
           xmlns:ext="http://example.org/extensions"
           xmlns:vc="http://www.w3.org/2007/XMLSchema-versioning">
  <xs:element name="astring" type="ShortString"/>
  <xs:simpleType name="ShortString">
    <xs:restriction base="xs:string">
      <ext:maxLengthWithoutWhitespace value="5"
            vc:facetAvailable="ext:maxLengthWithoutWhitespace"/>
    </xs:restriction>
  </xs:simpleType>
</xs:schema>
```

This would not have been appropriate for a prelexical facet like `saxon:preprocess`, however, because if the facet is simply ignored, the instruction to turn the value to upper case before validating it would be skipped. The resulting schema would have been stricter than intended when using a processor other than Saxon, because lowercase values would not be allowed.

XSD keywords

Appendix A

A.1 | Elements

Table A–1   all

Description	all model group, which allows elements in any order
Section	12.5.4 on p. 276
Possible parents	complexType, restriction, extension, group
Attributes	id, minOccurs, maxOccurs
Content model	annotation?, (element | [!]any | [!]group)*

Table A–2   `alternative`

Description	Alternative type for an element if a particular XPath test is true
Section	14.2.1 on p. 376
Possible parent	`element`
Attributes	`id, test, type, xpathDefaultNamespace`
Content model	`annotation?, (simpleType | complexType)?`

Table A–3   `annotation`

Description	Annotation that further documents a schema component
Section	21.8.1 on p. 581
Possible parents	all elements except `annotation`, `appinfo`, and `documentation`
Attribute	`id`
Content model	`(documentation | appinfo)*`

Table A–4   `any`

Description	Element wildcard
Section	12.7.1 on p. 285
Possible parents	`choice, sequence,` [1.1]`all,` [1.1]`openContent,` [1.1]`defaultOpenContent`
Attributes	`id, minOccurs, maxOccurs, namespace, processContents,` [1.1]`notNamespace,` [1.1]`notQName`
Content model	`annotation?`

Table A–5 `anyAttribute`

Description	Attribute wildcard
Section	12.7.3 on p. 298
Possible parents	`attributeGroup, complexType, extension, restriction`
Attributes	`id, namespace, processContents,` ▪1.1`notNamespace,` ▪1.1`notQName`
Content model	`annotation?`

Table A–6 `appinfo`

Description	Application information
Section	21.8.3 on p. 586
Possible parent	`annotation`
Attribute	`source`
Content model	any well-formed content

Table A–7 `assert`

Description	Assertion on a complex type
Section	14.1.2 on p. 365
Possible parents	`complexType, extension, restriction`
Attributes	`id,` **`test`**`, xpathDefaultNamespace`
Content model	`annotation?`

Table A–8 `assertion`

Description	Assertion on a simple type
Section	14.1.1 on p. 353
Possible parent	`restriction`
Attributes	`id`, **`test`**, `xpathDefaultNamespace`
Content model	`annotation?`

Table A–9 `attribute` (global declaration)

Description	Global attribute declaration
Section	7.2.1 on p. 115
Possible parents	`schema`, ▪️`override`
Attributes	`id`, **`name`**, `type`, `default`, `fixed`, ▪️`inheritable`
Content model	`annotation?, simpleType?`

Table A–10 `attribute` (local declaration)

Description	Local attribute declaration
Section	7.2.2 on p. 117
Possible parents	`attributeGroup, complexType, extension, restriction`
Attributes	`id`, **`name`**, `type`, `form`, `use`, `default`, `fixed`, ▪️`targetNamespace`, ▪️`inheritable`
Content model	`annotation?, simpleType?`

Table A–11 attribute (reference)

Description	Attribute reference
Section	12.6.2 on p. 282
Possible parents	attributeGroup, complexType, extension, restriction
Attributes	id, **ref**, use, default, fixed, ▪inheritable
Content model	annotation?

Table A–12 attributeGroup (definition)

Description	Attribute group definition
Section	15.3.1 on p. 393
Possible parents	schema, redefine, ▪override
Attributes	id, **name**
Content model	annotation?, (attribute | attributeGroup)*, anyAttribute?

Table A–13 attributeGroup (reference)

Description	Attribute group reference
Section	15.3.2.1 on p. 395
Possible parents	attributeGroup, complexType, extension, restriction
Attributes	id, **ref**
Content model	annotation?

Table A–14   `choice`

Description	`choice` group that allows a choice among elements
Section	12.5.2 on p. 273
Possible parents	`choice, complexType, extension, group, restriction, sequence`
Attributes	`id, minOccurs, maxOccurs`
Content model	`annotation?, (element | group | choice | sequence | any)*`

Table A–15   `complexContent`

Description	Complex content specification
Section	13.3.2 on p. 304
Possible parents	`complexType`
Attributes	`id, mixed`
Content model	`annotation?, (restriction | extension)`

Table A–16   `complexType` (named, global definition)

Description	Named complex type definition
Section	12.2.1 on p. 258
Possible parents	`schema, redefine,` [1.1]`override`
Attributes	`id,` **`name`**`, mixed, abstract, block, final,` [1.1]`defaultAttributesApply`
Content model	`annotation?, (simpleContent	complexContent	(`[1.1]`openContent?, (group | all | choice | sequence)?, ((attribute | attributeGroup)*, anyAttribute?),` [1.1]`assert*))`

Table A–17   `complexType` (anonymous, local definition)

Description	Anonymous complex type definition
Section	12.2.2 on p. 260
Possible parents	`element,` [1.1]`alternative`
Attributes	`id, mixed,` [1.1]`defaultAttributesApply`
Content model	`annotation?, (simpleContent	complexContent |` ([1.1]`openContent?, (group | all | choice | sequence)?, ((attribute | attributeGroup)*, anyAttribute?),` [1.1]`assert*))`

Table A–18   `defaultOpenContent`

Description	Default open content model
Section	12.7.2.2 on p. 295
Possible parent	`schema`
Attributes	`id, appliesToEmpty, mode`
Content model	`annotation?, any`

Table A–19   `documentation`

Description	Human-readable documentation of a schema component
Section	21.8.2 on p. 581
Possible parent	`annotation`
Attributes	`source, xml:lang`
Content model	any well-formed content

Table A–20   `element` (global declaration)

Description	Global element declaration
Section	6.1.1 on p. 89
Possible parents	`schema,` ▪️`override`
Attributes	`id,` **`name`**`, type, default, fixed, nillable, abstract, substitutionGroup, block, final`
Content model	`annotation?, (simpleType | complexType)?,` ▪️`alternative*, (key | keyref | unique)*`

Table A–21   `element` (local declaration)

Description	Local element declaration
Section	6.1.2 on p. 93
Possible parents	`all, choice, sequence`
Attributes	`id,` **`name`**`, form, type, minOccurs, maxOccurs, default, fixed, nillable, block,` ▪️`targetNamespace`
Content model	`annotation?, (simpleType | complexType)?,` ▪️`alternative*, (key | keyref | unique)*`

Table A–22   `element` (reference)

Description	Element reference
Section	12.4.2 on p. 267
Possible parents	`all, choice, sequence`
Attributes	`id,` **`ref`**`, minOccurs, maxOccurs`
Content model	`annotation?`

Table A–23   `enumeration`

Description	Facet specifying a valid value
Sections	8.4.4 on p. 145, 10.3.3.2 on p. 192
Possible parent	`restriction`
Attributes	`id,` **`value`**
Content model	`annotation?`

Table A–24   `explicitTimezone`

Description	Facet specifying whether a time zone is required, optional, or prohibited
Section	8.4.7 on p. 150
Possible parent	`restriction`
Attributes	`id, fixed,` **`value`**
Content model	`annotation?`

Table A–25   `extension` **(simple content)**

Description	Simple content extension
Section	13.4.1 on p. 306
Possible parent	`simpleContent`
Attributes	`id,` **`base`**
Content model	`annotation?, (attribute | attributeGroup)*,` `anyAttribute?,` 🔢`assert*`

Table A–26   `extension` **(complex content)**

Description	Complex content extension
Section	13.4.2 on p. 307
Possible parent	`complexContent`
Attributes	`id`, **`base`**
Content model	`annotation?,` ⬛`openContent?, (group | all | choice | sequence)?, (attribute | attributeGroup)*, anyAttribute?,` ⬛`assert*`

Table A–27   `field`

Description	Identity constraint field
Section	17.7.2 on p. 434
Possible parents	`key, keyref, unique`
Attributes	`id`, **`xpath`,** ⬛`xpathDefaultNamespace`
Content model	`annotation?`

Table A–28   `fractionDigits`

Description	Facet specifying the number of digits allowed after the decimal point
Section	8.4.3 on p. 145
Possible parent	`restriction`
Attributes	`id`, **`value`**, `fixed`
Content model	`annotation?`

Table A–29   group (definition)

Description	Named model group definition
Section	15.2.1 on p. 386
Possible parents	schema, redefine, **1.1**override
Attributes	id, **name**
Content model	annotation?, (all | choice | sequence)

Table A–30   group (reference)

Description	Named model group reference
Section	15.2.2.1 on p. 388
Possible parents	complexType, extension, restriction, sequence, choice, **1.1**all
Attributes	id, **ref**, minOccurs, maxOccurs
Content model	annotation?

Table A–31   import

Description	Import of another namespace
Section	4.3.2 on p. 66
Possible parent	schema
Attributes	id, namespace, schemaLocation
Content model	annotation?

Table A–32   `include`

Description	Include of another schema document
Section	4.3.1 on p. 62
Possible parent	`schema`
Attributes	`id`, **`schemaLocation`**
Content model	`annotation?`

Table A–33   `key` (key constraint)

Description	Key constraint
Section	17.5 on p. 428
Possible parent	`element`
Attributes	`id`, **`name`**
Content model	`annotation?`, `selector`, `field+`

Table A–34   `key` (reference to key constraint)

Description	Reference to key constraint
Section	17.10 on p. 442
Possible parent	`element`
Attributes	`id`, **`ref`**
Content model	`annotation?`

Table A–35 `keyref` (key reference)

Description	Key reference
Section	17.6 on p. 430
Possible parent	`element`
Attributes	`id`, **`name`**, **`refer`**
Content model	`annotation?, selector, field+`

Table A–36 `keyref` (reference to key reference)

Description	Reference to key reference
Section	17.10 on p. 442
Possible parent	`element`
Attributes	`id`, **`ref`**
Content model	`annotation?`

Table A–37 `length`

Description	Facet specifying the exact length of a value
Sections	8.4.2 on p. 143, 10.3.3.1 on p. 192
Possible parent	`restriction`
Attributes	`id`, **`value`**, `fixed`
Content model	`annotation?`

Table A–38   `list`

Description	List type that allows a space-separated list of values
Section	10.3.1 on p. 188
Possible parent	`simpleType`
Attributes	`id, itemType`
Content model	`annotation?, simpleType?`

Table A–39   `maxExclusive`

Description	Facet specifying the maximum allowed value (exclusive)
Section	8.4.1 on p. 142
Possible parent	`restriction`
Attributes	`id, `**`value`**`, fixed`
Content model	`annotation?`

Table A–40   `maxInclusive`

Description	Facet specifying the maximum allowed value (inclusive)
Section	8.4.1 on p. 142
Possible parent	`restriction`
Attributes	`id, `**`value`**`, fixed`
Content model	`annotation?`

Table A–41   maxLength

Description	Facet specifying the maximum length of the value
Sections	8.4.2 on p. 143, 10.3.3.1 on p. 192
Possible parent	restriction
Attributes	id, **value**, fixed
Content model	annotation?

Table A–42   minExclusive

Description	Facet specifying the minimum allowed value (exclusive)
Section	8.4.1 on p. 142
Possible parent	restriction
Attributes	id, **value**, fixed
Content model	annotation?

Table A–43   minInclusive

Description	Facet specifying the minimum allowed value (inclusive)
Section	8.4.1 on p. 142
Possible parent	restriction
Attributes	id, **value**, fixed
Content model	annotation?

Table A–44   `minLength`

Description	Facet specifying the minimum allowed length of the value
Sections	8.4.2 on p. 143, 10.3.3.1 on p. 192
Possible parent	`restriction`
Attributes	`id`, **`value`**, `fixed`
Content model	`annotation?`

Table A–45   `notation`

Description	Notation declaration
Section	19.7.1 on p. 494
Possible parents	`schema`, ᴵᴵ`override`
Attributes	`id`, **`name`**, `public`, `system`
Content model	`annotation?`

Table A–46   `openContent`

Description	Open content model
Section	12.7.2.1 on p. 292
Possible parents	`complexType`, `extension`, `restriction`
Attributes	`id`, `mode`
Content model	`annotation?`, `any?`

Table A–47 `override`

Description	Override of another schema document
Section	18.2.2 on p. 462
Possible parent	`schema`
Attributes	`id`, **`schemaLocation`**
Content model	`(annotation | simpleType | complexType | group | attributeGroup | element | attribute | notation)*`

Table A–48 `pattern`

Description	Facet specifying a regular expression
Sections	8.4.5 on p. 148, 10.3.3.3 on p. 194
Possible parent	`restriction`
Attributes	`id`, **`value`**
Content model	`annotation?`

Table A–49 `redefine`

Description	Redefinition of another schema document
Section	18.1.2 on p. 451
Possible parent	`schema`
Attributes	`id`, **`schemaLocation`**
Content model	`(annotation | attributeGroup | complexType | group | simpleType)*`

Table A–50   `restriction` (simple atomic type)

Description	Simple type restriction
Section	8.3.1 on p. 136
Possible parent	`simpleType`
Attributes	`id, base`
Content model	`annotation?, simpleType?, (minExclusive |` `minInclusive | maxExclusive | maxInclusive |` `length | minLength | maxLength | totalDigits |` `fractionDigits | enumeration | pattern |` `whiteSpace | ▣assertion | ▣explicitTimezone |` `▣`*{any element in another namespace})* `*`

Table A–51   `restriction` (list type)

Description	List type restriction
Section	10.3.3 on p. 190
Possible parent	`simpleType`
Attributes	`id, base`
Content model	`annotation?, simpleType?, (length | minLength |` `maxLength | pattern | enumeration | whiteSpace |` `▣assertion)*`

Table A–52   `restriction` (union type)

Description	Union type restriction
Section	10.2.2 on p. 185
Possible parent	`simpleType`
Attributes	`id, base`
Content model	`annotation?, simpleType?, (enumeration |` `pattern | ▣assertion)*`

Table A–53   restriction **(simple content)**

Description	Simple content restriction
Section	13.5.1 on p. 317
Possible parent	simpleContent
Attributes	id, **base**
Content model	annotation?, simpleType?, (enumeration | length | maxExclusive | maxInclusive | maxLength | minExclusive | minInclusive | minLength | pattern | totalDigits | fractionDigits | whiteSpace| pattern | ▣assertion | ▣explicitTimezone | ▣*{any element in another namespace})* *, (attribute | attributeGroup)*, anyAttribute?

Table A–54   restriction **(complex content)**

Description	Complex content restriction
Section	13.5.2 on p. 318
Possible parent	complexContent
Attributes	id, **base**
Content model	annotation?, ▣openContent?, (group | all | choice | sequence)?, (attribute | attributeGroup)*, anyAttribute?, ▣assert*

Table A–55 `schema`

Description	Schema document
Section	4.2 on p. 58
Possible parent	*none*
Attributes	`id`, `version`, `targetNamespace`, `attributeFormDefault`, `elementFormDefault`, `blockDefault`, `finalDefault`, `xml:lang`, ▥`defaultAttributes`, ▥`xpathDefaultNamespace`
Content model	`(include | import | redefine | `▥`override | annotation)*, `▥`defaultOpenContent?, (simpleType | complexType | group | attributeGroup | element | attribute | notation | annotation)*`

Table A–56 `selector`

Description	Identity constraint selector
Section	17.7.1 on p. 433
Possible parents	`key`, `keyref`, `unique`
Attributes	`id`, **`xpath`**, ▥`xpathDefaultNamespace`
Content model	`annotation?`

Table A–57 `sequence`

Description	`sequence` group that requires elements in a particular order
Section	12.5.1 on p. 270
Possible parents	`choice`, `complexType`, `extension`, `group`, `restriction`, `sequence`
Attributes	`id`, `minOccurs`, `maxOccurs`
Content model	`annotation?, (element | group | choice | sequence | any)*`

Table A–58 `simpleContent`

Description	Simple content specification
Section	13.3.1 on p. 303
Possible parent	`complexType`
Attributes	`id`
Content model	`annotation?, (restriction | extension)`

Table A–59 `simpleType` (named, global definition)

Description	Named simple type definition
Section	8.2.1 on p. 131
Possible parents	`schema, redefine,` ▣`override`
Attributes	`id,` **name**`, final`
Content model	`annotation?, (restriction | list | union)`

Table A–60 `simpleType` (anonymous, local definition)

Description	Anonymous simple type definition
Section	8.2.2 on p. 132
Possible parents	`attribute, element, list, restriction, union,` ▣`alternative`
Attribute	`id`
Content model	`annotation?, (restriction | list | union)`

Table A–61   `totalDigits`

Description	Facet specifying the total number of digits allowed in a value
Section	8.4.3 on p. 145
Possible parent	`restriction`
Attributes	`id`, **`value`**, `fixed`
Content model	`annotation?`

Table A–62   `union`

Description	Union type that allows values from multiple types
Section	10.2.1 on p. 183
Possible parent	`simpleType`
Attributes	`id`, `memberTypes`
Content model	`annotation?`, `simpleType*`

Table A–63   `unique` (uniqueness constraint)

Description	Uniqueness constraint
Section	17.4 on p. 426
Possible parent	`element`
Attributes	`id`, **`name`**
Content model	`annotation?`, `selector`, `field+`

Table A–64   `unique` (reference to uniqueness constraint)

Description	Reference to uniqueness constraint
Section	17.10 on p. 442
Possible parent	`element`
Attributes	`id`, **`ref`**
Content model	`annotation?`

Table A–65   `whiteSpace`

Description	Facet specifying how whitespace should be handled in values
Section	8.4.8 on p. 151
Possible parent	`restriction`
Attributes	`id`, **`value`**, `fixed`
Content model	`annotation?`

A.2 | Attributes

Table A–66   `abstract`

Description	Whether a type or element can be used in an instance
Sections	13.7.4 on p. 346, 16.7.3 on p. 420
Elements	`complexType`, `element`
Type/valid values	`boolean`
Default value	`false`

Table A–67 `appliesToEmpty`

Description	Whether the default open content model applies to empty content
Section	12.7.2.2 on p. 295
Element	`defaultOpenContent`
Type/valid values	`boolean`
Default value	`false`

Table A–68 `attributeFormDefault`

Description	Whether local attributes should be qualified in instances
Section	7.4 on p. 122
Element	`schema`
Type/valid values	`"qualified"` | `"unqualified"`
Default value	`unqualified`

Table A–69 `base`

Description	Base type of the derivation
Sections	various
Elements	`extension, restriction`
Type/valid values	`QName`

Table A–70 `block` **(complex type)**

Description	Whether to block type substitution in the instance
Section	13.7.2 on p. 344
Element	`complexType`
Type/valid values	`"#all"` or list of (`"extension"` | `"restriction"`)
Default value	defaults to `blockDefault` of `schema`

Table A–71 `block` **(element)**

Description	Whether type and/or element substitutions should be blocked from the instance
Sections	13.7.3 on p. 346, 16.7.2 on p. 419
Element	`element`
Type/valid values	`"#all"` or list of (`"extension"` | `"restriction"` | `"substitution"`)
Default value	defaults to `blockDefault` of `schema`

Table A–72 `blockDefault`

Description	Whether the use of derived types in instances should be blocked
Sections	13.7.2 on p. 344, 13.7.3 on p. 346
Element	`schema`
Type/valid values	`"#all"` or list of (`"extension"` | `"restriction"` | `"substitution"`)

Table A–73 `default`

Description	Default value for the element or attribute
Sections	6.4.1 on p. 102, 7.5.1 on p. 124
Elements	`attribute`, `element`
Type/valid values	`string`

Table A–74 `defaultAttributes`

Description	The default attribute group for all complex types in a schema document
Section	15.3.3 on p. 399
Element	`schema`
Type/valid values	`QName`

Table A–75 `defaultAttributesApply`

Description	Whether the default attribute group applies to a particular complex type
Section	15.3.3 on p. 399
Element	`complexType`
Type/valid values	`boolean`
Default value	`true`

Table A–76 `elementFormDefault`

Description	Whether local element names should be qualified in instances
Section	6.3.3 on p. 99
Element	`schema`
Type/valid values	`"qualified"` | `"unqualified"`
Default value	`unqualified`

Table A–77 `facetAvailable`[†]

Description	Facet(s) that must be available to include the component in the schema
Section	23.5.3 on p. 642
Elements	any element in the schema
Type/valid values	list of `QName`

[†] Namespace is `http://www.w3.org/2007/XMLSchema-versioning`, usually mapped to the prefix `vc`.

Table A–78 `facetUnavailable`[†]

Description	Facet(s) that must be unavailable to include the component in the schema
Section	23.5.3 on p. 642
Elements	any element in the schema
Type/valid values	list of `QName`

[†] Namespace is `http://www.w3.org/2007/XMLSchema-versioning`, usually mapped to the prefix `vc`.

Table A–79 `final` (complex type)

Description	Whether other types can be derived from this one
Section	13.7.1 on p. 343
Element	`complexType`
Type/valid values	`"#all"` or list of (`"extension"` | `"restriction"`)
Default value	defaults to `finalDefault` of `schema`

Table A–80   `final` **(element)**

Description	Whether the element declaration can be the head of a substitution group
Section	16.7.1 on p. 418
Element	`element`
Type/valid values	`"#all"` or list of (`"extension"` | `"restriction"`)
Default value	defaults to `finalDefault` of `schema`

Table A–81   `final` **(simple type)**

Description	Whether other types can be derived from this one
Section	8.5 on p. 152
Element	`simpleType`
Type/valid values	`"#all"` or list of (`"restriction"` | `"list"` | `"union"` | ▣`"extension"`)
Default value	defaults to `finalDefault` of `schema`

Table A–82   `finalDefault`

Description	Whether type derivation should be disallowed
Sections	8.5 on p. 152, 13.7.1 on p. 343, 16.7.1 on p. 418
Element	`schema`
Type/valid values	`"#all"` or list of (`"extension"` | `"restriction"` | `"list"` | `"union"`)

Table A–83 `fixed` (element/attribute)

Description	Fixed value for the element or attribute
Sections	6.4.2 on p. 103, 7.5.2 on p. 125
Elements	`attribute, element`
Type/valid values	`string`

Table A–84 `fixed` (facet)

Description	Whether the facet is fixed and therefore cannot be restricted further
Section	8.3.4 on p. 140
Elements	`fractionDigits, length, maxExclusive, maxInclusive, maxLength, minExclusive, minInclusive, minLength, totalDigits, whiteSpace,` 🔲`explicitTimezone`
Type/valid values	`boolean`
Default value	`false`

Table A–85 `form`

Description	Whether the element or attribute name must be qualified in the instance
Sections	6.3 on p. 98, 7.4 on p. 122
Elements	`attribute, element`
Type/valid values	`"qualified" | "unqualified"`
Default value	defaults to `attributeFormDefault` or `elementFormDefault` of `schema`

Table A–86   id

Description	Unique ID
Sections	various
Elements	all XSD elements except documentation and appinfo
Type/valid values	ID

Table A–87   inheritable

Description	Whether the value can be inherited by descendant elements
Section	7.6 on p. 126
Element	attribute
Type/valid values	boolean
Default value	false

Table A–88   itemType

Description	The simple type of each item in the list
Section	10.3.1 on p. 188
Element	list
Type/valid values	QName

Table A–89   lang†

Description	Natural language
Section	21.8.2 on p. 581
Elements	schema, documentation
Type/valid values	language

† Namespace is http://www.w3.org/XML/1998/namespace, mapped to the prefix xml.

Table A–90 `maxOccurs`

Description	Maximum number of element or group occurrences
Sections	12.4 on p. 266, 12.5 on p. 270
Elements	`all`, `any`, `choice`, `element`, `group`, `sequence`
Type/valid values	`nonNegativeInteger` | `"unbounded"`. For `all` group, must be `0` or `1`.
Default value	`1`

Table A–91 `maxVersion`[†]

Description	Maximum version supported by a component
Section	23.5.2 on p. 641
Elements	any element in the schema
Type/valid values	`decimal`

[†] Namespace is `http://www.w3.org/2007/XMLSchema-versioning`, usually mapped to the prefix `vc`.

Table A–92 `memberTypes`

Description	Member types that make up the union type
Section	10.2.1 on p. 183
Element	`union`
Type/valid values	list of `QName`

Table A–93   `minOccurs`

Description	Minimum number of element or group occurrences
Sections	12.4 on p. 266, 12.5 on p. 270
Elements	`all`, `any`, `choice`, `element`, `group`, `sequence`
Type/valid values	`nonNegativeInteger`. For `all` group, must be `0` or `1`.
Default value	`1`

Table A–94   `minVersion`[†]

Description	Minimum version supported by a component
Section	23.5.2 on p. 641
Elements	any element in the schema
Type/valid values	`decimal`

[†] Namespace is `http://www.w3.org/2007/XMLSchema-versioning`, usually mapped to the prefix `vc`.

Table A–95   `mixed`

Description	Whether the complex type allows mixed content
Sections	12.3.3 on p. 264, 13.3.2 on p. 304
Elements	`complexContent`, `complexType`
Type/valid values	`boolean`
Default value	`false` for `complexType`, for `complexContent` it defaults to the `mixed` value of the complex type

Table A–96 `mode`

Description	Where replacement elements can appear in an open content model
Sections	12.7.2 on p. 292, 12.7.2.2 on p. 295
Elements	`openContent, defaultOpenContent`
Type/valid values	`"none"` | `"interleave"` | `"suffix"` (`"none"` is not allowed for the `defaultOpenContent` element)
Default value	`interleave`

Table A–97 `name`

Description	Name of the schema component
Sections	various
Elements	`attribute, attributeGroup, complexType, element, group, key, keyref, notation, simpleType, unique`
Type/valid values	`NCName`

Table A–98 `namespace` **(wildcard)**

Description	Which namespace(s) the replacement elements/attributes may belong to
Sections	12.7.1 on p. 285, 12.7.3 on p. 298
Elements	`any, anyAttribute`
Type/valid values	`"##any"` or `"##other"` or list of (`anyURI` | `"##targetNamespace"` | `"##local"`)
Default value	`"##any"`

Table A–99   `namespace` (import)

Description	Namespace to be imported
Section	4.3.2 on p. 66
Element	`import`
Type/valid values	`anyURI`

Table A–100   `nil`[†]

Description	Whether the element's value is nil
Section	6.5 on p. 105
Elements	any instance element
Type/valid values	`boolean`
Default value	`false`

[†] Namespace is `http://www.w3.org/2001/XMLSchema-instance`, often mapped to the prefix `xsi`.

Table A–101   `nillable`

Description	Whether elements can be nilled, i.e. have the `xsi:nil` attribute
Section	6.5 on p. 105
Element	`element`
Type/valid values	`boolean`
Default value	`false`

Table A–102   noNamespaceSchemaLocation[†]

Description	Location of the schema in instances with no namespaces
Section	5.3.1.2 on p. 86
Elements	any instance element
Type/valid values	anyURI

[†] Namespace is http://www.w3.org/2001/XMLSchema-instance, often mapped to the prefix xsi.

Table A–103   notNamespace

Description	Disallowed namespaces for a wildcard
Sections	12.7.1 on p. 285, 12.7.3 on p. 298
Elements	any, anyAttribute
Type/valid values	list of (anyURI | "##targetNamespace" | "##local")

Table A–104   notQName

Description	Disallowed element or attribute names for a wildcard
Sections	12.7.1 on p. 285, 12.7.3 on p. 298
Elements	any, anyAttribute
Type/valid values	list of (QName | "##defined" | "##definedSibling"). Note that ##definedSibling cannot be used on anyAttribute.

Table A–105   `processContents`

Description	How strictly to validate the replacement elements or attributes
Sections	12.7.1 on p. 285, 12.7.3 on p. 298
Elements	`any, anyAttribute`
Type/valid values	`("lax" | "skip" | "strict")`
Default value	`strict`

Table A–106   `public`

Description	Public ID of a notation
Section	19.7.1 on p. 494
Element	`notation`
Type/valid values	token

Table A–107   `ref`

Description	Name of the schema component being referenced
Sections	various
Elements	`attribute, attributeGroup, element, group,` ▪key, ▪keyref, ▪unique
Type/valid values	QName

Table A–108   `refer`

Description	Name of the key being referenced
Section	17.6 on p. 430
Element	`keyref`
Type/valid values	QName

Table A–109   `schemaLocation` (import/include/redefine/override)

Description	Location of the schema which describes included or imported components
Section	4.3 on p. 61
Elements	`import, include, redefine,` `override`
Type/valid values	`anyURI`

Table A–110   `schemaLocation` (instance)†

Description	List of locations of the schemas that correspond to namespaces in an instance
Section	5.3.1.1 on p. 84
Elements	any instance element
Type/valid values	list of pairs of `anyURI` values

† Namespace is `http://www.w3.org/2001/XMLSchema-instance`, often mapped to the prefix `xsi`.

Table A–111   `source`

Description	Source of further documentation
Sections	21.8.2 on p. 581, 21.8.3 on p. 586
Elements	`appinfo, documentation`
Type/valid values	`anyURI`

Table A–112   `substitutionGroup`

Description	Head of the substitution group to which the element declaration belongs
Section	16.3 on p. 409
Element	`element`
Type/valid values	`QName` (list of `QName`)

Table A–113   `system`

Description	System ID of a notation
Section	19.7.1 on p. 494
Element	`notation`
Type/valid values	`anyURI`

Table A–114   `targetNamespace` **(schema)**

Description	Namespace to which all global schema components belong
Section	3.3.1 on p. 48
Element	`schema`
Type/valid values	`anyURI`

Table A–115   `targetNamespace` **(local declaration)**

Description	Namespace of a local element or attribute declaration being restricted
Section	13.5.7 on p. 337
Elements	`attribute, element`
Type/valid values	`anyURI`

Table A–116   `test`

Description	XPath assertion on a complex or simple type
Sections	14.2 on p. 375, 14.1.2 on p. 365, 14.1.1 on p. 353
Elements	`alternative, assert, assertion`
Type/valid values	XPath expression

Table A–117 `type` (element/attribute)

Description	Type of attributes or elements
Sections	6.2 on p. 96, 7.3 on p. 120
Elements	`attribute`, `element`, **1.1** `alternative`
Type/valid values	`QName`

Table A–118 `type` (instance)[†]

Description	Type of the element, used in type substitution and union types
Section	13.6 on p. 341
Elements	any instance element
Type/valid values	`QName`

[†] Namespace is `http://www.w3.org/2001/XMLSchema-instance`, often mapped to the prefix `xsi`.

Table A–119 `typeAvailable`[†]

Description	Type(s) that must be available to include the component in the schema
Section	23.5.3 on p. 642
Elements	any element in the schema
Type/valid values	list of `QName`

[†] Namespace is `http://www.w3.org/2007/XMLSchema-versioning`, usually mapped to the prefix `vc`.

Table A–120   typeUnavailable[†]

Description	Type(s) that must be unavailable to include the component in the schema
Section	23.5.3 on p. 642
Elements	any element in the schema
Type/valid values	list of QName

[†] Namespace is http://www.w3.org/2007/XMLSchema-versioning, usually mapped to the prefix vc.

Table A–121   use

Description	Whether an attribute is required or optional
Section	12.6 on p. 281
Element	attribute
Type/valid values	"optional" | "prohibited" | "required"
Default value	optional

Table A–122   value

Description	Value of the facet
Sections	8.4.1 on p. 142, 8.4.2 on p. 143, 8.4.3 on p. 145, 8.4.4 on p. 145, 8.4.5 on p. 148, 8.4.8 on p. 151
Elements	enumeration, fractionDigits, length, maxExclusive, maxInclusive, maxLength, minExclusive, minInclusive, minLength, pattern, totalDigits, whiteSpace, explicitTimezone
Type/valid values	various, depending on the facet and base type

Table A–123   version

Description	Version number of the schema
Section	23.2 on p. 626
Element	schema
Type/valid values	token

Table A–124   xpath

Description	XPath to the selected nodes or key field
Section	17.8 on p. 435
Elements	field, selector
Type/valid values	XPath subset

Table A–125   xpathDefaultNamespace

Description	The default namespace for XPath expressions
Sections	14.1.3.1 on p. 373, 17.9.1 on p. 441
Elements	alternative, assert, assertion, selector, field, schema
Type/valid values	anyURI | "##defaultNamespace" | "##targetNamespace" | "##local"

Built-in simple types

B.1 | Built-in simple types

Table B–1   Built-in simple types

Name	Description or range	Examples	Section
String and name types			
string	character string	This is a string!	11.2.1
normalizedString	character string with "replace" whitespace processing	This is a normalizedString!	11.2.1
token	character string with "collapse" whitespace processing	This is a token!	11.2.1
Name	valid XML name	size	11.2.2

(Continues)

Table B–1   (Continued)

Name	Description or range	Examples	Section
NCName	non-colonized (unprefixed) name	size	11.2.3
language	natural language identifier	en-GB, en-US, fr	11.2.4

Numeric types

Name	Description or range	Examples	Section
float	single-precision 32-bit floating-point number	-INF, -3E2, -0, 0, 24.3e-3, 12, 15.2, INF, NaN	11.3.1
double	double-precision 64-bit floating-point number	-INF, -3E2, -0, 0, 24.3e-3, 12, 15.2, INF, NaN	11.3.1
decimal	any decimal number	-3, +3.5, +.5, 3, 3., 003.0, 3.0000	11.3.2
integer	any integer	-3, 0, +3, 05, 4268	11.3.3
long	−9223372036854775808 to 9223372036854775807	-3000000000, +3, 699999999999999	11.3.3
int	−2147483648 to 2147483647	-2147483648, +3, 2147483647	11.3.3
short	−32768 to 32767	-32768, +3, 32767	11.3.3
byte	−128 to 127	-128, +3, 127	11.3.3
positiveInteger	1, 2, . . .	1, +426822752	11.3.3
nonPositive-Integer	. . . , −2, −1, 0	-426822752, -1, 0	11.3.3
negativeInteger	. . . , −2, −1	-426822752, -1	11.3.3
nonNegative-Integer	0, 1, 2, . . .	0, +1, 426822752	11.3.3

(Continues)

Table B–1   (Continued)

Name	Description or range	Examples	Section
unsignedLong	0 to 18446744073709551615	0, 70000000000000	11.3.3
unsignedInt	0 to 4294967295	0, 4294967295	11.3.3
unsignedShort	0 to 65535	0, 65535	11.3.3
unsignedByte	0 to 255	0, 255	11.3.3

Date and time types

Name	Description or range	Examples	Section
date	date, YYYY-MM-DD	2004-04-12	11.4.1
time	time, hh:mm:ss.sss	13:20:00.000, 13:20:00Z, 13:20:00-05:00	11.4.2
dateTime	date and time (YYYY-MMDDThh: mm:ss.sss) followed by an optional time zone	2004-04-12T13:20:00, 2004-04-12T13:20:00-05:00	11.4.3
1.1 dateTimeStamp	date and time (YYYY-MMDDThh: mm:ss.sss) followed by a required time zone	2004-04-12T13:20:00Z, 2004-04-12T13:20:00-05:00	11.4.4
gYear	specific year, YYYY	2004	11.4.5
gYearMonth	specific year and month, YYYY-MM	2004-04	11.4.6
gMonth	recurring month of the year, --MM	--04	11.4.7
gMonthDay	recurring day of the year, --MM-DD	--04-12	11.4.8

(Continues)

Table B–1   (Continued)

Name	Description or range	Examples	Section
gDay	recurring day of the month, ---DD	---12	11.4.9
duration	length of time, PnYnMnDTnHnMnS	P2Y6M5DT12H35M30.5S, P2Y	11.4.10
▣yearMonth-Duration	length of time in years and/or months, PnYnM	P2Y6M, P2Y, P12M	11.4.11
▣dayTime-Duration	length of time in days, hours, minutes, and/or seconds, PnDTnHnMnS	P5DT12H35M30.5S, P5D, PT12H	11.4.12

XML DTD types

ID	unique identifier		11.5.1
IDREF	reference to a unique identifier		11.5.2
IDREFS	list of IDREF		11.5.3
ENTITY	unparsed entity reference		11.5.4
ENTITIES	list of ENTITY		11.5.5
NMTOKEN	single token (no whitespace)	small	11.5.6
NMTOKENS	list of NMTOKEN	small medium large	11.5.7
NOTATION	notation reference		11.5.8

Other types

QName	qualified name (may be prefixed or unprefixed)	prod:size, size	11.6.1

(Continues)

Table B–1   (Continued)

Name	Description or range	Examples	Section
boolean	logical	true, false, 0, 1	11.6.2
hexBinary	binary with hex encoding	0FB8, 0fb8	11.6.3
base64Binary	binary with base64 encoding	0FB8, 0fb8	11.6.3
anyURI	URI reference (absolute or relative)	http://datypic.com, ../prod.html#shirt, urn:example:org	11.6.4

B.2 | Applicability of facets to built-in simple types

Table B–2   Applicability of facets to built-in simple types

Name	length	minLength	maxLength	minExclusive	minInclusive	maxInclusive	maxExclusive	totalDigits	fractionDigits	whiteSpace	pattern	enumeration	▣ assertion	▣ explicitTimezone
String and name types														
string	A	A	A							V	A	A	A	
normalizedString	A	A	A							V	A	A	A	
token	A	A	A							C	A	A	A	
Name	A	A	A							C	V	A	A	
NCName	A	A	A							C	V	A	A	

(Continues)

Table B–2   (Continued)

Name	length	minLength	maxLength	minExclusive	minInclusive	maxInclusive	maxExclusive	totalDigits	fractionDigits	whiteSpace	pattern	enumeration	assertion	explicitTimezone
language	A	A	A							C	V	A	A	
Numeric types														
float				A	A	A	A			C	A	A	A	
double				A	A	A	A			C	A	A	A	
decimal				A	A	A	A	A	A	C	A	A	A	
integer				A	A	A	A	A	0	C	V	A	A	
long				A	V	V	A	A	0	C	V	A	A	
int				A	V	V	A	A	0	C	V	A	A	
short				A	V	V	A	A	0	C	V	A	A	
byte				A	V	V	A	A	0	C	V	A	A	
positiveInteger				A	V	A	A	A	0	C	V	A	A	
nonPositiveInteger				A	A	V	A	A	0	C	V	A	A	
negativeInteger				A	A	V	A	A	0	C	V	A	A	
nonNegativeInteger				A	V	A	A	A	0	C	V	A	A	
unsignedLong				A	V	V	A	A	0	C	V	A	A	
unsignedInt				A	V	V	A	A	0	C	V	A	A	
unsignedShort				A	V	V	A	A	0	C	V	A	A	
unsignedByte				A	V	V	A	A	0	C	V	A	A	
Date and time types														
date				A	A	A	A			C	A	A	A	A

(Continues)

Table B–2   (Continued)

Name	length	minLength	maxLength	minExclusive	minInclusive	maxInclusive	maxExclusive	totalDigits	fractionDigits	whiteSpace	pattern	enumeration	assertion	explicitTimezone
time				A	A	A	A			C	A	A	A	A
dateTime				A	A	A	A			C	A	A	A	A
▣dateTimeStamp				A	A	A	A			C	A	A	A	V
gYear				A	A	A	A			C	A	A	A	A
gYearMonth				A	A	A	A			C	A	A	A	A
gMonth				A	A	A	A			C	A	A	A	A
gMonthDay				A	A	A	A			C	A	A	A	A
gDay				A	A	A	A			C	A	A	A	A
duration				A	A	A	A			C	A	A	A	
▣yearMonthDuration				A	A	A	A			C	A	A	A	
▣dayTimeDuration				A	A	A	A			C	A	A	A	
XML DTD types														
ID	A	A	A							C	V	A	A	
IDREF	A	A	A							C	V	A	A	
IDREFS	A	V	A							C	A	A	A	
ENTITY	A	A	A							C	V	A	A	
ENTITIES	A	V	A							C	A	A	A	
NMTOKEN	A	A	A							C	V	A	A	
NMTOKENS	A	V	A							C	A	A	A	
NOTATION	A	A	A							C	A	A	A	

(Continues)

Table B–2   (Continued)

Name	length	minLength	maxLength	minExclusive	minInclusive	maxInclusive	maxExclusive	totalDigits	fractionDigits	whiteSpace	pattern	enumeration	assertion	explicitTimezone
Other types														
QName	A	A	A							C	A	A	A	
boolean										C	A		A	
hexBinary	A	A	A							C	A	A	A	
base64Binary	A	A	A							C	A	A	A	
anyURI	A	A	A							C	A	A	A	
Other varieties														
List types	A	A	A							C	A	A	A	
Union types											A	A	A	

A — Facet is applicable to this type.

V — Facet has a value for this type, but it is not fixed.

0 — Facet is applicable to this type, but the only value that can be specified is 0.

C — Facet is applicable to this type, but the only value that can be specified is collapse.

Index

Index entries in gray refer to XML Schema 1.1.

Index entries in gray refer to XML Schema 1.1.

Index **entries in gray** refer to XML Schema 1.1.

Index **entries in gray** refer to XML Schema 1.1.

Index **entries in gray** refer to XML Schema 1.1.

Index entries in gray refer to XML Schema 1.1.

Index entries in gray refer to XML Schema 1.1.

Index **entries in gray** refer to XML Schema 1.1.

Index entries in gray refer to XML Schema 1.1.

Index **entries in gray** refer to XML Schema 1.1.

Index **entries in gray** refer to XML Schema 1.1.

Index **entries in gray** refer to XML Schema 1.1.

Index entries in gray refer to XML Schema 1.1.

overrides, 33, 459–471, 612–614
  and target namespace, 459–462, 572
  of attribute groups, 467, 491–492
  of complex types, 465
  of global declarations, 466
  of named model groups, 467
  of simple types, 464–465
  ripple effect of, 461–462
  risks of, 468–471
  vs. DTDs, 488
  vs. other extension mechanisms, 600

P

P
  in category escapes, 168
  in durations, 229–233
p element (HTML), 525
\p multicharacter escape, 161, 169–170, 177
\P multicharacter escape, 169–171
parameter entities (DTDs)
  external, 492
  for attribute extensions, 490–491
  for extensibility, 486–492
  for reuse, 483–486
  internal, 483–491
parent keyword (XPath), 438
parentheses. See ( )
particles (of complex type), 262
path expressions (XPath), 367–369, 435–440
  default namespace for, 60
  unprefixed names in, 440–441
pattern facet, 137, 139, 148–149
  changing restrictiveness of, 619–620
  for built-in types, 695–698
  for derived types, 140
  for duration types, 231
  for list types, 194
  for numeric types, 219
  for union types, 185
  multiple occurrences of, 148
  syntax of, 138, 665

#PCDATA specifier (DTDs), 474–475, 478
percent sign, in URIs, 251–252
performance, 82
period. See .
Perl programming language, 159
plus sign. See +
position function (XPath 2.0), 364
positiveInteger type, 217
  comparing values of, 254–255
  facets applicable to, 696
prefixed names, 40
  of attributes, 44–46, 120, 122
prefixes, 28, 37, 98
  in path expressions, 439
  mapping to:
    target namespace, 29, 53
    XML Schema Namespace, 38, 50–52
  naming rules for, 41
prelexical facets, 151
preprocess facet (Saxon), 155
preserve value (whiteSpace facet), 104, 125, 151–152, 205, 254
primitive types, 203
  additional, 203
processContents attribute
  and forward compatibility, 623
  lax value of, 288, 291, 602–603
    in open content, 605
  of attribute wildcard, 298, 315–316, 336–337, 602–603
  of element wildcard, 287–289
  skip value of, 287–289
  strict value of, 288–289
  syntax of, 684
prohibited value
  of use attribute, 283
  of value attribute, 150
proxy schemas, 74
public attribute (notation element), 493
  syntax of, 684

Index entries in gray refer to XML Schema 1.1.

Index **entries in gray** refer to XML Schema 1.1.

Index entries in gray refer to XML Schema 1.1.

Index **entries in gray** refer to XML Schema 1.1.

Index entries in gray refer to XML Schema 1.1.

Index entries in gray refer to XML Schema 1.1.

Index **entries in gray** refer to XML Schema 1.1.

Index entries in gray refer to XML Schema 1.1.